International Law and the

M000305324

Climate change and rising oil prices have thrust the Arctic to the top of the foreign policy agenda and raised difficult issues of sovereignty, security, and environmental protection. Improved access for shipping and resource development are leading to new international rules on safety, pollution prevention, and emergency response. Around the Arctic, maritime boundary disputes are being negotiated and resolved, and new international institutions, such as the Arctic Council, are mediating deep-rooted tensions between Russia and NATO and between nation states and indigenous peoples. *International Law and the Arctic* explains these developments and reveals a strong trend toward international cooperation and law-making. It thus contradicts the widespread misconception that the Arctic is an unregulated zone of potential conflict.

Michael Byers holds the Canada Research Chair in Global Politics and International Law at the University of British Columbia.

CAMBRIDGE STUDIES IN INTERNATIONAL AND COMPARATIVE LAW

Established in 1946, this series produces high-quality scholarship in the fields of public and private international law and comparative law. Although these are distinct legal sub-disciplines, developments since 1946 confirm their interrelations.

Comparative law is increasingly used as a tool in the making of law at national, regional, and international levels. Private international law is now often affected by international conventions, and the issues faced by classical conflicts rules are frequently dealt with by substantive harmonization of law under international auspices. Mixed international arbitrations, especially those involving state economic activity, raise mixed questions of public and private international law, while in many fields (such as the protection of human rights and democratic standards, investment guarantees and international criminal law) international and national systems interact. National constitutional arrangements relating to "foreign affairs," and to the implementation of international norms, are a focus of attention.

The Series welcomes works of a theoretical or interdisciplinary character, and those focusing on the new approaches to international or comparative law or conflicts of law. Studies of particular institutions or problems are equally welcome, as are translations of the best work published in other languages.

General Editors   James Crawford SC FBA *Whewell Professor of International Law, Faculty of Law, University of Cambridge*
John S. Bell FBA *Professor of Law, Faculty of Law, University of Cambridge*

A list of books in the series can be found at the end of this volume.

International Law and the Arctic

Michael Byers

With James Baker

CAMBRIDGE
UNIVERSITY PRESS

CAMBRIDGE
UNIVERSITY PRESS

University Printing House, Cambridge CB2 8BS, United Kingdom

Cambridge University Press is part of the University of Cambridge.

It furthers the University's mission by disseminating knowledge in the pursuit of education, learning and research at the highest international levels of excellence.

www.cambridge.org
Information on this title: www.cambridge.org/9781107470903

© Michael Byers 2013

This publication is in copyright. Subject to statutory exception and to the provisions of relevant collective licensing agreements, no reproduction of any part may take place without the written permission of Cambridge University Press.

First published 2013
Fifth printing 2014
First paperback edition 2014

A catalogue record for this publication is available from the British Library

Library of Congress Cataloguing in Publication data
Byers, Michael, 1966–
International law and the arctic / Michael Byers.
pages cm. – (Cambridge studies in international and comparative law ; 103)
Includes bibliographical references and index.
ISBN 978-1-107-04275-9 (hardback)
1. Arctic regions – International status. 2. Arctic regions – International cooperation. I. Title.
KZ4110.P65B94 2013
341.405091632–dc23
2013023187

ISBN 978-1-107-04275-9 Hardback
ISBN 978-1-107-47090-3 Paperback

Cambridge University Press has no responsibility for the persistence or accuracy of URLs for external or third-party internet websites referred to in this publication, and does not guarantee that any content on such websites is, or will remain, accurate or appropriate.

It is often said there are few truly untamed places left on Earth, but the windswept horizons of the Arctic surely qualify. Some political analysts maintain that the geopolitical landscape is equally harsh – a lawless region poised for conflict due to an accelerating "race for the North Pole."

We disagree. Instead, we firmly believe that the Arctic can be used to demonstrate just how much peace and collective interests can be served through the implementation of the international rule of law. Moreover, we believe that the challenges in the Arctic should inspire momentum in international relations, based on co-operation rather than rivalry and confrontation, and we believe that important steps have already been taken toward this goal.

Russian Foreign Minister Sergei Lavrov and Norwegian Foreign Minister Jonas Gahr Støre, "Canada, Take Note: Here's How to Resolve Maritime Disputes," *Globe and Mail*, September 21, 2010

Contents

Acknowledgements

This book is the culmination of an eight-year research project that began when I moved home to Canada after more than a decade of studying and teaching at Cambridge, Oxford, and Duke universities. Throughout this period, I have benefited from the encouragement and assistance of many people from across the Arctic and beyond, only some of whom can be thanked here.

First and foremost, I am grateful to the friends and colleagues who read and commented on draft chapters or sections: Betsy Baker, David Gray, Scott Highleyman, Bjørn Kunoy, Coalter Lathrop, John Merritt, Justin Nankivell, Joost Pauwelyn, Shayna Plaut, Joël Plouffe, Mark Stoller, several government officials, and two anonymous referees. All mistakes and omissions remain my own.

From Canada's Arctic, I am grateful for assistance and insights from Sheila Watt-Cloutier, John Amagoalik, Paul Okalik, Mary Simon, Udloriak Hanson, Letia Obed, Aaju Peter, Cindy Dickson, Arthur Yuan, Dennis Bevington, Tony Penikett, and the late Marty Bergmann. I am also grateful to the officers and crew of the CCGS *Amundsen*, Canada's research icebreaker, on which I have twice sailed the Northwest Passage.

Other Canadians who assisted in important ways include Terry Fenge, Louis Fortier, Martin Fortier, Shelley Wright, Lloyd Axworthy, Bill Rompkey, Ken Coates, Armand de Mestral, Franklyn Griffiths, Nigel Bankes, Peter Harrison, David Hik, Rob Huebert, Ron Macnab, Ted McDorman, Donald McRae, Donat Pharand, Ian Townsend-Gault, Robert Hage, Pierre Leblanc, Elizabeth Riddell-Dixon, Jacob Verhoef, Louis Simard, Trevor Taylor, Chris Westdal, Paul Heinbecker, Steve Staples, Peggy Mason, Fred Roots, Geoff Green, and the late Jack Layton.

From Russia, I am grateful to Anton Vasiliev, Roman Kolodkin, Artur Chilingarov, Sergey Rogov, Alexander Vylegzhanin, Vladimir Golitsyn, Sergei Proskurin, Vladislav Tolstykh, Evgeny Avdoshin, Alexander Shestakov, and Konstantin Timokhin. I am also grateful to the officers and crews of the MV *Lyubov Orlova* and *Akademik Ioffe*, the two ice-strengthened expedition ships on which I have lectured in the Arctic.

From the US, I benefited from the wisdom and support of Paul Cellucci, Scott Borgerson, Diddy Hitchens, Robert Corell, Frances Ulmer, Ashley Roach, Larry Mayer, Mead Treadwell, Oran Young, Elizabeth Elliot-Meisel, Bernard Oxman, Doug Nord, David Caron, Lawson Brigham, Brooks Yeager, and the late Jon Van Dyke and Christopher Joyner.

From Norway, I am grateful to Kjell Kristian Egge, Otto Mamelund, and Geir Ulfstein. From Denmark, I thank Poul Erik Dam Kristensen, Christian Marcussen, Thomas Winkler, and Jørgen Lilje-Jensen. From Sweden, I thank Gustaf Lind and Hans Corell.

From non-Arctic countries, I thank Charles Emmerson, James Crawford, Andrew Serdy, Martin Pratt, Nicholas Wheeler, Peiqing Guo, Keun-Gwan Lee, Donald Rothwell, Erik Frankx, Rüdiger Wolfrum, Georg Nolte, Stefan Oeter, Samantha Besson, Matthias Brinkmann, Kathrin Keil, and Michel Rocard.

I have benefited from two much-valued writing partnerships. The first is with Suzanne Lalonde of the University of Montreal, with whom I have co-authored several articles about the Northwest Passage. Chapter 5 draws on our collaborative work.

The second partnership is with James Baker, who is in the final stages of a Ph.D. at the University of British Columbia. Chapter 3 is based on a paper that James and I co-authored in *Ocean Development and International Law*, while the section on the Lomonosov Ridge is based on a workshop paper that was likewise co-authored with him.

Several other sections draw on an earlier book of mine entitled *Who Owns the Arctic?* That much slimmer volume, published in 2009, was written for a non-academic Canadian audience. I am grateful to Scott McIntyre for his support of that effort, as well as the idea of a follow-up academic book on the international law of the circumpolar Arctic.

Last, but not least, I am grateful to Dalaina Heiberg for two summers of superb research assistance; to John-Michael McColl for helping to organize two ArcticNet-funded workshops on issues central to this book; to Kathy and Mike Edmunds for providing the perfect writing environment; and to Bob Byers for many things – including a great deal of careful and patient editing.

Note on maps and measurements

This book contains only one map, specially prepared by Coalter Lathrop at Sovereign Geographic. It shows the different boundary lines preferred by the United States and Canada in the Beaufort Sea, and how those lines would continue beyond 200 nautical miles onto the extended continental shelf. Links to several other maps are provided in the footnotes. In particular, readers are encouraged to spend some time studying the following two maps:

(1) The International Boundary Research Unit at Durham University maintains a superb map on "Maritime jurisdiction and boundaries in the Arctic region," available at www.dur.ac. uk/resources/ibru/arctic.pdf.

(2) The "International Bathymetric Chart of the Arctic Ocean" has been produced with input from researchers from ten countries, including Canada, Denmark, Iceland, Norway, Russia, Sweden, and the US. It provides an up-to-date and relatively comprehensive picture of the ocean floor, including the main "seafloor highs," and is available at www.ngdc.noaa.gov/mgg/ bathymetry/arctic/arctic.html.

As for measurements, this book uses nautical miles for maritime distances and areas, as is standard in the law of the sea. All other distances and areas are in kilometers, while depths are measured in meters.

Abbreviations

AIBWC	Alaska and Inuvialuit Beluga Whale Committee
AMAP	Arctic Monitoring and Assessment Program
ASRC	Arctic Slope Regional Corporation
AWPPA	Arctic Waters Pollution Prevention Act
BEAC	Barents Euro-Arctic Council
BRC	Barents Regional Council
BWM	ballast water management
CITES	Convention on International Trade in Endangered Species
CLCS	Commission on the Limits of the Continental Shelf
ECOSOC	Economic and Social Council (UN)
EEZ	exclusive economic zone
EPA	Environmental Protection Agency
GATT	General Agreement on Tariffs and Trade
ICC	Inuit Circumpolar Council
ICJ	International Court of Justice
IMO	International Maritime Organization
INSROP	International Northern Sea Route Program
ISA	International Seabed Authority
ITLOS	International Tribunal for the Law of the Sea
IWC	International Whaling Commission
NAFO	Northwest Atlantic Fisheries Organization
NATO	North Atlantic Treaty Organization
NEAFC	North East Atlantic Fisheries Commission
NEB	National Energy Board (Canada)
NOAA	National Oceanic and Atmospheric Administration
NORAD	North American Aerospace Defense Command

NORDREG	Northern Canada Vessel Traffic Services Zone Regulations
OPRC	Convention on Oil Pollution Preparedness, Response and Cooperation
OSCE	Organization for Security and Cooperation in Europe
PEARL	Polar Environment Atmospheric Research Laboratory
POAC	International Conference on Port and Ocean Engineering under Arctic Conditions
PSI	Proliferation Security Initiative
RAIPON	Russian Association of Indigenous Peoples of the North, Siberia and Far East
SAR	search and rescue
SIPRI	Stockholm International Peace Research Institute
SLCP	short-lived climate pollutant
SRR	search-and-rescue region
TBT Agreement	Technical Barriers to Trade Agreement
UNEP	United Nations Environment Programme
UNESCO	United Nations Educational, Scientific and Cultural Organization
WMD	weapon of mass destruction
WTO	World Trade Organization

Introduction

Resolute Bay, an Inuit hamlet on Canada's Cornwallis Island, is a desolate but remarkable place – especially in mid-summer, as I discovered in June 2008. During a midnight stroll across a moonscape of frozen gravel, a powerful wind drove flecks of ice and sand into my face. At the same time, the sun was shining high in the sky, for Resolute Bay is located at 74 degrees north. I remember thinking that it was midday in India, and people there were enjoying the same sunlight as me. The only difference was that, in Resolute Bay, the light was shining directly over the North Pole.

No country will ever "own" the North Pole, which is located about 400 nautical miles north of Greenland and the northernmost islands of Canada and Russia. Although the water and seabed close to shore belong to the coastal states, the surface, water column, and at least some of the seabed of the central Arctic Ocean belong to all humanity. At the same time, many of the challenges there – including life-threatening accidents, oil spills, and overfishing – will necessarily be addressed first and foremost by the geographically proximate Arctic states. These challenges will increase rapidly in the years and decades ahead, as the climate changes, the sea-ice melts, and ships of all kinds gain access.

During the Cold War, the US and the Soviet Union squared off across the Arctic Ocean. Nuclear submarines prowled under the ice while long-range bombers patrolled high overhead. A more peaceful and cooperative approach emerged in 1990 when the two superpowers negotiated a maritime boundary in the Bering Sea, Bering Strait, and Chukchi Sea.[1]

---

[1] Agreement between the United States of America and the Union of Soviet Socialist Republics on the Maritime Boundary (1990) 29 ILM 941, available at www.state.gov/documents/organization/125431.pdf.

1

In 1996, the eight Arctic countries – the US, Russia, Canada, Denmark, Norway, Sweden, Finland, and Iceland – created the Arctic Council as an intergovernmental forum for discussing issues other than those of "military security."[2] At the same time, Russia accepted Western assistance with the decommissioning and disposal of Soviet-era nuclear reactors and warheads.[3] It also allowed many Soviet-era warships to degrade, while the US and Canada, for their part, chose not to replace aging icebreakers.[4]

More recently, climate change is fundamentally reshaping the Arctic.[5] In addition to rising temperatures caused by global greenhouse gas emissions, change is being driven by Arctic-specific "feedback loops" arising out of the delicate balance between frozen and liquid water. An increase of a fraction of a degree in the average annual temperature can change highly reflective sea-ice into dark, heat-absorbing open ocean. The same temperature increase can turn rock-hard biologically stable permafrost into a decomposing, methane-emitting morass of ancient plant material. In the Arctic, the average annual air temperature has already increased by more than two degrees Celsius.[6]

In September 2012, the area covered by Arctic sea-ice dropped to 3.6 million square kilometers, almost 50 percent below the 1979 to 2000 average.[7] It now seems possible that a complete, late-summer melt-out could occur as early as 2020.[8] The disappearance of thick, hard

---

[2] See www.arctic-council.org/. On the origins of the Arctic Council, see Evan T. Bloom, "Establishment of the Arctic Council" (1999) 93 *American Journal of International Law* 712.

[3] See Brian D. Finlay, "Russian Roulette: Canada's Role in the Race to Secure Loose Nuclear, Biological, and Chemical Weapons." (2006) 61 *International Journal* 411.

[4] See, e.g., *Polar Icebreakers in a Changing World: An Assessment of U.S. Needs (Report of the Committee on the Assessment of US Coast Guard Polar Icebreaker Roles and Future Needs, National Research Council)* (Washington, DC: National Academies Press, 2007), available at www. nap.edu/catalog.php?record_id=11753; Randy Boswell, "Shortsighted Politics, Forgotten Arctic Dreams: The Abandoned Polar 8 Icebreaker Ship Could Have Embodied Canada's Identity as a Circumpolar Power," *Ottawa Citizen*, August 10, 2007, A5.

[5] For the most comprehensive (though already dated) examination, see *Impacts of a Warming Arctic: Arctic Climate Impact Assessment* (Cambridge University Press, 2004), available at www.acia.uaf.edu/.

[6] "Sea Ice Loss Major Cause of Arctic Warming," *Independent*, April 30, 2010, available at www.independent.co.uk/environment/sea-ice-loss-major-cause-of-arctic-warming-1958815.html.

[7] US National Snow and Ice Data Center, "Arctic Sea Ice News and Analysis," available at http://nsidc.org/arcticseaicenews/.

[8] Margaret Munro, "Arctic Ice 'Rotten' to the North Pole, Scientist Says," *PostMedia News*, October 1, 2012, available at www.vancouversun.com/technology/Arctic+Rotten+North +Pole+scientist+says/7279382/story.html. For a useful discussion of different scientific

"multi-year" sea-ice would open up large areas of the Arctic to year-round navigation. The Arctic Ocean could soon resemble the Baltic Sea or the Gulf of St. Lawrence where ice-strengthened ships and icebreaker-escorted convoys operate in winter. This would reduce the costs of shipping between Asia and Europe and the Atlantic Seaboard of the United States and also facilitate resource exploration and extraction.

As easy-to-access conventional sources of oil are exhausted, companies are pursuing oil in less hospitable places, or developing non-conventional sources such as the tar sands of western Canada. As a result, the costs of finding, producing, and transporting oil to market will escalate. The price of oil rose to $140 before the 2008 global recession, and has since climbed back to above $100.[9] Some experts believe that "peak oil" – the point at which world demand exceeds remaining reserves – will soon be achieved, or perhaps has been reached already.[10] All of this explains the excitement when, in 2009, the US Geological Survey released projections of undiscovered oil and gas resources north of the Arctic Circle: 83 billion barrels of oil, enough to meet current world demand for three years; and 44 trillion cubic meters of natural gas, or roughly fourteen years of supply.[11]

The combination of melting sea-ice and high oil prices has led to concerns about possible struggles for Arctic territory and resources. In 2007, Artur Chilingarov, the then-deputy chair of the Russian Duma, caused a global media frenzy by planting a titanium flag on the seabed at the North Pole and declaring "the Arctic is Russian."[12] Peter MacKay, then Canada's foreign minister, responded in an equally colorful manner: "Look, this isn't the fifteenth century. You can't go around the world and just plant flags

predictions, see Katherine Leitzell, "When Will the Arctic Lose its Sea Ice?" US National Snow and Ice Data Center, May 3, 2011, available at http://nsidc.org/icelights/2011/05/03/when-will-the-arctic-lose-its-sea-ice/.

[9] International Energy Agency, "Oil Market Reports," available at http://omrpublic.iea.org/.

[10] John Collins Rudolf, "Is 'Peak Oil' Behind Us?" New York Times, November 14, 2010, http://green.blogs.nytimes.com/2010/11/14/is-peak-oil-behind-us/?partner=rssandemc=rss.

[11] Donald L. Gautier, et al., "Assessment of Undiscovered Oil and Gas in the Arctic." (2009) 324 (5931) Science 1175.

[12] Paul Reynolds, "Russia Ahead in Arctic 'Gold Rush'," BBC News, August 1, 2007, available at http://news.bbc.co.uk/2/hi/6925853.stm.

and say, 'We're claiming this territory.' Our claims over our Arctic are very well established."[13]

In 2008, the European Parliament stirred things up further by calling for a new multilateral convention for the Arctic modeled on the 1959 Antarctic Treaty.[14] In doing so, it was implicitly questioning the rights of Arctic Ocean coastal states under the law of the sea.[15] That same year, Scott Borgerson of the US Council on Foreign Relations described the situation in the Arctic as a "scramble" having potentially serious consequences: "The combination of new shipping routes, trillions of dollars in possible oil and gas resources, and a poorly defined picture of state ownership makes for a toxic brew."[16]

Fortunately, cooler heads have since prevailed. One of the Russian scientists involved in the North Pole flag-plant admitted that it was a publicity stunt lacking legal relevance.[17] Danish Foreign Minister Per Stig Møller invited his counterparts from the four other Arctic Ocean coastal states to Ilulissat, Greenland, where they reaffirmed their commitment to resolving any disputes within an existing framework of international law.[18] The European Union's Council of Ministers issued an Arctic policy that recognized the primacy of the law of the sea in a region that, unlike the Antarctic, is centered on an ocean.[19] US Secretary of State Hillary Clinton spoke of the need for Arctic countries

---

[13] "Canada Rejects Flag-Planting as 'Just a Show'," *Independent* online, August 3, 2012, available at www.iol.co.za/news/world/canada-rejects-flag-planting-as-just-a-show-1.364759#.UHgzYo4_5UQ.

[14] "European Parliament Resolution of 9 October 2008 on Arctic Governance," available at www.europarl.europa.eu/sides/getDoc.do?type=TA&reference=P6-TA-2008-0474&language=EN. For an excellent overview of similar proposals, see Timo Koivurova, "Alternatives for an Arctic Treaty – Evaluation and a New Proposal." (2008) 17 *Review of European Community and International Environmental Law* 14.

[15] The law of the sea is made up of rules of customary international law which were codified, and supplemented with other rules and institutions, in the 1982 United Nations Convention on the Law of the Sea, 1833 UNTS 397, available at www.un.org/Depts/los/convention_agreements/texts/unclos/closindx.htm.

[16] Scott Borgerson, "Arctic Meltdown." (2008) 87 *Foreign Affairs* 63, available at www.foreignaffairs.com/articles/63222/scott-g-borgerson/arctic-meltdown.

[17] Adrian Blomfield, "US Rises to Kremlin Bait," *Daily Telegraph*, August 4, 2007, available at www.telegraph.co.uk/news/worldnews/1559444/US-rises-to-Kremlin-bait.html.

[18] "The Ilulissat Declaration," May 29, 2008, available at http://uk.nanoq.gl/Emner/News/News_from_Parliament/2008/05/~/media/66562304FA464945BB621411BFFB6E12.ashx.

[19] Council of the European Union, "Council Conclusions on Arctic Issues," December 8, 2009, available at http://oceansnorth.org/resources/council-european-union-conclusions-arctic-issues. For an explanation of the shift in approach, see Njord Wegge, "The EU and the Arctic: European Foreign Policy in the Making." (2012) 3 *Arctic Review on Law and Politics* 6.

to work together: "We need all hands on deck because there is a huge amount to do, and not much time to do it."[20] Even the leaders of Canada and Russia, who are sometimes guilty of grandstanding on Arctic issues for domestic political purposes, adopted a decidedly more cooperative stance. In January 2010, Canadian Prime Minister Stephen Harper told NATO Secretary General Anders Fogh Rasmussen that "Canada has a good working relationship with Russia with respect to the Arctic" and "there is no likelihood of Arctic states going to war."[21] Eight months later, Harper's government released an Arctic Foreign Policy Statement that committed Canada to resolving its remaining Arctic boundary disputes.[22] In September 2010, Russian prime minister (now President) Vladimir Putin told an international conference of Arctic experts that: "If you stand alone you can't survive in the Arctic. Nature makes people and states to help each other."[23] Putin's comments came just one week after Russia and Norway signed a boundary treaty for the Barents Sea, where the two countries had previously disputed ownership of 50,000 square nautical miles of oil-and-gas-rich seabed.[24]

In short, there is no state-to-state competition for territory or resources in the Arctic, and no prospect of conflict either. Instead, the Arctic is becoming a region marked by cooperation and international law-making, during a period of significant geopolitical, environmental, and economic change.

With the insignificant exception of Hans Island, a rocky islet located halfway between Greenland and Canada, all of the land in the region belongs incontestably to one or another Arctic country. The Arctic Ocean itself is governed by rules of the law of the sea which apply globally, and which all countries including the United States accept as

---

[20] "Hillary Clinton Criticises Canada over Arctic talks," *BBC News*, March 30, 2010, available at http://news.bbc.co.uk/2/hi/8594291.stm.

[21] US State Department cable # VZCZCXR03302, January 20, 2010, available at http://aptn.ca/pages/news/2011/05/11/while-harper-talked-tough-with-nato-on-arctic-u-s-believed-pm-all-bark-no-bite/ (original cables are reproduced below the article).

[22] Statement on Canada's Arctic Foreign Policy, August 20, 2010, available at www.international.gc.ca/polar-polaire/assets/pdfs/CAFP_booklet-PECA_livret-eng.pdf.

[23] Luke Harding, "Vladimir Putin Calls for Arctic Claims to Be Resolved under UN Law," *Guardian*, September 23, 2010, available at www.guardian.co.uk/world/2010/sep/23/putin-arctic-claims-international-law.

[24] 2010 Treaty between the Kingdom of Norway and the Russian Federation Concerning Maritime Delimitation and Cooperation in the Barents Sea and the Arctic Ocean, English translation available at www.regjeringen.no/upload/ud/vedlegg/folkerett/avtale_engelsk.pdf.

customary international law.[25] Developed through centuries of state practice and *opinio juris*, these rules were codified in the 1982 United Nations Convention on the Law of the Sea (UNCLOS).[26]

As elsewhere in the world, the territorial seas of Arctic countries extend twelve nautical miles from shore. Within that band, coastal states have extensive regulatory powers over foreign shipping and absolute rights over fish and seabed resources. Between twelve and 200 nautical miles, in the exclusive economic zone (EEZ), coastal states have fewer powers over shipping but absolute rights over fish and seabed resources. Beyond 200 nautical miles, coastal states lose their rights over fish but may have rights over the seabed – if and where they can demonstrate scientifically that the ocean floor is a "natural prolongation" of their landmass. As Chapter 4 explains, this means that planting a flag on the seabed at the North Pole had no more legal consequence than a flag-plant on the Moon. It also means that most of the Arctic's offshore oil and gas is within the uncontested jurisdiction of one or another coastal state, since offshore oil and gas, which is derived from organic material, is usually found in sedimentary strata in continental shelves.

For decades, international law has played a central role in determining the boundaries between the maritime zones of adjacent coastal states. As mentioned above, the United States and the Soviet Union signed a boundary treaty for the Bering Sea, Bering Strait, and Chukchi Sea in 1990.[27] Twenty-one years later, Russia and Norway concluded a similar treaty for the Barents Sea.[28] As Chapter 3 explains, this leaves just one unresolved maritime boundary in the Arctic: in the Beaufort Sea between the United States and Canada.

As part of an effort to resolve that dispute, the United States and Canada have cooperated in the acquisition of geological and

[25] See, e.g., President Ronald Reagan, "Statement on United States Oceans Policy, March 10, 1983," available at www.oceanlaw.org/downloads/references/reagan/ReaganOceanPolicy-1983.pdf; National Oceanic and Atmospheric Administration (NOAA), Office of General Counsel, "Law of the Sea Convention," available at www.gc.noaa.gov/gcil_los.html ("While it is not yet a party, the US nevertheless observes the Convention as reflective of customary international law and practice"). The International Court of Justice recently ruled that Art. 76(1) of UNCLOS, on extended continental shelves, is part of customary international law. *Territorial and Maritime Dispute (Nicaragua v. Colombia)*, November 19, 2012, para. 118, available at www.icj-cij.org/docket/files/124/17164.pdf.

[26] n. 15, above.   [27] n. 1, above.   [28] n. 24, above.

geomorphological evidence concerning the outer limits of their continental shelves. As a party to UNCLOS, Canada will soon submit its data to
the Commission on the Limits of the Continental Shelf (CLCS), a body of
scientists that issues "recommendations" which serve to legitimize
well-supported proposed continental shelf limits. The same kind of
data will be relevant further north where the extended continental
shelves of Canada, Russia, and Denmark may overlap along several
underwater ridges. Since the Commission does not have the mandate
to resolve such overlaps, boundaries might eventually have to be negotiated in the central Arctic Ocean, though again, this will take place
within an existing framework of international law.

As Chapter 5 explains, there are also disputes over the legal status of
the Northwest Passage and the Northern Sea Route. Both disputes are
bilateral and both involve the United States, with Russia and Canada
each maintaining that these Arctic straits are "internal waters" subject
to their full jurisdiction and control. Russia has successfully deterred
any direct challenge to its legal position, while Canada has managed its
dispute for more than four decades, including by negotiating an Arctic
Cooperation Agreement in 1988 in which the United States promised to
seek permission before sending Coast Guard icebreakers through the
Northwest Passage.[29] Now, with the sea-ice receding and ships of all
kinds arriving, the agreement urgently needs updating.

Issues of ship safety, oil spill prevention, and fisheries management
also demand attention. Arctic conditions necessitate high standards of
ship construction, including ice-strengthening and double hulls as well
as fully enclosed lifeboats and state-of-the-art navigation and communication equipment. The International Maritime Organization spent
years negotiating a "Polar Code" for shipping, but the document was
downgraded to a set of guidelines before being adopted in 2002.[30]
Negotiations aimed at updating the guidelines and converting them to
a binding treaty are now underway.

Cleaning up a major oil spill in the Arctic would be an impossible task.
All eight Arctic countries have ratified the 1990 Convention on Oil

---

[29] Agreement between the Government of Canada and the Government of the United
States of America on Arctic Cooperation, Canada Treaty Series 1988, No. 29; available at
www.lexum.com/ca_us/en/cts.1988.29.en.html.
[30] The Guidelines were updated in 2009 but left unbinding. See Guidelines for Ships
Operating in Polar Waters, December 2, 2009, available at www.imo.org/blast/
blastDataHelper.asp?data_id=29985&filename=A1024(26).pdf.

Pollution Preparedness, Response and Cooperation (OPRC), which was negotiated under the auspices of the International Maritime Organization.[31] In addition to requiring measures such as the stockpiling of oil spill equipment, OPRC promotes the development of regional agreements. The Arctic Council has obliged with a draft treaty on Arctic marine oil pollution preparedness and response that should be adopted in 2013.[32] But the new treaty, which focuses on improving communication and coordination when accidents occur, is unlikely to go beyond the OPRC rules to address more difficult issues such as same-season relief wells and liability caps. What the Arctic really needs, as Chapter 6 explains, is a treaty on oil spill prevention.

At some point soon, long-range fishing fleets will explore the newly ice-free waters of the central Arctic Ocean. Around the world, fish stocks that exist on the high seas, or move between the high seas and the EEZs of coastal states, are acutely vulnerable to overexploitation. As Chapter 6 explains, a regional fisheries organization is needed for the Arctic Ocean – before commercial fishing begins.

Several regional organizations already exist in the Arctic. In 1993, Denmark, Finland, Iceland, Norway, Sweden, Russia, and the European Commission signed the "Kirkenes Declaration" establishing the Barents Euro-Arctic Council.[33] At the same time, provincial governments as well as indigenous groups signed a protocol establishing the Barents Regional Council. The two parallel organizations promote cooperation on matters of shared interest in a region where proximity and history have made it possible to achieve a particularly high level of trust and cooperation.

More recently, the Arctic Council has become the most comprehensive international body in the Arctic region. Since 1996, the Arctic Council has achieved a string of modest successes, including the 2004 Arctic Climate Impact Assessment[34] and the 2009 Arctic Marine Shipping Assessment.[35] In 2011, the eight member states created a permanent secretariat,

---

[31] 1990 International Convention on Oil Pollution Preparedness, Response and Co-operation, available at www.ifrc.org/docs/idrl/I245EN.pdf.

[32] See Task Force on Arctic Marine Oil Pollution Preparedness and Response, at www. arctic-council.org/index.php/en/about-us/task-forces/280-oil-spill-task-force.

[33] Declaration on Cooperation in the Barents Euro-Arctic Region, November 1, 1993, available at www.barentsinfo.fi/beac/docs/459_doc_KirkenesDeclaration.pdf.

[34] Arctic Climate Impact Assessment, n. 5, above.

[35] 2009 *Arctic Marine Shipping Assessment*, available at www.pame.is/index.php/amsa-2009-report.

arguably transforming the Arctic Council from an inter-governmental forum into an international organization.[36] They also negotiated a multilateral search-and-rescue treaty, the first legally binding instrument concluded under the auspices of the Arctic Council.[37]

Significantly, the Arctic Council has since its inception included indigenous peoples as "permanent participants." Together with the eight member states, they engage in an on-going, highly iterative process of consensus-based decision-making.[38] By creating a central forum for Arctic diplomacy and law-making, the Arctic Council has thus become the proverbial "town square" for an expanding transnational community of politicians, diplomats, and other experts who, through their repeated interactions, are gradually acquiring shared expectations, identities, and interests.[39] And this, in turn, is likely to promote even more cooperation and law-making.

Much like the midnight sun in Resolute Bay, this book tries to shine light on the growing role of law-based cooperation in a rapidly changing Arctic. In doing so, it deals with sometimes-quite-technical legal issues, seeking to explain them to lawyers and non-lawyers alike. Other aspects of the contemporary Arctic – post-Cold War geopolitics, the nascent institutions of regional governance, the fraught dynamic between hydrocarbons and climate change – are considered only insofar as they provide relevant context for the rules and rule-making processes. For the growth of international law-making in the Arctic is an important enough story, both in itself, and as a factual counterweight to the all-too-widespread narrative of unbridled competition and impending conflict.

---

[36] Nuuk Declaration, May 12, 2011, available at www.arctic-council.org/index.php/en/about/documents/category/5-declarations. Although the Arctic Council is based on a declaration rather than a founding treaty, such a treaty is not a necessary condition for an international organization. The Organization for Security and Cooperation in Europe (OSCE) is based on the "Helsinki Declaration" and has similarly evolved from an inter-governmental forum into an international organization. See Final Act of the Conference on Security and Cooperation in Europe, August 1, 1975, 14 ILM 1292, available at www1.umn.edu/humanrts/osce/basics/finact75.htm.

[37] Agreement on Aeronautical and Maritime Search and Rescue in the Arctic, May 12, 2011, available at www.arctic-council.org/index.php/en/about/documents/category/20-main-documents-from-nuuk.

[38] See discussion, Chapter 7, below.

[39] For more on the "constructivist" dynamics of diplomacy and international law-making, see Alexander Wendt, *Social Theory of International Politics* (Cambridge University Press, 1999); Michael Byers, *Custom, Power and the Power of Rules* (Cambridge University Press, 1999); Jutta Brunnée and Stephen Toope, *Legitimacy and Legality in International Law* (Cambridge University Press, 2010).

1   Territory

In August 2011, my eldest son and I rode a Zodiac through Bellot Strait, a narrow, winding, twenty-nautical-mile-long waterway in Canada's High Arctic. A seven-knot tidal rip made for an exhilarating trip. Our excitement peaked when, halfway through the strait, we landed on the most northerly extension of mainland North America. We knew that Zenith Point has been Canadian since Britain transferred its Arctic possessions to Canada in 1880 and that the islands to the north of Bellot Strait are just as unquestionably Canadian.[1] Yet the thrill of discovery still ran down our spines as we symbolically reclaimed the land for our country. This chapter focuses on territorial issues, including several of historic interest. It begins with the one remaining dispute over title to territory in the region.

1 Hans Island

A faded, wind-torn Danish flag is mounted on the wall in the office of Ambassador Thomas Winkler, legal adviser to the Danish foreign minister. Raised on Hans Island by Danish troops, the flag was later taken down by Canadian soldiers – and mailed back to Copenhagen.

Hans Island is a barren islet, just one kilometer across, located in the Kennedy Channel portion of Nares Strait between Ellesmere Island and

---

[1] An Order-in-Council dated July 31, 1880 transferred "all the British possessions on the North American continent, not hitherto annexed to any colony." See *Canada Gazette*, October 9, 1880; Ivan Head, "Canadian Claims to Territorial Sovereignty in the Arctic Regions." (1963) 9 *McGill Law Journal* 200 at 212.

northwest Greenland.[2] It was only in 1973, when Danish and Canadian diplomats were negotiating a 1,450-nautical-mile-long continental shelf boundary between Greenland and Canada,[3] that they became aware of a difference of opinion concerning title over the island. Instead of delaying their talks with this unexpected, almost inconsequential development, the negotiators simply drew the boundary line up to the low water mark on one side of the island and continued it from the low water mark on the other. Today, Hans Island, which is smaller than some of the icebergs that drift past it, is the only disputed land in the entire circumpolar Arctic.

Another Danish ambassador, Poul Kristensen, summarized his country's claim to Hans Island in a letter to the editor of the Ottawa Citizen newspaper in 2005:

It is generally accepted that Hans Island was first discovered in 1853 on an expedition done in agreement with the Danish authorities with the participation of the famous Greenlander Hans Hendrik of Fiskenæsset. His place in the expedition earned Hans Hendrik of Fiskenæsset a place in the history of exploration and the island was named after him – "Hans Ø" (Hans Island).

Since then it has been our view that the island, by virtue of its belonging to Greenland, is part of the Kingdom of Denmark. Relevant evidence in connection with defining the area of Greenland, such as geological and geomorphological evidence, clearly supports this point of view.

In 1933, when the Permanent Court of International Justice declared the legal status of Greenland in favor of Denmark, the Court did inter alia refer to the note from the British Government, acting on behalf of Canada, which in 1920 assured the Danish Government that it recognized Danish sovereignty over Greenland.[4]

Tom Høyem, a former Danish minister for Greenland, advanced another component of the claim:

Hans Island has been used for centuries by Greenlandic Inuit as an ideal vantage point to get an overview of the ice situation and of the hunting prospects, especially for polar bears and seals. The Canadian Inuit have never used the

---

[2] David H. Gray, "Canada's Unresolved Maritime Boundaries." (1997) 5(3) *IBRU Boundary and Security Bulletin* 61 at 68–69, available at www.dur.ac.uk/resources/ibru/publications/full/bsb5-3_gray.pdf.

[3] For more on the Danish–Canadian maritime boundary, see Chapter 2, below.

[4] Poul E.D. Kristensen, *Ambassador of Denmark, Letter to the Editor* ("Hans Island: Denmark Responds"), *Ottawa Citizen*, July 28, 2005.

island. . . . Hans Island is, in fact, an integrated part of the Thule-Inuit hunting area. They even gave it its local name, Tartupaluk, which means kidney.[5]

However, none of these arguments stands up well to scrutiny. Ambassador Kristensen failed to mention that Hans Hendrik was participating in an American expedition, though the United States has never claimed Hans Island. Geological and geomorphological evidence is relevant when it comes to extended continental shelves more than 200 nautical miles from shore, but irrelevant with respect to an island that lies within sight of opposing coastlines.[6] Britain's 1920 recognition of Danish title to Greenland does bind Canada, since Britain was responsible for Canada's foreign relations until 1931, but only with respect to Greenland. The use of Hans Island by the Greenland Inuit is the only Danish argument that carries any weight, though it is hardly decisive. The same Inuit often traveled to Ellesmere Island, which is universally regarded as Canadian territory.

Canada's claim to Hans Island is based on the transfer of North America's High Arctic islands (excluding Greenland) from Britain in 1880. The claim also relies on "use and occupation," since international law requires that title to territory be consolidated and maintained by regular activity.[7] Hans Island was home to a Canadian scientific base for a brief period during the Second World War. In 1950, the Canadian Permanent Committee on Geographical Names formally adopted the name "Hans Island." Three years later, Eric Fry of the Topographical Survey of Canada surveyed Hans Island and built a cairn, in which he left a note claiming the island for Canada. In 1972, Fry's survey point, along with survey points on Greenland, was linked by angle and distance measurements to Canada's control survey network by a Canadian government survey party that included Danish government surveyors.[8]

---

[5] Tom Høyem, "Mr. Graham, You Should Have Told Us You Were Coming," *Globe and Mail*, July 29, 2005.

[6] In the 1985 *Libya–Malta Case*, the ICJ made it clear that the evolution of distance-related foundations for maritime zones, most significantly in the form of the 200-nautical-mile EEZ, meant that geological and geomorphological features were to play no part in maritime delimitations where opposite coasts are less than 400 nautical miles apart. Indeed, it went so far as to specify that even evidence of a fundamental break in the continental shelf would not affect such delimitation. *Case Concerning the Continental Shelf* (1985) ICJ Reports 13 at 33 and 35, paras. 34 and 39, available at www.icj-cij.org/docket/files/68/6415.pdf. For more on extended continental shelves, see Chapter 4, below.

[7] *Island of Palmas Case (US v. Netherlands)*, Permanent Court of Arbitration, April 4, 1928, p. 35, available at www.pca-cpa.org/showfile.asp?fil_id=168.

[8] Gray, n. 2, above, at 69.

The dispute achieved its "critical date" - the point when the differing positions became clear and subsequent attempts to bolster them became inconsequential to the legal analysis - in 1973, when the seabed boundary between Greenland and Canada was being negotiated.[9] From that point onwards, a diplomatic protest by one country is usually sufficient to prevent the acquisition of sovereign rights by another country through the protested act. Notwithstanding this legal reality, the almost insignificant dispute over Hans Island has prompted some ridiculous and expensive forms of posturing, including the deployment of military aircraft and ships over long distances.

In the early 1980s, the Canadian government issued a land use permit to Dome Petroleum, a Canadian company, for the establishment of a scientific camp to study the impact of sea-ice and icebergs being pushed by strong currents against Hans Island's north shore. The study was intended to assist in the design of platforms and artificial islands for offshore drilling rigs. When Federal Land Use Administrator Joe Ballantyne inspected the camp in 1983, Danish military jets buzzed the island - and "scared the day-lights out of the scientists."[10]

The next year, Tom Høyem, the Danish minister for Greenland, flew to Hans Island by helicopter and planted a Danish flag. The Canadian government issued a diplomatic protest. Additional Danish flag-plants - and Canadian protests - followed in 1988, 1995, 2002, 2003, and 2004. In 2000, a team of geologists from the Geographical Society of Canada visited the island, mapped its location, and took geological samples. Despite all the activity, both sides maintained a sense of humor about the dispute. As Peter Taksoe-Jensen said when he was legal adviser to the Danish foreign minister: "When Danish military go there, they leave a bottle of schnapps. And when [Canadian] military forces come there, they leave a bottle of Canadian Club [whisky] and a sign saying, 'Welcome to Canada.'"[11]

---

[9] Gerald Fitzmaurice defined the critical date as "the date after which the actions of the parties can no longer affect the issue." Fitzmaurice, *The Law and Procedure of the International Court of Justice*, vol. 1 (Cambridge University Press, 1995), 260. See also *Minquiers and Ecrehos Case* (1953) ICJ Reports 59-60; L.F.E. Goldie, "The Critical Date." (1963) 12 *International and Comparative Law Quarterly* 1251; Robert Jennings and Arthur Watts, *Oppenheim's International Law*, 9th edn (London: Longman, 1992), 711-712; Marcelo Kohen, *Possession contestée et souveraineté territoriale* (Paris: Presses universitaires de France, 1997), 169-183; *Sovereignty over Pulau Ligitan and Pulau Sipadan* (Indonesia/Malaysia), Judgment (2002) ICJ Reports 625 at 682, para. 135.

[10] Joe Ballantyne, *Sovereignty and Development in the Arctic: Selected Exploration Programs in the 1980s* (Whitehorse: self-published, 2009) 7 (on file with author).

[11] Christopher J. Chipello, "It's Time to Plant the Flag Again in the Frozen North," *Wall Street Journal*, May 6, 2004.

In Canada, the dispute began attracting public attention only in 2002 as the result of an alarmist op-ed article in the *Globe and Mail* newspaper entitled "The Return of the Vikings."[12] The previous summer, the Danish ice-strengthened frigate *Vædderen* had landed sailors on Hans Island. The island was devoid of other visitors at the time, and the Canadian government responded with the standard diplomatic protest. But in the newspaper the Danes were described as "invading hordes" – a curious choice of words for close NATO allies. Unfortunately, the escalation of the dispute in the media played directly into the hands of politicians seeking electoral advantage.

The *Vædderen* had sailed to Hans Island just a couple of months before the Danish general election of November 2001. The 2002, 2003, and 2004 flag-plants further strengthened the Danish government's nationalist credentials in the lead-up to the next general election in February 2005. Canada's most dramatic response – a flag-plant in July 2005, followed one week later by the arrival of Defence Minister Bill Graham – occurred as Prime Minister Paul Martin's minority Liberal government was staggering from one domestic crisis to another.

The role of domestic politics becomes more apparent when one considers that the dispute has no implications for the location of the maritime boundary between Canada and Greenland, or for Canadian or Danish rights elsewhere. When Canada and Denmark delimited the continental shelf between Canada and Greenland in 1973, they left a gap of just 875 meters between the end points on the north and south shores of Hans Island. As a result, any resolution of the dispute will not affect the surrounding seabed, which has already been divided by treaty.[13] Nor will it have any consequence for the surrounding waters, since both countries have used the same line to define their fisheries zones.

The almost complete irrelevance of the dispute makes it easier to resolve, which may explain why, in September 2005, Canada and Denmark issued the following joint statement:

We acknowledge that we hold very different views on the question of the sovereignty of Hans Island. This is a territorial dispute that has persisted since the early 1970s, when agreement was reached on the maritime boundary between Canada and Greenland. We underscore that this issue relates only to the island as such, and has no impact on that agreement.

[12] Rob Huebert, "The Return of the Vikings," *Globe and Mail*, December 28, 2002.
[13] For more on the Danish–Canadian maritime boundary, see Chapter 2, below.

Firmly committed as we are to the peaceful resolution of disputes, including territorial disputes, we consistently support this principle here at the United Nations, and around the world. To this end, we will continue our efforts to reach a long-term solution to the Hans Island dispute. Our officials will meet again in the near future to discuss ways to resolve the matter, and will report back to Ministers on their progress.

While we pursue these efforts, we have decided that, without prejudice to our respective legal claims, we will inform each other of activities related to Hans Island. Likewise, all contact by either side with Hans Island will be carried out in a low key and restrained manner.[14]

Solving the dispute should be as easy as drawing a straight line: from the end of the seabed delimitation line on one side of Hans Island, to the continuation of that line on the other. Under this approach, each country would secure title over approximately 50 percent of the island, and Canada and Denmark would share a short and very remote land border. And recent reports suggest that an agreement is imminent, with one possible outcome being the division of Hans Island in half.[15]

Another solution would be to declare Hans Island a condominium, in the sense that Canada and Denmark would share sovereignty over all of it. A number of such arrangements exist elsewhere, including Pheasant Island in the middle of the Bidasoa River between France and Spain.[16] Those two countries share sovereignty, with administrative responsibility alternating every six months between the French municipality of Hendaye and the Spanish municipality of Irún.[17]

[14] Canada–Denmark Joint Statement on Hans Island, September 19, 2005, New York, available at http://byers.typepad.com/arctic/canadadenmark-joint-statement-on-hans-island.html.

[15] John Ibbitson, "Dispute over Hans Island Nears Resolution. Now for the Beaufort Sea," *Globe and Mail*, January 27, 2011, available at www.theglobeandmail.com/news/politics/dispute-over-hans-island-nears-resolution-now-for-the-beaufort-sea/article563692/; Adrian Humphreys, "New Proposal Would See Hans Island Split Equally between Canada and Denmark," *National Post*, April 11, 2012, available at http://news.nationalpost.com/2012/04/11/new-proposal-would-see-hans-island-split-equally-between-canada-and-denmark/.

[16] On condominiums generally, see Joel H. Samuels, "Condominium Arrangements in International Practice: Reviving an Abandoned Concept of Boundary Dispute Resolution." (2007–2008) 29 *Michigan Journal of International Law* 727. Most recently, the ICJ utilized the instrument of condominium in a maritime context in the *Land, Island and Maritime Frontier Dispute* (El Salvador/Honduras: Nicaragua intervening) (1992) ICJ Reports 350 at 601–604.

[17] The Pheasant Island condominium was created by the 1659 Treaty of the Pyrenees. See Luis Careaga, "Un condominium franco-espagnol: L'île des faisans ou de la conférence," thesis, Faculté de droit et des sciences politiques, University of Strasbourg, 1932; Peter Sahlins, Boundaries: The Making of France and Spain in the Pyrenees (Berkeley: University of California Press, 1989); Frank Jacobs, "The World's Most Exclusive

Whatever the solution, Inuit in Canada and Greenland should be involved, as was suggested by Høyem in 2005: "[B]oth Canadians and Danes should respect and involve the local population, not only in resolving this small dispute, but also in developing future Arctic strategy."[18] For instance, the governments of Greenland and Nunavut might wish to assume responsibility for managing the new border or condominium. They might even wish to create an international park, along the lines of Waterton-Glacier International Peace Park, which straddles the border between the Canadian province of Alberta and the US state of Montana.[19]

In advance of any negotiated solution between Canada and Denmark, the Inuit may even wish to argue that they hold title over Hans Island. Such an argument would turn on the fact that neither Canada nor Denmark realized the existence of their dispute until 1973, and have contested each other's claim ever since. It is therefore possible that neither state has perfected its title; in other words, that Hans Island might never have been colonized. If so, the Inuit arguably retain any pre-existing, pre-colonial rights. Nomadic people are capable of holding certain rights over territory, as the International Court of Justice recognized in its advisory opinion in the *Western Sahara Case*.[20] Although these rights are not equivalent to statehood, they do prevent the land from being *terra nullius* – that is, territory belonging to no one and therefore open to the acquisition of title through occupation.[21]

The only dispute over title to territory in the Arctic thus creates opportunities for states and indigenous peoples to think about sovereignty in creative ways. For inspiration and another possible model, they need look no further than the Svalbard archipelago – just 800 nautical miles away.

2 Svalbard

The Svalbard archipelago is located in the Barents Sea halfway between the Norwegian mainland and the North Pole.[22] Spitsbergen (Dutch for

Condominium," *New York Times* online, January 23, 2012, http://opinionator.blogs.nytimes.com/2012/01/23/the-worlds-most-exclusive-condominium/.
[18] Tom Høyem, "Mr. Graham, You Should Have Told Us You Were Coming," *Globe and Mail*, July 29, 2005.
[19] See the UNESCO website at http://whc.unesco.org/en/list/354.
[20] *Western Sahara, Advisory Opinion* (1975) ICJ Reports 12 at 38–39, paras. 79–80.
[21] Ibid.
[22] For a map of Svalbard, see http://ngm.nationalgeographic.com/2009/04/svalbard/svalbard-map.

"jagged mountains") was the original name of the entire archipelago and the name used in the 1920 Spitsbergen Treaty. Svalbard (Norwegian for "land with the cold coasts") is the modern name, with Spitsbergen now being used to refer to the largest of the islands, and the treaty increasingly being referred to as the Svalbard Treaty, as will be done here.

Svalbard is a land of fjords and ice-capped mountains, with roughly half of the archipelago being covered by glaciers. A total landmass of 62,000 square kilometers makes Svalbard about twice the size of Belgium, albeit with a much smaller population. Only 2,500 people live there, all of them on the island of Spitsbergen. There are no indigenous peoples.

Coal has been mined on the island of Spitsbergen for more than a century, with about four million tonnes still being shipped to Europe each year. The Gulf Stream confers relatively mild temperatures and seasonally ice-free waters, while good infrastructure and flight connections with Europe make Svalbard one of the easier and more comfortable places for tourists to experience the Arctic. Each summer now, dozens of cruise ships operate within the archipelago, some of them carrying more than 3,000 passengers. Svalbard has also become a center for Arctic science, with many countries – including China and India – operating research stations there. It is home to the Svalbard Global Seed Vault, where hundreds of thousands of seed samples from around the world are preserved deep in a permanently frozen mountainside: the ultimate security policy for global crop diversity.[23]

Sovereignty over territory is usually a matter of customary international law, but in this case the 1920 Svalbard Treaty is determinative.[24] In the nineteenth century, Svalbard was widely considered to be *terra nullius* and therefore open to all. However, the exploitation of Svalbard's rich coal deposits by companies from a number of countries necessitated some kind of management regime. Three options were considered: retaining the *terra nullius* status but giving governance powers to a trilateral commission made up of Norway, Sweden, and Russia; designating the archipelago a Norwegian mandate under the League of Nations; or recognizing Norwegian sovereignty but making it subject

---

[23] See Svalbard Global Seed Vault at www.croptrust.org/content/svalbard-global-seed-vault.

[24] Treaty concerning the Archipelago of Spitsbergen ("Svalbard Treaty") (February 9, 1920) 2 *League of Nations Treaty Series* 7, available at www.lovdata.no/traktater/texte/tre-19200209-001.html#map0.

to specified treaty rights of economic access on the part of other states. The last option was chosen at the Paris Peace Conference of 1919; the Svalbard Treaty was signed in February 1920 and entered into force five years later.

Forty countries have ratified the Svalbard Treaty, including Britain, Canada, China, Denmark, France, Germany, India, Norway, Russia, and the United States.[25] Norway takes the view that its sovereignty over Svalbard is opposable to non-parties under customary international law, as a result of its effective occupation and the lack of protests from other states. Non-parties cannot claim rights under the treaty but, as Geir Ulfstein points out, they are still "free to ratify the Svalbard Treaty and thereby benefit from its provisions, first and foremost the right of non-discriminatory access to economic exploitation of the archipelago."[26]

Russia is the only treaty party to take significant advantage of its rights on land and a Russian-owned coalmine has been operating at Barentsburg on the island of Spitsbergen since 1932. The 500 inhabitants of Barentsburg are almost all Russian or Ukrainian and there is no road connection to the Norwegian town of Longyearbyen, just fifty kilometers away.

The Svalbard Treaty's prohibition on discrimination does not prevent Norway from regulating or even prohibiting activities such as mining, tourism, and scientific research, provided that the rules apply equally to Norwegians. As Ulfstein explains: "Norway's sovereignty implies the right to adopt laws and regulations on Svalbard, and their enforcement. Norway has no more duty to consult with other States on the government of Svalbard than any other State about the management of its territory."[27] These powers have been exercised extensively for the purposes of environmental protection, with parks and nature preserves now covering roughly 65 percent of the archipelago. The wide-reaching use of Norway's powers could conceivably create future tension, with Charles Emmerson warning that "Norway's right to impose strong environmental regulations threatens to collide with signatory states' rights of equal access."[28]

---

[25] See "Traité concernant le Spitsberg," at www.lovdata.no/cgi-bin/udoffles?doc=tra-1920-02-09-001.txt&.

[26] Geir Ulfstein, "Spitsbergen/Svalbard," in Rudiger Wolfrum (ed.), *Max Planck Encyclopedia of Public International Law* (Oxford University Press, 2012), sec. 1, para. 24.

[27] Ibid., para. 23.

[28] Charles Emmerson, *The Future History of the Arctic* (New York: Public Affairs, 2010), p. 93.

Norway is also entitled to levy taxes against foreign nationals, provided the same taxes are levied on Norwegian nationals and "devoted
exclusively to the said territories and shall not exceed what is required
for the object in view," namely the administration of the archipelago.[29]
As Ulfstein points out, this latter limitation is inconsequential today,
since the costs of administration greatly exceed the tax revenue.[30] It
could become important, however, if oil and gas exploitation were to
occur on or around Svalbard on a major scale.[31]

The only current dispute over Svalbard concerns whether the right
to non-discriminatory economic access extends beyond the twelve-
nautical-mile territorial sea. This issue first arose in 1977 when
Norway began regulating fishing in a 200-nautical-mile zone around
the archipelago, arguing that the provision concerning equal economic
access only applied to the islands and their territorial waters, and not
the EEZ. It has since accorded quotas within the EEZ to several other
states, based on their traditional fishing activities there, but not to other
parties to the Svalbard Treaty such as Iceland. On several occasions,
Norway has arrested Russian fishing boats within 200 nautical miles of
Svalbard, creating some diplomatic friction.[32] The dispute has more
recently grown to encompass the seabed, including areas of extended
continental shelf beyond 200 nautical miles, and the potential for oil
and gas exploitation there.[33]

Several provisions of the Svalbard Treaty clearly stipulate that the
right of non-discriminatory economic access extends to the territorial
sea.[34] At the time of the treaty's conclusion, Norway claimed a four-
nautical-mile territorial sea. In 1970, the Norwegian government drew
straight baselines around the archipelago; in 2001, it modified those
baselines; and in 2003, it adopted a twelve-nautical-mile territorial sea.

---

[29] Treaty concerning the Archipelago of Spitsbergen, n. 24, above, Art. 8.
[30] Ulfstein, n. 26, above, sec. 4, para. 31.   [31] Ibid.
[32] See, e.g., Charles Digges, "Arrested Russian Fishing Trawler Flees for Home with Two
Detained Norwegian Coast Guard Inspectors," October 18, 2005, Bellona Foundation
(Norway), available at www.bellona.org/english_import_area/international/russia/
nuke_industry/co-operation/40320.
[33] For more on extended continental shelves, see Chapter 4, below.
[34] Art. 2 reads, in part: "Ships and nationals of all the High Contracting Parties shall enjoy
equally the rights of fishing and hunting in the territories specified in Article 1 and in
their territorial waters." Art. 3 reads, in part: "The nationals of all the High Contracting
Parties . . . shall be admitted under the same conditions of equality to the exercise and
practice of all maritime, industrial, mining or commercial enterprises both on land and
in the territorial waters, and no monopoly shall be established on any account or for
any enterprise whatever." Svalbard Treaty, n. 24, above.

However, Norway has also explicitly accepted that the non-discriminatory rights in the Svalbard Treaty apply within – though not beyond – that expanded coastal zone.

In 1920, the concepts of the EEZ and continental shelf had not yet entered international law. Today, Norway argues that the limits on its sovereign rights set out in the Svalbard Treaty must be interpreted restrictively and not extended, without any written basis, to apply to new zones beyond the territorial sea. It has also argued that the continental shelf around Svalbard is in fact an extension of the continental shelf of the mainland Norwegian coast and, for this additional reason, not subject to the non-discriminatory rights of the Svalbard Treaty.[35]

Two positions were adopted in opposition to Norway's claims. The first, held until recently by Iceland and Russia, is that Norwegian sovereignty is limited not just in substance but also in geographic scope by the Svalbard Treaty and, as a result, Norway has no rights – no EEZ or continental shelf – beyond the territorial sea. A second, more nuanced position is held by the United Kingdom, which argues that the Svalbard Treaty must be read according to the usual rules of interpretation set out in the 1969 Vienna Convention on the Law of Treaties. Since the non-discriminatory rights were set out in the same sentence as the recognition of Norwegian sovereignty, it follows that the intent of the parties was to extend non-discriminatory rights to the full geographic extent of that sovereignty. Accordingly, the non-discriminatory rights expanded to include the EEZ and continental shelf when Norwegian sovereignty was extended to those new zones. The United Kingdom also argues that the EEZ and continental shelf are functional extensions of the territorial sea, that any other conclusion would create a strange situation where Norway would have more rights beyond twelve nautical miles than within that distance, and that Norway did not itself treat the continental shelf north of Svalbard as an extension of the continental shelf of the mainland coast when it negotiated a maritime boundary with Denmark (Greenland) and filed its submission concerning an extended continental shelf with the CLCS in 2006.[36]

---

[35] See, generally, Torbjørn Pedersen, "The Svalbard Continental Shelf Controversy: Legal Disputes and Political Rivalries." (2006) 37 *Ocean Development and International Law* 339.

[36] For a cogent expression of these arguments, see David H. Anderson, "The Status under International Law of the Maritime Areas around Svalbard." (2009) 40 *Ocean Development and International Law* 373. For the executive summary of the Norwegian submission, see www.un.org/depts/los/clcs_new/submissions_files/nor06/nor_exec_sum.pdf.

It now appears that Russia and Iceland have abandoned their hard-line position. In 2009, the CLCS responded favorably to a Norwegian submission that used Svalbard as a basis for asserting sovereignty rights over a substantial area of extended continental shelf northwards of the archipelago.[37] Significantly, neither Russia nor Iceland nor any other country has expressed opposition to the CLCS's recommendations, which means those recommendations are now final and binding. Russia and Norway then concluded a boundary treaty for the Barents Sea in 2011 that implicitly accepts that Svalbard generates a Norwegian 200-nautical-mile EEZ.[38]

However, the British position remains alive and well, for if the non-discriminatory rights set out in the Svalbard Treaty apply beyond twelve nautical miles, they apply to the full extent of the continental shelf also. Of course, so too will the Norwegian rights to regulate environmental protection, including the right to impose strict conditions on oil and gas exploitation or even to ban it outright. Relations between the United Kingdom and Norway on this issue may be slightly strained. In 2006, the United Kingdom reportedly held a meeting of some key parties to the Svalbard Treaty, including Russia and the United States. Norwegian officials were unaware of the meeting until after it had taken place. When they did become aware, an "enraged" Foreign Minister Johan Gahr Støre immediately called his British counterpart for an explanation.[39]

A final aspect of the Svalbard Treaty is that it effectively demilitarizes the archipelago by prohibiting the establishment of any "naval base" or "fortification" and stating that it "may never be used for warlike pur-poses."[40] During the Cold War, the Soviet Union argued that these constraints were violated when Norwegian military vessels and aircraft visited Svalbard, and when the archipelago was placed under NATO command.[41] These tensions have since dissipated. However, as the

---

[37] "Summary of the Recommendations of the Commission on the Limits of the Continental Shelf in Regard to the Submission Made by Norway in Respect of Areas in the Arctic Ocean, the Barents Sea and the Norwegian Sea on 27 November 2006," March 27, 2009, available at www.un.org/Depts/los/clcs_new/submissions_files/nor06/nor_rec_summ.pdf.

[38] Tore Henriksen and Geir Ulfstein, "Maritime Delimitation in the Arctic: The Barents Sea Treaty." (2011) 42 *Ocean Development and International Law* 1 at 9.

[39] "Big Powers Discussed Spitsbergen Without Norway," April 18, 2007, www.spitsbergen-svalbard.info/topical.html.

[40] Treaty concerning the Archipelago of Spitsbergen, n. 24, above, Art. 9.

[41] Ulfstein, n. 26, above, sec. B, para. 15.

first instrument to demilitarize part of the Arctic, the Svalbard Treaty constitutes a small but relevant precedent for advocates of an Arctic-wide nuclear-weapon-free zone or other, intermediary steps toward that goal.[42]

If Svalbard is an example of shared sovereignty, or at least the limitation of sovereignty through the according of treaty rights to other states, Greenland is an example of sovereignty approaching a transition point. For the largest island in the world not considered to be a continent, is well on its way to becoming the first Inuit-governed state.

3 Greenland

Greenland, at 2.1 million square kilometers, is larger than France, Germany, Italy, and Spain combined.[43] According to the Icelandic sagas, Erik the Red discovered the island in the tenth century and named it Greenland in order to attract settlers. There was a degree of misrepresentation involved, because a vast ice sheet covers 80 percent of the island.

Denmark's long-standing claim to Greenland took on more significance in 1916 when Denmark agreed to sell the Virgin Islands to the United States. As part of the deal, US Secretary of State Robert Lansing publicly declared: "[T]he Government of the United States will not object to the Danish government extending their political and economic interests to the whole of Greenland."[44]

When Norway proclaimed sovereignty over Eastern Greenland in 1931, Denmark took the matter to the Permanent Court of International Justice. Two years later, the Court found in favor of Denmark, holding that sovereignty could be established and maintained through "very little in the way of actual exercise of sovereign rights, provided that the other state could not make out a superior claim. This is particularly true in the case of claims to sovereignty over areas in thinly populated or unsettled countries."[45]

---

[42] See discussion, Chapter 8, below.

[43] For a map of Greenland, showing its proximity to Canada, Iceland, and the Norwegian island of Jan Mayen, see www.slaw.ca/wp-content/uploads/2009/06/canada-greenland.png.

[44] Convention between the United States and Denmark: Cession of the Danish West Indies, US Treaty Series No. 269, 39 Stat. 1706.

[45] *Legal Status of Eastern Greenland Case (Denmark v. Norway)* (1933) PCIJ Reports, Series A/B, No. 53, p. 46, available at www.icj-cij.org/pcij/serie_AB/AB_53/01_Groenland_Oriental_Arret.pdf.

In 1941, Denmark and the United States signed an "Agreement Relating to the Defense of Greenland" whereby the latter country took over responsibility for the island until the end of the Second World War.[46] In 1953, Greenland became an integral part of the Kingdom of Denmark. The island was granted home rule in 1979 and six years later it exercised its new powers by leaving the European Economic Community (EEC) over concerns about commercial fishing regulations and a ban on sealskin products.[47] As a result, Greenland is not a member of the European Union today.

In 2008, a referendum on greater autonomy resulted in Greenland taking on responsibility for judicial affairs, policing, and natural resources.[48] For the moment, Denmark retains control of foreign and defense policy and represents Greenland at the United Nations and other international organizations, including the Arctic Council.

The new separation of powers has caused some confusion with respect to oil and gas development in offshore areas. In 2010, after a Scottish oil company began drilling on the Greenland side of Baffin Bay, Canadian diplomats expressed uncertainty as to whether a 1983 agreement with Denmark on the marine environment still applied.[49] They later concluded that Greenland had succeeded to Denmark's obligations under the agreement.[50] In 2012, the separation of powers also affected the negotiation of a boundary treaty for the Lincoln Sea. The delimitation aspects of the treaty were dealt with between the governments of Canada and Denmark, before negotiations on a joint management regime for straddling hydrocarbons began between Canada and the government of Greenland.

Natural resources will likely drive further changes in the relationship between Greenland and Denmark, with one senior Greenlandic official

[46] 1941 Agreement Relating to the Defense of Greenland. (1941) 35(3) *American Journal of International Law Supplement* 129.
[47] See "Greenland Out of EEC," *New York Times,* February 4, 1985, available at www.nytimes.com/1985/02/04/business/greenland-out-of-eec.html.
[48] 2009 Act on Greenland Self-Government, available at http://uk.nanoq.gl/~/media/f74bab3359074b29aab8c1e12aa1ecfe.ashx.
[49] Canadian Press, "Drilling Plans Near Greenland Spark Concern," April 30, 2010, available at www.ctv.ca/CTVNews/Canada/20100430/Greenland-drilling-warning-100430/.
[50] See the website of the Canadian Department of Foreign Affairs, "Denmark (Faroe Islands/Greenland)," at www.international.gc.ca/arctic-arctigue/partners-international-partenaires.aspx?lang=eng ("As a successor to the 1983 Danish–Canadian Agreement for Cooperation Relating to the Marine Environment, Greenland cooperates with Canada to develop effective oil and gas guidelines and prevent oil spills").

saying that the island is "just one big oil strike away" from independence.[51] Indeed, the self-government agreement foresees that the annual transfer of 3.4 billion Danish krone (approximately $580 million) from the Danish to the Greenland government will be reduced as natural resource revenues increase.[52] The self-government agreement also foresees that Greenland will eventually become independent, though it emphasizes that this outcome will result through negotiations – and not, therefore, a unilateral declaration.[53] Since 88 percent of Greenlanders are Inuit, the territory is well on its way to becoming the world's first Inuit-governed state. This development will be important, not just for the Inuit of Greenland, but also – as Chapter 7 explains – for the rights of indigenous peoples in international law.

There will also be a small element of irony in Greenland's achievement of independence. As was explained above, Denmark has not hesitated to invoke the Greenlandic Inuit's historic "use and occupancy" of Hans Island in support of its own claim to sovereignty there. Nor, as the following example shows, has Denmark been the only Arctic country to behave in this way.

4 Sverdrup Islands

Incredibly remote and historically besieged with ice, the Sverdrup Islands of northern Nunavut were initially discovered, mapped, and claimed for Norway by Otto Sverdrup, the famed Norwegian explorer, who had sailed there on his purpose-built ship the *Fram* between 1898 and 1902.[54] Although the Norwegian government had shown little interest in Sverdrup's claim, in 1930, the Canadian government decided to close off that possibility. Negotiations were initiated, with the British government acting as an intermediary because the Statute of Westminster – which accorded Canada independence in foreign policy – would not be adopted until the following year. An offer was made to purchase Sverdrup's maps and papers concerning his voyage, ostensibly

---

[51] *Environmental News Service*, "Wikileaks Cables: 'Cold Peace' Among Resource-Hungry Arctic Nations," May 18, 2011, available at www.ens-newswire.com/ens/may2011/2011-05-18-01.html.

[52] 2009 Act on Greenland Self-Government, n. 48, above, chap. 3, secs. 5 and 8.

[53] Ibid., chap. 8, sec. 21.

[54] The Fram Museum in Oslo, where the historic ship is housed, provides a useful summary of Sverdrup's expedition: www.frammuseum.no/Polar-Heroes/Main-Heroes/Main-Hero-3.aspx.

to assist him in his retirement, in return for Norway formally recognizing Canadian sovereignty. A lump sum payment of $67,000 was agreed upon, after the Canadian government had decided that annual payments might cost too much if the seventy-six-year-old explorer lived an unusually long life.[55] As it happened, Sverdrup died just two weeks after the settlement was announced. But Canada did much better in the settlement itself, which took the form of an "exchange of notes" – a kind of international treaty comprising a series of letters expressing an agreement between states. The letters are worth reading, for they demonstrate just how easily claims can be extinguished, and also the early emergence of indigenous rights in Arctic international law.

In a letter written on 8 August 1930, the Norwegian chargé d'affaires in London asked the British foreign secretary to "inform His Majesty's Government in Canada that the Norwegian Government, who do not as far as they are concerned claim sovereignty over the Sverdrup Islands, formally recognise the sovereignty of His Britannic Majesty over these islands."[56] The Canadian diplomats had achieved their goal quickly and at relatively little cost, but the Norwegian chargé d'affaires had stumbled badly. Almost immediately, he wrote a second letter:

With reference to my note of to-day in regard to my Government's recognition of the sovereignty of His Britannic Majesty over the Sverdrup Islands, I have the honour, under instructions from my Government, to inform you that the said note has been despatched on the assumption on the part of the Norwegian Government that His Britannic Majesty's Government in Canada will declare themselves willing not to interpose any obstacles to Norwegian fishing, hunting or industrial and trading activities in the areas which the recognition comprises.[57]

Canadian sovereignty had already been recognized, however, and so there was nothing left to negotiate. The Canadians could have dismissed

---

[55] It has been suggested that a side-deal also existed between Norway and the United Kingdom, with Norway recognizing Canadian sovereignty over the Sverdrup Islands in return for the United Kingdom recognizing Norwegian sovereignty over the island of Jan Mayen. See Thorleif Tobias Thorleifsson, "Norway 'must really drop their absurd claims such as that to the Otto Sverdrup Islands.' Bi-Polar International Diplomacy: The Sverdrup Islands Question, 1902–1930," MA thesis, Simon Fraser University, 2006, available at http://ir.lib.sfu.ca/retrieve/3720/etd2367.pdf. For a discussion of Jan Mayen, see Chapter 2, below.

[56] Exchange of Notes regarding the Recognition by the Norwegian Government of the Sovereignty of His Majesty over the Sverdrup Islands, Canada Treaty Series 1930, No. 17, available at http://byers.typepad.com/arctic/1930.html.

[57] Ibid.

the second letter out of hand, but instead they offered a reason for denying the request. On November 5, 1930, the British chargé d'affaires in Oslo wrote to the Norwegian Minister for Foreign Affairs:

[I]t is the established policy of the Government of Canada, as set forth in an Order in Council of July 19, 1926, and subsequent Orders, to protect the Arctic areas as hunting and trapping preserves for the sole use of the aboriginal population of the Northwest Territories, in order to avert the danger of want and starvation through the exploitation of the wild life by white hunters and traders. Except with the permission of the Commissioner of the Northwest Territories, no person other than native Indians or Eskimos [i.e., Inuit] is allowed to hunt, trap, trade, or traffic for any purpose whatsoever in a large area of the mainland and in the whole Arctic island area, with the exception of the southern portion of Baffin Island.[58]

Significantly, non-aboriginals were thereby prohibited not just from hunting and trapping in the High Arctic but from all commercial activities there.

The letter from the British chargé d'affaires concluded with a conciliatory but meaningless offer:

Should, however, the regulations be altered at any time in the future, His Majesty's Government in Canada would treat with the most friendly consideration any application by Norwegians to share in any fishing, hunting, industrial, or trading activities in the areas which the recognition comprises.[59]

The phrase "friendly consideration" did not create a legal right of Norwegian access to the Sverdrup Islands, though Norwegian companies are certainly free to participate in the Canadian resource sector according to the normal rules governing foreign investment. And Statoil, a Norwegian state-owned company that is already active in the tar sands of Western Canada, may well wish to look north. Thanks to exploration work carried out in the 1970s and 80s, the Sverdrup Islands are known to contain at least $1 trillion worth of oil and gas deposits.[60]

5 Summary

Title to territory is hardly a major issue in Arctic politics, with tiny Hans Island being the only disputed land in the entire circumpolar region.

---

[58] Ibid.   [59] Ibid.
[60] See, e.g., Zhuoheng Chen, et al., "Petroleum Potential in Western Sverdrup Basin, Canadian Arctic Archipelago." (December 2000) 48(4) *Bulletin of Canadian Petroleum Geology* 323–338.

The dispute could easily be solved by connecting the maritime boundary on one side of the island with the maritime boundary on the other. Another solution would be for Denmark and Canada to create a condominium, which would make Hans Island the second example of shared or limited sovereignty rights in the Arctic. Since 1920, Norway's title over the Svalbard archipelago has been subject to economic access rights on the part of other states, including Russia, which operates a coalmine there. Greenland, on the other hand, is approaching the point where it might soon transition from being sovereign Danish territory to being a fully independent, Inuit-governed state. However, around Hans Island, Svalbard, Greenland, and the rest of the Arctic, the most difficult and pressing issues of international law concern the maritime domain.

2 Maritime boundaries

James Baker's Ph.D. thesis is about the assumption – widespread within the discipline of international relations – that the history and politics of boundaries at sea are similar to those of borders on land. As he has discovered, there are in fact important differences. Most notably, maritime boundaries have never been defined through force and conquest, but rather by the development and application of rules of international law that conceive of offshore rights as derivative of rights on land.

Baker's analysis is of critical importance in the Arctic. For unlike the Antarctic, a continent surrounded by oceans, the Arctic is an ocean surrounded by continents. For this reason, it is governed in large part by the law of the sea – the body of unwritten but nevertheless binding rules of customary international law that were codified in the 1982 United Nations Convention on the Law of the Sea (UNCLOS).[1] So far, 164 countries have ratified this so-called "constitution of the oceans," including four of the five Arctic Ocean coastal states: Canada, Denmark (Greenland), Norway, and Russia.[2] The remaining Arctic Ocean country, the United States, accepts the key provisions of UNCLOS as customary international law.[3] The United States might also ratify UNCLOS soon, with its concerns about the national security implications of accepting limits on the freedom of the seas having been superseded by concerns about terrorism and shipments of "weapons of mass destruction" (WMDs), as well as by a desire to secure international recognition of

---

[1] See Introduction, n. 15, above.
[2] See "Table Recapitulating the Status of the Convention and of the Related Agreements, as at 6 November 2012," available at www.un.org/Depts/los/reference_files/status2010.pdf.
[3] See Introduction, n. 25, above.

28

its sovereign rights over large areas of so-called "extended continental shelf."

As was explained in the Introduction, each coastal state has the right to claim a twelve-nautical-mile territorial sea. Each coastal state also has the right to claim an exclusive economic zone (EEZ) from twelve to 200 nautical miles offshore where, as the name suggests, it holds exclusive rights over the natural resources of the water column and seabed. A parallel rule provides each coastal state with inherent rights over resource exploitation on any adjoining continental shelf, the relatively shallow area of ocean floor extending from most landmasses. By the early 1970s, it had become clear that new technologies and higher prices would eventually lead to the exploitation of oil and gas reserves more than 200 nautical miles from shore. As a result, Article 76 of UNCLOS specifies that a coastal state may exercise sovereign rights over an extended continental shelf beyond 200 nautical miles – if the depth and shape of the seabed and the thickness of underlying sediments indicate a "natural prolongation" of the coastal state's landmass.[4]

The boundaries between coastal states that adjoin or oppose (i.e., across a bay, strait, or other portion of ocean) each other in these different maritime zones have featured prominently in third-party dispute settlement, including in approximately one-fifth of the cases heard by the International Court of Justice since 1947.[5] However, most maritime boundaries are the result of negotiations leading to treaties and, as the following overview shows, this is certainly the case in the Arctic. There are also numerous maritime boundaries around the world that remain unresolved, including one in the Arctic.[6]

1 1973 Canada–Denmark Boundary Treaty

After the super-tanker SS *Manhattan* transited the Northwest Passage in 1969,[7] Canada extended its territorial sea from three to twelve nautical

---

[4] The interpretation and application of Article 76 is discussed in Chapter 3, below.
[5] For a list of ICJ cases, see www.icj-cij.org/docket/index.php?p1=3andp2=2.
[6] For a visual depiction of the general situation, the Durham University International Boundary Research Unit map on "Maritime Jurisdiction and Boundaries in the Arctic Region" is an excellent place to start, available at www.dur.ac.uk/resources/ibru/arctic.pdf.
[7] For more on the Northwest Passage dispute, see Chapter 5, below.

miles.[8] In doing so, it overlooked that the new limit extended beyond a "median" line between Ellesmere Island and Greenland.[9] Once this consequence was realized, boundary negotiations with Denmark commenced. In 1973, the two countries agreed to divide the ocean floor between Canada and Greenland using a median or "equidistance" line, i.e., a line that at every point – in this case 109 of the 127 agreed "turning points" – is an equal distance from the nearest point on each of the two opposing coasts.[10] Since then, they have also used the resulting 1,450-nautical-mile boundary to define their fishing zones, meaning that the continental shelf delimitation has informally become an all-purpose maritime boundary.[11]

One interesting aspect of the treaty is how it deals with the issue of Hans Island – the disputed islet between Ellesmere Island and Greenland – without even making reference to it.[12] The treaty uses two series of geodesic lines to define the dividing line in Nares Strait, the first of which stops at turning point 122 (located at 80°49.2′N, 66°29.0′W) and the second of which begins at turning point 123 (located just half a mile away at 80°49.8′N, 66°26.3′W).[13] The negotiators quite deliberately placed turning point 122 at the low water mark on the south shore of Hans Island, and turning point 123 at the low water mark on the north shore of the island.[14] But since the treaty concerns

---

[8] Act to Amend the Territorial Sea and Fishing Zones Act, 1969–1970 Statutes of Canada, chap. 68, sec. 1243. The change, which was motivated at least partly by fisheries concerns elsewhere, took advantage of a developing rule of customary international law allowing states to claim twelve-mile territorial seas; by 1970, nearly sixty states had done just that. See Pierre Trudeau, "Remarks to the Press Following the Introduction of Legislation on Arctic Pollution, Territorial Sea and Fishing Zones in the Canadian House of Commons on April 8, 1970." (1970) 9 ILM 600.

[9] David H. Gray, "Canada's Unresolved Maritime Boundaries." (Autumn 1997) 5(3) *IBRU Boundary and Security Bulletin* 61 at 68, available at www.dur.ac.uk/resources/ibru/publications/full/bsb5-3_gray.pdf.

[10] Agreement between the Government of Canada and the Government of the Kingdom of Denmark Relating to the Delimitation of the Continental Shelf between Greenland and Canada, December 17, 1973, available at www.un.org/depts/los/LEGISLATIONANDTREATIES/PDFFILES/TREATIES/DNK-CAN1973CS.PDF. The other points were either adjusted from the true equidistance line (110–113) or arbitrarily picked near the center of the channel (114–127).

[11] Gray, n. 9, above, at 68.   [12] For more on Hans Island, see Chapter 1, above.

[13] Agreement between the Government of Canada and the Government of the Kingdom of Denmark, n. 10, above.

[14] Although the two turning points later turned out to be just slightly off the low water marks, the common intent – to delimit the entire maritime boundary – was clear.

the delimitation of continental shelf rather than land, the negotiators apparently saw no need to mention this.

The treaty also has provisions concerning the possible discovery of hydrocarbons along or near the boundary. Article 3 addresses the less-than-exact character of the new line:

In view of the inadequacies of existing hydrographic charts for certain areas and failing a precise determination of the low-water line in all sectors along the coast of Greenland and the eastern coasts of the Canadian Arctic Islands, neither Party shall issue licences for exploitation of mineral resources in areas border-ing the dividing line without the prior agreement of the other Party as to exact determination of the geographic co-ordinates of points of that part of the dividing line bordering upon the areas in question.[15]

Relatedly, the treaty addresses the complex but not uncommon issue of differing geodetic coordinate systems, as David Gray explained in 1997:

From a surveying stand-point, the interesting aspect is the fact that the Canadian maps and charts were drawn on the North American Datum (NAD) 1927 and the Danish maps and charts on the Qornoq Datum which uses a different ellipsoid. The technical experts knew that there was a difference between the geodetic coordinate systems but had no way of knowing the magnitudes. So the practical solution was to set the problem aside for future consideration and to assume that the two coordinate systems were identical. Provision was made in the agreement to re-open the agreement when geodetic data was available to relate the two geodetic datums and if new surveys located new turning points from which one could compute the equidistance line.

In 1982, the two countries agreed to re-open the computation of the equi-distance line south of 75°N and the work has been going on ever since [conclud-ing in 2003].

Because there is now the capability to interrelate the Qornoq Datum, NAD 1927, NAD 1983 and World Geodetic System 1984, it is probable that the future amendment to the coordinates will be provided in several datums and may reduce the number of turning points of the boundary from the present 113 points (south of 75°N).[16]

This process is specifically provided for in the treaty, with Article 4(2) laying out the consequences:

---

[15] Agreement between the Government of Canada and the Government of the Kingdom of Denmark, n. 10, above, emphasis added.

[16] Gray, n. 9, above, at 68. In the end, only the southern 109 points were recomputed, and only on WGS-84, although NAD-83 is equivalent for all practical purposes. Personal communication from David Gray, November 2012.

If new surveys or resulting charts or maps should indicate that the dividing line requires adjustment, the Parties agree that an adjustment will be carried out on the basis of the same principles as those used in determining the dividing line, and such adjustment shall be provided for in a Protocol to this Agreement.[17]

Article 5 addresses the possibility of hydrocarbon reserves or other exploitable seabed resources straddling the new boundary even after it has been more precisely defined. But, unlike some boundary treaties,[18] it only requires that the parties negotiate in these circumstances, rather than providing a process or mechanism for resolving the matter:

If any single geological petroleum structure or field, or any single geological structure or field of any other mineral deposit, including sand and gravel, extends across the dividing line and the part of such structure or field which is situated on one side of the dividing line is exploitable, wholly or in part, from the other side of the dividing line, the Parties shall seek to reach an agreement as to the exploitation of such structure or field.[19]

Finally, the negotiators chose not to delineate a boundary north of 82°13.0′N where Nares Strait opens into the Lincoln Sea off Ellesmere Island and Greenland. This decision led to two further issues. The first is dealt with later in this chapter, and concerns two small lens-shaped disputed areas within 200 nautical miles from shore that resulted from a difference of opinion as to whether Beaumont Island off northwest Greenland could be used for the purposes of determining Denmark's straight baselines. The second issue is addressed in Chapter 4, and concerns the location of the boundary between the adjoining extended continental shelves of Canada and Denmark beyond 200 nautical miles from shore. The Canada–Denmark Boundary Treaty itself, however, is a fairly standard instrument. Based on the equidistance principle and an on-going cooperative relationship between close allies, it delivered all that was needed at the time – and nothing more.

2 1990 Bering Sea Treaty

There is no Arctic boundary dispute between Russia and the United States because the two countries negotiated a 1,600-nautical-mile

---

[17] Agreement between the Government of Canada and the Government of the Kingdom of Denmark, n. 10, above.

[18] See, e.g., the Norway–Russia Barents Sea Treaty discussed later in this chapter.

[19] Agreement between the Government of Canada and the Government of the Kingdom of Denmark, n. 10, above.

all-purpose maritime boundary in the Bering Sea, Bering Strait, and Chukchi Sea in 1990.[20] Named the "Baker–Shevardnadze Line" after its signatories, US Secretary of State James Baker and Soviet Foreign Minister Eduard Shevardnadze, the boundary is based on a line described in the 1867 treaty by which the United States purchased Alaska from Russia:

The western limit within which the territories and dominion conveyed, are contained, passes through a point in Behring's straits on the parallel of sixty-five degrees thirty minutes north latitude, at its intersection by the meridian which passes midway between the islands of Krusenstern, or Ignalook, and the island of Ratmanoff, or Noonarbook, and proceeds due north, without limitation, into the same Frozen ocean. The same western limit, beginning at the same initial point, proceeds thence in a course nearly southwest through Behring's straits and Behring's sea, so as to pass midway between the northwest point of the island of St. Lawrence and the southeast point of Cape Choukotski, to the meridian of one hundred and seventy-two west longitude; thence, from the intersection of that meridian, in a south-westerly direction, so as to pass midway between the island of Attou and the Copper island of the Kormandorski couplet or group in the North Pacific ocean, to the meridian of one hundred and ninety-three degrees west longitude, so as to include in the territory conveyed the whole of the Aleutian islands east of that meridian.[21]

However, the 1867 Convention was silent on the type of line, map projection, and horizontal datum to be used in depicting the boundary. The two countries, which took different approaches to mapping, were consequently unable to agree on the precise location of the line. As Vlad Kaczynski explains:

Cartographers normally use two types of lines to delineate marine boundaries. These are rhomb [rhumb] lines and geodetic lines (also known as great circle arcs) that are used on two common map projections, Mercator and conical. Depending on the type of line and map projection used, lines will either appear as straight or curved lines. For example, a rhomb line will be a straight line on a Mercator projection, whereas a geodetic line is curved. Because each country interpreted the line described in the 1867 Treaty as a straight line, the Soviet

[20] Agreement between the United States of America and the Union of Soviet Socialist Republics on the Maritime Boundary (1990) 29 ILM 941, available at www.state.gov/documents/organization/125431.pdf; See, generally, Robert W. Smith, "United States–Russia Maritime Boundary," in Gerald Henry Blake (ed.), *Maritime Boundaries* (London: Routledge, 1994), 91.
[21] Treaty concerning the Cession of the Russian Possessions in North America, June 20, 1867, Art. 1, available at http://avalon.law.yale.edu/19th_century/treatywi.asp.

Union depicted the Bering Sea marine boundary as a rhomb line on a Mercator projection whereas the US used a geodetic line on a conical projection. While both appear as straight lines on their respective map projections, each country's claim maximized the amount of ocean area and seafloor under their respective control.[22]

The result was a disputed zone of approximately 15,000 square nautical miles.[23]

The 1990 treaty divided that disputed zone roughly in half, with the new line explicitly delimiting jurisdiction over both fisheries and seabed resources. The United States was quick to ratify the treaty, with the Senate giving its advice and consent to ratification in 1991. However, the treaty attracted considerable opposition within the Soviet Union and later Russia, based on the fact that the boundary set by the treaty in the Bering Sea runs significantly to the west of where an equidistance line – the default approach in international law – would be located.[24] Opponents of the treaty attribute this result to the weak negotiating position of the Soviet Union, which was literally disintegrating as the talks were taking place, and feel the interests of fishermen in Russia's Far East were not protected.[25]

Concurrent with the signature of the 1990 treaty, the Soviet Union and the United States entered into an exchange of notes whereby, "pending the entry into force of that Agreement, the two Governments agree to abide by the terms of that Agreement as of June 15, 1990."[26] The exchange of notes is consistent with Article 25(1) of the 1969 Vienna Convention on the Law of Treaties, which reads: "A treaty or a part of a treaty is applied provisionally pending its entry into force if: the treaty itself so provides; or the negotiating States have in some

---

[22] Vlad M. Kaczynski, "US–Russian Bering Sea Marine Border Dispute: Conflict over Strategic Assets, Fisheries and Energy Resources." (May 2007) 20 *Russian Analytical Digest* 2, available at www.laender-analysen.de/russland/rad/pdf/Russian_Analytical_Digest _20.pdf.

[23] For a map showing the difference between the rhumb line on a Mercator projection and the geodetic line on a conical projection, see Figure 1 in Kaczynski, ibid., p. 3. The equidistance principle is applied – and sometimes modified – through a three-step approach. See discussion, Chapter 3, below.

[24] For a map showing the difference between the 1990 boundary and an equidistance line, see Figure 3 in Kaczynski, ibid., p. 5.

[25] Ibid., pp. 3–4.

[26] The exchange of notes is reproduced in Alex G. Oude Elferink, "The 1990 USSR–USA Maritime Boundary Agreement." (1991) 6 *International Journal of Estuarine and Coastal Law* 41, Annexes 2 and 3.

other manner so agreed."[27] In addition, both countries continue to behave as if the treaty is in force and, in 2007, Kaczynski reported that discussions had been re-opened in "an attempt to resolve the issue."[28]

One currently relevant aspect of the treaty concerns the fact that, northwards from a point in the center of the Bering Strait (65°30'00"N, 168°58'37"W), the boundary follows the 168°58'37"W meridian into the Arctic Ocean "as far as permitted under international law." Of course, what is permitted under international law can change over time. For instance, UNCLOS was concluded in 1982 but did not come into force until 1994. This meant that at the time the Bering Sea Treaty was concluded Article 76 of UNCLOS was not yet binding on either state, nor would its content have become part of customary international law. Today, it is recognized that coastal states may exercise sovereign rights over extended continental shelves beyond 200 nautical miles, with Article 76 providing criteria for determining the outer limit in any particular location.[29] The negotiators of the Bering Sea Treaty anticipated these changes and provided a boundary that would follow them northwards.

That said, and as Chapter 3 explains, it is possible that a resolution of the United States–Canada boundary dispute in the Beaufort Sea could result in Canadian sovereign rights over the extended continental shelf reaching as far west as the 168°58'37"W meridian. In this scenario, the Russia–United States boundary would logically extend only as far north as US jurisdiction (i.e., the point where the Russia–United States boundary intersected with the Canada–United States boundary), leaving an unresolved boundary between Russian and Canadian extended continental shelves further to the north.

The Bering Sea Treaty also contains some important innovations, such as the use of "special areas." In these areas, sovereign rights generated as the result of proximity to one treaty partner's coastline but cut off from that coastline by the newly agreed boundary, are transferred to the other treaty partner so as to maximize their combined areas of national jurisdiction. This approach enabled the Soviet Union

---

[27] 1969 Vienna Convention on the Law of Treaties, 1155 UNTS 331, 8 ILM 679, available at http://untreaty.un.org/ilc/texts/instruments/english/conventions/1_1_1969.pdf.

[28] Kaczynski, n. 22, above, p. 5.

[29] The International Court of Justice recently ruled that Article 76(1) is part of customary international law: *Territorial and Maritime Dispute (Nicaragua v. Colombia)*, Introduction, n. 25, above, para. 118. For more on the interpretation and application of Article 76, see Chapters 3 and 4, below.

and the United States to agree on a line that comes closer than 200 nautical miles to the Soviet/Russian coastline at several points, while remaining more than 200 nautical miles from the US coastline.[30] Arguably, such a line would normally have had the effect of transforming those outward portions of the Soviet/Russian EEZ into high seas. But the negotiators were able to avoid this outcome by designating several special areas where Soviet EEZ rights were assigned to the United States notwithstanding that those rights were generated by the Soviet/Russian coastline.[31] A similar but smaller special area was created toward the northern end of the boundary in the Chukchi Sea, where the line comes within 200 nautical miles of the US coastline in an area well beyond 200 nautical miles of the Soviet/Russian coast. In that case, EEZ rights generated by the US coastline were assigned to the Soviet Union.

This approach raises the question of whether such assignments of EEZ rights are opposable to third states. At least one Russian international lawyer has argued that the attempt to use special areas is contrary to customary international law and UNCLOS.[32] The answer to the question might lie in prescription, since third states have not protested these special areas. Two decades later, it seems open to the United States and Russia to argue that the rights have become generally opposable as a result of acquiescence, in a process akin to the acquisition of territory through prescription as well as to the creation of customary international law.[33]

3 Maritime boundaries around Jan Mayen

Jan Mayen is a relatively small (373 km^2) island located roughly 250 nautical miles east of Greenland, 360 nautical miles northeast of Iceland and 600 nautical miles from Norway. In the early seventeenth century, it served as a base for Dutch whalers. The Norwegian Meteorological Institute established a station on Jan Mayen in 1921 and Norway

---

[30] Agreement between the United States of America and the Union of Soviet Socialist Republics on the Maritime Boundary, n. 20, above.

[31] The map included in the treaty (ibid.) provides a useful visual image of the "special areas."

[32] Aleksandr Antonovich Kovalev, *Contemporary Issues of the Law of the Sea: Modern Russian Approaches* (trans. W. E. Butler) (Utrecht: Eleven International Publishing, 2004), pp. 67–68.

[33] For a similar view, see Kaczynski, n. 22, above, p. 5. On prescription, see Jennings and Watts, *Oppenheim's International Law*, Chapter 1, n. 9, above, pp. 705–712. On customary international law, see Byers, *Custom, Power and the Power of Rules*, Introduction, n. 39, above.

annexed the island four years later. The government of Norway formally incorporated the island into the Kingdom of Norway in 1930, but only after ensuring – perhaps contingent on Norway's recognition of Canadian sovereignty over the Sverdrup Islands[34] – that Britain would recognize the claim. Today, only a few dozen people live on Jan Mayen, all of them employees of the Norwegian Armed Forces or the Norwegian Meteorological Institute. However, the EEZ around Jan Mayen supports a sizeable fishery.

In a case initiated by Denmark, the International Court of Justice delimited a single maritime boundary between Greenland and Jan Mayen in 1993.[35] The Court began with a median line, on a provisional basis, and then considered whether "special circumstances" justified any adjustments in order to achieve an "equitable result." The Court concluded that the much greater length of the Greenland coast was a special circumstance requiring a delimitation that tracked closer to Jan Mayen; and that the line should also be shifted somewhat eastwards to allow Denmark equitable access to certain fish stocks.

Other forms of dispute resolution have been applied to the waters and seabed between Jan Mayen and Iceland, which, again, is located 360 nautical miles away. In 1981, Norway and Iceland concluded a treaty whereby they agreed that Iceland's EEZ and continental shelf extend to the full 200 nautical miles from the Icelandic coast in the area between Jan Mayen and Iceland, despite the proximity of the Norwegian island.[36] However, the treaty also gave Norway the right to 25 percent participation in oil and gas exploration on a portion of Iceland's continental shelf south of the new boundary, and Iceland the right to 25 percent participation in oil and gas exploration on a portion of Jan Mayen's continental shelf north of the new boundary.[37] The treaty provides for the creation of a unitization agreement in the case of oil and gas deposits that straddle the boundary.[38]

In 2008, the two countries adopted follow-up treaties setting out more-detailed frameworks for cooperative oil and gas exploration of

---

[34] See Thorleifsson, Chapter 1, n. 55, above. For more on the Sverdrup Islands, see Chapter 1, above.

[35] *Maritime Delimitation in the Area between Greenland and Jan Mayen (Denmark v. Norway)* (1993) ICJ Reports 38, available at www.icj-cij.org/docket/files/78/6743.pdf.

[36] Agreement on the Continental Shelf between Iceland and Jan Mayen, October 22, 1981, available at www.un.org/depts/los/LEGISLATIONANDTREATIES/PDFFILES/TREATIES/ISL-NOR1981CS.PDF.

[37] Ibid., Arts. 5 and 6.   [38] Ibid., Art. 8.

straddling deposits[39] and within the two zones of 25 percent participation.[40] Although the resulting joint hydrocarbon regime was not unprecedented, it was the first to be established in Arctic waters – and as such
could provide a model for the United States–Canada dispute in the
Beaufort Sea as well as possible overlapping Canadian, Danish, and
Russian submissions concerning extended continental shelf rights in
the central Arctic Ocean.[41] According to Norwegian Foreign Minister
Jonas Gahr Støre, the arrangement provides the predictability that oil
companies need.[42]

4 2006 Greenland–Svalbard Boundary Treaty

In 2006, Denmark and Norway negotiated an all-purpose maritime
boundary between Greenland and the Norwegian Arctic archipelago
of Svalbard.[43] Roughly 430 nautical miles long, the boundary is based
on an equidistance line, adjusted slightly to take into account the
presence of Denmark's Tobias Island some thirty-eight nautical miles
off the Greenland coast.[44] By concluding the treaty, Denmark implicitly
recognized Norway's claim – discussed in Chapter 1 – that Svalbard
generates an EEZ and continental shelf. The treaty includes a provision
on straddling mineral depositions, whereby either party can initiate

---

[39] Agreement between Iceland and Norway concerning Transboundary Hydrocarbon
Deposits, November 3, 2008, available at www.nea.is/media/olia/
JM_unitisation_agreement_Iceland_Norway_2008.pdf.

[40] Agreed Minutes concerning the Right of Participation pursuant to Articles 5 and 6 of the
Agreement of 22 October 1981 between Iceland and Norway on the Continental Shelf in
the Area between Iceland and Jan Mayen, November 3, 2008, available at www.nea.is/
media/olia/JM_agreed_minutes_Iceland_Norway_2008.pdf.

[41] See Chapter 3 (Beaufort Sea) and Chapter 4, below (extended continental shelf).

[42] Jonas Karlsbakk, "Norway and Iceland Sign Border Treaty," *BarentsObserver.com*,
November 5, 2008, available at http://barentsobserver.com/en/node/20950. According
to the same report, the new treaty was signed just three days after the Norwegian Bank
gave the Icelandic government a loan of approximately 1 million euros as part of
Norway's assistance to Iceland during the global financial crisis.

[43] Agreement between the Government of the Kingdom of Norway on the one hand, and
the Government of the Kingdom of Denmark together with the Home Rule
Government of Greenland on the other hand, concerning the delimitation of the
continental shelf and the fisheries zones in the area between Greenland and Svalbard,
Copenhagen, February 20, 2006, UNTS, vol. 2378, I-42887, p. 21, available at http://
treaties.un.org/doc/Publication/UNTS/Volume%202378/v2378.pdf.

[44] See, generally, Alex G. Oude Elferink, "Maritime Delimitation between Denmark/
Greenland and Norway." (2007) 38 *Ocean Development and International Law* 375.

negotiations on possible cooperative solutions – without committing the two parties to any result.

5 2010 Barents Sea Boundary Treaty

The Barents Sea lies north of Norway's Finnmark region and Russia's Kola Peninsula, between Norway's Svalbard archipelago to the northwest and two Russian archipelagos – Franz Josef Land and Novaya Zemlya – to the northeast and east. Roughly 400,000 square nautical miles in size, it has an average depth of only 230 meters. The entire seabed constitutes continental shelf, making the Barents Sea a prime location for fish, oil, and natural gas. The Snøhvit gas field off northwest Norway is already producing and has estimated reserves of 193 billion cubic meters.[45] The gas is piped 140 kilometers along the ocean floor to a liquefaction plant at Hammerfest and then loaded into super-cooled tankers bound for Japan, France, and Spain.[46] Further to the east, but still within Norwegian jurisdiction, the Goliat oil field has estimated recoverable reserves of 174 million barrels.[47] On the Russian side of the Barents Sea, the massive Shtokman gas field has an estimated 3.8 trillion cubic meters of natural gas and 37 million tons of natural gas condensates.[48]

For more than three decades, Oslo and Moscow contested roughly 50,000 square nautical miles, or about 10 percent of the Barents Sea. Moscow argued that a number of "special circumstances" were relevant to the boundary delimitation: the length and shape of Russia's coast; the size of the respective populations in the adjacent areas; ice conditions; fishing, shipping and other economic interests; and strategic concerns. It also argued that the 1920 Svalbard Treaty prevented any points on that archipelago from influencing the delimitation.[49] In Moscow's view, all these factors combined to justify a sector line along the 32°04'35"E

---

[45] See "Offshore Field Development Projects: Snohvit," at www.subseaiq.com/data/Project.aspx?project_id=223.

[46] See "Snøhvit – Unlocking Resources in the Frozen North," at www.statoil.com/en/OurOperations/ExplorationProd/ncs/Pages/SnohvitNewEnergyHistoryInTheNorth.aspx.

[47] See "Offshore Field Development Projects: Goliat," at www.subseaiq.com/data/Project.aspx?project_id=400.

[48] See "Offshore Field Development Projects: Shtokman," at www.subseaiq.com/data/Project.aspx?project_id=476.

[49] For more on the Svalbard Treaty, see Chapter 1, above.

meridian, with that line being adjusted east of Svalbard only, so as not to infringe on the area defined under the Svalbard Treaty.[50]

Oslo responded that the Soviet Union had drawn the sector line in 1926 for the sole purpose of defining the territorial status of several offshore islands, without any intention of delimiting maritime zones. It argued that a median line should instead be drawn from the termination of the Norway–Russia land border at the head of the Varangerfjord, the narrow inlet between Finnmark and the Kola Peninsula. Such a line would be equidistant, at all points, from the Norwegian and Russian mainland coasts; further out, it would be equidistant from Svalbard in the west and Novaya Zemlya and Franz Josef Land in the east.[51]

The dispute arose in the 1960s when Norway and the Soviet Union both relied on the 1958 Geneva Convention on the Continental Shelf to claim offshore rights.[52] It acquired greater consequence in 1977 when the two countries asserted 200-nautical-mile EEZs encompassing both fish and seabed resources.[53] Then, in 1996 and 1997 respectively, Norway and Russia ratified UNCLOS, Article 76 of which recognizes that a coastal state may exercise sovereign rights over an extended continental shelf more than 200 nautical miles from shore, if and where it can demonstrate a "natural prolongation" of its land mass.[54] However, Article 83 of UNCLOS also stipulates that continental shelf delimitation between states with opposite or adjacent coasts "shall be affected by agreement on the basis of international law … in order to achieve an equitable solution." The same stipulation is made in Article 74, which deals with the delimitation of overlapping EEZs.

Despite the size and importance of the dispute, and the fact that the two countries were on opposite sides of the Cold War, Norway, the Soviet Union and later Russia behaved with commendable restraint. In 1975, Oslo and Moscow concluded an Agreement on Cooperation in the Fishing Industry that emphasized the principles of conservation and rational utilization of the Barents Sea fisheries and established a Joint

---

[50] Robin Churchill and Geir Ulfstein, *Marine Management in Disputed Areas: The Case of the Barents Sea* (London: Routledge, 1992), 63.

[51] Ibid.

[52] 1958 Convention on the Continental Shelf, 499 UNTS 311, available at http://untreaty. un.org/ilc/texts/instruments/english/conventions/8_1_1958_continental_shelf.pdf. See Tore Henriksen and Geir Ulfstein, "Maritime Delimitation in the Arctic: The Barents Sea Treaty." (2011) 42 *Ocean Development and International Law* 1 at 2.

[53] Henriksen and Ulfstein, "Maritime Delimitation in the Arctic."

[54] For more on the interpretation and application of Article 76, see Chapters 3 and 4, below.

Fisheries Commission.[55] The Commission, relying on scientific advice from the International Council for the Exploration of the Sea, has recommended annual "total allowable catches" for various species.[56] The total allowable catch is divided equally between Norway and Russia. In 1976, a follow-up agreement explicitly recognized that both Norway and the Soviet Union had coastal state fisheries jurisdiction out to 200 nautical miles from shore. Significantly, the agreement also granted each country access to the other country's EEZ.[57] In 1978, the two countries moved to regulate fisheries in the area where their claims overlapped. The so-called "Grey Zone Agreement" began by stipulating that it was without prejudice to either party's legal position.[58] It recognized that Norwegian vessels in the disputed zone were under Norway's exclusive jurisdiction, and that Russian vessels were under Russia's exclusive jurisdiction. It then provided that third-party fishing vessels could enter the disputed zone if authorized to do so by either Norway or Russia. In these situations, Norway had jurisdiction over those vessels that it admitted, while Russia had jurisdiction over those that it admitted. The Grey Zone Agreement has worked well for more than three decades and been renewed on an annual basis.

At the same time, the extension of the two countries' fisheries jurisdiction left a roughly 25,000 square nautical mile area of high seas in the middle of the Barents Sea. By the 1990s, overfishing by Icelandic vessels in this unregulated area had depleted straddling stocks and created tensions with both Norway and Russia. In 1999, Norway, Russia, and Iceland concluded the so-called "Loophole Agreement," which included bilateral protocols between Norway and Iceland and between Russia

---

[55] Agreement between the Government of the Kingdom of Norway and the Government of the Union of Soviet Socialist Republics on Co-operation in the Fishing Industry, April 11, 1975, 983 UNTS 8, available at http://treaties.un.org/doc/Publication/UNTS/Volume%20983/volume-983-I-14331-English.pdf.

[56] See Norwegian Ministry of Fisheries and Coastal Affairs, "Fisheries Collaboration with Russia," available at www.fisheries.no/resource_management/International_cooperation/Fisheries_collaboration_with_Russia/.

[57] Agreement between the Government of the Union of Soviet Socialist Republics and the Government of the Kingdom of Norway concerning Mutual Relations in the Field of Fisheries, October 15, 1976, 1157 UNTS 147, Art. 1, available at http://treaties.un.org/doc/Publication/UNTS/Volume%201157/volume-1157-I-18273-English.pdf.

[58] Agreement on an Interim Practical Arrangement for Fishing in an Adjoining Area in the Barents Sea, January 11, 1978, original Norwegian text at (1978) *Overenskomster med fremmede stater* 436. See also Kristoffer Stabrun, "The Grey Zone Agreement of 1978: Fishery Concerns, Security Challenges and Territorial Interests," Fridtjof Nansen Institute Report 13/2009, available at www.fni.no/doc&pdf/FNI-R1309.pdf.

and Iceland.[59] Under the new regime, Iceland received fishing quotas in the Norwegian and Russian EEZs. In return, Norwegian fishermen obtained access to Iceland's EEZ, Russia received cash payments, and all three countries were required to prevent their nationals from fishing in the Barents Sea under flags of convenience or landing catches without a quota.

Norway and the Soviet Union also agreed to postpone all oil and gas activity in the disputed zone, and to renew efforts to negotiate a maritime boundary. In 1957, the two countries had successfully delimited a territorial sea boundary within the Varangerfjord. Informal negotiations over the maritime boundary further out began in 1970, followed by formal negotiations in 1974.[60] But it was not until 2007 that Norwegian and Russian negotiators finally succeeded in delimiting the first twenty nautical miles of a maritime boundary beyond the territorial sea.[61]

The breakthrough on the rest of the boundary came in April 2010 when Norwegian Foreign Minister Jonas Gahr Støre and Russian Foreign Minister Sergey Lavrov signed an agreement in Oslo. The agreement committed the two countries to an all-purpose boundary that would be drawn "on the basis of international law in order to achieve an equitable solution," recognizing "relevant factors . . . including the effect of major disparities in respective coastal lengths" while dividing "the overall disputed area in two parts of approximately the same size."[62] The resulting treaty – with geodetic lines connecting eight defined points – was signed five months later and ratified by the Norwegian Parliament and Russian Duma in February and March 2011, respectively.[63]

---

[59] Agreement between the Government of Iceland, the Government of Norway and the Government of the Russian Federation concerning Certain Aspects of Co-operation in the Area of Fisheries, May 15, 1999, 2070 UNTS 204, available at http://treaties.un.org/doc/Publication/UNTS/Volume%202070/v2070.pdf.

[60] Churchill and Ulfstein, n. 50, above, pp. 54 and 63.

[61] Agreement between the Russian Federation and the Kingdom of Norway on the Maritime Delimitation in the Varangerfjord Area, July 11, 2007, 67 UN Law of the Sea Bulletin 42, available at http://treaties.un.org/doc/Publication/UNTS/No%20Volume/45114/Part/I-45114–08000002801f5bf2.pdf.

[62] "Joint Statement on Maritime Delimitation and Cooperation in the Barents Sea and the Arctic Ocean," Oslo, April 27, 2010, available at www.regjeringen.no/upload/UD/Vedlegg/Folkerett/030427_english_4.pdf.

[63] 2010 Treaty between the Kingdom of Norway and the Russian Federation concerning Maritime Delimitation and Cooperation in the Barents Sea and the Arctic Ocean, English translation available at www.regjeringen.no/upload/ud/vedlegg/folkerett/avtale_engelsk.pdf. See also Henriksen and Ulfstein, n. 52, above; Thilo Neumann,

The treaty sets a single maritime boundary for both the EEZ and continental shelf within 200 nautical miles from shore and for the extended continental shelf beyond that. It is a question of only limited interest as to "whether the agreed boundary is best described as a modified median line (as argued by Norway) or a modified sector line (as argued by Russia),"[64] since the treaty divides the previously disputed sector almost exactly in half. If anything, the line seems to have resulted from a straightforward application of the principle of equity, which in the case of judicial or arbitral decisions involving maritime boundaries has frequently resulted in a splitting of the difference between opposing claims.[65]

The agreement is a model for bilateral cooperation in other respects. As the Soviet Union and the United States did in the 1990 Bering Sea Treaty,[66] the two parties created a "special area" to maximize the combined extent of their sovereign rights. Article 3(1) reads:

In the area east of the maritime delimitation line that lies within 200 nautical miles of the baselines from which the breadth of the territorial sea of mainland Norway is measured but beyond 200 nautical miles of the baselines from which the breadth of the territorial sea of the Russian Federation is measured (hereinafter "the Special Area"), the Russian Federation shall, from the day of the entry into force of the present Treaty, be entitled to exercise such sovereign rights and jurisdiction derived from exclusive economic zone jurisdiction that Norway would otherwise be entitled to exercise under international law.

Article 3(2) further recognizes that:

To the extent that the Russian Federation exercises the sovereign rights or jurisdiction in the Special Area as provided for in this Article, such exercise of sovereign rights or jurisdiction derives from the agreement of the Parties and does not constitute an extension of its exclusive economic zone. To this end, the Russian Federation shall take the necessary steps to ensure that any exercise on its part of such sovereign rights or jurisdiction in the Special Area shall be so characterized in its relevant laws, regulations and charts.

"Norway and Russia Agree on Maritime Boundary in the Barents Sea and the Arctic Ocean." (November 9, 2010) 14(34) *ASIL Insight*, available at www.asil.org/files/2010/insights/insights_101109.pdf. On the prompt ratifications, see Walter Gibbs, "Norway Hails Barents Treaty OK by Russian Duma," *Reuters*, March 26, 2011, available at www.reuters.com/article/2011/03/26/barentstreaty-idUSLDE72P0HY20110326. For a map of the new boundary line, see www.regjeringen.no/upload/UD/kart/kart_100914_ny.gif.

[64] Henriksen and Ulfstein, n. 52, above, at 7.

[65] See, e.g., Prosper Weil, *The Law of Maritime Delimitation – Reflections* (Cambridge: Grotius Publications, 1989), 9–14.

[66] See discussion, above, pp. 35–36.

As with the Bering Sea Treaty, this approach raises the question whether such special areas are opposable to third states.[67]

Foreseeing that some hydrocarbons might straddle the boundary, Norway and Russia agreed to co-manage such deposits. Article 5 stipulates: "If the existence of a hydrocarbon deposit on the continental shelf of one of the Parties is established and the other Party is of the opinion that the said deposit extends to its continental shelf, the latter Party may notify the former Party and shall submit the data on which it bases its opinion." At that point, the two countries are required to "initiate discussions on the extent of the hydrocarbon deposit and the possibility for exploitation of the deposit as a unit" with both making "their best efforts to ensure that all relevant information is made available for the purposes of these discussions." If it turns out that the deposit extends across the boundary and that its exploitation by one party would affect the interests of the other, either party may request the conclusion of a "unitization agreement" under which the deposit would be exploited as a single whole. At this point, the treaty imposes stringent obligations on both countries to enable private companies to secure drilling rights on either side of the boundary and enter into a "joint operating agreement" whereby a "unit operator" oversees the exploration and exploitation of the deposit.

This agreement between two corporations operates at the level of private law but is inextricably linked to the unitization agreement, which as a state-to-state agreement is part of public international law. For instance, Norway and Russia have prohibited themselves, by way of the treaty, from altering without prior consultation with the other state, the right of a corporation to explore for and extract hydrocarbons from a deposit. Moreover, since consultation sometimes cannot resolve all differences of opinion, the treaty sets out dispute settlement procedures – including the appointment of an arbitral tribunal in the event of a failure to reach a unitization agreement, and an independent expert in the event of a failure to agree on the apportionment of a hydrocarbon deposit. In both situations, the treaty deems that the outcome of the dispute settlement "shall be binding upon the Parties."

Norway and Russia also agreed to continue their decades-long practice of co-managing the fisheries within the previously contested area, as well as in the loophole of high seas that is enclosed by their surrounding EEZs. Article 4 of the treaty reads:

[67] See discussion, above, p. 36.

1   The fishing opportunities of either Party shall not be adversely affected by the conclusion of the present Treaty.

2   To this end, the Parties shall pursue close cooperation in the sphere of fisheries, with a view to maintain their existing respective shares of total allowable catch volumes and to ensure relative stability of their fishing activities for each of the stocks concerned.

3   The Parties shall apply the precautionary approach widely to conservation, management and exploitation of shared fish stocks, including straddling fish stocks, in order to protect the living marine resources and preserve the marine environment.

4   Except as provided for in this Article and in Annex I, nothing in this Treaty shall affect the application of agreements on fisheries cooperation between the Parties.

As Tore Henriksen and Geir Ulfstein explain, the term "relative stability" is drawn from the Common Fisheries Policy of the European Union and refers to the allocation of fishing opportunities based on predictable shares.[68] The paragraph on the "precautionary approach," a principle central to international environmental law, is taken directly from Article 6 of the 1995 UN Agreement on Straddling Fish Stocks and Highly Migratory Fish Stocks.[69] The task of applying both approaches concurrently remains with the Joint Fisheries Commission, which, as mentioned above, has operated successfully for nearly four decades.[70]

It would be difficult to overstate the importance of the Barents Sea Treaty. Again, Norway and Russia were for decades on opposite sides of the Cold War. Norway is a long-standing NATO member with modern frigates and F-16 fighter jets; most of Russia's remaining nuclear missile submarines are based along the Barents Sea. Resolving the last disputed Arctic boundary between a NATO state and Russia is a major contribution to "resetting" the relationship between the former adversaries, an objective – championed by US President Barack Obama – that also led to

---

[68] Henriksen and Ulfstein, n. 52, above, p. 8.

[69] 1995 UN Agreement for the Implementation of the Provisions of the United Nations Convention on the Law of the Sea of 10 December 1982 Relating to the Conservation and Management of Straddling Fish Stocks and Highly Migratory Fish Stocks, available at www.un.org/Depts/los/convention_agreements/convention_overview_fish_stocks.htm. For discussion of a proposed regional fisheries organization for the Arctic Ocean, see Chapter 6, below.

[70] Annex I extends the application of the 1975 and 1976 Norwegian–Russian fisheries agreements by fifteen years while also providing for an additional six years of provisional application.

the conclusion of a deep-reaching nuclear arms reduction treaty between Russia and the United States.[71]

The Barents Sea Treaty has implications for other Arctic boundary disputes, as the foreign ministers of Russia and Norway reminded the government of Canada in September 2010 when they co-authored an op-ed article in the *Globe and Mail* entitled "Canada, Take Note: Here's How to Resolve Maritime Disputes."[72] Certainly, if little Norway (population 5 million) can negotiate a win–win boundary agreement with powerful Russia (population 140 million), there is no reason for any other Arctic boundary dispute to remain unresolved. And, as the following example shows, it appears Canada is now following that advice.

6 Lincoln Sea boundary

The Lincoln Sea is that portion of the Arctic Ocean located directly to the north of Greenland and Ellesmere Island. The Arctic's thickest sea-ice is found there, pushed into the space between the two islands and held there for years by prevailing winds and ocean currents. As mentioned above, the negotiators who delimited the maritime boundary between Canada and Greenland in 1973 stopped at 82°13′N where Nares Strait opens into the Lincoln Sea.[73] As a result, nearly 200 nautical miles of continental shelf (and later EEZ) boundary to the north were left unresolved.

In 1977, Canada claimed a 200-nautical-mile fisheries zone along its Arctic Ocean coastline. The zone was bounded in the east by an equidistance line that used the low water line of the coasts of Ellesmere Island and Greenland and several fringing islands as base points.[74] Denmark adopted its own equidistance line three years later, but only after drawing straight baselines – two of which used Beaumont Island as

---

[71] For more on the geopolitical context of the "reset," see Chapter 8, below. See also New START Treaty ("Treaty between the United States of America and the Russia Federation on Measures for the Further Reduction and Limitation of Strategic Offensive Arms"), April 8, 2010, available at www.state.gov/documents/organization/140035.pdf; Peter Baker and Dan Bilefsky, "Russia and US Sign Nuclear Arms Reduction Pact." *New York Times*, April 8, 2010.

[72] Sergei Lavrov and Jonas Gahr Støre, "Canada, Take Note: Here's How to Resolve Maritime Disputes." *Globe and Mail*, September 21, 2010, available at www. theglobeandmail.com/commentary/canada-take-note-heres-how-to-resolve-maritime-disputes/article4326372/.

[73] See discussion, above, p. 32.   [74] Gray, n. 2, above, at 68.

a base point.[75] Beaumont Island is just over ten square kilometers in size and located more than twelve but less than twenty-four nautical miles from the Greenland coast. The first of the resulting baselines was 42.6 nautical miles long and ran from Cape Bryant at 82°20.4′N, 55°13.0′W to the northwest point of Beaumont Island at 82°45.2′N, 50°46.0′W. The second baseline was 40.9 nautical miles long and ran from the same point on Beaumont Island to Cape Distant at 83°08.2′N, 46°12.0′W. The use of straight baselines and Beaumont Island had the effect of pushing the equidistance line slightly westward, adding two isolated lens-shaped areas of thirty-one square nautical miles and thirty-four square nautical miles to the Danish (Greenland) claim.

Canada quickly objected to the Danish straight baselines and particularly the use of Beaumont Island as a base point, for four reasons: "Beaumont Island is somewhat west of the other islands, thus it is not part of a fringe of islands; the straight baselines are long; they do not follow the trend of the coast; they do not cross the mouths of the intervening fjords but are farther offshore."[76] These reasons seem to be derived from the seminal International Court of Justice decision on straight baselines, namely the 1951 *Anglo-Norwegian Fisheries Case*.[77]

The scope of the Lincoln Sea boundary dispute was reduced in 2004 when Denmark modified its straight baselines, using more precise base points and replacing the 40.9-nautical-mile baseline east of Beaumont Island with a series of shorter baselines, including one that connects Beaumont Island to John Murray Island, the next island in the chain.[78] Also in 2004, Denmark adopted a new "Royal Decree on the Entry into Force of Act on Exclusive Economic Zones for Greenland" in which it repeated its position that:

[75] See Executive Order No. 176 of 14 May 1980 on the fishing territory of Northern Greenland, available at http://faolex.fao.org/docs/pdf/den99033E.pdf.

[76] Gray, n. 9, above, at 68.   [77] *Anglo-Norwegian Fisheries Case* (1951) ICJ Reports 116.

[78] "Royal Decree on Amendment of Royal Decree on Delimitation of the Territorial Waters of Greenland, 15 October 2004" (2005) 56 *Law of the Sea Bulletin* 126 at 128, available at www.un.org/Depts/los/doalos_publications/LOSBulletins/bulletinpdf/bulletin56e.pdf. The new base points are as follow: Cape Bryant 82°20′.234 N, 55°14′.984 W; Northernmost point of Beaumont Island 82°45′.346 N, 50°47′.051 W; Northernmost point of John Murray Island 82°50′.190 N, 49°03′.203 W; Cape Benét 82°59′.816 N, 47°16′.698 W; Cape Payer 83°05′.275 N, 46°15′.167 W; Cape Ramsay 83°10′.915 N, 44°53′.891 W. Cape Distant is no longer used as a base point and now falls within the straight baseline connecting Cape Payer to Cape Ramsay. A useful map of the baselines is available in "Royal Decree," p. 132. Beaumont Island is almost bisected by the fiftieth meridian toward the top of the page.

The delimitation of the exclusive economic zone in Lincoln Hav [Sea], where the coasts of Greenland and Canada lie opposite each other at a distance of less than 400 nautical miles, in the absence of any special agreement relating thereto, shall follow the line which from point 127 [the northernmost point on the 1973 agreed boundary] in any direction is equidistant from the nearest points on the baselines of the coasts in question (the median line).[79]

The Danish changes succeeded in reducing the size of the northernmost disputed sector, almost to the point of eliminating it, while also strengthening the case for using Beaumont Island as a base point.[80]

Subsequent to Denmark's initial adoption of straight baselines, and Canada's protest, the rules identified in the *Anglo-Norwegian Fisheries Case* were codified in Article 7 of UNCLOS. Specifically, Article 7(1) reads: "In localities where the coastline is deeply indented and cut into, or if there is a fringe of islands along the coast in its immediate vicinity, the method of straight baselines joining appropriate points may be employed in drawing the baseline from which the breadth of the territorial sea is measured." That said, and as a United Nations study of straight baselines observed: "There is no uniformly identifiable objective test which will identify for everyone islands which constitute a fringe in the immediate vicinity of the coast. States should, however, be guided by the general spirit of article 7."[81]

As the International Court of Justice later made clear in the *Black Sea Case*, one country's drawing of baselines for the purpose of establishing the extent of the continental shelf and EEZ does not mean that those same baselines are necessarily appropriate for delimiting the

---

[79] "Royal Decree," p. 135.

[80] For a map showing the Danish equidistance line post-2004, see the map of the "Outer Limits of the Exclusive Economic Zone of Greenland," in "Executive Order on the Exclusive Economic Zone of Greenland, 20 October 2004" (2005) 56 *Law of the Sea Bulletin* 133 at 136, available at www.un.org/Depts/los/doalos_publications/LOSBulletins/ bulletinpdf/bulletin56e.pdf.

[81] Office for Ocean Affairs and the Law of the Sea, The Law of the Sea – Baselines: An Examination of the Relevant Provisions of the United Nations Convention on the Law of the Sea (United Nations: New York, 1989), p. 21, para. 42, available at www.un.org/ depts/los/doalos_publications/publicationstexts/The%20Law%20of%20the% 20Sea_Baselines.pdf. The State practice on the interpretation of Article 7 is mixed, with Asian states being especially liberal with their straight baselines. See Sam Bateman and Clive Schofield, "State Practice Regarding Straight Baselines in East Asia – Legal, Technical and Political Issues in a Changing Environment." Paper prepared for a conference at the International Hydrographic Bureau, Monaco, October 16–17, 2008, available at www.gmat.unsw.edu.au/ablos/ABLOS08Folder/Session7-Paper1-Bateman. pdf.

continental shelf and EEZ between adjacent or opposite states. As the Court wrote:

In the second case, the delimitation of the maritime areas involving two or more States, the Court should not base itself solely on the choice of base points made by one of those Parties. The Court must, when delimiting the continental shelf and exclusive economic zones, select base points by reference to the physical geography of the relevant coasts.[82]

In any event, Canada's position on the Lincoln Sea boundary was never particularly strong. Beaumont Island is indeed to the west of the other islands along northwest Greenland, but it is one of four islands that extend in a chain more-or-less parallel to a coastline indented with several deep fjords. Critically, it is also less than twenty-four nautical miles from the next island to the east and less than twenty-four nautical miles from the mainland. On this point, the UN study said: "The descriptive phrase 'in its (the coast's) immediate vicinity' is a concept which has a clear meaning but for which there is no absolute test. . . . It is generally agreed that with a 12-mile territorial sea, a distance of 24 miles would satisfy the conditions."[83]

Neither UNCLOS nor the UN study specifies a maximum length for straight baselines connecting fringing islands. However, a US State Department study has recommended: "No individual straight baseline segment should exceed 48 nautical miles in length."[84] Again, the original Beaumont Island baselines fit within this recommended constraint.

As for baselines following the trend of the coast, Article 7(3) of UNCLOS states: "The drawing of straight baselines must not depart to any appreciable extent from the general direction of the coast." But what does "appreciable extent" actually mean? The US State Department study recommended that

[t]he directional trend of the outermost islands (i.e., the islands on which the straight baseline turning points will be situated) should not deviate more than 20° from the opposite mainland coastline (including any closing lines that may properly be drawn across bays, river mouths and harbors), or from the general

---

[82] *Case Concerning Maritime Delimitation in the Black Sea* (2009) ICJ Reports 44 at 108, para. 137, available at www.icj-cij.org/docket/files/132/14987.pdf.

[83] Ibid., p. 22, para. 46.

[84] US State Department, *Limits in the Sea (No. 106): Developing Standard Guidelines for Evaluating Straight Baselines* (1987), 6, available at www.state.gov/documents/organization/59584.pdf.

direction of the opposite mainland coastline, whichever more nearly parallels the relevant islands.[85]

In the case of Beaumont Island and the rest of the island chain, the directional trend deviates less than ten degrees from the general direction of the Greenland coast.

As for Canada's concern that the straight baselines "do not cross the mouths of the intervening fjords but are farther offshore," Article 7(1) indicates that straight baselines may be used "where the coastline is deeply indented and cut into, or if there is a fringe of islands." In locations where the two geographic situations coexist, the coastal state would seem to have a choice, and Denmark cannot be faulted for choosing the approach that favored it most.

On coastal indentations, the relatively conservative US State Department study recommends that "baseline segments accounting for at least 70% of the total length of the relevant baselines should each have at least a 6:10 ratio of coastal penetration to segment length" and there should be "at least three significant indentations in any given locality."[86] On the issue of a fringe, the study recommends that the islands "should mask 50% of the opposite mainland coastline."[87] The first recommendation is clearly met around Beaumont Island; the second is not met but the degree of masking is still substantial – around 25 to 30 percent.

Nor could it successfully be argued that using straight baselines for the purposes of boundary delimitation is inconsistent with international law. After a review of state practice concerning maritime boundary agreements, Louis Sohn reported that "there were some 20 cases in which systems of straight baselines were expressly taken into account" and "some 50 instances [in which] they were disregarded, in whole or in part."[88] The tribunal in the Eritrea–Yemen Arbitration relied upon the straight baseline system that had been adopted by Ethiopia (prior to Eritrean independence), and rejected the use of one feature as a base point because of the criteria set out for straight baselines in Article 7(4) of UNCLOS.[89] In the *Qatar v. Bahrain Case*, the International Court of

---

[85] Ibid., p. 16.   [86] Ibid., p. 6.   [87] Ibid., p. 16.

[88] Louis B. Sohn, "Baseline Considerations," in Jonathan I. Charney and Lewis M. Alexander (eds.), *International Maritime Boundaries*, vol. 1 (Dordrecht: Martinus Nijhoff, 1993), 153 at 157.

[89] *Award of the Arbitral Tribunal in the Second Stage of the Proceedings between Eritrea and Yemen (Maritime Delimitation)* (1999), 22 Reports of International Arbitration Awards 335 at 366–367, available at http://untreaty.un.org/cod/riaa/cases/vol_XXII/335-410.pdf. Article

Justice was clearly open to applying an existing straight baseline system for the purposes of delimiting a boundary between the two countries' territorial seas, because it rejected the Bahrain system on the substantive grounds that a cluster of islands off the coast of its main islands was too small in number and insufficiently distinct from the main islands to be considered a "fringe of islands along the coast."[90]

Finally, David Gray has suggested that, "As an isolated, uninhabited island of about 4 square miles [10.3 km^2] it could be argued that the island [Beaumont] cannot generate an exclusive economic zone in its own right under Article 121(3) of the Law of the Sea Convention."[91] To understand this argument, one must begin with Article 121(1) of UNCLOS, which defines an "island" as "a naturally formed area of land, surrounded by water, which is above water at high tide." According to Article 121(2), islands generate a territorial sea, contiguous zone, EEZ, and continental shelf rights in the same way as other land. Article 121(3) then identifies an exception to the category of islands, namely: "Rocks which cannot sustain human habitation or economic life of their own shall have no exclusive economic zone or continental shelf."[92] These "rocks" generate a territorial sea and contiguous zone but no EEZ or continental shelf rights; as a result, they cannot be used for straight baselines.

For the moment, Beaumont Island is devoid of human habitation and economic life. However, Jonathan Charney examined the *travaux pré-paratoires* to Article 121 and concluded: "[A] feature does not need both human habitation and an economic life of its own. Only one of these qualifications must be met to remove the feature from the restrictions of Article 121(3)."[93] Charney also found that "human habitation does not require that people reside permanently on the feature," while economic life does not require that it "be capable of sustaining a

7(4) reads: "Straight baselines shall not be drawn to and from low-tide elevations, unless lighthouses or similar installations which are permanently above sea level have been built on them or in instances where the drawing of straight baselines to and from such elevations has received general international recognition."

[90] *Maritime Delimitation and Territorial Questions between Qatar and Bahrain* (2001) ICJ Reports 40 at 67, para. 214, available at www.icj-cij.org/docket/files/87/7027.pdf.

[91] Gray, n. 9, above, p. 68.   [92] See Introduction, n. 15, above.

[93] Jonathan I. Charney, "Rocks that Cannot Sustain Human Habitation." (1999) 93 *American Journal of International Law* 863 at 868. See also Clive Schofield, "The Trouble with Islands: The Definition and Role of Islands and Rocks in Maritime Boundary Delimitation," in S. Y. Hong and Jon Van Dyke (eds.), *Maritime Boundary Disputes, Settlement Processes, and the Law of the Sea* (The Hague: Martinus Nijhoff, 2009), 19.

human being throughout the year."[94] Instead, "[t]he phrase seems merely to require proof that the rock actually has some capacity for human habitation or economic value for society,"[95] which in the context of the considerable resource potential of the Arctic region, would hardly seem an impossible test for Denmark.

The size of the feature may also be relevant, as Charney explained:

> The travaux préparatoires further show that terms such as "islets" and "small islands" were originally used to define the features that would fall within the provision that ultimately became Article 121(3). Some delegates contended that islets of less than 1 square kilometer, or no larger than a "pinhead," should not be entitled to any maritime areas. Others claimed that islands of less than 10 square kilometers should not be entitled to maritime areas other than a 12-nautical-mile territorial sea. However, the ultimate redaction of Article 121(3) seems to apply to an even narrower range of small features than these – only "rocks" that cannot sustain human habitation or have an economic life of their own.[96]

Beaumont Island, again, is just over ten square kilometers in size. Although Charney's views are hardly definitive, it is likely an "island" for the purposes of the law of the sea, and, for this reason, also a reasonable point for straight baselines.

Despite the relative weakness of its position vis-à-vis Denmark's straight baselines, Canada could still consider itself fortunate. For a straightforward application of equidistance in the Lincoln Sea might be somewhat generous, given the seemingly different lengths of the "relevant coasts" on either side of the Lincoln Sea.[97] On the Canadian side, the coast of Ellesmere Island turns away from the Lincoln Sea around Cape Columbia (the northernmost portion of Canadian land territory), roughly 190 kilometers to the northwest of Robeson Channel (the northernmost portion of Nares Strait). On the Danish side, the coast does not turn away from the Lincoln Sea until Cape Morris Jesup, the northernmost point on Greenland, located more than 380 kilometers to the northeast of Robeson Channel. A court or arbitral tribunal might consider these different lengths of coasts to be a "relevant circumstance" and shift the line westwards as a result.

---

[94] Charney, ibid.   [95] Ibid.   [96] Ibid., p. 869.
[97] See Alex G. Oude Elferink, "Arctic Maritime Delimitations: The Preponderance of Similarities with Other Regions," in Elferink and Donald Rothwell (eds.), *The Law of the Sea and Polar Maritime Delimitation and Jurisdiction* (Dordrecht: Kluwer Law International, 2001), 179 at 194.

Coastal lengths have been deemed relevant circumstances in some previous maritime boundary delimitations, including the *Jan Mayen*,[98] *Libya-Malta*[99] and *Gulf of Maine Cases*.[100] And in the *Tunisia-Libya Case*, the International Court of Justice held that:

[T]here comes a point on the coast of each of the two Parties beyond which the coast in question no longer has a relationship with the coast of the other Party relevant for submarine delimitation. The sea-bed areas off the coast beyond that point cannot therefore constitute an area of overlap of the extensions of the territories of the two Parties, and are therefore not relevant to the delimitation.[101]

Similarly, in the *Black Sea Case*, the International Court disregarded some portions of the Ukrainian coast because they did not project on the area being delimited.[102]

Canada may even have undermined its position in the Lincoln Sea by drawing its own straight baselines along the coast of Ellesmere Island. In 1973, the delimitation of the continental shelf boundary between Canada and Greenland was done using straight baselines along the east coast of Ellesmere Island.[103] In 1985, those and other baselines around Canada's High Arctic islands were publicly announced.[104] Some of those baselines proved controversial for reasons that include their unusual length and possible departure from the general direction of the coast: two of the very same reasons that Canada cited in its 1980 protest against the Danish straight baselines.

---

[98] *Maritime Delimitation in the Area between Greenland and Jan Mayen (Denmark v. Norway)* (1993) ICJ Reports 38 at 69, para. 69, available at www.icj-cij.org/docket/files/78/6743.pdf.

[99] *Case Concerning the Continental Shelf (Libya/Malta)* (1985) ICJ Reports 13 at 50, para. 68, available at www.icj-cij.org/docket/files/68/6415.pdf.

[100] *Gulf of Maine Case (Canada v. United States)* (1984) ICJ Reports 246 at 334–335, para. 218, available at www.icj-cij.org/docket/files/67/6369.pdf.

[101] *Case Concerning the Continental Shelf (Libya v. Tunisia)* (1982) ICJ Reports 62, para. 75, available at www.icj-cij.org/docket/files/63/6267.pdf.

[102] *Case Concerning Maritime Delimitation in the Black Sea*, n. 82, above, para. 99–100.

[103] "Report Number 1-1, Canada–Denmark (Greenland)," in Jonathan Charney and Lewis Alexander (eds.), *International Maritime Boundaries: Volume I* (Dordrecht: American Society of International Law/Martinus Nijhoff, 1993), 375 (Canada "established construction lines along its coast facing Greenland, up to the northeasternmost point of Ellesmere Island. It was not until September 1985, however, that Canada announced it considered the construction lines to be official straight baselines along its arctic archipelago").

[104] For a discussion of the relevance of the straight baselines to the Northwest Passage dispute, see Chapter 5.

Finally, and most importantly, it is possible that the Lincoln Sea boundary dispute has ceased to exist, for one or both of two reasons. First, it is unclear whether Canada protested the modified straight baselines adopted by Denmark in 2004.[105] Although a diplomatic note may have been sent, no public record of a protest exists. Arguably, this means that there is already an implicit agreement on base points and therefore on an equidistance line. Second, and perhaps relatedly, Canadian Foreign Minister John Baird and Danish Foreign Minister Villy Søvndal announced in November 2012 that negotiators "have reached a tentative agreement on where to establish the maritime boundary in the Lincoln Sea."[106]

Apparently, the only outstanding issue for negotiation is a joint management regime for any straddling hydrocarbon deposits. This issue could not be dealt with solely by the Danish and Canadian negotiators, for while Denmark retains control over Greenland's foreign policy, the Greenland government has since 2008 exercised control over natural resources – including on the continental shelf.[107] Nevertheless, it seems likely that a Lincoln Sea Boundary Treaty will be signed in 2013 or 2014. Joint management regimes have become a standard part of maritime boundary treaties, including between Iceland and Jan Mayen and in the Barents Sea, meaning that models of best practice are easy to find.[108]

Whatever happens, the Lincoln Sea boundary dispute is of little practical significance. There has never been any difference of opinion over the location where the adjoining Canadian and Danish jurisdictions meet at 200 nautical miles from shore. This means that any dispute within 200 nautical miles of shore is of little legal relevance to a delimitation of the extended continental shelf, which is the focus of Chapter 4.

[105] See discussion, above, pp. 47–48.
[106] "Canada and Kingdom of Denmark Reach Tentative Agreement on Lincoln Sea Boundary," News Release, Canadian Department of Foreign Affairs, 28 November 2012 (with backgrounder), available at www.international.gc.ca/media/aff/news-communiques/2012/11/28a.aspx?lang=eng. See also Kim Mackrael, "Canada, Denmark a step closer to settling border dispute," Globe and Mail, November 30, 2012, available at www.theglobeandmail.com/news/national/canada-denmark-a-step-closer-to-settling-border-dispute/article5831571/.
[107] 2009 Act on Greenland Self-Government, available at http://uk.nanoq.gl/~/media/f74bab3359074b29aab8c1e12aa1ecfe.ashx.
[108] See discussions above, pp. 37–38 and 44.

7 Summary

Most maritime boundaries result from negotiations, and this is certainly the case in the Arctic. In 1973, Canada and Denmark delimited a 1,450-nautical-mile boundary between Canada and Greenland. In 1990, the United States and the Soviet Union negotiated a 1,600-nautical-mile boundary in the Bering Sea, Bering Strait, and Chukchi Sea. In 2006, Denmark and Norway agreed upon a boundary between Greenland and the Norwegian Arctic archipelago of Svalbard. These efforts set the stage for the resolution of the largest of the Arctic maritime boundary disputes, namely 50,000 square nautical miles of contested water column and seabed in the Barents Sea north of Norway and Russia. In 2010, those two countries concluded a treaty that set an agreed boundary, maintained existing cooperative measures on fisheries management, and created a joint management regime for straddling hydrocarbon deposits. It would be difficult to overstate the importance of the Barents Sea Treaty, for it bridged the old Cold War divide and set Russia on the track toward international cooperation in the Arctic. Finally, a small boundary dispute in the Lincoln Sea north of Greenland and Ellesmere Island is about to be resolved. A tentative agreement was announced by Canada and Denmark in November 2012, with the only outstanding issue for negotiation being a joint management regime for straddling hydrocarbons – for which models of best practice are now readily available, in the Barents Sea and elsewhere.

3   Beaufort Sea boundary

Ah, for just one time I would take the Northwest Passage
To find the hand of Franklin reaching for the Beaufort Sea
Stan Rogers, "Northwest Passage"[1]

Every summer from 2008 through 2011, two powerful icebreakers – one American, the other Canadian – met up in the Beaufort Sea north of Alaska and Canada's Yukon Territory.[2] The United States' *Healy* is equipped with an advanced multi-beam sonar system that provides detailed bathymetry, i.e., information about the shape of the ocean floor. Canada's *Louis S. St-Laurent* carries a sophisticated seismic array that measures the character and thickness of seabed sediments. Since vibrations from icebreaking can affect the accuracy of these instruments, the two ships took turns clearing a path for each other, with the resulting sonar and seismic data being shared between the United States and Canada.[3] It was a partnership born of necessity, since neither country has two icebreakers capable of the task. Moreover, and as will be discussed at some length in Chapter 4, both countries require a complete

---

[1] "Stan Rogers," in *The Canadian Encyclopedia*, available at www.thecanadianencyclopedia.com/articles/stan-rogers.

[2] Randy Boswell, "'Astonishing' Data Boost Arctic Claim," *Ottawa Citizen*, November 12, 2008, at A3; Sian Griffiths, "US–Canada Arctic Border Dispute Key to Maritime Riches," *BBC News*, August 2, 2010, available at www.bbc.co.uk/news/world-United States–Canada-10834006.

[3] The quality of the data can also be affected by cavitation (i.e., air pockets) as well as chunks of ice passing along the bottom of the hull. Moreover, it is sometimes necessary for a ship to reverse when operating in ice, and this is difficult to do while towing a seismic array.

56

scientific picture of the seabed in order to determine the geographic extent of their sovereign rights to an "extended continental shelf" more than 200 nautical miles from shore.

Additional to that, the collaborative mapping beyond 200 nautical miles has opened the door to the resolution of the only significant boundary dispute in the entire circumpolar Arctic. For nearly four decades, the United States and Canada have contested a wedge of maritime space extending 200 nautical miles northwards from the terminus of the Alaska–Yukon land border, that is, to the limit of the two coastal states' EEZs. The recent seabed mapping, however, has brought into focus the possibility that extended continental shelves might exist in the Beaufort Sea that stretch 350 nautical miles or even further from shore. Although neither the United States nor Canada has articulated a position on the boundary beyond 200 nautical miles, it would – curiously and significantly – not necessarily benefit either of them simply to extend their present claimed line on the same basis they use to justify it within 200 nautical miles.

1 Background

The Beaufort Sea is that shallow portion of the Arctic Ocean located between Alaska and Canada's High Arctic islands, just to the north of the Mackenzie River delta. As far back as the 1970s, seismic surveys and exploratory wells established that the seabed sediments there contain hydrocarbons.[4] In 2006, Devon Canada discovered a potential 240 million barrels of oil north of Tuktoyaktuk, a small Inuvialuit community in the Northwest Territories.[5] The next year, Imperial Oil and ExxonMobil Canada committed to spending $585 million in return for exploration rights over a nearby area of seabed.[6] Then, in 2008, BP agreed to spend $1.2 billion in exploring an area adjacent to the

---

[4] For the 2011 "disposition map" of the Beaufort Sea and Mackenzie Delta produced by Aboriginal Affairs and Northern Development Canada, showing past discoveries and "shows," see www.aadnc-aandc.gc.ca/DAM/DAM-INTER-HQ/STAGING/texte-text/ nog_mp_bsmd_pg_1317059161670_eng.pdf.

[5] Gary Park, "Beaufort Find Is Oil, Not Gas," October 21, 2007, *Petroleum News* 12, available at www.petroleumnews.com/pntruncate/304958258.shtml.

[6] Dina O'Meara, "Imperial Oil, Exxon–Mobil Canada Bet C$585M on Offshore Arctic Oil and Gas," July 19, 2007, *Resource Investor*, available at www.resourceinvestor.com/2007/ 07/19/imperial-oil-exxonmobil-canada-bet-c585m-on-offsho.

Imperial–Exxon–Mobil leases.[7] In 2010, the three companies concluded a joint venture to explore for oil and gas in the two offshore parcels.[8] On the US side of the Beaufort Sea, Shell spent billions of dollars preparing for exploratory drilling that was initially planned for 2010; regulatory concerns arising from the BP spill in the Gulf of Mexico then postponed the plans until the summer of 2012,[9] which later slipped to 2013.[10] As a result of all this attention to the Beaufort Sea from oil companies, there has been a recent surge of interest in the disputed boundary between the United States and Canada – because companies need to know which permitting and regulatory authority is responsible for any particular area where they might wish to drill.

The two countries have disagreed on the location of the Beaufort Sea boundary since 1976 when the United States protested the boundary line that Canada was using while issuing oil and gas concessions.[11] The existence of the dispute was confirmed the following year when both countries delineated exclusive fishing zones out to 200 nautical miles, and used different lines.[12]

The dispute itself arises from the wording of an 1825 Treaty between Russia and Britain (the United States took on Russia's treaty rights when it purchased Alaska in 1867; Canada acquired Britain's rights in 1880).[13] The treaty sets the eastern border of Alaska at the "meridian line of the

---

[7] Scott Haggett, "BP Bids Big for Canadian Arctic Drilling Rights," *Reuters*, June 9, 2008, available at http://uk.reuters.com/article/2008/06/09/uk-energy-arctic-idUKN0947438920080609.

[8] Shaun Polczer, "Firms Team Up in Arctic," *Calgary Herald*, July 31, 2010, available at www2.canada.com/calgaryherald/news/calgarybusiness/story.html?id=a3a43f92-a51d-4402-a76d-61362b8105b8.

[9] Kim Murphy, "Arctic Drilling: Beaufort Sea Oil Spill Response Plan Approved," *Los Angeles Times*, March 28, 2012, available at www.latimes.com/news/nation/nationnow/la-na-nn-arctic-drilling-20120328,0,2904392.story.

[10] Kim Murphy, "Drill Rigs Wind up Operations in Arctic Alaska Seas," *Los Angeles Times*, October 31, 2012, available at www.latimes.com/news/nation/nationnow/la-na-nn-arctic-drill-alaska-20121031,0,6809964.story.

[11] See Ted L. McDorman, *Salt Water Neighbors: International Ocean Law Relations between the United States and Canada* (New York: Oxford University Press, 2009), 184 (referring to Diplomatic Note, in *Gulf of Maine Pleadings*, 103 (May 20, 1976), vol. 5, Annex 8 to Reply of the United States, 529–530).

[12] Gray, Chapter 2, n. 9, above, p. 62.

[13] Great Britain/Russia: Limits of their Respective Possessions on the North-West Coast of America and the Navigation of the Pacific Ocean, February 16, 1825, 75 *Consolidated Treaty Series* 95.

141st degree, in its prolongation as far as the frozen ocean."[14] Canada claims this treaty provision establishes both the land border and the maritime boundary, and that both must follow the 141°W meridian straight north. In contrast, the United States argues that the treaty's delimitation applies to land only, that regular methods of maritime boundary delimitation apply beyond the coastline, and that in the case of the Beaufort Sea an equidistance line – where every point on the line is an equal distance from the nearest point on the coasts on either side – is the legally and geographically appropriate approach.[15] Since the coast of Alaska, the Yukon, and the Northwest Territories slants east-southeast from Point Barrow, Alaska, to the mouth of the Mackenzie River, such an equidistance line trends progressively further east of the Canadian-preferred line at the 141°W meridian, running in a roughly north-northeast direction from the terminus of the land border to the 200-nautical-mile limit. As a result, within that distance from shore, an approximately 6,250-square-nautical-mile pie-shaped disputed sector has been created.[16]

As mentioned above, states are also entitled to sovereign rights over the resources of the seabed beyond 200 nautical miles, if and where the continental shelf appertaining to their landmass stretches beyond that limit. Article 76 of the 1982 United Nations Convention on the Law of the Sea (UNCLOS) sets out scientific criteria that states are to utilize in determining the outer limits of their jurisdiction over the extended continental shelf.[17] Although the United States has not yet acceded to UNCLOS, it has repeatedly stated that the convention's major provisions reflect customary international law.[18]

UNCLOS also created the Commission on the Limits of the Continental Shelf (CLCS), which is empowered to provide recommendations as to the sufficiency of the scientific data submitted to it by states and therefore pronounce on the legitimacy of their delineations

---

[14] Ibid., Art. 3. The 1825 treaty was written in French only, but the 1867 treaty both repeats the relevant passage in French *and* uses this English translation in an authentic text. Treaty concerning the Cession of the Russian Possessions in North America, Art. 1, Chapter 2, n. 21, above.

[15] See, e.g., US Department of State, Public Notice 2237, Exclusive Economic Zone and Maritime Boundaries (1995) 60 Fed. Reg. 43825–43829.

[16] See McDorman, n. 11, above, pp. 181–190 for the definitive presentation of the dispute as previously understood.

[17] See Introduction, n. 15, above.   [18] See Introduction, n. 25, above.

of the outer limits of the extended continental shelf.[19] All states wishing to assert rights over seabed beyond 200 nautical miles are expected to submit data to the CLCS within ten years of ratifying UNCLOS, although, as will be discussed below, states may choose to make partial or pre-liminary submissions that can then be updated after the ten-year period has passed.[20] The joint US–Canadian mapping beyond 200 nautical miles in the Beaufort Sea has been conducted in preparation for the two countries asserting jurisdiction over portions of the extended con-tinental shelf and, in Canada's case, submitting its data to the CLCS by the end of its ten-year period in 2013.[21]

The introduction of the extended continental shelf into the equation creates a curious twist to the Beaufort Sea boundary dispute, for if one extends the equidistance line preferred by the United States beyond 200 nautical miles, it soon changes direction and begins tracking toward the northwest (see Map 1). It does so because of a change in direction of the Canadian coast on the eastern side of the Mackenzie River delta and even more so because of the presence of Banks Island, a large feature on the eastern side of the Beaufort Sea. The effect of Banks Island is so strong that the equidistance line crosses over the 141°W meridian (which, naturally, continues straight north to the Pole) and heads toward the maritime boundary between the United States and Russia.[22] This would seem to leave a large and as-yet-unspoken-for area of extended continental shelf to the west of the 141°W meridian and east of the equidistance line, essentially the reverse of the disputed sector further south. In simple spatial terms, the US line appears to favor Canada beyond 200 nautical miles, and vice versa.

So far, neither the United States nor Canada has publicly expressed a position as to its rights beyond the limits of the EEZ. Therefore, one cannot assume that either or both countries consider their arguments within 200 nautical miles to be determinate of their positions beyond

[19] See Introduction, n. 15, above; Commission on the Limits of the Continental Shelf, available at www.un.org/Depts/los/clcs_new/clcs_home.htm.

[20] See below, pp. 84–85. See also Coalter Lathrop, "Continental Shelf Delimitation Beyond 200 Nautical Miles: Approaches Taken by Coastal States Before the Commission on the Limits of the Continental Shelf," in David A. Colson and Robert W. Smith (eds.), International Maritime Boundaries (Leiden: American Society of International Law/ Martinus Nijhoff, 2011), 4139.

[21] See US Extended Continental Shelf Project, at http://continentalshelf.gov/; Canadian Extended Continental Shelf Program, at www.international.gc.ca/continental/index. aspx?lang=engandmenu_id=7andmenu=R.

[22] On the boundary between the United States and Russia, see Chapter 2, above.

Map 1 Beaufort Sea: US and Canadian claims

that zone, though Canada's meridian-based claim would seem to lack any logical mechanism for differentiating between the line within that limit and beyond it. In the case of the United States, the possibility of different arguments within and beyond 200 nautical miles is

augmented by possible differences between the legal principles relevant to maritime boundary delimitation in the two areas. Most importantly, the extension of the dispute beyond 200 nautical miles appears
conducive to a negotiated solution.

2 Resolution efforts

In the late 1970s, the United States and Canada sought to resolve the
Beaufort Sea dispute along with their other maritime boundary disputes.[23] At the time, Canada indicated a willingness to approach the
disputes as a package, and that it would trade losses in the Beaufort Sea
for gains elsewhere.[24] The parties also investigated the possibility of
setting up a joint hydrocarbon development zone, an approach that is
discussed at more length below.[25] Ultimately, neither side was willing
to compromise on its legal position for fear of prejudicing its
approaches to other delimitations, and the two countries subsequently
focused on the most pressing boundary dispute, in the Gulf of Maine,
which they agreed to refer to a chamber of the International Court of
Justice.[26] Nevertheless, the Beaufort Sea dispute has remained well
managed, with both countries adhering to a de facto moratorium on
oil and gas exploration in the disputed area.[27]

As mentioned above, the introduction of extended continental
shelves into the equation has only recently created a new bargaining
environment, with the traditional US legal position conceivably
favoring Canada and the traditional Canadian legal position conceivably favoring the United States. In other words, what appeared to be a
zero-sum negotiating situation now offers opportunities for creative
trade-offs. A probable overlap in the two states' views of the areas
subject to their extended continental shelf rights was cited by an official
from the Canadian Department of Foreign Affairs in February 2010 as
the main reason for a renewed effort to resolve the Beaufort Sea

---

[23] McDorman, n. 11, above, pp. 188–189.

[24] Lorne Clark, Deputy Negotiator for Maritime Boundaries Canada/United States,
Minutes of Proceedings and Evidence of the Standing Committee on Fisheries and
Forestry, April 11, 1978, 30th Parliament, 3rd Session (1977–1978), No. 15 at 8, cited in
McDorman, n. 11, above, p. 120.

[25] See Christopher Kirkey, "Delineating Maritime Boundaries: The 1977–1978 Canada–US
Beaufort Sea Continental Shelf Delimitation Boundary Negotiations." (1995) 25
Canadian Review of American Studies 49; McDorman, n. 11, above, p. 188; discussion,
below, pp. 88–90.

[26] *Gulf of Maine Case*, Chapter 2, n. 100, above.   [27] Gray, Chapter 2, n. 9, above, p. 63.

boundary dispute.[28] Then, in the "Speech from the Throne" in March 2010, the Canadian government signaled its desire to "work with other northern countries to settle boundary disagreements."[29] This was followed by a public invitation to open negotiations specifically on the Beaufort Sea boundary, delivered in May 2010 by then Foreign Affairs Minister Lawrence Cannon during a speech in Washington, DC.[30] By the time Cannon released Canada's "Arctic Foreign Policy Statement" in August 2010, reiterating the commitment to resolving boundary disputes, at least one meeting between US and Canadian diplomats had already taken place.[31] Although the discussions are being conducted behind closed doors, the two countries' existing legal positions have likely provided starting points.

3 Canada's legal position

Canada could advance several arguments in support of its position that the 1825 treaty delimits the maritime boundary north of Alaska and the Yukon, in addition to the border on land. First, the treaty negotiations were prompted by Russian Czar Alexander II who in 1821 claimed the right to exclude foreigners from within 100 Italian miles of the coast of northwest North America. As British Foreign Secretary George Canning said at the time: "It is not on our part essentially a negotiation about limits. It is a demand of the repeal of an offensive and unjustifiable allegation of exclusive jurisdiction over an ocean of unmeasured extent ... We negotiate about territory to cover the remonstrance upon principle."[32] As a result, Canada could argue that the 1825 treaty's

---

[28] Randy Boswell, "Beaufort Sea Breakthrough," *Vancouver Sun*, February 17, 2010, available at http://byers.typepad.com/arctic/2010/02/beaufort-sea-breakthrough.html.

[29] Speech from the Throne, March 3, 2010, available at www.speech.gc.ca/eng/media.asp?id=1388.

[30] Randy Boswell, "Canada Ready to Settle Beaufort Sea Dispute with US: Cannon," *Vancouver Sun*, May 14, 2010, available at http://byers.typepad.com/arctic/2010/05/canada-ready-to-settle-beaufort-sea-dispute-with-us-cannon.html.

[31] See Department of Foreign Affairs, "Statement on Canada's Arctic Foreign Policy: Exercising Sovereignty and Promoting Canada's Northern Strategy Abroad." (2010), available at www.international.gc.ca/polar-polaire/assets/pdfs/CAFP_booklet-PECA_livret-eng.pdf; Randy Boswell, "Work Underway to Resolve Beaufort Sea Boundary Dispute," *Vancouver Sun*, July 26, 2010, available at http://byers.typepad.com/arctic/2010/07/work-underway-to-resolve-beaufort-sea-boundary-dispute.html.

[32] Quoted in Charles B. Bourne and Donald M. McRae, "Maritime Jurisdiction in the Dixon Entrance: The Alaska Boundary Re-examined." (1976) 14 *Canadian Yearbook of International Law* 183.

application to the maritime boundary in the Beaufort Sea is consistent with its "object and purpose," which is one of the guiding principles of treaty interpretation, both in customary international law and in the 1969 Vienna Convention on the Law of Treaties.[33] That said, when Charles Bourne and Donald McRae investigated the history of the negotiations leading to the 1825 treaty, they could find no evidence that the parties intended to delimit a maritime boundary.[34] Additionally, the Russian claim of maritime jurisdiction was not in the Beaufort Sea but rather in the North Pacific Ocean.

Second, Canada could point to the fact that the authentic text of the 1825 treaty is in French. Article 33 of the 1969 Vienna Convention on the Law of Treaties requires that an authenticated text of the treaty must be used for the purposes of interpretation (unless the treaty provides, or the parties agree, that a text in another language shall be considered an authentic text).[35] Moreover, Article 31 of the Vienna Convention requires that the interpretation be consistent with the "ordinary meaning of the terms."[36] Canada could argue that, in French, the preposition "jusqu'à" in the phrase "dans son prolongation jusqu'à la Mer Glaciale" would normally be interpreted as inclusive of the object to which it relates. In other words, in French, "as far as the frozen ocean" includes the ocean.[37]

Third, Canada could point to the fact that the 1867 Treaty of Cessation of Alaska to the United States,[38] which referred explicitly to the 1825 treaty, has been used as the basis for the Russian–US maritime boundary in the Bering and Chukchi Seas.[39] In Article I, the 1867 treaty refers to the eastern limit of the territories as that demarcated in the 1825

---

[33] Vienna Convention on the Law of Treaties, Article 31(1), Chapter 2, n. 27, above; Lord McNair, *The Law of Treaties* (Oxford University Press, 1961), 366–382.

[34] Bourne and McRae, n. 32, above, pp. 175–223.

[35] Vienna Convention on the Law of Treaties, Chapter 2, n. 27, above.   [36] Ibid.

[37] Contrary views have been expressed by Donat Pharand, "Delimitation Problems of Canada (Second Part)," in Donat Pharand and Umberto Leanza (eds.), *The Continental Shelf and the Exclusive Economic Zone: Delimitation and Legal Regime* (Dordrecht: Martinus Nijhoff, 1993), 171 at 174–176; Karin L. Lawson, "Delimiting Continental Shelf Boundaries in the Arctic: The United States–Canada Beaufort Sea Boundary." (1981) 22 *Virginia Journal of International Law* 221 at 231–232.

[38] Treaty concerning the Cession of the Russian Possessions in North America, Chapter 2, n. 21, above.

[39] See Mark B. Feldman and David Colson, "The Maritime Boundaries of the United States." (1981) 75 *American Journal of International Law* 729 at 751–753.

treaty, repeating the boundary's position as the "meridian line of the 141st degree, in its prolongation as far as the Frozen Ocean."[40] Article I continues:

The western limit within which the territories and dominion conveyed, are contained, passes through a point in Behring's straits on the parallel of sixty-five degrees thirty minutes north latitude, at its intersection by the meridian which passes midway between the islands of Krusenstern of Ignalook, and the island of Ratmanoff, or Noonarbook, and proceeds due north without limitation, into the same Frozen Ocean.

For more than a century, the parties accepted that the 1867 treaty defined a maritime boundary,[41] and in 1990, the United States and the Soviet Union accepted and updated the treaty using the 168°58'37"W meridian "into the Arctic Ocean as far as permitted by international law."[42]

The International Court of Justice rejected a similar argument in the 1993 *Jan Mayen Case* between Norway and Denmark, to the effect that the island's boundary with Greenland would have to be on similar terms to those agreed by Norway for its boundary with Iceland.[43] However, the situation in the Beaufort Sea is arguably distinct, in that the party which contests the application of the 1825 treaty to one maritime zone has already accepted that, in effect, the very same treaty defines a maritime boundary elsewhere. As Camille Antinori observed in 1987: "The United States is virtually saying that the same treaty that delimits a maritime boundary in the west does not delimit a maritime boundary in the east."[44]

Fourth, Canada could argue that the United States initially acquiesced to its use of the 141°W meridian as the maritime boundary. In the late 1960s, Canada issued oil and gas exploration permits in the now-disputed

---

[40] Treaty concerning the Cession of the Russian Possessions in North America, Chapter 2, n. 21, above.

[41] Feldman and Colson, n. 39, above, p. 752.

[42] 1990 US–USSR Maritime Boundary Agreement, Chapter 2, n. 20, above. For more on the 1990 treaty, see Chapter 2, above.

[43] *Maritime Delimitation in the Area between Greenland and Jan Mayen* (1993) ICJ Reports 38 at 76–77, para. 86, available at www.icj-cij.org/docket/files/78/6743.pdf.

[44] Camille M. Antinori, "The Bering Sea: A Maritime Delimitation Dispute between the United States and the Soviet Union." (1987) 18 *Ocean Development and International Law* 1 at 34. Ted McDorman has suggested that, even if the parties cannot agree on whether the 1825 treaty applies as a treaty in the Beaufort Sea, the US maritime boundary with Russia in western Alaska at least indicates "what the United States might consider an equitable result" in eastern Alaska. McDorman, n. 11, above, p. 187.

area without eliciting a protest from the United States.[45] In 1970, Canada asserted environmental protection jurisdiction in the now-disputed area through the Arctic Waters Pollution Prevention Act.[46] The Act itself elicited a protest from the United States, but the protest was not directed against the use of the 141°W meridian in the Beaufort Sea.[47] It was only in 1976, when Canada issued more oil and gas concessions, that the United States delivered its first protest and, after Canada used the 141°W meridian to delimit a 200-nautical-mile fishing zone later that year, proclaimed its own fishing zone using an equidistance line.[48] That said, the delay between the issuing of the first exploration permits and the US protest against such permits was less than ten years, and none of the permits resulted in any drilling in the disputed area. As for the Arctic Waters Pollution Prevention Act, it is questionable whether the United States needed to protest one specific and relatively small area of application when protesting the legislation as a whole.

Finally, Canada cannot and does not rely on the fact that, during the early twentieth century, it used the 141°W meridian in conjunction with the so-called "sector theory" to define its jurisdiction all the way to the North Pole,[49] so as to argue that early invocations of the sector theory were also, concurrently, unopposed assertions of Canada's preferred interpretation of the 1825 treaty. For Canada's attitude toward the sector theory soon shifted to studied ambiguity,[50] where it remained until 2006 when Prime Minister Stephen Harper abandoned the theory definitively.[51]

---

[45] Donat Pharand, *Canada's Arctic Waters in International Law* (Cambridge University Press, 1988), 58.

[46] Arctic Waters Pollution Prevention Act, 1969–70 Statutes of Canada, chap. 47, sec. 2, available at http://laws-lois.justice.gc.ca/eng/acts/A-12/FullText.html.

[47] McDorman, n. 11, above, p. 184.   [48] Ibid.

[49] Robert S. Reid, "The Canadian Claim to Sovereignty over the Waters of the Arctic." (1974) 12 *Canadian Yearbook of International Law* 115; Lester B. Pearson, "Canada Looks Down North." (1946) 24 *Foreign Affairs* 639.

[50] See K. M. Shusterich, "International Jurisdictional Issues in the Arctic Ocean," in W. E. Westermeyer and K. M. Shusterich (eds.), *United States Arctic Interests: The 1980s and 1990s* (New York: Springer-Verlag, 1984), at 253, cited in McDorman, n. 11, above, p. 184.

[51] Stephen Harper, "Securing Canadian Sovereignty in the Arctic," speech delivered at Iqaluit, Nunavut, August 12, 2006, available at http://byers.typepad.com/arctic/2009/03/securing-canadian-sovereignty-in-the-arctic.html.

4 United States' legal position

The United States has not made its position on Canada's legal arguments explicit, but it could counter the Canadian position on several
grounds. First, it too could argue that a literal construction of the 1825
treaty is required, consistent with the "ordinary meaning of the terms"
approach codified in the Vienna Convention on the Law of Treaties.[52]
Applying such an approach to the English translation, the border set by
the 1825 treaty ends at the coastline of the Beaufort Sea where the water
is frozen for much of the year.[53] But, as was explained above, the
authentic text of the treaty is in French, and so the United States has
to argue that applying the "ordinary meaning" approach to "dans son
prolongation jusqu'à la Mer Glaciale" generates the same result.[54] It
might also argue that the English translation of that phrase in the 1867
treaty should be treated as authoritative, though of course that treaty
was with Russia instead of Britain.

Second, the United States could point to the fact that national jurisdiction in the early nineteenth century extended only a short distance
offshore, and that the negotiators of the 1825 treaty could not possibly
have sought to delimit a boundary they did not know existed. Some
support for this argument is found in the 1985 Guinea–Guinea Bissau
Arbitration, where a cautious approach to historical treaties was
adopted.[55]

Finally, the United States could point to the difference in language
between the 1825 and 1867 treaties as indicating the different purposes
behind them. Whereas the 1825 treaty sets the line between Alaska and
the Yukon "jusqu'à la Mer Glaciale," the 1867 treaty establishes the
boundary between Alaska and Russia "into the same Frozen Ocean."
The latter formulation is clearly intended to delimit a maritime boundary, while the former is hardly clear.[56]

---

[52] Vienna Convention on the Law of Treaties, Chapter 2, n. 27, above.
[53] Conceivably, the United States could argue the boundary terminates wherever the sea
becomes covered in ice at any given point during the year, but this would produce an
unprecedented and impractical result: a boundary that terminates at different places
depending on the season and the on-going effects of climate change.
[54] See discussion, above, p. 64.
[55] *Guinea–Guinea Bissau Dispute Concerning the Delimitation of the Maritime Boundary* (1985) 25
ILM 251.
[56] See Lawson, n. 37, above, p. 232. David Colson and Mark Feldman have further
suggested that the terms of the 1867 treaty, which transferred "territory and dominion"
rather than simply "possessions" as used in the 1825 treaty, can be understood to apply

If the US arguments are convincing, the next step is to consider the international law of maritime boundary delimitation, first as it applies within 200 nautical miles from shore, and second as it applies to extended continental shelves beyond that distance.

5 Law of maritime boundary delimitation within 200 nautical miles

The international law of maritime boundary delimitation becomes relevant to the Beaufort Sea dispute only if the US position concerning the inapplicability of the 1825 treaty prevails, or if that interpretation comes up as a factor during negotiations – as is likely. During the nearly four decades that the dispute has existed, the rules of maritime boundary delimitation have traversed several stages of evolution, influenced by multilateral treaties, case law, and dispute-specific negotiations.

In 1958, the Geneva Convention on the Continental Shelf favored an "equidistance/special circumstances" approach to delimitation.[57] This meant that in the absence of an agreed boundary, an equidistance line was to be used, with that line normally being modified if special circumstances so justified. In 1982, a somewhat different approach was taken in UNCLOS, Article 83(1) of which provides that: "The delimitation of the continental shelf between States with opposite or adjacent coasts shall be effected by agreement on the basis of international law . . . in order to achieve an equitable solution."[58] This change was also seen in the case law, with the International Court of Justice consistently refusing to accept that it was bound by any rule or principle of delimitation, instead treating each case on its merits in order to arrive at an equitable result.[59] Although the jurisprudence was initially criticized for not

---

to continental shelf rights. Colson and Feldman, n. 39, above, pp. 750–751. Bourne and McRae, however, see no significance in the different wording and refer to the decision in the 1893 *Bering Sea Seal Fishery Arbitration*, which held that Russia had no exclusive fishing rights beyond the territorial sea. Bourne and McRae, n. 32, above, pp. 199–200.

[57] 1958 Convention on the Continental Shelf, 499 UNTS 311, available at http://untreaty. un.org/ilc/texts/instruments/english/conventions/8_1_1958_continental_shelf.pdf.

[58] See Introduction, n. 15, above, Art. 74 (relating to the EEZ) and Art. 83 (relating to the continental shelf).

[59] This practice began in the *North Sea Continental Shelf Cases (Netherlands v. Germany; Denmark v. Germany)* (1969) ICJ Reports 3, available at www.icj-cij.org/docket/files/51/5535.pdf. See, generally, Prosper Weil, *The Law of Maritime Delimitation – Reflections* (Cambridge: Grotius Publications, 1989), 9–14.

providing a set of general criteria that apply across cases,[60] more recent decisions evince greater coherence and even provide something of a formula for arriving at maritime boundary delimitations.

In the 2009 *Black Sea Case*, the International Court of Justice described the process as consisting of three stages.[61] In most cases, "the first stage of the Court's approach is to establish the provisional equidistance line."[62] The Court will then "consider whether there are factors calling for the adjustment or shifting of the provisional equidistance line."[63] In the third and final stage, the Court will check that there is no marked disproportionality in maritime areas, as compared to the ratio of the relative coastal lengths of the parties.[64] In the 2012 *Nicaragua–Colombia Case*, the Court used the same three-stage approach to boundary delimitation.[65]

The factors or "relevant circumstances" the International Court of Justice has drawn on to adjust provisional lines have been overwhelmingly geographical in character. Consistent with the principle that it is sovereignty over land territory that generates rights to maritime jurisdiction,[66] the Court has determined that it is the geography of the "coastal opening" that governs maritime boundary delimitations.[67] The coastal opening relates to the configuration of the coastline itself and is distinguished from other geographical factors such as the size of the land territory of a state.[68] Anomalous features such as islands, different coastal lengths, or the concave nature of a coastline can have disproportionate effects on an equidistance line, and all have been treated as relevant circumstances in cases of maritime delimitation.[69]

---

[60] See Gilbert Guillaume, "Speech to the Sixth Committee of the General Assembly of the United Nations," October 31, 2001, available at www.icj-cij.org/court/index.php? pr=81andpt=3andp1=1andp2=3andp3=1andPHPSESSID.

[61] *Case Concerning Maritime Delimitation in the Black Sea*, Chapter 2, n. 82, above, paras. 118–122.

[62] Ibid., para. 118.   [63] Ibid., para. 120.   [64] Ibid., para. 122.

[65] *Territorial and Maritime Dispute (Nicaragua v. Colombia)*, November 19, 2012, paras. 190–193, available at www.icj-cij.org/docket/files/124/17164.pdf.

[66] See *North Sea Continental Shelf Cases*, n. 59, above.

[67] *Case Concerning the Continental Shelf (Libya/Malta)* (1985) ICJ Reports 13 at 39–40, para. 49, available at www.icj-cij.org/docket/files/68/6415.pdf.

[68] Ibid.

[69] On islands, see Arbitration between the United Kingdom and France Concerning the Continental Shelf Boundary in the English Channel and South-Western Approaches (1979) 54 International Law Reports 6; *Case Concerning Maritime Delimitation and Territorial Questions (Qatar v. Bahrain)* (2001) ICJ Reports 68. On different coastal lengths, see *Libya/Malta Continental Shelf Case*, ibid.; *In the Matter of the Arbitration between Barbados and Trinidad and Tobago*, Permanent Court of Arbitration, April 11, 2006, para. 334, available at www.

This focus on geographical features has been at the expense of other factors that parties have sometimes argued should be relevant. In the *Gulf of Maine Case*, a chamber of the International Court of Justice wrote that provisional lines should not be adjusted for economic or security reasons, unless failing to do so would have catastrophic consequences:

[T]he respective scale of activities connected with fishing – or navigation, defence or, for that matter, petroleum exploration and exploitation – cannot be taken into account as a relevant circumstance or, if the term is preferred, as an equitable criterion to be applied in determining the delimitation line. What the Chamber would regard as a legitimate scruple lies rather in concern lest the overall result, even though achieved through the application of equitable criteria and the use of appropriate methods for giving them concrete effect, should unexpectedly be revealed as radically inequitable, that is to say, as likely to entail catastrophic repercussions for the livelihood and economic well-being of the population of the countries concerned.[70]

Geographical features also played a major part in the earlier jurisprudence relating to the delimitation of the continental shelf, national rights over which pre-dated the creation of the EEZ. In the 1969 *North Sea Continental Shelf Cases*, the International Court of Justice outlined the doctrinal basis of the entitlement of states to jurisdiction over their continental shelf:

What confers the ipso jure title which international law attributes to the coastal State in respect of its continental shelf, is the fact that the submarine areas concerned may be deemed to be actually part of the territory over which the coastal State already has dominion, – in the sense that, although covered with water, they are a prolongation or continuation of that territory, an extension of it under the sea.[71]

This notion that the continental shelf is the natural prolongation of a state's land territory also found its way into UNCLOS, Article 76(1) of which states: "The continental shelf of a coastal State comprises the seabed and subsoil of the submarine areas that extend beyond its territorial sea throughout the natural prolongation of its land territory to the outer

pca-cpa.org/showpage.asp?pag_id=1152; and *Gulf of Maine Case*, Chapter 2, n. 100, above. On the concave nature of a given coastline, see *North Sea Continental Shelf Cases*, n. 59, above. State practice increasingly reflects this approach, including in the Arctic. In 2010, Norway and Russia took "major disparities in the parties' coastal lengths" into account when negotiating the 2010 Barents Sea Treaty. See Norwegian Ministry of Foreign Affairs, "The Background to the Treaty," available at www.regjeringen.no/en/dep/ud/kampanjer/delelinje/forhistorie.html?id=614274; discussion, Chapter 2, above.

[70] See, e.g., *Gulf of Maine Case*, Chapter 2, n. 100, above, p. 100, para. 237.
[71] See *North Sea Continental Shelf Cases*, n. 59, above, p. 31, para. 43.

edge of the continental margin."[72] This language led several states to advance claims to maritime jurisdiction, within 200 nautical miles, based on the geological and geomorphological characteristics of the seabed.[73] But, in the 1985 *Libya–Malta Case*, the International Court of Justice made it clear that the evolution of distance-related foundations for maritime zones, most significantly in the form of the EEZ, meant that geological and geomorphological features are to play no part in maritime delimitations where opposite coasts are less than 400 nautical miles apart.[74] It went so far as to specify that even evidence of a fundamental break in the continental shelf would not affect such delimitations.[75]

6 Law of maritime boundary delimitation beyond 200 nautical miles

The decision in the 1985 *Libya–Malta Case* has generated debate over the degree to which geological and geomorphological considerations remain relevant to maritime boundary delimitations beyond 200 nautical miles from shore. The International Court of Justice stated that privileging the status of distance in the delimitation of overlapping EEZs was "not to suggest that the idea of natural prolongation is now superseded by that of distance."[76] However, there have been no further decisions of the International Court of Justice that clarify how geological and geomorphological characteristics may influence delimitation beyond the EEZ.

Earlier negotiated delimitations of the extended continental shelf took no account of geomorphological and geological factors because the parties had insufficient information about the characteristics of the seabed.[77] In 2003, after examining seven such agreements, David

---

[72] Chapter 2, n. 100, above.

[73] See *Gulf of Maine Case*, Introduction, n. 15, above; *Libya/Malta Continental Shelf Case*, n. 67, above; see also Anthony Bergin, "The Australian-Indonesian Timor Gap Maritime Boundary Agreement." (1990) 5 *International Journal of Estuarine and Coastal Law* 383.

[74] *Libya/Malta Continental Shelf Case*, n. 67, above, pp. 33–35, paras. 34 and 39.   [75] Ibid.

[76] Ibid.

[77] Australia–France: Agreement on Maritime Delimitation, January 4, 1982, 1329 UNTS 107; Ireland–United Kingdom: Agreement Concerning the Delimitation of Areas of the Continental Shelf, November 7, 1988, 1564 UNTS 218; Trinidad and Tobago–Venezuela: Treaty on the Delimitation of Marine and Submarine Areas, April 18, 1990, 1654 UNTS 301; US–Russia Maritime Boundary Treaty, Chapter 2, n. 20, above.; United States–Mexico: Treaty on the Delimitation of the Continental Shelf in the Western Gulf of Mexico Beyond 200 Nautical Miles, June 9, 2000, S. Treaty Doc. No. 106–39; Treaty between the Government of Australia and the Government of New Zealand

Colson concluded that they had several commonalities, among them that the delimitation methodology applied within 200 nautical miles did not change beyond that point, and that Article 76 criteria were employed to determine the end point of the boundary rather than its course.[78] Insufficient information about the seabed was also part of the reason why the tribunal in the Guinea–Guinea Bissau Arbitration took no account of the seabed characteristics in drawing that extended continental shelf boundary.[79]

It does seem that the 2004 boundary treaty between Australia and New Zealand took some geomorphological and geological factors into account beyond 200 nautical miles, because New Zealand gained more seabed than if a median line had been used.[80] Clive Schofield suggests that the negotiators treated the Three Kings Ridge as an extension of the New Zealand mainland, though the distance between the mainland and the relevant Australian islands also played a part.[81]

Most recently, the International Tribunal for the Law of the Sea addressed the delimitation of extended continental shelves in the *Bay of Bengal Case* between Bangladesh and Myanmar.[82] Bangladesh argued that Myanmar was not entitled to an extended continental shelf because there was a geological discontinuity, in the form of a tectonic plate boundary between the seabed of the Bay of Bengal and the landmass of Myanmar within 200 nautical miles of the coast.[83] Bangladesh's position was that the mention of "natural prolongation" in Article 76(1) of the Convention was to be given a geological interpretation and that an area of continental shelf without a natural geological affinity with Myanmar, such as that beyond the plate boundary, could not

Establishing Certain Exclusive Economic Zone and Continental Shelf Boundaries, July 25, 2004, No. 4 Australia Treaty Series, 2006.

[78] David Colson, "The Delimitation of the Outer Continental Shelf between Neighboring States." (2003) 97 *American Journal of International Law* 96.

[79] Guinea–Guinea Bissau Arbitration, n. 55, above, p. 300.

[80] Australia–New Zealand Maritime Boundary Agreement, n. 77, above.

[81] Clive Schofield, "Australia's Final Frontiers?: Developments in the Delimitation of Australia's International Maritime Boundaries." (2008) 158 *Maritime Studies* 2 at 6. It is noteworthy that Australia relies on a natural prolongation argument elsewhere, in its delimitation with Indonesia, where it continues to press for the boundary to follow the Timor Trough between it and Timor-Leste. See Bergin, n. 73, above.

[82] *Dispute Concerning Delimitation of the Maritime Boundary between Bangladesh and Myanmar in the Bay of Bengal* (Bangladesh/Myanmar), International Tribunal for the Law of the Sea, Case No. 16, March 14, 2012, p. 76, para. 240, available at www.itlos.org/fileadmin/itlos/ documents/cases/case_no_16/C16_Judgment_14_03_2012_rev.pdf.

[83] Ibid., p. 112, para. 417.

possibly fall under that country's jurisdiction. The tribunal rejected the argument, stating that "no elaboration of the notion of natural prolongation referred to in article 76, paragraph 1, is to be found"[84] and that it could not accept that natural prolongation "constitutes a separate and independent criterion a coastal State must satisfy in order to be entitled to a continental shelf beyond 200 nm."[85] The tribunal held that Article 76 of UNCLOS is concerned with whether "the continental shelf of a coastal State can extend either to the outer edge of the continental margin or to a distance of 200 nm, depending on where the outer edge is situated."[86] Since the Convention contains a definition of the outer limit of the continental shelf, based on the geomorphological characteristics of the seabed, it is this definition to which effect should be given. Myanmar was able to demonstrate a geomorphological continuity between it and the seabed in the Bay of Bengal, because sediments had covered the plate tectonic boundary, and was therefore entitled to a continental shelf beyond 200 nautical miles. Moreover, the origin of those sediments was immaterial to the entitlement of both Bangladesh and Myanmar to assert rights to an extended continental shelf.

The tribunal in the *Bay of Bengal Case* thus found that it had to delimit a continental shelf that was subject to overlapping claims by the parties. Crucially, it decided that the "method to be employed in the present case for the continental shelf beyond 200 nautical miles should not differ from that within 200 nm. Accordingly, the equidistance/relevant circumstances method continues to apply for the delimitation of the continental shelf beyond 200 nm." Rejecting further geological arguments from Bangladesh, to the effect that the tectonic composition and origin of the sediments in the Bay of Bengal constituted a special circumstance because they were more naturally associated with its territory, the tribunal decided that the same reasons for adjusting the equidistance line within 200 nautical miles – based on coastal geography – merited the line's adjustment beyond that distance.[87]

In sum, the International Tribunal for the Law of the Sea has helped to clarify the role of geological factors within 200 nautical miles in terms of both extended continental shelf entitlement and maritime

---

[84] Ibid., para. 432.
[85] Ibid., para. 435. This part of the decision was not unanimous. See, e.g., Judge Gao's separate decision, available at www.itlos.org/fileadmin/itlos/documents/cases/case_no_16/C16.sep_op.Gao.rev.Ewith_maps.pdf.
[86] Ibid., p. 126, para. 429.   [87] Ibid., p. 133, para. 461.

delimitation beyond 200 nautical miles. The geomorphology of the seabed rather than its geological relationship to landmass determines whether a coastal state's rights extend beyond the EEZ. However, when it comes to delimitations between adjoining or opposing states in cases of shared extended continental shelves, the characteristics of the coastline – rather than geomorphology – are the material factors to be taken into account.

However, the *Bay of Bengal Case* concerned a situation without a submarine ridge or a submarine elevation. As is explained at more length in Chapter 4, coastal state rights are limited to 350 nautical miles from shore in the case of submarine ridges, but not in the case of submarine elevations. On submarine elevations, which differ from submarine ridges in being "natural components of the continental shelf," a "2,500-metre isobath plus 100 nautical mile" constraint line may be used.[88] In the western Beaufort Sea, a large submarine feature called the Chukchi Plateau would seem to extend more than 350 nautical miles from shore. As far back as 1980, the United States expressed the view that, under the terms of UNCLOS, the Chukchi Plateau is a submarine elevation and therefore not subject to the 350-nautical-mile limitation.[89]

At the moment, the case law and state practice with respect to the delimitation of extended continental shelves remain too limited and variable to provide clarity on whether and how a submarine elevation, extending off a common continental margin on one side of a land border, might be considered relevant by an international court or tribunal charged with delineating a maritime boundary. The fact that Canada and the United States have cooperatively mapped the extended continental shelf in the area means, however, that a lack of information will not be an impediment to using geomorphological and geological features in either a negotiated or an adjudicated solution.

7 Potential negotiating positions

7.1 Unilateral recognition of the other state's position

The curious situation outlined earlier – that the legal positions of both Canada and the United States within 200 nautical miles might, if extended beyond the EEZ, actually favor the other country – could

---

[88] See Introduction, n. 15, above, Art. 76(6).
[89] Elliot Richardson, US Ambassador, "Statement," April 3, 1980 (1981) 13 *Official Records of the Third United Nations Conference on the Law of the Sea* 43.

lead to an immediate solution to the Beaufort Sea boundary dispute. Either state could unilaterally recognize the other's position, on the explicit basis that it applied both within and beyond 200 nautical miles. Such a move would pre-empt any change in position by the other state, and perhaps discourage it from arguing that different methods of delimitation should apply to the two zones. It would, however, require the state making the move to accept a still uncertain trade-off between a loss (or gain) in the EEZ, and a gain (or loss) in the extended continental shelf. The uncertainty results from several factors: better ice conditions, shallower water, and shorter distances to shore facilities are likely to make the disputed triangle within 200 nautical miles more immediately valuable than the new, as-yet-unspoken-for triangle beyond the EEZ. Moreover, until seismic surveys have been conducted and test wells sunk in the two triangles, the existence and location of hydrocarbons remains speculative. One additional element of uncertainty applies in the outside triangle, namely, how far offshore the legal continental shelf actually extends. In these circumstances, a unilateral recognition seems unlikely, and the cooperation between the United States and Canada on seabed mapping takes on new importance.

A more detailed scientific understanding of the seabed beyond 200 nautical miles will, along with the newly appreciated importance of the extended continental shelf, likely lead to a reformulation of each country's legal position as a precursor to serious negotiations. Alternatively, each party might maintain its position within the EEZ and advance a view of the extended continental shelf that is grounded on a different legal argument. However, as mentioned above, Canada's existing position does not lend itself to this kind of distinction, given that it is based on the use of a meridian – in a treaty that pre-dated the concept of a 200-nautical-mile limit by 150 years. If Canada is right and the 1825 treaty was meant to delimit a maritime boundary, that boundary has no logical endpoint other than the ultimate limits of national jurisdiction.

7.2 Coastal length

While adhering to its position on the 141°W meridian, Canada will likely also formulate an alternative argument – one that accepts the principle of equidistance but construes the coastal geography in Canada's favor. The first element in this approach involves coastal length.

Coastal length has been deemed a relevant circumstance in several cases of maritime boundary delimitation. In the *Jan Mayen Case*, the

International Court of Justice recognized that significant differences in the lengths of coastlines had to be taken into account when drawing a boundary line.[90] The Court came to a similar conclusion in the *Libya–Malta*[91] and *Gulf of Maine Cases*,[92] as did the tribunal in the Barbados–Trinidad and Tobago Arbitration.[93] In the *Gulf of Maine Case*, even a relatively small discrepancy in coastal length between Canada and the United States – a ratio of 1.38 to 1[94] – affected the location of the line chosen for part of the boundary, though the general characteristics of the area reinforced this conclusion. In all the other cases, much larger discrepancies existed.[95]

In the *Black Sea Case*, the International Court of Justice dismissed the Ukraine's argument that the greater length of its coastline – 2.8 times longer than Romania's – entitled it to a larger share of the delimitation area.[96] However, the Court clearly considered it relevant that several portions of the longer Ukrainian coastline projected onto the same maritime area, therefore "strengthening but not spatially expanding the Ukrainian entitlement."[97] In all these cases, the Court has been careful to emphasize that coastal length cannot determine in any mathematically mechanical way the offshore entitlements of a state.

A mathematical calculation is, however, at the heart of the test of proportionality the Court has applied in the third, verification, stage of delimitation. Here the court has calculated the ratio of the respective coastal lengths of the parties to the dispute and compared it to the extent of the maritime areas awarded to them by a proposed delimitation line, so as to ensure there is no marked disproportionality.[98]

---

[90] *Jan Mayen Case*, Chapter 2, n. 35, above, para. 69.

[91] *Libya/Malta Continental Shelf Case*, n. 67, above, para. 68.

[92] *Gulf of Maine Case*, Chapter 2, n. 100, above, para. 218.

[93] *In the Matter of the Arbitration between Barbados and Trinidad and Tobago*, n. 69, above.

[94] *Gulf of Maine Case*, Chapter 2, n. 100, above, para. 222. The ratio was 1.32 to 1 when Seal and Mud Islands were included.

[95] Trinidad and Tobago had cited the difference between its coastal length and that of Barbados as being of a ratio of 8.2:1. *In the Matter of the Arbitration between Barbados and Trinidad and Tobago*, n. 69, above, para. 326. In the *Libya/Malta Continental Shelf Case*, n. 67, above, para. 68, the International Court of Justice calculated the length of Malta's relevant coasts at twenty-four miles as opposed to 192 miles for those of Libya. In the 2012 *Nicaragua–Columbia Case*, n. 65, above, the ratio was 8.2 to 1 in favor of Nicaragua yet the adjudicated line is only three times further from Nicaragua than from the Colombian islands.

[96] *Black Sea Case*, Chapter 2, n. 82, above, para. 215.   [97] Ibid., para. 168.

[98] For a discussion of the three-stage formula, see above, p. 69.

The relevance of coastal length to delimitations involving the extended continental shelf is unclear, though it did play a role in the Barbados-Trinidad and Tobago Arbitration.[99] However, the tribunal made it clear that the longer coastline of Trinidad and Tobago was relevant only because it directly abutted the area subject to delimitation.[100] Establishing the stretches of coastline that are relevant to the delimitation area is a critical step – indeed, the critical step – in establishing the relevance of coastal length and the proportionality of the result. For instance, Canada might argue that the discrepancy between the length of the northwest flank of its High Arctic archipelago and the length of the northern coastline of Alaska requires an adjustment of the provisional equidistance line in its favor. However, the United States could counter-argue that the breaks between the Canadian islands cannot be counted as coastline for the purposes of length, and only a much shorter stretch of Canadian coastline is relevant to the delimitation.

Various cases have identified how to determine the coastlines relevant to delimitation. In the *Tunisia-Libya Case*, the International Court of Justice wrote:

[T]here comes a point on the coast of each of the two Parties beyond which the coast in question no longer has a relationship with the coast of the other Party relevant for submarine delimitation. The sea-bed areas off the coast beyond that point cannot therefore constitute an area of overlap of the extensions of the territories of the two Parties, and are therefore not relevant to the delimitation.[101]

The Court went on to define the relevant lengths of coast as those ending at Ras Kaboudia on the Tunisian coast and at Ras Tajoura on the Libyan coast, both being locations where the coastlines turn slightly away from the delimitation area.[102] In the *Black Sea Case*, the Court similarly disregarded some portions of the Ukrainian coast because they did not face the delimitation area.[103] For this reason, it might be argued that the only portions of the Canadian coastline relevant to the delimitation are the mainland, the west coast of Banks Island, and perhaps the southwest corner of Prince Patrick Island. Similarly, it might be argued that the relevant portion of the US coastline extends

---

[99] *In the Matter of the Arbitration between Barbados and Trinidad and Tobago*, see n. 69, above.
[100] Ibid., para. 331.
[101] *Case Concerning the Continental Shelf (Libya v. Tunisia)* (1982) ICJ Reports 62, para. 75.
[102] Ibid.   [103] *Black Sea Case*, Chapter 2, n. 82, above, para. 99.

only to Point Barrow where the coastline turns away from the Beaufort Sea. In these scenarios, the discrepancy in coastal lengths is minimal and could be considered insignificant.

7.3 Relevance of islands

The effect of islands on the placement of lines is a perennial issue in maritime boundary delimitation. As was explained in Chapter 2, "islands" are capable of generating a full suite of their own maritime zones, in contrast to "rocks" that are incapable of sustaining a population or economic life of their own and which are only entitled to a territorial sea.[104] At 70,000 square kilometers, Banks Island is clearly entitled to its own continental shelf and EEZ. The effect of its coastline on the placement of any equidistance line is therefore justified on that basis. Although the International Court of Justice and arbitral tribunals have accorded less than full effect to islands off the shores of a continental state, they have done so only in cases where those islands are either at some distance from the coastline or very small. For example, in the Anglo-French Arbitration, the tribunal "enclaved" the Channel Islands because they were off the French coast, distant from the United Kingdom and therefore well beyond the median line of the English Channel.[105] Banks Island, by contrast, is less than twenty-four nautical miles from Victoria Island, which is itself less than twelve nautical miles from the Canadian mainland. Moreover, Banks Island is hardly an insignificant feature; its presence creates a major anomaly in an equidistance line that would otherwise be defined by the two countries' mainland coasts.

7.4 Concavity of the coastline

One final characteristic of the coastline might require that any provisional equidistance line be adjusted in Canada's favor. The mainland coast arguably becomes concave near the mouth of the Mackenzie River, east of the terminus of the land border between Alaska and the Yukon. The concavity becomes more marked when the coastline of Banks Island is taken into account. Concave coastlines have been recognized as a relevant factor by the International Court of Justice in maritime boundary delimitations, most notably in the *North Sea*

---

[104] Introduction, n. 15, above, Art. 121. For a discussion of 'rocks' and 'islands' in the context of the Lincoln Sea, see Chapter 2, above.

[105] *Anglo-French Arbitration* (1979) 18 ILM 397, para. 202.

Continental Shelf Cases between Germany and Denmark and Germany and the Netherlands, all of which have similar coastal lengths.[106] The Court stated: "What is unacceptable in this instance is that a State should enjoy continental shelf rights considerably different from those of its neighbors merely because in the one case the coastline is roughly convex in form and in the other it is markedly concave, although those coastlines are comparable in length."[107] The Court concluded that an equitable solution, which corrected for the concave nature of the German coastline, could be arrived at by drawing a straight baseline "between the extreme points at either end of the coast concerned" and constructing a boundary based on it rather than the real German coastline.[108] This approach provided Germany with considerably more maritime space than would have been the case if equidistance lines were used.

If Canada argued that the concavity of its coastline needs to be taken into account and a similar approach taken, the question would arise as to where the end points of such a "closing line" should be placed – since it is those points which determine the line's seaward reach. One possibility would be to use Cape Bathurst on the south side of the entrance to Amundsen Gulf, as the eastern point for a line extending westwards to the terminus of the Canada–US land border. If that closing line and the Alaskan coast from the 141°W meridian to Port Barrow were then treated as the relevant coasts, they would be of roughly equal length. Such an approach would benefit Canada within 200 nautical miles from shore while possibly benefiting the United States further out, since Banks Island would be removed from the equidistance calculation. Whatever approach is taken, and while the Beaufort Sea dispute can be distinguished from the *North Sea Continental Shelf Cases* on the basis that Canada is not disadvantaged on both sides of the delimitation area, the concavity of the coastline will likely feature prominently in Canada's negotiating position.

7.5 Canada's position beyond the EEZ

Given the presence of the Chukchi Plateau, it seems likely that the natural prolongation of the continental shelf is longer on the US side

---

[106] For a similar, more recent result, see *Dispute Concerning Delimitation of the Maritime Boundary between Bangladesh and Myanmar in the Bay of Bengal*, n. 82, above, paras. 290–297.

[107] See *North Sea Continental Shelf Cases*, n. 59, above, p. 50, para. 91.

[108] Ibid. at p. 52, para. 98.

of the 141°W meridian than on the Canadian side.[109] However, Canada can argue that the continental shelf regime is of a unified character – with the consequence being that geological and geomorphological factors are of no relevance to the delimitation, and the same delimitation principles apply both within and beyond 200 nautical miles. As explained above, this was precisely what the International Tribunal for the Law of the Sea concluded with regard to the geology, geomorphology, and international law applicable in the *Bay of Bengal Case*.[110] Geology and geomorphology would seem to play a role in the delimitation of continental shelves only where two distinct continental margins exist, as will often be the case in situations involving opposite states, but only rarely in situations involving adjacent states. For this reason, it is possible that Canada will have sovereign rights over at least part of the Chukchi Plateau, with the equidistance line (especially an adjusted one) cutting across that feature.

However, this outcome also depends on the application of Article 76(5) of UNCLOS, which – as Chapter 4 explains – imposes a series of constraints on the outer limit of a coastal state's extended continental shelf. As a result, it is just as possible that Canada's jurisdiction ends somewhere east of the Chukchi Plateau, regardless of the likely existence of a common continental margin.

7.6 Inuvialuit Final Agreement: a complicating factor

Canada does face an important domestic impediment to altering its position on the location of the international boundary in the Beaufort Sea. In 1984, in the Inuvialuit Final Agreement – a constitutionally recognized land claims agreement – the Canadian government used the 141°W meridian to define the western edge of the Inuvialuit Settlement Region.[111] In the Settlement Region and specifically an area called the "Yukon North Slope," which includes the offshore to the northeast of the terminus of the international land border, Canada

---

[109] See discussion, above, p. 74.   [110] See discussion, above, pp. 72–74.

[111] See 1984 Inuvialuit Final Agreement (as amended), available at www.daair.gov.nt.ca/_live/documents/documentManagerUpload/InuvialuitFinalAgreement1984.pdf. Under section 35 of the Constitution Act 1982, "rights that now exist by way of land claims agreements or may be so acquired" are "recognized and affirmed." See http://laws.justice.gc.ca/eng/Const/page-12.html#sc:7_II.

recognized Inuvialuit harvesting rights over fish and game and promised to protect the area.[112]

Under international law, Canada could enter into a maritime boundary treaty with the United States that would likely be valid and binding regardless of the domestic rights of the Inuvialuit.[113] However, under Canadian law, the federal government has a duty to consult, limit any infringement of aboriginal rights as much as possible, make any such limitation clear through an Act of Parliament, and provide compensation.[114] For this reason, the Canadian government would be wise to consult closely and continuously with the Inuvialuit regarding the boundary delimitation, and to compromise as little as possible over the placement of the line during negotiations with the United States.

Canada could, for instance, argue that the Inuvialuit Final Agreement is a relevant circumstance that would require the adjustment of any provisional equidistance line toward the west. The United States might respond that the Final Agreement was concluded eight years after the boundary dispute's "critical date," when subsequent attempts to bolster one or the other side's position become inconsequential to the legal analysis.[115] Canada might then argue that the Final Agreement simply recognizes pre-existing indigenous rights vested before 1976 in Canadian citizens.

[112] Inuvialuit Final Agreement, ibid., especially at sec. 12(2): "The Yukon North Slope shall fall under a special conservation regime whose dominant purpose is the conservation of wildlife, habitat and traditional native use." Curiously, the Inuvialuit Settlement Area extends more than 600 nautical miles northward into the Beaufort Sea, well beyond Canada's exclusive jurisdiction over the living resources of the EEZ, though it is unclear whether Canada (in 1984 or at any time since) purports to exercise any exclusive jurisdiction beyond 200 nautical miles. For a map of the Inuvialuit Settlement Area, see www.aadnc-aandc.gc.ca/eng/1100100031121/1100100031129#chp7.

[113] Vienna Convention on the Law of Treaties, Chapter 2, n. 27, above, Art. 46(1): "A State may not invoke the fact that its consent to be bound by a treaty has been expressed in violation of a provision of its internal law regarding competence to conclude treaties as invalidating its consent unless that violation was manifest and concerned a rule of its internal law of fundamental importance."

[114] See the Constitution Act 1982, n. 111, above, sec. 35; R. v. Sparrow, [1990] SCR 20 (Canada); Haida Nation v. British Columbia (Minister of Forests), [2004] SCR 73; and Mikisew Cree First Nation v. Canada (Minister of Canadian Heritage), [2005] SCR 69. In 2010, the Nunavut Supreme Court issued an injunction against seismic testing in Lancaster Sound on the grounds that the obligation to consult had not been fulfilled. See discussion, Chapter 7, below; Josh Wingrove, "Lancaster Sound: A Seismic Victory for the Inuit," Globe and Mail, August 14, 2010, available at www.theglobeandmail.com/news/politics/lancaster-sound-a-seismic-victory-for-the-inuit/article1377067/.

[115] On the critical date principle, see references, Chapter 1, n. 9, above.

Indeed, the Inuvialuit have long hunted seals and beluga and bow-head whales in the Beaufort Sea, and traveled and lived on the ice at certain times of the year.[116] The ability of indigenous peoples to acquire and transfer sovereign rights was recognized by the International Court of Justice in the *Western Sahara Case*, though that case did not involve a maritime boundary.[117] Perhaps more on point is the decision in the Barbados–Trinidad and Tobago Arbitration, where the tribunal suggested that historical usage of an area was an insufficient reason to modify an equidistance line except when the population on one side is overwhelmingly dependent on fisheries there.[118] Moreover, the tribunal concluded that it would be appropriate, indeed legally required, for transboundary access rights to be negotiated after the drawing of the boundary, as part of the duty placed on states in UNCLOS to agree on measures to conserve and develop straddling fish stocks.[119]

For this reason, one possible outcome of negotiations over the Beaufort Sea boundary is the creation of new rights and obligations between the Canadian Inuvialuit and the US government with respect to any area falling between the 141°W meridian and an agreed international boundary to the east of that line. Such an agreement would free the Canadian government to make concessions within 200 nautical miles from shore, in return, presumably, for US concessions further out. But, again, to achieve this result, the Inuvialuit will need to be involved in the negotiations.

7.7 United States' position beyond the EEZ

As mentioned above, in 1980, a US diplomat expressed the view that the Chukchi Plateau is a submarine elevation over which sovereign rights can extend more than 350 nautical miles offshore.[120] The United States could now take the position that an equidistance line, whether adjusted

---

[116] That said, the Inupiat, the closely related indigenous people on the US side of the boundary, have also engaged in hunting and fishing activities in the disputed area.

[117] See *Western Sahara, Advisory Opinion* (1975) ICJ Reports 12, para. 79, recognizing that territories inhabited by indigenous peoples having a measure of social and political organization are not *terra nullius*, and thus conferring a limited but no less real international legal status on such groups.

[118] *In the Matter of the Arbitration between Barbados and Trinidad and Tobago*, n. 69, above, para. 327.

[119] Ibid. Also, in the *Qatar–Bahrain Case*, n. 69, above, para. 236, the Court found that pearling banks were not a relevant circumstance for adjusting a line, even though the Bahrainis argued they had predominantly engaged in diving there.

[120] Richardson, n. 89, above. For more on submarine elevations, see Chapter 4, below.

or not, is only appropriate within 200 nautical miles and that geological and geomorphological features should determine the boundary further out. This position is supported by the dictum of the International Court of Justice in the *Libya–Malta Case*[121] and not contradicted by the decision of the International Tribunal for the Law of the Sea in the *Bay of Bengal Case*.[122]

Alternatively, the United States could argue that the Beaufort Sea is a situation of opposite continental shelves. Colson has argued that in such situations extensions could be delimited based on the location of the foot of the slope, with an equidistance line being placed between them.[123] But while this approach might be practicable where states are genuinely opposite it does not translate so easily in a situation such as the Beaufort Sea where the parties are essentially in a mixed "adjacent–opposite" relationship. While Banks and Prince Patrick Islands are more or less opposite the northeast coast of Alaska, this opposition arises only after a considerable length of adjacent coastline closer to the land border.

Finally, either the United States or Canada may seek to make different arguments regarding the line within and beyond 200 nautical miles on the basis that the line is the product of an adjacent coastal relationship out to that point, and the product of an essentially opposite relationship beyond there. The International Court adopted this approach in both the *Gulf of Maine*[124] and *Tunisia–Libya Cases*,[125] although arguably the distinction between the factors relevant to opposite and adjacent delimitation has more recently become blurred.[126]

8 Options for United States–Canada cooperation

None of the potential opening negotiating positions identified above will necessarily reduce the size of the disputed area. However, negotiations are recognized by most states as the most suitable method for resolving overlapping maritime claims. Negotiations allow parties to retain control of the process of delimitation and to bring into

[121] *Libya/Malta Continental Shelf Case*, n. 67, above, para. 34.
[122] *Dispute Concerning Delimitation of the Maritime Boundary between Bangladesh and Myanmar in the Bay of Bengal*, n. 82, above.
[123] See Colson, n. 78, above.   [124] *Gulf of Maine Case*, Chapter 2, n. 100, above, para. 216.
[125] *Tunisia–Libya Case*, n. 101, above, para.126.
[126] See *In the Matter of the Arbitration between Barbados and Trinidad and Tobago*, n. 69, above, para. 315.

consideration more factors than a strict application of the law by a court or tribunal would allow.[127] That said, the outcomes of past maritime boundary negotiations suggest the final result will more or less split the difference between the respective claims of the parties, whether they are based on the positions outlined here or not. In the event that negotiations become difficult, however, there are several more-innovative options the parties might consider – especially as Canada moves into the CLCS process in 2013.

8.1 Canada makes a preliminary or partial submission to the Commission on the Limits of the Continental Shelf

The CLCS can provide recommendations on the sufficiency of scientific data presented to it with regard to areas of extended continental shelf that are subject to competing submissions. However, such recommendations are without prejudice to existing maritime delimitation matters, and it is always possible for the other disputing state to indicate to the CLCS that because of the dispute it may not proceed.[128] In light of this risk of the CLCS being blocked by a disputant state, a coastal state may choose to submit only "preliminary information indicative of the outer limits ... and a description of the status of preparation and intended date for making a submission."[129] Alternatively, a coastal state may choose to make only a partial submission that excludes data with respect to a disputed zone – thus meeting the ten-year filing expectation, holding its place in the queue, and enabling the CLCS to proceed with its review of those areas for which data has been submitted.[130] Both these options will have been considered by Canada as it

---

[127] Litigation or arbitration of the Beaufort Sea dispute seems particularly unlikely given US disappointment over the result in the 1984 *Gulf of Maine Case.* See A. L. Springer, "Do Fences Make Good Neighbours? The Gulf of Maine Revisited." (1994) 6 *International Environmental Affairs* 231; and McDorman, n. 11, above, pp. 148–149.

[128] Introduction, n. 15, above, Art. 76(10).

[129] Eighteenth Meeting of the States Parties, "Decision Regarding the Workload of the Commission and the Ability of States to Fulfil the Requirements of Article 4 of Annex II," Doc. SPLOS/183, June 20, 2008, paragraph 1, available at www.un.org/Depts/los/meeting_states_parties/SPLOS_documents.htm. This document records the decision, by the parties to UNCLOS, that a preliminary submission is sufficient to meet the expectation of a submission within ten years of ratifying.

[130] The Commission on the Limits of the Continental Shelf (CLCS) has indicated that submissions will be "queued in the order they are received." See "Statement by the Chairman of the Commission on the Limits of the Continental Shelf on the Progress of Work in the Commission, 6 October 2006," at para. 38, available at http://

prepares for a submission in 2013. But, while they may seem attractive at first glance, these options have the unfortunate consequence of leaving the outer limit of the extended continental shelf undetermined in an area where the problem that the CLCS is intended to prevent – uncertainty and potential contestation of maritime zones – already exists and could well worsen.[131]

8.2 United States sends a "no objection statement" to the Commission on the Limits of the Continental Shelf

Countries will sometimes agree *not* to object to the CLCS considering data with respect to a disputed area. Ideally, such an agreement will be proactively communicated to the CLCS through a "no objection statement" – though the Commission, so far, has been willing to treat silence as consent. Norway consented to the CLCS's examination of Russia's first submission in 2002, and in 2009, a number of members of the Economic Community of West African States agreed to send a no objection statement concerning extended continental shelf boundaries to the CLCS.[132] It will often be in a country's interest to provide such a statement, since the CLCS recommendations will identify the maximum area susceptible to coastal-state jurisdiction and therefore open to a negotiated division. Should the United States and Canada not be able to agree on more extensive cooperation, they would be wise to take this approach, with the former sending a no objection statement to the CLCS with respect to the latter's submission.

8.3 Canada and United States maximize combined EEZ rights with a "special area"

In maritime boundary negotiations, areas over which one country would normally have jurisdiction and the other country would not, have in some instances been assigned by the first country to the second

daccess-dds-ny.un.org/doc/UNDOC/GEN/N06/558/82/PDF/N0655882.pdf?OpenElement. See also Alex G. Oude Elferink and Constance Johnson, "Outer Limits of the Continental Shelf and 'Disputed Areas': State Practice Concerning Article 76(10) of the LOS Convention." (2004) 21 *International Journal of Marine and Coastal Law* 466. Cf. Bjørn Kunoy, "Disputed Areas and the 10-Year Time Frame: A Legal Lacuna?" (2010) 41 *Ocean Development and International Law* 112.

[131] Lathrop, n. 20, above.

[132] Permanent Mission of Norway to the Secretary-General of the United Nations, "Norway: Notification Regarding the Submission Made by the Russian Federation to the Commission on the Limits of the Continental Shelf," 2002, available at www.un.org/Depts/los/clcs_new/submissions_files/rus01/CLCS_01_2001_LOS__NORtext.pdf; Lathrop, n. 20, above, p. 4155.

country by treaty – in order to preserve those jurisdictional rights as part of the negotiated package. As was explained in Chapter 2, at several points along the boundary set by the 1990 treaty between the United States and the Soviet Union in the Bering Sea, the agreed line comes closer than 200 nautical miles to the Soviet (now Russian) coastline while remaining more than 200 nautical miles from the US coastline.[133] Arguably, such a boundary line would have had the effect of transforming those outward portions of the Soviet EEZ into high seas. To avoid this possible outcome, the negotiators designated several "special areas" where the Soviet Union assigned its EEZ rights to the United States, notwithstanding that those rights were generated by the Soviet coastline. Norway and Russia followed the same approach in the 2010 Barents Sea Treaty, with an area of ocean within 200 nautical miles of the Norwegian coastline but on the eastern side of the new boundary being explicitly assigned to Russia, despite being more than 200 nautical miles from the Russian coast.[134]

A similar approach will likely be followed by the United States and Canada within 200 nautical miles from shore, if they negotiate a Beaufort Sea boundary that runs west of the equidistance line. For as a result of the concave nature of the coast, such a shift in the line would otherwise cause a small area of water column that is within 200 nautical miles of the US coastline and currently within the US-claimed EEZ, arguably to become high seas.[135] A transfer of rights would not be needed to bring the seabed rights in that same area within Canadian jurisdiction, since they would presumably fall to Canada as extended continental shelf. Nevertheless, the simplest way to deal with the situation, again, would be for the United States to transfer some EEZ rights to Canada through the inclusion of a small "special area" within the boundary treaty.

8.4 Multifunctional delimitation

Canada and the United States might seek to negotiate a multifunctional delimitation treaty with separate boundary lines for different zones. Australia and Papua New Guinea took such an approach in the Torres Strait Treaty of 1978, delimiting separate boundaries for rights to exploit the resources of the water column and seabed.[136] Such an

---

[133] US–Russia Maritime Boundary Treaty, Chapter 2, n. 20, above.
[134] Norway–Russia Barents Sea and Arctic Ocean Maritime Boundary Agreement, Chapter 2, n. 63, above, Art. 3.
[135] See the map, above, p. 61.
[136] Torres Strait Treaty (Australia–Papua New Guinea), No. 4, 1985 Australia Treaty Series.

approach might accommodate some of the rights recognized in the Inuvialuit Final Agreement. For example, if Canada maintained sovereign rights to exploit the resources of the water column up to the 141°W meridian and out to 200 nautical miles, the sustenance harvesting rights of the Inuvialuit would arguably remain intact – even if the United States had jurisdiction over the seabed.[137] However, it is equally arguable that such a compromise would not provide Canada with the extent of jurisdiction needed to fulfill all its obligations to the Inuvialuit, such as protecting their hunting and fishing rights from the negative effects of oil and gas exploration.[138] Problems similar to this might explain why the Torres Strait Treaty is a rare exception to a general practice of negotiating single maritime boundaries.[139]

8.5 Provision of economic access rights

As mentioned above, if Canada and the United States wish to delimit a boundary that falls within the Inuvialuit Settlement Region, one part of the compromise could see the United States agreeing to allow Canadian Inuvialuit to exercise their traditional rights up to the 141°W meridian despite the fact that at least some of the Inuvialuit Settlement Area would now fall within US maritime jurisdiction. Elsewhere in the world, states have sometimes agreed to continue to permit the nationals of neighboring states to fish in their waters after the delimitation of a maritime boundary, usually for a limited period of time to enable the fishing industry to adapt to the new circumstances.[140] This is the approach taken in the Torres Strait Treaty where Torres Strait Islanders and the coastal peoples of Papua New Guinea are entitled to continue their traditional activities in specially designated protected

---

[137] See discussion, above, pp. 80–82.

[138] See, e.g., Inuvialuit Final Agreement, n. 111, above, Art. 13(12): "The Government agrees that every proposed development of consequence to the Inuvialuit Settlement Region that is within its jurisdiction and that could have a significant negative impact on wildlife habitat or on present or future wildlife harvesting will be authorized only after due scrutiny of and attention to all environmental concerns and subject to reasonable mitigative and remedial provisions being imposed."

[139] In the Matter of the Arbitration between Barbados and Trinidad and Tobago, n. 69, above, para. 235.

[140] For example, the China–Vietnam Fisheries Agreement, which accompanied the 2000 Gulf of Tonkin Boundary Treaty, provides for a transitional period of four years to enable Chinese fishermen to adjust to new fishing patterns. See Zou Keyuan, "The Sino-Vietnamese Agreement on Maritime Boundary Delimitation in the Gulf of Tonkin." (2005) 36 Ocean Development and International Law 16-21.

zones without regard to international boundaries.[141] Again, economic access rights probably would not satisfy the full requirements of the Inuvialuit Final Agreement, but they could contribute toward securing the agreement of the Inuvialuit to a new boundary treaty – a matter, again, of no small importance for the Canadian government.

8.6 Joint development arrangement

Ted McDorman has written that the "Beaufort Sea boundary dispute area has long been seen as a candidate for the development of some type of hydrocarbon joint development regime."[142] As mentioned above, Canada and the United States considered a type of joint development area for the Beaufort Sea during maritime boundary negotiations in the 1970s.[143] Joint management regimes of larger regional scope already apply in the disputed zone with respect to beluga whales and polar bears – though these agreements were concluded between the indigenous peoples on both sides of the boundary as well as the Alaskan rather than the Canadian and US governments.[144]

Joint development arrangements for oil and gas have been a relatively popular solution to otherwise intractable maritime boundary disputes in other parts of the world. They can be adopted either alongside a final delimitation or in its absence. Hazel Fox, et al. have identified three general types:

---

[141] See Torres Strait Treaty, n. 136, above, Art. 10.

[142] McDorman, n. 11, above, p. 188, citing as examples Dawn Russell, "International Ocean Boundary Issues and Management Arrangements," in David VanderZwaag (ed.), Canadian Ocean Law and Policy (Toronto: Butterworths, 1992), 496–498; Donald M. McRae, "Canada and the Delimitation of Maritime Boundaries," in Donald M. McRae and Gordon Munro (eds.), Canadian Oceans Policy: National Strategies and the New Law of the Sea (Vancouver, University of British Columbia Press, 1989), 159–160; and Donald R. Rothwell, Maritime Boundaries and Resource Development: Options for the Beaufort Sea (Calgary: Canadian Institute of Resources Law, 1988), 45–57.

[143] McDorman, n. 11, above, p. 189, explains: "The idea was that shared-access zones would be created adjacent to a negotiated maritime boundary. Although each State would have exclusive authority over the hydrocarbon activities within the zone on its side of the maritime boundary, each State would have a right of purchase to obtain one-half of the volume of the hydrocarbons produced within each shared-access zone."

[144] See Marie Adams, Kathryn J. Frostz, and Lois A. Harwood, "Alaska and Inuvialuit Beluga Whale Committee (AIBWC) – An Initiative in At Home Management." (1993) 46 Arctic 134; and Inuvialuit-Inupiat Polar Bear Management Agreement in the Southern Beaufort Sea, 2000, available at http://pbsg.npolar.no/en/agreements/USA-Canada. html. See also, discussion, Chapter 6, below.

Model 1:   A system of compulsory joint ventures between the states or their nationals;

Model 2:   A joint authority with licensing and regulatory powers manages development of the joint development zone on behalf of the states;

Model 3:   One state manages development of the joint zone on behalf of both with the other state's participation confined to revenue sharing and monitoring.[145]

In reality, these models are pure types and there may be substantial overlap between them. Each also involves varying levels of delegation to joint bodies and harmonization of legislation as it applies to the joint development area. These issues are likely to be important to states that opt to negotiate some form of joint development regime, but, regardless of the model, the difficulties of reaching agreement on the details are sometimes as significant as those involved in delimiting a final boundary.[146] That said, joint development remains a possibility should the parties fail to agree on the location of a final boundary, and perhaps even if they succeed.

As was explained in Chapter 2, both the 1981 Iceland–Norway boundary treaty between Iceland and Jan Mayen as well as the 2010 Norway–Russia Barents Sea Treaty created systems for joint management of straddling oil and gas deposits.[147] A joint development regime might also be considered if the parties are, through negotiation, only able to reduce the size of any disputed area.[148] Finally, "model 3" (where one state manages development on behalf of both states) might be a creative way in which Canada could uphold its commitments in the

---

[145] Hazel Fox, et al., Joint Development of Offshore Oil and Gas: A Model Agreement for States for Joint Development with Explanatory Commentary (London: British Institute of International and Comparative Law, 1989).

[146] This situation is exemplified by the difficulties in setting up a "model 2" joint development zone between Thailand and Malaysia, which led to an eleven-year hiatus between the signing of the memorandum of understanding that expressed a desire for cooperation and its actual implementation in a considerably watered-down form. See David M. Ong, "The 1979 and 1990 Malaysia-Thailand Joint Development Agreements: A Model for International Legal Co-operation in Common Offshore Petroleum Deposits?" (1999) 14 International Journal of Marine and Coastal Law 207.

[147] Agreement on the Continental Shelf between Iceland and Jan Mayen, n. 36, above; Norway–Russia Barents Sea and Arctic Ocean Maritime Boundary Agreement, Chapter 2, n. 63, above, Annex II.

[148] This seems to have been the intent of the negotiators during the 1977 talks on the Beaufort Sea boundary who failed to reach agreement "as regards the number, size or configuration" of shared access zones. Lorne Clark, n. 24, above, p. 13, cited in McDorman n. 11, above, p. 189.

Inuvialuit Final Agreement. In short, Canada could manage development in the southern portion of the disputed zone, in consultation with the Inuvialuit, and simply pay the United States a proportion of the revenue from exploitation activities there.

9 Russia–Canada maritime boundary in the Beaufort Sea?

One final curiosity remains about the effects of any maritime delimitation between the United States and Canada in the Beaufort Sea, namely, the potential for a boundary dispute between Canada and Russia. As was explained in Chapter 2, the United States has already agreed on a boundary with the Soviet Union (now Russia) that follows the 168°58′37″W meridian "as far as permitted by international law."[149] If the United States were now to agree on a boundary with Canada that was based on equidistance or modified equidistance, the US boundary with Russia would naturally terminate at the point at which it met the new United States–Canada line – provided, again, that Canada is able to demonstrate that its rights to an extended continental shelf stretch that far. This might then necessitate the negotiation of a maritime boundary between Canada and Russia, unless those two countries simply continue to use the 168°58′37″W meridian. As Chapter 4 explains, Russia respected that line all the way to the North Pole when making its initial submission to the CLCS in 2001.[150] However, in the event that a new United States–Canada boundary placed a northern limit on US jurisdiction, it is possible that Russia would seek to expand its jurisdiction eastwards of 168°58′37″W, for instance, along the Alpha/Mendeleev Ridge.[151] Likewise, there is no bar to Canada seeking to extend its jurisdiction beyond the line in the opposite direction, if geological and geomorphological circumstances allow.

10 Summary

The Beaufort Sea boundary dispute has recently become more salient as the result of melting sea-ice, greater access to offshore oil and gas, and the realization that the disputed area could extend beyond 200 nautical

---

[149] US–Russia Maritime Boundary Agreement, Chapter 20, n. 20, above, Art. 2(1).
[150] "Submission by the Russian Federation: Summary," 2001, available at www.un.org/depts/los/clcs_new/submissions_files/submission_rus.htm.
[151] For more on the Alpha/Mendeleev Ridge, see Chapter 4, below.

miles onto the extended continental shelf. Canada and the United States have not yet publicized their legal positions on the boundary beyond 200 nautical miles, and the development of those positions will be complicated by the curious fact that each of their positions within 200 nautical miles would seem to favor the other party further out. Although the expanded dispute offers greater possibilities for a negotiated agreement, during any negotiations the parties will naturally seek to maximize their gains. For this reason, it is possible that either or both parties will partially or wholly abandon their existing legal positions, and formulate new ones.

Canada, for instance, might adopt the position that an equidistance line is appropriate – if it is modified to take into account the concave nature of its coastline in the east of the delimitation area, and only if it is also used to delimit the extended continental shelf. The United States, on the other hand, might maintain its position on equidistance within the EEZ and argue that geological and geomorphological characteristics should determine the course of the boundary further out. For instance, it might argue that the Chukchi Plateau is a "submarine elevation" over which it could potentially have sovereign rights beyond 350 nautical miles, and that this should be considered relevant to any delimitation. Such positions are not likely to reduce the size of the area in dispute, but they do create room for a negotiated solution that, unlike litigation or arbitration, enables the parties to retain control over the delimitation process. Creative solutions that do not involve a single maritime boundary are also available, though some might be quite difficult to negotiate. The extension of the Inuvialuit Settlement Region into the disputed area complicates matters only insofar as the Inuvialuit will have to be closely consulted and ideally involved in any negotiations between Canada and the United States, so as to ensure that their existing harvesting rights are protected within any outcome.

4   Extended continental shelves

"The Arctic is Russian."[1] With a few simple words, Artur Chilingarov, who led the expedition that planted a titanium flag on the ocean floor at the North Pole, commanded global media attention in August 2007. Observers of Russian politics knew that Chilingarov was a member of the Russian Duma in the midst of an election campaign and that – as one of the Russian scientists involved later admitted – the North Pole flag-plant was a publicity stunt lacking legal relevance.[2] However, Canadian Foreign Minister Peter MacKay took the bait. "Look, this isn't the fifteenth century," he exclaimed. "You can't go around the world and just plant flags and say, 'We're claiming this territory.' Our claims over our Arctic are very well established."[3] MacKay's statement obscured the fact that Canada has never claimed the North Pole. It was also somewhat ironic, because Canadian soldiers had flown to Hans Island to plant a Canadian flag just two years earlier.[4]

Russian, Canadian, and Danish politicians have learned that asserting sovereign rights in the Arctic is good election fodder. However, Arctic sovereignty is never just a domestic issue; it centrally involves relations with other, sometimes quite powerful states. Playing the sovereignty card badly can have a negative impact on seemingly unrelated matters of global importance, such as nuclear disarmament talks between

---

[1] Paul Reynolds, "Russia Ahead in Arctic 'Gold Rush'," *BBC News*, August 1, 2007, available at http://news.bbc.co.uk/2/hi/6925853.stm.

[2] Adrian Blomfield, "US Rises to Kremlin Bait," *Daily Telegraph*, August 4, 2007, available at www.telegraph.co.uk/news/worldnews/1559444/US-rises-to-Kremlin-bait.html.

[3] "Canada Rejects Flag-Planting as 'Just a Show'," *Independent* online, August 3, 2012, available at www.iol.co.za/news/world/canada-rejects-flag-planting-as-just-a-show-1.364759#.UHgzYo4_5UQ.

[4] For more on Hans Island, see Chapter 1, above.

Russia and the United States. The negative impact can be magnified when journalists pay more attention to the possibility of confrontation than the reality of cooperation. Chilingarov and MacKay's comments led to a rush of excited reporting about an upcoming conflict over Arctic resources; some headlines portrayed a North that was on the brink of war.

In a deliberate response to all the misreporting, the Danish government invited the foreign ministers of the four other Arctic Ocean coastal states to Ilulissat, Greenland, in May 2008.

The summit culminated in the Ilulissat Declaration, in which all five states reaffirmed their commitment to working together within an existing framework of international law.[5] "We have politically committed ourselves to resolve all differences through negotiations," explained Danish Foreign Minister Per Stig Møller. "And thus we have hopefully, once and for all, killed all the myths of a 'race to the North Pole.' The rules are in place. And the five states have now declared that they will abide by them."[6]

Møller was right: The rules are in place, and they have been for some time.

1 Continental shelf regime

The North Pole is located more than 400 nautical miles from the northernmost islands of Canada, Denmark, Norway, and Russia. Under international law, coastal state rights over the water column are limited to 200 nautical miles; beyond that the ocean's surface and water column are "high seas" open to exploitation by any state. If sovereign rights extend beyond 200 nautical miles, they can only concern the seabed and subsoil – under the continental shelf regime.

States' rights to the resources of the continental shelf have their origins in the first half of the twentieth century. Though some exploitation of seabed resources such as pearls had taken place for centuries, the extension of coastal state authority over the continental shelf began in earnest with the 1945 Truman Proclamation on the Continental

---

[5] "The Ilulissat Declaration," Arctic Ocean Conference, Ilulissat, Greenland, May 27–29, 2008, available at http://byers.typepad.com/arctic/ilulissat-declaration-may-28-2008.html.

[6] Andrew C. Revkin, "Countries Agree to Talk Over the Arctic," New York Times, May 29, 2008, available at www.nytimes.com/2008/05/29/science/earth/29arctic.html.

Shelf.[7] In the Truman Proclamation, the United States claimed that all coastal states have the exclusive right to the resources of the continental shelf offshore their territory. The reciprocally available nature of the claim led many other states to extend their own jurisdiction within just a few years.[8] By 1958, the Geneva Convention on the Continental Shelf sought to define the spatial extent of that jurisdiction as well as the content and application of coastal state rights.[9] The convention specified that coastal states had sovereign rights over continental shelf resources up to a depth of 200 meters or (crucially and ambiguously) to a point where the depth of the water admitted of exploitation. As mentioned in Chapter 3, the International Court of Justice provided a rationale for all this in the 1969 *North Sea Continental Shelf Cases*, namely that "the submarine areas concerned may be deemed to be actually part of the territory over which the coastal State already has dominion, – in the sense that, although covered with water, they are a prolongation or continuation of that territory, an extension of it under the sea."[10] However, the true catalyst for the effort to establish a definite boundary between the continental shelf and the deep ocean floor came in 1967 when Maltese diplomat Arvid Pardo called for the deep seabed and its resources to be declared the "Common Heritage of Mankind."[11]

The current legal regime of the continental shelf was negotiated during the Third UN Conference on the Law of the Sea and set out in Part VI of the 1982 UN Convention on the Law of the Sea (UNCLOS).[12] Each coastal state is entitled to exploit the seabed and subsoil up to a distance of 200 nautical miles from its territorial sea baselines as part of the regime of the exclusive economic zone (EEZ). Those states whose

---

[7] "Policy of the United States with Respect to the Natural Resources of the Subsoil and Sea Bed of the Continental Shelf," reproduced in (1946) 40 *American Journal of International Law* 45, available at www.ibiblio.org/pha/policy/1945/450928a.html.

[8] James Crawford and Thomas Viles, "International Law on a Given Day," in Konrad Ginther, et al. (eds.), *Völkerrecht zwischen normativem Anspruch und politischer Realität. Festschrift für Karl Zemanek zum 65. Geburtstag* (Berlin: Duncker and Humblot, 1994), 65; reprinted in James Crawford, *International Law as an Open System: Selected Essays* (London: Cameron and May, 2002), 69. See also Byers, *Custom, Power and the Power of Rules*, Introduction, n. 39, above, pp. 90–92.

[9] 1958 Geneva Convention on the Continental Shelf, 499 UNTS 311, available at http://un treaty.un.org/ilc/texts/instruments/english/conventions/8_1_1958_continental_shelf.pdf.

[10] *North Sea Continental Shelf Cases*, Chapter 3, n. 59, above, p. 31, para. 43.

[11] 1st Committee, 22nd Session, UN GAOR meeting., UN Doc. A/C.1/PV.1515 (November 1, 1967), available at www.un.org/Depts/los/convention_agreements/texts/pardo_ga1967.pdf.

[12] UN Doc. A/CONF.62/122 (1982), reproduced in (1982) 21 ILM 1261, available at www.un. org/Depts/los/convention_agreements/texts/unclos/closindx.htm.

outer edge of the continental margin extends beyond 200 nautical miles may extend their exploitation rights further. Article 76(1) states: "The continental shelf of a coastal State comprises the seabed and subsoil of the submarine areas that extend beyond its territorial sea throughout the natural prolongation of its land territory to the outer edge of the continental margin."[13] The continental shelf is still conceived, therefore, as a continuous geomorphological feature. Although the scientific and legal definitions of the continental shelf diverge,[14] the contemporary legal regime uses both the geological and geomorphological characteristics of the seabed to define the theory and limits of the legal continental shelf. The continental margin is defined as "the submerged prolongation of the land mass of the coastal State, and consists of the seabed and subsoil of the shelf, the slope and the rise."[15]

Any party to UNCLOS wishing to establish rights beyond 200 nautical miles is expected to submit scientific data concerning its proposed extended continental shelf limits to the CLCS[16] within ten years of ratifying the convention. Once the CLCS issues recommendations in response, limits established on the basis of those recommendations become final and binding on the other parties to UNCLOS.[17] But, again, a state is only required to submit data if its continental margin extends beyond 200 nautical miles; otherwise, it can simply claim out to 200 nautical miles under the EEZ regime (Arts. 55–77) or the second clause of Article 76(1).[18]

Article 76 provides a set of formulae for submissions. States may determine the seaward limits of their legal continental shelf on the

---

[13] Ibid.

[14] See Philip A. Symonds and Harald Brekke, "The Ridge Provisions of Article 76 of the UN Convention on the Law of the Sea," in Myron H. Nordquist, John Norton Moore, and Tomas H. Heidar (eds.), *Legal and Scientific Aspects of Continental Shelf Limits* (Dordrecht: Martinus Nijhoff, 2004), 170.

[15] UNCLOS, n. 12, above, Art. 76(3).

[16] Ibid., Annex II, Art. 4. The CLCS is a body of scientists elected by the UNCLOS parties to issue recommendations on submissions concerning the outer limits of coastal states' rights over extended continental shelves.

[17] Ted McDorman argues that the limits only become final and binding on the coastal state, with other states only becoming bound to respect such limits if they do not protest them and the limits become generally accepted. Ted L. McDorman, "The Role of the Commission on the Limits of the Continental Shelf: A Technical Body in a Political World." (2002) 17 *International Journal of Marine and Coastal Law* 301 at 315.

[18] The second clause reads: "or to a distance of 200 nautical miles from the baselines from which the breadth of the territorial sea is measured where the outer edge of the continental margin does not extend up to that distance." UNCLOS, n. 12, above.

basis of either (1) sediment thickness or (2) the distance from the "foot" of the continental slope, which, unless there is evidence to the contrary, is defined as the point of maximum change in gradient at its base. The limits must be marked by lines that are no longer than sixty nautical miles, connecting fixed points at which either (1) the thickness of sediments is no more than 1 percent of the distance back to the foot of the slope, or (2) the distance to the foot of the slope is no more than sixty nautical miles. A state may use either approach at any given point, and will generally choose whichever is most advantageous to it. Complicating things further, a coastal state's extended continental shelf may not reach beyond the furthest of two constraint lines: either (1) 100 nautical miles from the 2,500 meter "isobath" (i.e., underwater depth contour line); or (2) 350 nautical miles from the territorial sea baselines. On classic continental margins, such as those in the Atlantic Ocean, these formulae are relatively easy to apply. Other continental shelves are more complex and therefore more challenging – a situation that prevails in the Arctic Ocean.

2 Seafloor highs

One way in which complexity is increased is through the presence of ridges and other seafloor "highs," which Ron Macnab likens to "wild cards" in terms of their role in the Article 76 process.[19] Together, these highs constitute a greater proportion of the Earth's seafloor than the continental margins themselves, covering 1.7 times more area.[20] They have varying characteristics and origins, as well as varying geological and geomorphological relationships with the continental margin. Philip A. Symonds, *et al.* provide the following list of highs that occur in "non-convergent settings," i.e., situations where tectonic plates are not being pushed together:

Spreading ridges are the product of seafloor spreading at extension plate tectonic boundaries, which may be active or extinct.
Fracture zone ridges may be present along translational plate boundaries.
Microcontinents may form when continents break up.

---

[19] Ron Macnab, "Submarine Elevations and Ridges: Wild Card in the Poker Game of UNCLOS Article 76" (2008) 39 *Ocean Development and International Law* 223.
[20] Harald Brekke and Philip A. Symonds, "A Scientific Overview of Ridges," in Nordquist, *et al.*, n. 14, above, p. 152.

Oceanic plateaus represent the impact of a mantle hot spot.
Hot spot ridges represent the track of a mantle hot spot.[21]

In "convergent settings," subduction-related "island arc systems" and collision-related "orogenic belts" may be present (*convergent ridges*), or *accreted ridges* may occur due to the attachment of pre-existing ridges to the continental margin. The geographical names of these features may vary and their geological and geomorphological characteristics will not always be apparent from the names.

Article 76 includes three categories of seafloor features with different rules concerning the extent to which national jurisdiction may be exercised over them. Oceanic ridges may not be reduced to national jurisdiction.[22] As mentioned in Chapter 3, submarine ridges may provide a valid basis for establishing the outer limit of the continental shelf and thus be subject to national jurisdiction, but not beyond 350 nautical miles from shore – thus removing the "2,500 metre plus 100 nautical mile" option.[23] Submarine elevations that are natural components of the continental margin, such as plateaux, rises, caps, banks, and spurs, may also provide a valid basis for establishing the outer limit of the continental shelf. But they differ from submarine ridges in that either constraint line may be adopted when calculating the limits of jurisdiction.[24] UNCLOS does not define these features further, nor does it define key terms such as "natural components of the continental margin."

2.1 Oceanic ridges

Oceanic ridges are associated with the deep ocean and have been defined by the International Hydrographic Organization as "long elevation[s] of the deep ocean floor with either irregular or smooth topography and steep sides."[25] They are ordinarily composed of oceanic crust and lie completely beyond the geomorphological continental shelf.

---

[21] Philip A. Symonds, *et al.*, "Ridge Issues," in Peter J. Cook and Chris Carleton, *Continental Shelf Limits: The Scientific and Legal Interface* (New York: Oxford University Press, 2000), 285 at 288.

[22] UNCLOS, n. 12, above, Art. 76(3).

[23] Ibid., Art. 76(6). However, Kunoy, *et al.* argue that CLCS practice is inconsistent on this point. See Bjørn Kunoy, Martin V. Heinesen, and Finn Mørk, "Appraisal of Applicable Depth Constraint for the Purpose of Establishing the Outer Limits of the Continental Shelf." (2010) 41 *Ocean Development and International Law* 357.

[24] Ibid.

[25] International Hydrographic Organization, *A Manual on Technical Aspects of the United Nations Convention on the Law of the Sea – 1982*, 4th edn., Special Publication No. 51 (2006), Appendix I-21, available at www.gmat.unsw.edu.au/ablos/TALOS_ed4.pdf.

Sometimes islands sit on top of such ridges, as is the case with Iceland and the Azores. Some authors are of the view that the geology of these ridges is determinative and such islands cannot generate a legal continental shelf beyond 200 nautical miles.[26] Others consider that such islands, having been created by the same processes as the ridge on which they sit, can take advantage of the provision on submarine ridges to extend their continental shelf rights out to 350 nautical miles.[27] Complicating matters, ridges composed of oceanic crust may sometimes be geomorphologically connected to the continental margin in convergent settings, and the issue of whether and when such ridges may be reduced to national jurisdiction has yet to be resolved.[28]

In 1999, the CLCS published guidelines on how it would interpret Article 76, including its provisions on oceanic and submarine ridges and submarine elevations.[29] With regard to the general categories of seafloor highs, the CLCS wrote:

Article 76 makes no systematic reference to the different types of the earth's crust. Instead it only makes reference to the two terms: "the natural prolongation of . . . land territory" and "the submerged prolongation of the land mass" of coastal states as opposed to oceanic ridges of the deep ocean floor. The terms "land mass" and "land territory" are both neutral terms with regard to crustal types in the geological sense. Therefore, the Commission feels that geological crust types cannot be the sole qualifier in the classification of ridges and elevations of the sea floor into the legal categories of paragraph 6 of article 76, even in the case of island States.[30]

In 2010, in its recommendations regarding the United Kingdom's submission concerning the extended continental shelf around Ascension Island, the CLCS confirmed that it would not prevent or limit the assertion of rights over oceanic ridges solely because of their crust type.[31] Rather, it would establish a view based on considerations such as "whether a ridge is a natural prolongation of land territory and land mass, [the] morphology of ridges and their relation to the continental

[26] See Symonds, *et al.*, "Ridge Issues," n. 21, above, p. 300.   [27] Ibid.   [28] Ibid.
[29] "Scientific and Technical Guidelines of the Commission on the Limits of the Continental Shelf," CLCS/11, May 13, 1999, available at www.un.org/depts/los/clcs_new/commission_documents.htm#Guidelines.
[30] Ibid., p. 54.
[31] "Summary of Recommendations of the Commission on the Limits of the Continental Shelf in Regard to the Submission Made by the United Kingdom of Great Britain and Northern Ireland in Respect of Ascension Island on 9 May 2008," April 15, 2010, at paras. 22 and 23, available at www.un.org/Depts/los/clcs_new/submissions_files/gbr08/gbr_asc_isl_rec_summ.pdf.

margin as defined in paragraph 4 [of Article 76], and continuity of ridges."[32] The CLCS stressed that the determination of whether a ridge falls into the oceanic or submarine category would be made on a case-by-case basis.

2.2 Submarine ridges and submarine elevations

The distinction between submarine ridges and submarine elevations has been controversial. A commonly cited definition of the term "submarine ridge" is: "an elongated elevation of the sea floor, with either irregular or relatively smooth topography and steep sides which constitutes a natural prolongation of land territory."[33] The fact that they are natural prolongations of land territory is one of the keys to distinguishing submarine ridges from oceanic ridges. For this reason, it is relatively well established that submarine ridges must lie within the geomorphological continental margin – that is, within the "foot of the slope" envelope as defined in Article 76(4) – in order to be subject to sovereign rights.[34] Any other ridge would be unable to contribute to the outer limit of the continental shelf regardless of crust type.[35] Additionally, in cases where there is a "saddle" area that divides upper and lower portions of the continental shelf, sufficient geomorphological continuity must be shown so as to establish that the saddle is not a component of the deep ocean floor.[36]

UNCLOS could be interpreted as barring the use of the "2,500-metre plus 100 nautical mile" constraint line on all ridge-like features, on the

---

[32] Ibid.   [33] International Hydrographic Organization, n. 25, above.

[34] Harald Brekke and Philip A. Symonds, "Submarine Ridges and Elevations of Article 76 in Light of Published Summaries of Recommendations of the Commission on the Limits of the Continental Shelf." (2011) 42 *Ocean Development and International Law* 292.

[35] Symonds and Brekke, "The Ridge Provisions of Article 76 of the UN Convention on the Law of the Sea," n. 14, above, p. 185.

[36] Brekke and Symonds note that Norway attempted to use foot of the slope points on the Mohns-Knipovich Ridge system, claiming that it was a submarine ridge because it was geomorphologically connected to Norway's continental margin by the Bjørnøya Fan. However, the CLCS decided that the seafloor in the area was too flat, and concluded that "the Mohns-Knipovich Ridge system, including its central valley, is considered to be part of the deep ocean floor and/or rise provinces on morphological and geological grounds." Similarly, the CLCS concluded that the United Kingdom could not use foot of the slope points on the mid-Atlantic Ridge because "Ascension Island is distinct from the surrounding ocean floor, morphologically, geologically, geophysically and geochemically." See "Summary of Recommendations of the Commission on the Limits of the Continental Shelf in Regard to the Submission Made by the United Kingdom of Great Britain and Northern Ireland in Respect of Ascension Island on 9 May 2008," n. 31, above, para. 47; Brekke and Symonds, n. 14, above, p. 292.

basis that such features are necessarily either submarine ridges or oceanic ridges. However, another interpretation is that the definition of a ridge is indistinguishable from that of a "spur" and, therefore, UNCLOS admits of some ridge-like structures being "submarine elevations that are natural components of the continental margin."[37] Significantly, the CLCS took the latter approach in its recommendations on New Zealand's submission, recognizing several long ridge-like features as submarine elevations.[38] As Symonds, *et al.* explain: "[T]here are a variety of ridge-like submarine elevations throughout the world's oceans. Some exhibit clear continental affinities, others oceanic affinities, and some both."[39] This then raises the question of the relevance of crust type to the classification of seafloor highs as either submarine ridges or submarine elevations in circumstances where they are geomorphologically adjacent to the continental margin.

In its 1999 Guidelines, the CLCS stated:

The term "submarine elevations" in paragraph 6 includes a selection of highs: "such as plateaux, rises, caps, banks and spurs". The phrase "such as" implies that the list is not complete. Common to all of these elevations is that they are natural components of the continental margin. This makes it relevant to consider the processes that form the continental margins and how continents grow. ... Consequently, the Commission will base its views on "submarine elevations" mainly on the following considerations:

(a) In the active margins, a natural process by which a continent grows is the accretion of sediments and crustal material of oceanic, island arc or continental origin onto the continental margin. Therefore, any crustal fragment or sedimentary wedge that is accreted to the continental margin should be regarded as a natural component of that continental margin.

(b) In the passive margins, the natural process by which a continent breaks up prior to the separation by seafloor spreading involves thinning, extension and rifting of the continental crust and extensive intrusion of magma into and extensive extrusion of magma through that crust. This process adds to the growth of the continents. Therefore, seafloor highs that are formed by this breakup process should be regarded as natural components of the

---

[37] Tomasz Gorski, "A Note on Submarine Ridges and Elevations with Special Reference to the Russian Federation and the Arctic Ridges." (2009) 40 *Ocean Development and International Law* 56.

[38] "Recommendations of the Commission on the Limits of the Continental Shelf in Regard to the Submission Made by New Zealand 19 April 2006," August 22, 2008, available at www.mfat.govt.nz/downloads/global-issues/cont-shelf-recommendations.pdf.

[39] Symonds, *et al.*, n. 21, above, p. 286.

continental margin where such highs constitute an integral part of the prolongation of the land mass.[40]

The origins and geological character of these features, as well as their geomorphological relationship to the continental margin, are therefore all relevant to their legal status. However, the CLCS still failed to specify whether, and up to what point, a feature that arose from one of the above processes and took on the character of a ridge could still be considered a submarine elevation.[41]

Part of the problem is that Article 76 was a compromise between two competing goals: (1) preventing coastal states from asserting sovereign rights over deep seabed resources constituting the Common Heritage of Mankind;[42] and (2) providing broad margin coastal states with an entitlement to extended continental shelves. This tension was apparent in the negotiations relating to ridges: the Soviet Union suggested that "the limit of the shelf in areas containing submerged oceanic ridges shall not extend farther than the ... 350-mile distance."[43] However, the delegates were discussing long, narrow highs formed of oceanic crust, as was reflected in a Japanese proposal that ridges composed of oceanic crust could not be included in the legal continental shelf.[44] This conclusion is supported by Tomasz Gorski, who reports that the singular 350-nautical-mile constraint on submarine ridges was designed to limit the sovereign rights generated by islands that are located on top of mid-ocean ridges.[45] The International Law Association's Outer Continental Shelf Committee likewise interprets the term "submarine ridge" as "applicable to ridges that are (predominantly) oceanic in origin and that are the natural prolongation of the land territory of a coastal state."[46] However, Harald Brekke and Symonds conclude that the failure to include language related to crust type means that ridges

[40] "Scientific and Technical Guidelines," n. 29, above.
[41] Macnab, n. 19, above, p. 224.
[42] Part XI of UNCLOS specifies that the "Area" beyond the continental shelf is the "Common Heritage of Mankind" and that "No State shall claim or exercise sovereignty or sovereign rights over any part of the Area or its resources, nor shall any State or natural or juridical person appropriate any part thereof. ... All rights in the resources of the Area are vested in mankind as a whole, on whose behalf the Authority shall act," n. 12, above, Arts. 136 and 137.
[43] Symonds, et al., n. 21, above, p. 287.   [44] Ibid.   [45] Gorski, n. 37, above, pp. 51–60.
[46] International Law Association, "Legal Issues of the Outer Continental Shelf," 2nd Report, Toronto Conference, 2006, p. 4, available at www.ila-hq.org/download.cfm/docid/435A6BA1-4F85-47B3-9ED23A6F64924414.

composed of oceanic crust may be included in the continental margin as natural components, if they have a morphological and geological relationship with the margin.[47]

During the negotiations leading to UNCLOS, broad margin coastal states had advocated that certain highs be included in the legal continental shelf. As mentioned in Chapter 3, the United States insisted that the Chukchi Plateau was a natural component of its continental margin.[48] Australia suggested that "plateaux, rises, banks and spurs" were examples of submarine elevations that formed part of the continental margin.[49] Denmark later explained that it considered highs that "belong fundamentally to the same geological structure as the land territory" to be natural components of the continental margin.[50]

This differentiation of submarine elevations from submarine ridges leads Brekke and Symonds to conclude that the latter "must be ridges that are not natural components of the continental margin but still integral parts of the continental margin because they fall within the common envelope of the foot of the continental slope."[51] Such ridges are geologically associated with the continental margin at their landward extent and also with the deep ocean floor further seaward, while being geomorphologically integral to the continental margin. Brekke and Symonds therefore suggest that those ridges which are geomorphologically but not geologically continuous with the continental margin throughout their full extent be considered submarine ridges, and those which are both geologically and geomorphologically continuous be considered submarine elevations.[52] They also suggest that geological continuity should be interpreted in terms of both general geological character and origin.[53]

In short, given that the definition of a spur is essentially indistinguishable from that of a ridge and that the final list of submarine elevations incorporated into UNCLOS is not exhaustive, there would seem to be no bar to ridge-like features being treated as natural components of the continental margin.[54] As a consequence, it would appear that either constraint line is available for use from foot of the slope points calculated from a ridge-like feature, so long as the feature in

---

[47] Brekke and Symonds, n. 14, above, p. 192.   [48] Richardson, Chapter 3, n. 89, above.
[49] Symonds, et al., n. 21, above, p. 287.   [50] Ibid.
[51] Brekke and Symonds, n. 14, above, p. 186.   [52] Ibid. at p. 192.   [53] Ibid.
[54] Weiguo Wang, "Geological Structures of Ridges with Relation to the Definition of Three Types of Seafloor Highs Stipulated in Article 76" (2011) 30 *Acta Oceanologica Sinica* 125 at 137.

question has, throughout its full extent, both geomorphological and geological affinity with the continental margin – in which case it is properly called a submarine elevation.[55]

This is the approach adopted by the CLCS in a number of cases, as Bjørn Kunoy explains:

[T]he Commission has on geological grounds either disqualified or qualified the classification of a seafloor high as a submarine elevation that is a natural component of the continental margin, which has a bearing on the extent of seaward limits of the relevant coastal state. In its recommendations to Australia, the Commission dismissed the application of the depth constraint with regard to the Williams Ridge "since the nature of the submarine high with regard to Article 76, paragraph 6, is not considered proven." In other words, because of the absence of geological processes, the classification of the Williams Ridge as a submarine elevation that is a natural component of the continental margin was not accepted. Further, it seems that Australia also argued that Joey Rise was a submarine elevation that is a natural component of the continental margin "on morphology only." Despite recognizing that Joey Rise was part of the submerged prolongation of the land mass of Australia, the Commission did not accept the view that it was a submarine elevation that is a natural component of the continental margin on the basis of the submitted data concerning the origin of Joey Rise, which were considered "too sparse to be conclusive." By contrast, on the basis of geological considerations, the Central Kerguelen Plateau, Southern Kerguelen Plateau and the Elan Bank were "considered natural components of the continental margin of the Heard and MacDonald Islands" and therefore "subject to the application of the depth criterion constraint."[56]

According to Symonds and Brekke, "the CLCS makes an assessment as to what extent such an elevation is geologically associated or continuous with the landmass of the coastal state, and to what extent it is geologically different to the surrounding deep ocean floor."[57] At the same time, they point out that some countries disagree with this approach.[58] Australia was particularly keen to prevent the development of a precedent by the CLCS, preferring that it continue to decide the

---

[55] Wang agrees that geological continuity is essential. Ibid., p. 136.

[56] Bjørn Kunoy, "The Terms of Reference of the Commission on the Limits of the Continental Shelf: A Creeping Legal Mandate." (2012) 25 Leiden Journal of International Law 109 at 120–121. See also Brekke and Symonds, n. 14, above, p. 299.

[57] See Brekke and Symonds, n. 56, above, ibid.

[58] Ibid. Australia argued that the geological test is relevant only in the case of ridges, with all other features being considered natural components of the continental margin on the basis of geomorphology alone. This approach seems problematic, given the non-exhaustive nature of the list and the definition of a spur.

status of ridges on a case-by-case basis.[59] Yet as Mel Weber rightly concludes, ultimately the practice of the CLCS will combine with state practice to determine the outcome of this debate.[60]

To sum up this highly technical section, the UNCLOS provisions on seafloor highs are complex, but some consensus on their meaning is emerging. Oceanic ridges are usually, but not always, composed of oceanic crust, lie beyond the geomorphological continental margin and are therefore associated with the deep ocean floor. They cannot contribute to the establishment of the outer limit of the continental shelf. Submarine ridges are geomorphologically related to the continental margin while being geologically discontinuous from it, and national jurisdiction is limited to 350 nautical miles from shore. Submarine elevations are both geomorphologically related and geologically continuous with the landmass of the coastal state, in terms of crust type and/or geological origin. They are therefore natural components of the continental margin and national jurisdiction is limited to either 350 nautical miles or 100 nautical miles beyond the 2,500-meter isobath, whichever is (at any given point) further from shore. Despite this emerging consensus, however, it must always be remembered that the CLCS's characterization of seafloor highs is conducted on a case-by-case basis, which maintains an on-going element of uncertainty in the process.

3 Geomorphological and geological characteristics of the central Arctic Ocean

The seafloor of the central Arctic Ocean includes four ridge-like structures: the Gakkel, Lomonosov, Alpha, and Mendeleev Ridges. The Gakkel Ridge is located in the Eurasian Basin on the European side of the Arctic Ocean. The Lomonosov Ridge separates the Eurasian Basin from the Amerasian Basin; it extends northwards from an area proximate to the continental shelf of Greenland and Canada's Ellesmere Island, passing near but not over the North Pole, and southwards from there to an area proximate to the continental shelf of Russia's New Siberian Islands. The Alpha and Mendeleev Ridges, which may be the same feature and are here referred to as the Alpha/Mendeleev Ridge, are

---

[59] Ibid.
[60] Mel Weber, "Defining the Outer Limits of the Continental Shelf across the Arctic Basin: The Russian Submission, States' Rights, Boundary Delimitation and Arctic Regional Cooperation." (2009) 24 *International Journal Marine and Coastal Law* 653 at 669.

located in the Amerasian Basin on the other side of the Lomonosov Ridge.[61]

3.1 Lomonosov Ridge

The Lomonosov Ridge is roughly 900 nautical miles long and varies from 24 to 108 nautical miles in width and from 400 to 4,000 meters in height above the seafloor.[62] Although a "trough" or "saddle" separates the continental crust on the edge of the Ellesmere Island and Greenland margin, Canada and Denmark conducted a joint survey of the area in 2006, which built on a 1979 survey that established the general characteristics of the Lomonosov Ridge. According to the Canadian Department of Foreign Affairs and International Trade, the objective of the 2006 survey "was to use seismometers to record the sound velocities of the sedimentary and crustal layers in order to show that the Ridge has an affinity with the nearby continental region."[63]

In 2010, an article written by Canadian government scientists was published in *Geophysical Journal International*.[64] It reported that the geology of the saddle area is different from the surrounding deep ocean floor, there is a continuity of continental crust across the saddle, and the Lomonosov Ridge is incorporated into the North American margin by a continuous foot of the slope envelope.[65] The article also reported that, although sea-ice has prevented geological sampling on large parts of the ridge, the collection of samples containing the mineral zircon supports the hypothesis that it is a "double-sided continental margin" that is geomorphologically appurtenant to both the Canadian and/or Danish continental margin and that of Russia.[66] The saddle is around 1,000 meters higher than the deep seafloor, and the CLCS has already accepted a difference of similar

---

[61] The International Bathymetric Chart of the Arctic Ocean provides the most up-to-date and comprehensive picture, with the latest version dating to June 2012. International Bathymetric Chart of the Arctic Ocean, Version 3.0, June 8, 2012, available at www. ngdc.noaa.gov/mgg/bathymetry/arctic/arctic.html.

[62] H. Ruth Jackson, Trine Dahl-Jensen, and the LORITA working group, "Sedimentary and Crustal Structure from the Ellesmere Island and Greenland Continental Shelves onto the Lomonosov Ridge, Arctic Ocean." (2010) 182 *Geophysical Journal International* 11.

[63] Department of Foreign Affairs, "Extended Continental Shelf: International Cooperation," www.international.gc.ca/continental/collaboration.aspx?view=d. Presumably, the participating scientists would have conducted their research without any such pre-ordained conclusion.

[64] H. Ruth Jackson, *et al.*, n. 62, above, p. 11.   [65] Ibid.

[66] Ibid., p. 13. See also Ruth Jackson, *et al.*, "The Structure of the Lomonosov Ridge, Arctic Ocean," American Geophysical Union, Fall Meeting 2010, abstract #T31A-2122, available at http://adsabs.harvard.edu/abs/2010AGUFM.T31A2122J.

proportions with respect to Australia's extended continental shelf submission.[67] An area of similar geomorphology exists toward the Russian end of the Lomonosov Ridge where it meets the Siberian continental margin, and Russian scientists report that the ridge is included within the foot of the slope envelope there also.[68]

3.2 Alpha/Mendeleev Ridge

In 2011, the US and Canadian icebreakers Healy and Louis S. St. Laurent extended their joint seabed mapping to the Alpha Ridge, a 1,100-nautical-mile-long range of underwater mountains running from the northwest flank of Canada's Ellesmere Island toward Russia's Wrangel Island. The Alpha Ridge is located on the opposite side of the Lomonosov Ridge from the geographic North Pole. A key question concerns whether the Alpha Ridge terminates somewhere in the middle of the Arctic Ocean, or connects to another range of underwater mountains called the Mendeleev Ridge which extends northwards from Siberia. The Russians are asking the same question and have sent the nuclear-powered icebreaker Rossiya and the research vessel Akademik Fedorov to map the area. The Rossiya is equipped with a seismic array and the Akademik Fedorov with a multi-beam sonar system, and they worked in tandem just like the Healy and Louis S. St. Laurent.[69] Early reports indicate that Russia, as in its 2001 submission to the CLCS,[70] remains willing to limit its assertion of sovereign rights to those areas west of the 168°58′37″W meridian (which the Soviet Union and the United States agreed in 1990 constituted the boundary between their continental shelf rights "as far as permitted under international law").[71] This self-limitation, however, cannot be assumed to continue if and when

---

[67] In the Australian submission, the CLCS was presented with a number of seafloor highs separated from other parts of the continental margin by a saddle. The Commission was satisfied with a depth difference of 2,000 m. and 700 m. above the deep ocean floor for the two saddle areas that connect the Macquarie Ridge Complex and the Australian continent (para. 71) and a difference of 1,000 m. for the saddle area that joins the South Tasman Saddle to the Australian continent (para. 94). See "Summary of the Recommendations of the Commission on the Limits of the Continental Shelf (CLCS) in Regard to the Submission Made by Australia on 15 November 2004: Recommendations Adopted by CLCS on 9 April 2008," available at www.un.org/Depts/los/clcs_new/submissions_files/aus04/aus_summary_of_recommendations.pdf.

[68] Macnab, n. 19, above, p. 226.

[69] On the joint US–Canada mapping in the Beaufort Sea, see Chapter 3, above.

[70] See discussion, next section.

[71] See Alexandra Zakharova and Vitaly Radnayev, "Russia Proves Mendeleev Ridge Is Eurasian Continent Extension," Voice of Russia, November 1, 2012, available at http://

Canada asserts rights over the Alpha/Mendeleev Ridge also, and will certainly not continue if Canada asserts rights west of 168°58'37"W. For this reason, the options for cooperation identified below with respect to possible coordination and cooperation between Russia, Denmark, and Canada along the Lomonosov Ridge apply, *mutatis mutandis*, to Russia and Canada on the Alpha/Mendeleev Ridge.

3.3 Submissions, responses, and diplomacy

Again, Russia submitted data to the CLCS in 2001 just four years after ratifying UNCLOS. As per the rules of procedure, the submission was confidential and only a summary and accompanying map were published.[72] According to the map, Russia asserted that a large part of the Arctic Ocean seabed – amounting to some 102,000 square nautical miles and extending right up to the North Pole – was a natural prolongation of its territory.[73]

In March 2002, during his presentation of Russia's submission to the CLCS, the Deputy Minister for Natural Resources of the Russian Federation stated:

The integrated interpretation of the deep seismic sounding and seismic reflection sounding along the SLO-92 geotraverse passing across Lomonosov ridge provided data on the velocity characteristics, layering and thickness of the earth's crust which are characteristic of a continental-type crust. This conclusion is consistent with generally accepted concepts.[74]

The submission expressed the view that both the Lomonosov Ridge and the Alpha/Mendeleev Ridge are natural components of Russia's continental margin, but by stopping at the North Pole it also suggested that Russia was willing to limit its assertion of sovereign rights.[75] As men-

---

english.ruvr.ru/2012_11_01/Russia-proves-Mendeleev-Ridge-is-Eurasian-continent-extension/. On the Russia–US boundary, see Chapter 2, above.

[72] "Submission by the Russian Federation: Summary," available at www.un.org/depts/los/clcs_new/submissions_files/submission_rus.htm.

[73] "Area of the Continental Shelf of the Russian Federation in the Arctic Ocean beyond 200-Nautical-Mile Zone," available at www.un.org/depts/los/clcs_new/submissions_files/rus01/RUS_CLCS_01_2001_LOS_2.jpg.

[74] "Statement Made by the Deputy Minister for Natural Resources of the Russian Federation during Presentation of the Submission Made by the Russian Federation to the Commission on 28 March 2002," Doc. CLCS/31, 5 April 2002, at p. 5, available at http://daccess-dds-ny.un.org/doc/UNDOC/GEN/N02/318/60/PDF/N0231860.pdf?OpenElement.

[75] See Ted L. McDorman, "The Continental Shelf Beyond 200 nm: Law and Politics in the Arctic Ocean." (2009) 18 *Journal of Transnational Law and Policy* 155 at 176–177.

tioned above, the Russian submission used the 168°58'37"W meridian set by the 1990 maritime boundary treaty with the United States as its eastern limit all the way across the Amerasia Basin, Alpha/Mendeleev Ridge, and Lomonosov Ridge, while applying the "2,500-metre isobath plus 100 nautical mile" constraint line from both the Lomonosov Ridge and the Siberian shelf in the west.[76]

Although the submission might well have been more extensive, not all of Russia's maritime neighbors were willing to allow the CLCS process to move forward without protest. Norway did consent to the CLCS considering the Russian submission in an area over which it also planned to assert rights,[77] while Denmark said it could not formulate an opinion on whether the submission overlapped with areas over which it might later assert rights.[78] Both Denmark and Canada stated that the CLCS's examination of the Russian data did not imply their acquiescence to the submission and that it was without prejudice to any final delimitation of maritime boundaries between themselves and Russia.[79] Most significantly, the United States disputed that the Lomonosov Ridge was a submarine ridge or elevation. Despite not being a party to UNCLOS, it submitted a protest that stated the Lomonosov Ridge "is a free-standing feature in the deep, oceanic part of the Arctic Ocean Basin, and not a natural component of the continental margins of either Russia or any other State."[80] The CLCS subsequently requested more

---

[76] Weber, n. 60, above, p. 660.

[77] Permanent Mission of Norway to the Secretary-General of the United Nations, Chapter 3, n. 132, above.

[78] Permanent Mission of Denmark to the United Nations, "Denmark: Notification Regarding the Submission Made by the Russian Federation to the Commission on the Limits of the Continental Shelf," 2002, available at www.un.org/Depts/los/clcs_new/submissions_files/submission_rus.htm.

[79] Ibid.; Permanent Mission of Canada to the United Nations, "Canada: Notification Regarding the Submission Made by the Russian Federation to the Commission on the Limits of the Continental Shelf," 2002, available at www.un.org/Depts/los/clcs_new/submissions_files/submission_rus.htm.

[80] "Letter from the Permanent Representative of the United States of America to the United Nations," UN Doc. CLCS.01.2001.LOS/USA, 28 February 2002, p. 3, available at www.un.org/depts/los/clcs_new/submissions_files/rus01/CLCS_01_2001_LOS__USAtext.pdf. The US view has apparently evolved more recently in light of new scientific data, and it might now be willing to consider the Lomonosov Ridge as susceptible to national jurisdiction. See Betsy Baker, "Law, Science, and the Continental Shelf: The Russian Federation and the Promise of Arctic Cooperation." (2010) 25 *American University International Law Review* 251 at 269–270.

data from Russia, saying that it was unable to make a firm determination on the basis of the amount of information provided.[81]

Denmark has also expressed an interest in an area of the Lomonosov Ridge that extends from Greenland past the North Pole, and is planning to include the Pole in its submission to the CLCS.[82] However, Denmark has not engaged in seabed mapping beyond the median line between the Greenland and Russian coasts, which is located on the Russian side of the North Pole. This means that its submission will not include the entire Lomonosov Ridge. But Denmark could make a further submission at some point, until outer limits have been established, or unless and until maritime boundaries are agreed.

Canada is also preparing a submission that includes a significant portion of the Lomonosov Ridge, but, like Denmark, it has not collected data beyond the median line with Russia. All of this creates the possibility of two or three at least partially overlapping submissions in the area between the 168°58′37″W meridian and the median line (between the Greenland/Ellesmere Island and Russian coasts), which, according to Mel Weber, amounts to just 22,000 square nautical miles.[83] For these reasons, as Russia, Denmark, and Canada move into the CLCS process, they will wish to consider their options – some of which could facilitate the avoidance, management, or resolution of otherwise potentially difficult disputes over what, objectively speaking, would be relatively small, incredibly remote areas of seabed.

4 Options for submissions to the Commission on the Limits of the Continental Shelf

Although Article 76(10) of UNCLOS states that CLCS recommendations are without prejudice to questions of delimitation,[84] the Commission's own rules of procedure preclude consideration of a submission in areas where land or maritime disputes exist – unless all the parties to the dispute have given prior consent.[85] Several procedures serve to inform the CLCS and potentially affected states of any problems. A submitting

---

[81] See "Oceans and the Law of the Sea: Report of the Secretary General, Addendum," UN Doc. A/57/57/Add.1, 8 October 2002, at para. 41, available at www.un.org/Depts/los/ general_assembly/general_assembly_reports.htm.

[82] See Danish Continental Shelf Project at http://a76.dk/lng_uk/main.html.

[83] Weber, n. 60, above, p. 672.   [84] UNCLOS, n. 12, above.

[85] Rules of Procedure, Annex 1, Art. 5(a), available at www.un.org/Depts/los/clcs_new/ commission_rules.htm.

state is obliged to notify the CLCS of any active dispute and reassure it that the submission will not prejudice the matter.[86] Additionally, an executive summary of the submission is published for the purpose of enabling other states to determine if it encroaches on an area over which they also assert rights.[87] Yet the publication of the executive summary has also enabled the CLCS to be more flexible than its own rules suggest, treating any failure to object by the second, non-submitting state involved in a dispute as consent to having data from the disputed area considered and recommendations issued.

At the same time, there are a number of possible approaches to making submissions where disputes exist (or potentially exist) and the parties do not wish to resolve them prior to submission. It is important to note that a combination of approaches may be used with respect to a single area.

4.1 Full submission without coordination with other states

It is open to any state to make a full submission to the CLCS without any coordination with other states. However, as mentioned above, a state that includes data on a disputed or potentially disputed area within its submission risks having one or more other states object to the CLCS considering the submission. The Commission would then be unable to consider the data,[88] which could delay any resolution of the matter and leave it as an on-going, possible source of tension.[89] For these reasons, it would be unwise for Russia, Denmark, or Canada to make submissions that create overlaps in the central Arctic Ocean without coordinating with each other.

---

[86] Ibid., sec. 2.   [87] Lathrop, Chapter 3, n. 20, above.

[88] The CLCS would likely be quite prompt in declaring itself unable to consider the data, as it did with regard to the UK submissions regarding the Hatton Rockall and Falkland Islands areas. On Rockall, see "Statement by the Chairman of the Commission on the Limits of the Continental Shelf on the Progress of Work in the Commission," October 1, 2009, paras. 41–46, available at http://daccess-dds-ny.un.org/doc/UNDOC/GEN/N09/536/21/PDF/N0953621.pdf. On the Falkland Islands, see "Statement by the Chairman of the Commission on the Limits of the Continental Shelf on the Progress of Work in the Commission," April 30, 2010, paras. 55–60, available at http://daccess-dds-ny.un.org/doc/UNDOC/GEN/N10/337/97/PDF/N1033797.pdf.

[89] The CLCS is already experiencing a substantial backlog. See "Delegates Offer Differing Views Regarding Workload of Commission on Limits of Continental Shelf as States Parties Continue Twenty-First Meeting," SEA/1954, June 14, 2011, available at www.un.org/News/Press/docs//2011/sea1954.doc.htm.

4.2 Exclude any disputed or potentially disputed area from the submission

A second option would be for Russia, Denmark, and Canada to make only partial submissions to the CLCS, thus excluding any potentially disputed area.[90] This would enable them to continue with submissions on the rest of their continental shelf limits, thus meeting their ten-year timelines, while deferring consideration of the limits in areas of possible overlap. This approach is most useful in cases of intractable overlapping assertions of rights where neither side wishes the other to make any move relating to the disputed area. It requires minimal cooperation and communication, apart from the sharing of information on the extent of the existing or potential assertions. It also raises the possibility of a later, joint submission on the disputed or potentially disputed area – an option discussed below.

In some countries, however, excluding a disputed or potentially disputed area from a CLCS submission might carry domestic political risks, since the government could be portrayed as asserting rights over a less-than-maximum area – even if it would retain the option of making a further submission at a later date.[91] It would also miss an opportunity to make at least some progress toward finalizing boundaries, with all the risks that delay and uncertainty might entail. Finally, this option would seem to run counter to the stated intentions of Russia, Denmark, and Canada to use the CLCS process to identify the seaward extent of their sovereign rights and resolve any disputes according to the law of the sea.[92]

4.3 Agree not to object to the Commission on the Limits of the Continental Shelf considering data

As was explained in Chapter 3, countries will sometimes agree *not* to object to the CLCS considering data with respect to a disputed area. Ideally, such an agreement will be proactively communicated to the CLCS through a "no objection statement." Such agreements still lead to separate submissions, but without the attendant risk of the process being interrupted or delayed. And while the Commission's

---

[90] See discussion, above, pp. 84–85.

[91] Lathrop, Chapter 3, n. 20, above, pp. 4151–4152.

[92] See "The Ilulissat Declaration," Arctic Ocean Conference, Ilulissat, Greenland, May 27–29, 2008, available at http://byers.typepad.com/arctic/ilulissat-declaration-may-28-2008.html; "Russia, Canada Back Science to Resolve Dispute over Arctic Claims," RIA Novosti, September 16, 2010, available at http://en.rian.ru/world/20100916/160615112.html.

recommendations will be without prejudice to any delimitation, they can, at the same time, provide information about the outer limits of national jurisdiction that is useful to the parties if and when they decide to negotiate a solution. For this reason, Russia, Denmark, and Canada could usefully agree not to object when their respective submissions or resubmissions are made, and ideally issue no objection statements.

4.4 Coordinated submissions

A further option is to coordinate submissions more closely by sharing geomorphological and geological data and advancing common interpretations of them, albeit within the context of separate submissions. Such coordination could result in Russia, Denmark, and Canada advancing a common view of the geological history of the Arctic Ocean seabed, as well as a common view of the character of the Lomonosov and Alpha/Mendeleev Ridges based on shared interpretations of Article 76's language on submarine elevations. Coordination of this kind would seem to optimize the chances for the success of CLCS submissions, while contributing to a longer-lasting cooperative dynamic that might benefit future delimitation efforts.

4.5 Joint submission

Canada, Denmark, and Russia (or any two of the three countries) could make a joint submission to the CLCS, and preliminary discussions of this option have reportedly taken place.[93] As Coalter Lathrop explains, a joint submission internalizes any unresolved dispute within the group of submitting states, thus ensuring that the CLCS will consider data that might otherwise be precluded.[94] This approach offers many other potential benefits: cost-sharing and division of labor, a more complete and rigorous data set, enhanced transparency, and a cooperative dynamic that could facilitate future agreement on a boundary or boundaries. A joint submission would also help to prevent a worsening of the dispute – or the media and public perceptions of it – while the three countries wait the decade or more that the CLCS will likely take to consider the matter and issue recommendations.

---

[93] Randy Boswell, "Thaw May Be Underway in Ottawa–Moscow Arctic Issues," *Vancouver Sun*, May 12, 2009, available at http://byers.typepad.com/arctic/2009/05/thaw-may-be-underway-in-ottawa-moscow-arctic-issues.html.
[94] Lathrop, Chapter 3, n. 20, above, p. 4147.

On the negative side of the equation, a joint submission may not offer benefits such as cost-sharing if, as is the case in the Arctic, a great deal of data has already been collected by the individual states. Pooling of data may also be difficult to achieve if the parties are at different stages in the data-gathering process, have different understandings of the geological history of the area, or employ different methods to determine issues such as foot of the slope points or sediment thickness. Moreover, it could take years to integrate scientific projects that have, until now, been proceeding separately. Given that Canada and Denmark are expected to make submissions in 2013 and 2014, respectively, there might be insufficient time left to prepare a joint submission – unless they make only partial submissions that leave any potential overlaps to be dealt with at a later date.

There is also the issue of Russia's place in the CLCS queue. Russia is currently entitled to have its resubmitted data considered prior to all the submissions that were made by other states after the first Russian submission. However, it would lose that right if it submitted the same data as part of a joint submission. Nor is the history of joint submissions entirely positive. When the coastal states around the Bay of Biscay decided to submit pooled data, they were asked by the CLCS to present the data for their individual assertions separately, in order to prove their independent entitlements to shelf areas.[95] The Commission ultimately disallowed a portion of the submission, concluding that the area falling under the jurisdiction of the coastal states as a group, could not be larger than the area they could have asserted rights over with individual submissions.[96] After all, Article 76 speaks of "coastal state" in the singular, suggesting that any particular entitlement to continental shelf may only be generated by one state.

[95] "Statement by the Chairman of the Commission on the Limits of the Continental Shelf on the Progress of Work in the Commission," October 4, 2007, at paras. 26–29, available at http://daccess-dds-ny.un.org/doc/UNDOC/GEN/N07/529/89/PDF/N0752989.pdf.

[96] Commission on the Limits of the Continental Shelf, "Summary of the Recommendations of the Commission on the Limits of the Continental Shelf in Regard to the Joint Submission Made by France, Ireland, Spain, and the United Kingdom of Great Britain and Northern Ireland in Respect of the Area of the Celtic Sea and the Bay of Biscay on 19 May 2006," March 24, 2009, at paras. 26 and 27, available at www.un.org/depts/los/clcs_new/submissions_files/frgbires06/fisu_clcs_recommendations_summary2009.pdf.

5 Negotiating temporary lines or permanent boundaries before submitting

In addition to the various options for self-limitation or cooperation with respect to CLCS submissions, Russia, Denmark, and Canada will wish to consider the options for negotiating temporary lines or permanent boundaries before submissions are made.

5.1 Negotiate temporary lines in advance of Commission on the Limits of the Continental Shelf submissions

Russia, Denmark, and Canada could negotiate temporary "constraint lines" for the purposes of making their submissions to the CLCS. Indeed, UNCLOS strongly encourages the use of "provisional arrangements of a practical nature" pending a final agreement on the delimitation of a continental shelf, and specifies that such arrangements "shall be without prejudice to the final delimitation."[97] Any set of lines could plausibly be used for a temporary delimitation, with one obvious possibility being a sector-based division of the central Arctic Ocean – obvious because Russia chose this avenue in its 2001 submission. Denmark, having expressed an interest in areas on the Russian side of the North Pole, might be expected to resist this approach.[98] Moreover, applying the sector approach across the central Arctic Ocean could artificially implicate the United States into the question of jurisdiction over the Lomonosov and Alpha/Mendeleev Ridges. For, while the extended continental shelf off Alaska is unlikely to reach that far, sector-based temporary lines would assign parts of both of those ridges to a country that had no real prospect of ever perfecting the allocation.

A better approach might be for the Russian sector to be used as that country's temporary constraint line, with the rest of the seabed around the Alpha/Mendeleev Ridge being temporarily assigned to Canada, and the rest of the seabed around the Lomonosov Ridge to Canada and Denmark. A temporary delimitation between the latter two countries could follow either the crest of the Lomonosov Ridge, an equidistance line between the "foot of the slope" on either side, or – most easily and therefore preferably – an equidistance line based on the northern coasts of Greenland and Canada's High Arctic islands. The issue of a

---

[97] UNCLOS, n. 12, above, Art. 83(3).
[98] See the Danish Continental Shelf Project, at www.a76.dk/.

Canadian–Danish boundary along the Lomonosov Ridge is discussed in more detail below.[99]

A more general problem with temporary lines relates to Lathrop's observation that "in some instances it is only after full consideration of a submission that a State will know whether or to what extent boundaries need be agreed with neighbors."[100] It is possible that the CLCS will eventually recommend that one or more of the parties may not extend its jurisdiction using the Lomonosov Ridge or Alpha/Mendeleev Ridge, and that due to temporary lines the other party (or parties) may not have made a submission that extends to the point at which the other party's (or parties') national jurisdiction ends. This would leave that state or states in the unfortunate position of either terminating their jurisdiction short of their actual natural prolongation, or having to submit new data to the CLCS – with all the attendant delays. Denmark, Iceland, and Norway dealt with this problem, in the context of the so-called "Southern Banana Hole" in the Northeast Atlantic, by submitting data with respect to areas beyond the temporary lines they had agreed.[101] In the event that the CLCS decided that a party did not have rights in a particular area, that party would simply drop out in favor of the others, and the boundaries would be adjusted accordingly.

There are several other ways in which states might agree in advance on how different CLCS recommendations would affect temporary lines. It could be agreed that the temporary lines would automatically become permanent maritime boundaries if the recommendations were consistent with them. Similarly, and perhaps additionally, it could be agreed that the lines would be shifted as a result of the CLCS's recommendations in accordance with specific formulae. For example, it might be agreed that if an area were determined to be subject to overlapping rights from two or more states the line or lines would be adjusted so as to divide the overlap proportionately between them.

5.2 Negotiate permanent boundaries in advance of Commission on the Limits of the Continental Shelf submissions

A final option would be for Russia and Canada to agree to a permanent boundary on the Alpha/Mendeleev Ridge and for Russia, Canada, and Denmark to agree to permanent boundaries on the Lomonosov Ridge, coupled with agreements to submit all of their data to the CLCS along

---

[99] See discussion, below, pp. 120–122.   [100] Lathrop, Chapter 3, n. 20, above, p. 4146.
[101] Ibid.

with notifications of their intent to use the full complement of their combined juridical entitlements in support of the agreed boundaries. In the event the CLCS recommended that one or more of the ridges was an extension of the continental margin of just one country, the rights of that country would then be transferred to its treaty partner or partners on the other side of the agreed boundary, much like rights over seabed and water column within 200 nautical miles from shore are sometimes transferred as so-called "special areas" within the context of maritime boundary treaties – as was explained in Chapter 2.

Admittedly, using this approach with respect to extended continental shelves would run counter to the idea of the continental shelf as the natural prolongation of a coastal state. It might also seem overly generous to the party that gained continental shelf to which it would not under normal circumstances be entitled. But it does have several advantages. First, pre-submission permanent boundaries would provide a high degree of certainty and stability, and do so fairly quickly. Second, they would provide some protection against the risk of the CLCS concluding that a particular coastal state has no rights on the Alpha/ Mendeleev and/or Lomonosov Ridges. In this sense, negotiating permanent boundaries before CLCS recommendations creates a "veil of ignorance" that makes it easier to achieve distributional fairness during negotiations.[102] That said, after the veil of ignorance has been lifted, the apportionment of maritime space to an otherwise unentitled state could conceivably result in political tensions.

It is also important to note that submissions to the CLCS will be required, not just to support the agreed permanent boundaries, but also to determine the extent of sovereign rights into the central Arctic Ocean along the flanks of the two ridges – delimitations that the relevant state will then adjust, as necessary, to comply with the CLCS's recommendations. Finally, a recommendation by the CLCS that the Alpha/Mendeleev and/or Lomonosov Ridges are either oceanic ridges or submarine ridges (as opposed to submarine elevations) would nullify the relevant agreed boundaries, since all or part of the ridge in question would fall beyond national jurisdiction. This risk, and the time and effort involved in negotiating boundaries, might nevertheless be justifiable on the basis of the stability that would be created in the meantime, while the CLCS works through its already considerable backlog.

---

[102] See, e.g., John Rawls, *A Theory of Justice* (New York: Basic Books, 1974).

6 Options for maritime boundary delimitation

Temporary boundaries, formulae for adjusting temporary boundaries, and permanent boundaries all require extensive negotiations. As Chapters 2 and 3 explained, negotiations over maritime boundaries take place within the context of legal rules. But, while one might expect that the normal rules of boundary delimitation would apply to the extended continental shelves of the central Arctic Ocean, several academic studies have instead assumed that all the seabed there will be distributed based on either: (1) the sector principle, where boundaries following meridian lines are drawn from the termini of land or maritime boundaries straight to the North Pole; or (2) the equidistance principle, where each point of an extended continental shelf boundary is an equal distance from the nearest points on the respective opposite or adjacent coastlines.[103]

Neither approach finds support in the current practice of Arctic states. The sector theory was propounded by Russia for decades but not even mentioned in the 2010 Barents Sea Treaty with Norway.[104] Canada maintained an ambiguous stance on the sector theory for decades, before definitively abandoning it in 2006.[105] Norway has already obtained recommendations from the CLCS that set the outer limits of its continental shelf far to the south of the North Pole.[106] Denmark has finished collecting data in preparation for a submission to the CLCS, while the United States seems to be treating Article 76 as reflective of customary international law, despite not being bound by it as a treaty obligation.[107] Moreover, as was explained in Chapter 3, the decision of the International Tribunal on the Law of the Sea in the *Bay of Bengal Case* might not provide much guidance for the central Arctic Ocean, because

---

[103] See, e.g., Weber, n. 60, above.

[104] See Tore Henriksen and Geir Ulfstein, "Maritime Delimitation in the Arctic: The Barents Sea Treaty." (2011) 42 *Ocean Development and International Law* 1 at 6.

[105] Stephen Harper, "Securing Canadian Sovereignty in the Arctic, Speech Given at Iqaluit, Nunavut, 12 August 2006," available at www.byers.typepad.com/arctic/2009/03/securing-canadian-sovereignty-in-the-arctic.html.

[106] See "Summary of the Recommendations of the Commission on the Limits of the Continental Shelf in Regard to the Submission Made by Norway in Respect of Areas in the Arctic Ocean, the Barents Sea and the Norwegian Sea on 27 November 2006," March 27, 2009, available at www.un.org/Depts/los/clcs_new/submissions_files/nor06/nor_rec_summ.pdf.

[107] The International Court of Justice has ruled that Article 76(1) of UNCLOS is part of customary international law. See *Territorial and Maritime Dispute (Nicaragua v. Colombia)*, November 19, 2012, Chapter 3, n. 65, above, para. 118.

it did not involve a situation where submarine ridges or submarine elevations were present. For all these reasons, it is necessary to consider which, if any, rules of international law apply to the delimitation of that area.

6.1 Delimitation of seafloor highs

With Canada, Denmark, and Russia all considering the Lomonosov Ridge to be a natural component of their respective continental margins, it is important to consider what the implications would be if the ridge is (as was suggested above) geomorphologically appurtenant to *both* the Canadian and/or Danish continental margin *and* that of Russia. Logically, similar implications will pertain to the Alpha/Mendeleev Ridge should Canada and Russia produce similar scientific evidence there.

Recent science certainly points in the direction of a geomorphologically shared Lomonosov Ridge, with scientists working for the Russian government claiming that the ridge is a fragment of an ancient continent named Arctida which formed a tectonic bridge between Eurasia and North America,[108] and scientists working for the Canadian and Danish governments suggesting that it is a "double-sided continental margin" that rifted at a time when the North American and Eurasian landmasses were indistinct.[109] This raises the question: could a ridge be legally considered a natural component of more than one continental margin and thus subject to the jurisdiction of two or more opposing coastal states?

Neither UNCLOS nor the CLCS Guidelines would seem to preclude this possibility. The Guidelines simply suggest that ridges in passive margins that were formed by the break-up process prior to seafloor spreading are likely to be considered natural components of the continental margin, without addressing the possibility of such a ridge being connected to two continental margins.[110] Thus, a ridge that is

---

[108] See, e.g., E. V. Verzhbitskii, *et al.*, "Age of the Alpha–Mendeleev and Lomonosov Ridges (Amerasian Basin)" (2011) 441 *Doklady Earth Sciences* 1587; N. P. Lavero, *et al.*, "Basic Model of Tectonic Development of the Arctic as a Basis for Preparation of the Updated Submission of Russia to the UN Commission concerning the Establishment of the Outer Limits of the Continental Shelf." (2012) 2(6) *The Arctic: Ecology and Economy* 4 (in Russian).

[109] See, e.g., Ruth Jackson, *et al.*, "The Structure of the Lomonosov Ridge, Arctic Ocean," n. 66, above.

[110] See discussion, above, pp. 100–101.

appurtenant to more than one continental margin could conceivably be judged a natural component of all the margins to which it is geomorphologically attached.

As mentioned above, the fact that Russia's 2001 submission to the CLCS terminated at the North Pole suggests that Moscow, at least, is not interested in asserting rights over the entire ridge. Canada and Denmark's lack of mapping beyond the median line also suggests that they will not claim the entire feature. It is therefore possible that some or all of the Arctic Ocean states would prefer to divide the Lomonosov Ridge into Eurasian and North American portions using some sort of distance or sector formulae.

6.2 Delimiting ridges with sector or distance formulae

Adopting either a sector-based or distance-based approach to the lateral delimitation of the Lomonosov Ridge could reduce the potential for scientific disagreements to complicate or otherwise disrupt the achievement of a mutually agreed solution. The fact that the 2001 Russian submission stopped at the North Pole could be taken as an offer – extended in the hope that Canada and Denmark would likewise consider it reasonable to use the Pole as an artificial boundary, either on the basis of the sector theory in its full sense, or in recognition of the symbolic significance of the location. In the latter case, it might be considered reasonable to draw a lateral boundary across the portion of the ridge that is closest to the Pole.[111] A distance-based approach, in contrast, would draw a median (i.e., equidistance) line across the ridge based on the opposing coastlines of Russia and Greenland/Ellesmere Island.

The first question, then, is whether either or both Canada and Denmark would in fact accept the North Pole as the basis for some sort of lateral boundary. Clearly, they would be less likely to do so if the entire Lomonosov Ridge were an extension of solely their continental margin, and more likely to do so if the ridge were a natural component of both their and Russia's continental margins. But, even in the latter circumstance, it might be considered relevant that the area of the Lomonosov Ridge nearest to the North Pole is significantly closer to

---

[111] Conceivably, such a lateral line could follow the 168°58′37″W meridian, consistent with the 1990 Russia–US boundary treaty and Russia's 2001 submission to the CLCS, or be based on a modified equidistance line that tracked the contours of the Russian and Canadian/Greenland coasts.

Greenland and Ellesmere Island than it is to the coast of Russia. Again, Weber states that the discrepancy between a sector-based division and median lines would amount to some 22,000 square nautical miles.[112] Everything else being equal, using the North Pole as the basis for some sort of an artificial boundary would seem to benefit Russia. In support of this, Russia could point to the fact that it has a longer Arctic Ocean coastline than either Canada or Denmark, consistent with the "equidistance plus relevant circumstances" approach adopted by regular maritime boundary law within the EEZ.[113] On the other hand, Alex G. Oude Elferink has suggested that Denmark and/or Canada might seek an adjustment of the equidistance line on the basis that the distance of some of Russia's smaller islands from other areas of its coast might necessitate their being discounted or given reduced effect.[114]

In sum, if Canada, Denmark, and Russia wished to delimit permanent maritime boundaries in the central Arctic Ocean, they could do so either on the basis of advice from the CLCS or in its absence. If the parties continued to believe, with or without CLCS recommendations, that the Lomonosov Ridge is a natural component of each of their continental margins, they could delimit the ridge and surrounding seabed laterally using either a line (sector or otherwise) related to the North Pole, or perhaps a median line (which might then be adjusted). In addition to the lateral delimitation, the North American end of the Ridge would require some sort of longitudinal delimitation between Canada and Denmark, and it is to this issue that we now turn.

6.3 Canada–Denmark boundary along the Lomonosov Ridge

As explained in Chapter 2, Canada and Denmark delimited a 1,450-nautical-mile boundary between Greenland and the northeast coast of Canada in 1973. The boundary terminated at the point where Nares Strait opens into the Lincoln Sea, leaving unresolved what was then thought to be nearly 200 nautical miles of continental shelf (and later EEZ) boundary to the north. In November 2012, the Canadian and Danish foreign ministers announced that negotiators had "reached a tentative agreement on where to establish the maritime boundary in

---

[112] Weber, n. 60, above, p. 672.
[113] On the law of maritime boundary delimitation within 200 nautical miles from shore, see Chapter 3, above.
[114] The islands in question are Henrietta and Jeannette Islands, which are only 3.4 and 11.9 square kilometers in size. Alex G. Oude Elferink, "Arctic Maritime Delimitations," Chapter 2, n. 97, above.

the Lincoln Sea."[115] But while the imminent conclusion of a final treaty on the location of the line within 200 nautical miles may create momentum for further negotiations, it is of little *legal* relevance to a delimitation of the extended continental shelf – because there has been no dispute as to the location where the adjoining Canadian and Danish jurisdictions meet at 200 nautical miles.

Canada and Denmark will only have to negotiate a boundary beyond 200 nautical miles if their respective jurisdictions extend that far. As was explained above, both countries believe this to be the case, and it is open to them to initiate maritime boundary negotiations before they make their submissions to the CLCS, or after they submit but before the CLCS issues its recommendations. Moreover, there is no reason why negotiations between Canada and Denmark have to wait for negotiations between those two countries and Russia. The uncertain legal status of the Lomonosov Ridge might necessitate that the boundary be provisional in nature, and it might be considered prudent to terminate it (for the moment) at a point 350 nautical miles from shore. Or, perhaps better yet, it could simply be stipulated that the boundary will continue along the same method of delimitation "as far as permitted under international law" – as was done in the 1990 Bering Sea boundary treaty between the Soviet Union and the United States.[116]

The first delimitation method available to Canada and Denmark is a meridian-based (i.e., "sector") line, though the fact that both countries have already relied on the equidistance method within 200 nautical miles of Ellesmere Island and Greenland might render this problematic or at least inconsistent.[117] Second, an equidistance line could also be used beyond 200 nautical miles, although determining base points can become more technically difficult the further one moves offshore. Moreover, both the meridian and equidistance methods ignore the potential relevance of geological and geomorphological features to the delimitation of extended continental shelves involving submarine

---

[115] "Canada and Kingdom of Denmark Reach Tentative Agreement on Lincoln Sea Boundary," News Release, Canadian Department of Foreign Affairs, November 28, 2012 (with backgrounder), available at www.international.gc.ca/media/aff/news-communiques/2012/11/28a.aspx?lang=engandview=d. See also Kim Mackrael, "Canada, Denmark a Step Closer to Settling Border Dispute," *Globe and Mail*, November 30, 2012, available at www.theglobeandmail.com/news/national/canada-denmark-a-step-closer-to-settling-border-dispute/article5831571/.

[116] Chapter 2, n. 20, above, Art. 2(1).

[117] On the maritime boundary in the Lincoln Sea, see Chapter 2, above.

ridges or submarine elevations. It might therefore be considered preferable for the ridge to be divided, either along its crest, or along a line equidistant from the foot of the slope points along each flank of the ridge.

However, determining the crest of the ridge might be difficult along some of the flatter stretches, while drawing an equidistance line based on foot of the slope points off the flanks of the ridge would be rendered difficult by the paucity of scientific data in those areas, which is due to the continued prevalence of challenging ice conditions there. Fortunately, these challenges may not need to be overcome, since by sheer coincidence of political and physical geography, an equidistance line drawn using coastal base points would track more-or-less down the middle of the Lomonosov Ridge. An equidistance line based on coastal base points can therefore be recommended as the best and easiest way of defining a boundary in this instance.

Regardless of which method is adopted, Canada and Denmark will wish to provide for the joint management of any hydrocarbon and mineral deposits that straddle the boundary – as discussed in both Chapters 2 and 3. As discussed earlier in this chapter, they should also consider including a provision on "special areas" within any boundary agreement, so as to guard against the risk of the CLCS recommending that one or the other state has no sovereign rights on the Lomonosov Ridge.[118] Since Russia, the United States, and Norway have already used special areas in the Arctic, albeit within 200 nautical miles from shore, they might well acquiesce in their use by Canada and Denmark beyond that distance.

6.4 Third-party dispute resolution

If Russia, Denmark, and Canada are unable to negotiate their boundaries, they could choose between several forms of third-party binding dispute resolution. Options include the International Court of Justice, International Tribunal for the Law of the Sea (ITLOS), Permanent Court of Arbitration, or an ad hoc tribunal appointed especially to deal with the issue.[119] Adjudication or arbitration can avoid the domestic political costs associated with negotiated concessions, but entail a loss of control

---

[118] On special areas generally, see Chapter 2, above.

[119] See, generally, Natalie Klein, *Dispute Settlement in the UN Convention on the Law of the Sea* (Cambridge University Press, 2004).

and prevent non-legal factors from being taken into account – which may or may not be considered advantageous.

Adjudication or arbitration might be one way to clarify the legal status of the Lomonosov Ridge. Russia, Denmark, and Canada could, by way of a "special agreement," submit that specific question to the court or tribunal, without asking the court or tribunal to delimit boundaries. After the judgment, the parties would be in a position to negotiate boundaries on a more concrete legal basis. Alternatively, the three countries could ask the court or tribunal to determine the status of the ridge and to delimit their boundaries.

It might also be possible for Canada or Denmark to initiate a case against each other on the basis of the compulsory jurisdiction of the International Court of Justice, since both have made the necessary declarations under the so-called "Optional Clause."[120] However, Russia has not made a comparable declaration and might object to the status of the Lomonosov Ridge being determined without its consent, as per the principle identified in the 1953 *Monetary Gold Case*.[121] Perhaps more importantly, each of the three states has made wide-reaching declarations excluding maritime boundary disputes from compulsory dispute resolution under Part XV of UNCLOS, which could exclude any of them initiating proceedings relating to the central Arctic Ocean in any court or tribunal without the consent of the other party or parties.[122] They do, however, retain the option of taking one another to conciliation under the procedures in Annex V, section 2 of UNCLOS, in the event that no agreement arises from negotiations in a reasonable period of time.[123]

Another important question arises with respect to any recourse to adjudication or arbitration: Would any international court or tribunal feel competent to advise or rule on these issues before the CLCS has made recommendations? In the *Bay of Bengal Case*, ITLOS concluded that it could and should proceed with a delimitation of the extended continental shelf in advance. As it explained:

---

[120] For Canada's declaration, see www.icj-cij.org/jurisdiction/index.php?p1=5andp2=1andp3=3andcode=CA. For Denmark's, see www.icj-cij.org/jurisdiction/index.php?p1=5andp2=1andp3=3andcode=DK.

[121] *Monetary Gold Removed from Rome in 1943 (Italy v. France, UK and USA)* (1954) ICJ Reports 19.

[122] See Declarations of States Parties Relating to Settlement of Disputes in Accordance with Article 298 (optional exceptions to the applicability of Part XV, Section 2, of the Convention). www.itlos.org/fileadmin/itlos/documents/basic_texts/298_declarations_June_2011_english.pdf.

[123] UNCLOS, n. 12, above, Art. 298(1)(a)(i).

There is nothing in the Convention or in the Rules of Procedure of the Commission or in its practice to indicate that delimitation of the continental shelf constitutes an impediment to the performance by the Commission of its functions. Article 76, paragraph 10, of the Convention states that "[t]he provisions of this article are without prejudice to the question of delimitation of the continental shelf between States with opposite or adjacent coasts" ... Just as the functions of the Commission are without prejudice to the question of delimitation of the continental shelf between States with opposite or adjacent coasts, so the exercise by international courts and tribunals of their jurisdiction regarding the delimitation of maritime boundaries, including that of the continental shelf, is without prejudice to the exercise by the Commission of its functions on matters related to the delineation of the outer limits of the continental shelf.[124]

In short, there is an important distinction between the determination of the outer limit of the continental shelf and the delimitation of a maritime boundary, with the former being the domain of the CLCS and the latter being the responsibility of the relevant coastal states. Those states may delimit a boundary at any point, including by submitting the matter to adjudication or arbitration. That said, the tribunal did signal that it would have been hesitant to delimit a boundary beyond 200 nautical miles had it "concluded that there was significant uncertainty as to the existence of a continental margin in the area in question."[125] A CLCS recommendation to this effect is at least conceivable with regard to the central Arctic Ocean, after the request for more data from Russia following its first submission in 2001.

A commitment to adjudication or arbitration might also be included in any agreement on a joint submission to the CLCS. For example, Canada, Denmark, and Russia could agree to submit all of their data to the CLCS on the explicit understanding that its recommendations, when received, would immediately be transmitted to the International Court of Justice, ITLOS, Permanent Court of Arbitration, or some other tribunal for the purposes of the boundary delimitation. This would have the advantage of de-politicizing the entire issue of central Arctic Ocean seabed jurisdiction by leaving it entirely in the hands of competent third-party institutions, and doing so without pre-empting the role of the CLCS.

---

[124] *Dispute Concerning Delimitation of the Maritime Boundary between Bangladesh and Myanmar in the Bay of Bengal* (Bangladesh/Myanmar), Chapter 3, n. 82, above, pp. 111-112, paras. 377–379.

[125] Ibid. at p. 129, para. 443.

7 Non-Arctic states and Arctic continental shelves

Several non-Arctic states have signaled an interest in the central Arctic Ocean, with China indicating a specific concern for the integrity of the area beyond national jurisdiction.[126] As China's Assistant Minister of Foreign Affairs Hu Zhengyue said in 2009:

> When determining the delimitation of outer continental shelves, the Arctic states need to not only properly handle relationships among themselves, but must also consider the relationship between the outer continental shelf and the international submarine area that is the common human heritage, to ensure a balance of coastal countries' interests and the common interests of the international community.[127]

It is therefore possible that one or more non-Arctic state could protest the Canadian, Danish, and updated Russian submissions to the CLCS. Protests from non-Arctic states cannot be based on delimitation disputes as such states do not have sovereign rights in the area, and so they would not affect the CLCS's legal authority to make recommendations. However, McDorman has argued that the CLCS is not the representative of any state or group of states and that all states, therefore, retain the right to protest its recommendations or the actions of coastal states in delineating their continental shelves.[128] He concludes that the only way in which continental shelf limits can become binding *erga omnes* is for them to be generally accepted by the international community for a reasonable period of time.[129] Even if McDorman is incorrect, the possibility of protests from non-Arctic states could have a *political* effect on the CLCS, dampening any willingness to approve

---

[126] "China's Perspective on Arctic Matters." (2009) 55(15) *Shijie Zhishi*, translated in Linda Jakobson, "China Prepares for an Ice-Free Arctic." *SIPRI Insights on Peace and Security*, No. 2010/2, March 2010, available at http://books.sipri.org/files/insight/SIPRIInsight1002.pdf.

[127] Ibid. The next year, Assistant Foreign Minister Liu Zhenmin said: "In accordance with the United Nations Convention on the Law of the Sea and other relevant international laws, Arctic states have sovereign rights and jurisdiction in their respective areas in the Arctic region, while non-Arctic states also enjoy rights of scientific research and navigation. To develop a partnership of cooperation, Arctic and non-Arctic states should, first and foremost, recognize and respect each other's rights under the international law." See Liu Z., "China's View on Arctic Cooperation," July 30, 2010, available at www.fmprc.gov.cn/eng/wjb/zzjg/tyfls/tfsxw/t812046.htm.

[128] Ted L. McDorman, "The Role of the Commission on the Limits of the Continental Shelf: A Technical Body in a Political World." (2002) 17 *International Journal of Marine and Coastal Law* 301 at 313.

[129] Ibid., p. 317.

especially ambitious submissions. It might also provide a reason for the Arctic Ocean states to exercise restraint in their submissions and to consider carefully their various options within and around the CLCS process.

At the same time, UNCLOS applies globally and many non-Arctic states will have the opportunity to make submissions concerning extended continental shelves off their own coastlines. China, for instance, uses Article 76 on extended continental shelves to support its far-reaching claims in the East China Sea.[130] It also intends to benefit from the rules set out in Part XI of UNCLOS, which give all states the right to engage in deep seabed mining beyond the extended continental shelf.[131] The same is true of the non-Arctic European countries. The United Kingdom relies on Article 76 to assert sovereign rights over extended continental shelves around South Georgia and South Shetland Islands.[132] France uses Article 76 off its Atlantic coast and around La Réunion Island in the Indian Ocean.[133] And so on. The reciprocal nature of these rules ensures that non-Arctic countries will accept their application to the Arctic.

8 Summary

The seabed of the central Arctic Ocean features a number of seafloor highs, prominently including the Lomonosov Ridge. UNCLOS provides formulae for coastal states to use to determine their jurisdiction over different kinds of seafloor highs. Canada, Denmark, and Russia may be legally entitled to claim part or all of the Lomonosov Ridge as a natural component of their continental margins (or what is termed a "submarine elevation") while Canada and Russia may be legally entitled to claim part or all of the Alpha/Mendeleev Ridge. This might allow these

---

[130] See Alexander M. Peterson, "Sino-Japanese Cooperation in the East China Sea: A Lasting Arrangement?" (2009) 42 *Cornell International Law Journal* 441. China's disputes in the South China Sea revolve around quite different issues of title to land territory, in the form of islands and shoals, and the entitlements of such features to maritime zones.

[131] On deep seabed mining, see Chapter 6, below.

[132] Submission by the United Kingdom of Great Britain and Northern Ireland in Respect of South Georgia and the South Sandwich Islands, 2009, available at www.un.org/Depts/los/clcs_new/submissions_files/gbr45_09/gbr2009fgs_executive%20summary.pdf.

[133] Submission by the French Republic in Respect of La Réunion Island and Saint-Paul and Amsterdam Islands, 2009, available at www.un.org/Depts/los/clcs_new/submissions_files/submission_fra_40_2009.htm.

countries, along with the United States, to extend their seabed jurisdictions to all but two small areas of the Arctic Ocean. However, arriving at that result will be a lengthy and perhaps difficult process unless the different countries cooperate with one another. Canada, Denmark, and Russia could usefully coordinate their submissions to the CLCS, perhaps even making a joint submission, in order to ensure that the CLCS can provide them with the information necessary permanently to resolve the legal status of the two ridges. Canada, Denmark, and/or Russia may even wish to delimit temporary or permanent maritime boundaries in order to create a greater level of certainty and stability while they wait for CLCS recommendations. Two or more of the three countries could also have recourse to adjudication or arbitration to help resolve the legal uncertainties that currently prevail. Whichever of these steps is taken, they will only help to sustain the healthy dynamic of cooperation that has characterized Arctic Ocean politics to date.

5   Arctic Straits

"For the first time in my life, I'm trying to find ice." Alex McIntyre was standing on the bridge of the *Akademik Ioffe* as the Russian-flagged ice-strengthened ship traversed Larsen Sound in August 2011. A Canadian ice-pilot with four decades of Arctic experience, McIntyre remembers when the route was choked with sea-ice that was ten meters thick. Now, the eighty eco-tourists on board were keen to witness sea-ice and the marine life that congregates around it, but Larsen Sound, unexpectedly, was completely ice-free. The previous day we had passed through Bellot Strait, a historically ice-filled chokepoint of the Northwest Passage located 600 kilometers north of the Arctic Circle. The strait is narrow, with strong tidal flows, but in the absence of ice no more difficult to navigate than the Bosporus and Dardanelles in western Turkey, or the Øresund between Denmark and Sweden.

For decades, shipping through the Northwest Passage was restricted to heavy icebreakers by the year-round presence of thick, hard "multi-year" sea-ice. The same was true of the Northern Sea Route along the northern coast of Russia, which is sometimes referred to as the Northeast Passage. But climate change, which is advancing more rapidly in the Arctic than anywhere else on Earth, is causing the ice to thin and recede. In September 2007, an unprecedented melting of Arctic sea-ice took the lowest coverage that season to 4.17 million square kilometers, a full 1.5 million square kilometers below the previous record set in 2005.[1] For the first time, both the Northwest Passage and Northern Sea Route were temporarily free of ice and open to non-icebreaking vessels. The record was shattered again in September 2012, when the area

---

[1] See US National Snow and Ice Data Center, "Arctic Sea Ice News and Analysis," at http://nsidc.org/arcticseaicenews/.

covered by Arctic sea-ice plunged to just 3.41 million square kilometers, fully 49 percent below the 1979 to 2000 average.[2] Nor were 2007 and 2012 aberrations; the six lowest extents of Arctic sea-ice on record all occurred in the six years from 2007 to 2012.[3]

It now seems that the Arctic could experience a complete, late season melt-out of sea-ice by 2020, and with it a permanent loss of multi-year ice.[4] In 2011, imagery from the European Space Agency's new Cryosat satellite showed that the multi-year ice was already gone from much of the Arctic Ocean and thinning rapidly wherever it remained.[5] Before long, the waterways along the northern coastlines of Canada and Russia could resemble the Baltic Sea or Gulf of St. Lawrence, where ice-strengthened vessels and icebreaker-escorted convoys can operate throughout the year. Already, we are seeing a sharp upturn in Arctic shipping. During the first century of navigation through the Northwest Passage, from 1906 to 2005, there were just 69 transits.[6] Yet it took just five more years, from 2006 to 2010, for the next 69 transits, with 18 taking place in each of 2009 and 2010. The increase has continued, with 22 transits in 2011 and 30 transits in 2012.[7]

Increased shipping brings with it environmental and security risks that in such a large and remote region can only adequately be addressed by the nearest coastal state. These risks include life-threatening accidents, oil spills, smuggling, illegal immigration, piracy, and terrorism.[8] Yet the extent of coastal state jurisdiction in the Northwest Passage and the Northern Sea Route is contested, in both instances by the United States, which claims that the narrowest stretches of both waterways are "international straits" through which vessels from all countries may pass freely.

---

[2] Ibid.   [3] Ibid.
[4] Peter Wadhams, "Arctic Ice Cover, Ice Thickness and Tipping Points." (2012) 41 *AMBIO: A Journal of the Human Environment* 1 at 31.
[5] "Cryosat Mission Delivers First Sea-Ice Map," *BBC News*, June 21, 2011, available at www.bbc.co.uk/news/science-environment-13829785.
[6] Donat Pharand, "The Arctic Waters and the Northwest Passage: A Final Revisit." (2007) 38 *Ocean Development and International Law* 3 at 38.
[7] Emails from John North, Marine Communications and Traffic Services, Canadian Coast Guard, December 15, 2011 and November 29, 2012 (on file with author). The post-2005 numbers do not include vessels under 300 tons which are not required to register with Transport Canada before entering Arctic waters. Already, dozens of smaller vessels, mostly private yachts, sail the Northwest Passage each summer.
[8] See the discussion of the 2009 Arctic Marine Shipping Assessment in Chapter 6, below.

The criteria for an international strait, according to the International Court of Justice in the 1949 *Corfu Channel Case*, are its "geographical situation as connecting two parts of the high seas and the fact of its being used for international navigation."[9] Foreign vessels sailing through an international strait necessarily pass within twelve nautical miles of one or more coastal states, but instead of the regular right of "innocent passage" through territorial waters they benefit from an enhanced right of "transit passage."[10] This entitles them to pass through the strait without coastal state permission, while also freeing them from other constraints.[11] For instance, foreign submarines may sail submerged through an international strait – something they are not permitted to do in regular territorial waters.[12]

Both Canada and Russia maintain that the straits and channels along their northern coastlines constitute "internal waters." Internal waters are not territorial waters and there is no right to access them without the permission of the coastal state. When foreign ships enter internal waters with permission, which is what ships do every time they enter a port in another country, their presence does not undermine the internal waters claim.

Internal waters arise in bays or along fragmented coastlines through the long-term acquiescence of other countries, or by the drawing of "straight baselines" between headlands and fringing islands in accordance with customary international law and the judgment of

---

[9] *Corfu Channel Case (UK v. Albania)* (1949) ICJ Reports 4 at 28. The Court held that the test was not one of volume, while noting that 2,884 ships had passed through the Corfu Channel in a twenty-one-month period. Nor did the test concern the waterway's "greater or lesser importance for international navigation," providing that it is a "useful route for international maritime traffic."

[10] Art. 38, UNCLOS, Chapter 4, n. 12, above.

[11] The precise extent of freedom of navigation in international straits remains contested, with some authors questioning whether the relevant provisions of UNCLOS accurately reflect customary international law. See, e.g., Tullio Scovazzi, *The Evolution of the International Law of the Sea: New Issues, New Challenges* (The Hague: Martinus Nijhoff, 2001), 174; Nihan Ünlü, *The Legal Regime of the Turkish Straits* (The Hague: Martinus Nijhoff, 2002), 75.

[12] Article 39(1)(c) of UNCLOS states that ships exercising the right of transit passage "shall refrain from any activities other than those incident to their normal modes of continuous and expeditious transit unless rendered necessary by *force majeure* or by distress." Submarines, by definition, normally sail submerged. In contrast, Article 20 of UNCLOS states: "In the territorial sea, submarines and other underwater vehicles are required to navigate on the surface and to show their flag." UNCLOS, Chapter 4, n. 12, above.

the International Court of Justice in the 1951 *Anglo-Norwegian Fisheries Case*.[13]

The disputes over the legal status of the Northwest Passage and the Northern Sea Route mattered little when only powerful icebreakers could pass through. But due to the rapidly melting ice and increasing volume of shipping they already matter a great deal more than before – and could cause tensions in future. This chapter explains the legal issues within their geopolitical context before making a series of recommendations as to how these Arctic straits could be transformed into safe, reliable, efficient, and contention-free shipping routes through cooperation between coastal and shipping states. Ideally, such cooperation would lead to treaties that recognize the straits as Russian and Canadian internal waters, in return for assured access and significant investments in services and infrastructure.

1 Northwest Passage

The Northwest Passage consists of several possible shipping routes through Canada's High Arctic islands. The thousands of islands themselves have been Canadian since the United Kingdom transferred title over them in 1880, while the nearly impenetrable sea-ice meant that the issue of ownership and control over the water was never discussed – until the acquisition of powerful icebreakers by the United States and, more recently, the dramatic melting of sea-ice.

If the Northwest Passage constitutes Canadian internal waters, the full force of Canada's domestic law applies. As mentioned above, internal waters are not territorial waters, and ships have no right to access them without the permission of the coastal state. Internal waters arise through the long-term acquiescence of other states, or by the drawing of straight baselines in accordance with customary international law and the *Anglo-Norwegian Fisheries Case*.[14]

In 1985, Canada drew straight baselines around the High Arctic islands. It also argued that the waters are internal as a result of historic usage, including thousands of years of use and occupation of the sea-ice by the Inuit, a largely maritime indigenous people. As then Foreign Minister Joe Clark told the House of Commons:

---

[13] *Fisheries Case (UK v. Norway)* (1951) ICJ Reports 116 at 128–129.
[14] Ibid. Parties to the 1982 UNCLOS (Chapter 4, n. 12, above) wishing to draw straight baselines are subject to Articles 7 and 8. But Canada did not ratify UNCLOS until 2003.

Canada's sovereignty in the Arctic is indivisible. It embraces land, sea and ice. It extends without interruption to the seaward facing coasts of the Arctic islands. These islands are joined, and not divided, by the waters between them. They are bridged for most of the year by ice. From time immemorial Canada's Inuit people have used and occupied the ice as they have used and occupied the land.[15]

Prior to the negotiation of the 1993 Nunavut Land Claims Agreement,[16] Inuit from across the Canadian Arctic were interviewed about traditional hunting and traveling patterns. The resulting map confirmed that the ice-covered waters south of Ellesmere Island and the Sverdrup Islands, including the eastern and central portions of the Northwest Passage, were virtual highways for the Inuit and their sled dogs.[17] More recently, the Inuit Heritage Trust has interviewed elders about place names in Inuktitut (the Inuit language) along the Northwest Passage.[18] The many thousands of names confirm the centrality of the waterway to the Inuit language, culture, history, and identity.

In addition to contributing to historic usage and thus Canada's internal waters claim, it can be argued that the Inuit acquired rights over the Northwest Passage before the arrival of the Europeans, which they subsequently transferred to Canada.[19] In the 1975 *Western Sahara Advisory Opinion*, the International Court of Justice recognized that territories inhabited by indigenous peoples who have a measure of social and political organization are not *terra nullius*; as a result, these human *collectivités* possess a limited but no less real international legal status.[20]

To succeed with such an argument, Canada would have to persuade other states or an international court or tribunal, that: (1) sea-ice can be subject to occupancy and appropriation like land; (2) under

---

[15] Joe Clark, Secretary of State for External Affairs, Statement on Sovereignty, September 10, 1985, reprinted in Franklyn Griffiths (ed.), *Politics of the Northwest Passage* (Kingston and Montreal: McGill–Queen's University Press, 1987), 269 at 270.

[16] 1993 Nunavut Land Claims Agreement, available at http://nlca.tunngavik.com/. In Canada, land claims agreements are "recognized and affirmed" by Section 35 of the Constitution Act 1982. See http://laws.justice.gc.ca/eng/Const/page-12.html#sc:7_II.

[17] The map is reproduced in Donat Pharand, *Canada's Arctic Waters in International Law* (Cambridge University Press, 1988), 165.

[18] Inuit Heritage Trust, Place Names Project, at www.ihti.ca/eng/iht-proj-plac.html.

[19] For an argument to this effect, see José Woehrling, "Les Revendications du Canada sur les eaux de l'archipel de l'Arctique et l'utilisation immémoriale des glaces par les Inuit." (1987) 30 *German Yearbook of International Law* 120 at 139.

[20] *Western Sahara*, Advisory Opinion (1975) ICJ Reports 12, paras. 79–80.

international law, indigenous people can acquire and transfer sovereign rights to states; and (3) the Inuit ceded such rights to Canada. The first point is the most difficult to argue, though the nearly year-round presence of the ice and its centrality to the traditional Inuit way of life make the situation unique and therefore more compelling.[21] The second point requires an expansive interpretation of the *Western Sahara Case*; one made easier by recent developments such as the adoption of the UN Declaration on the Rights of Indigenous People.[22] The last point is the easiest to prove, since the Nunavut Land Claims Agreement affirms the intent of the Inuit to transfer to Canada any rights they might have over the Northwest Passage under international law.[23]

In 1986, the United States protested Canada's adoption of straight baselines in the Arctic, with the State Department compilation of US maritime claims reproducing the following excerpt from a letter to a US senator as evidence of its position:

On September 10, 1985, the Government of Canada claimed all the waters among its Arctic islands as internal waters, and drew straight baselines around its Arctic islands to establish its claim. The United States position is that there is no basis in international law to support the Canadian claim. The United States

---

[21] Susan B. Boyd, "The Legal Status of the Arctic Sea Ice: A Comparative Study and a Proposal." (1984) 22 *Canadian Yearbook of International Law* 98 at 105. The argument for the Inuit having rights over sea-ice is comparable to (and probably stronger than) similar arguments in favor of indigenous rights in the open water of Torres Strait between Australia and Papua New Guinea. See Monica Mulrennan and Colin Scott, "Indigenous Rights in Saltwater Environments." (2000) 31 *Development and Change* 681; Colin Scott and Monica Mulrennan, "Reconfiguring Mare Nullius: Torres Strait Islanders, Indigenous Sea Rights and the Divergence of Domestic and International Norms," in Mario Blaser, *et al.* (eds.), *Indigenous Peoples and Autonomy: Insights for a Global Age* (Vancouver: UBC Press, 2010), 148.

[22] See discussion, Chapter 7, below. The 2007 UN Declaration on the Rights of Indigenous Peoples is available at www.un.org/esa/socdev/unpfii/documents/DRIPS_en.pdf. The UN Declaration may now be contributing to the development of customary international law. See, e.g., Mauro Barelli, "The Role of Soft Law in the International Legal System: The Case of the United Nations Declaration on the Rights of Indigenous Peoples." (2009) 58 *International and Comparative Law Quarterly* 957. However, the only reference to "waters and coastal seas" in the UN Declaration is in the context of "spiritual relationships." Ibid., Art. 25.

[23] 1993 Nunavut Land Claims Agreement, n. 16, above, sec. 15.1.1(c) ("Canada's sovereignty over the waters of the arctic archipelago is supported by Inuit use and occupancy") and sec. 2.7.1(a) ("In consideration of the rights and benefits provided to Inuit by the Agreement, Inuit hereby: cede, release and surrender to Her Majesty The Queen in Right of Canada, all their aboriginal claims, rights, title and interests, if any, in and to lands and waters anywhere within Canada and adjacent offshore areas within the sovereignty or jurisdiction of Canada").

cannot accept the Canadian claim because to do so would constitute acceptance of full Canadian control of the Northwest Passage and would terminate US navigation rights through the Passage under international law.[24]

Regardless of the merits of the US position, the letter was incorrect that an acceptance of Canada's straight baselines would necessarily terminate any right of transit passage, since straight baselines cannot have the effect of closing-off an existing international strait.[25] As a result, a critical aspect of the dispute between Canada and the United States concerns whether the Northwest Passage was "used for international navigation" before the straight baselines were drawn in 1985.

It is even possible that 1969 is the "critical date" with respect to the Northwest Passage, that is to say, the point at which the dispute became clear and any subsequent attempts to bolster the respective positions became legally inconsequential.[26]

1.1 *Voyage of the SS* Manhattan

In 1969, Exxon sent the SS *Manhattan*, an ice-strengthened super-tanker, to test the feasibility of the Northwest Passage as a route for shipping oil from Alaska to the Atlantic Seaboard of the United States.[27] The US government sent a Coast Guard icebreaker, the USCGC *Northwind*, to assist. Neither Exxon nor the US government sought Canada's permission for the voyage. Concerned that a precedent might be created, the Canadian government decided the best response was a friendly offense. It focused on the fact that some consultation had taken place, and then provided its consent in the form of aerial reconnaissance and the assistance of a powerful Canadian icebreaker.[28]

---

[24] "Letter from James W. Dyer, Acting Assistant Secretary of State for Legislative and Intergovernmental Affairs, to Senator Charles Mathias, Jr. (R. Maryland), February 26, 1986," reproduced in Office of Ocean Affairs, *Limits in the Seas No. 112: United States Responses to Excessive National Maritime Claims* (Washington, DC: US State Department, 1992), 30, available at www.state.gov/documents/organization/58381.pdf.

[25] Arts. 8(2) and 35(1), UNCLOS, Chapter 4, n. 12, above.

[26] See references, Chapter 1, n. 9, above.

[27] Bern Keating, *The Northwest Passage: From the Mathew to the Manhattan, 1497–1969* (Chicago: Rand McNally and Company, 1970), 140.

[28] As Prime Minister Pierre Trudeau told the House of Commons: "The legal status of the waters of Canada's Arctic archipelago is not at issue in the proposed transit of the Northwest Passage by the ships involved in the *Manhattan* project . . . The oil companies concerned and the United States Coast Guard have consulted with appropriate Canadian authorities in the planning of the operation. The government will support the trials with the Canadian Coast Guard ice-breaker *John A. Macdonald* . . . and will also

Washington's failure to request permission was based on a belief that the SS *Manhattan* and the USCGC *Northwind* would not have to enter areas under Canadian jurisdiction. At the time, Canada claimed only a three-mile territorial sea, which left a "high seas" corridor through the Northwest Passage.[29] American officials had therefore intended that the two vessels would remain on the high seas throughout the voyage, entering the Northwest Passage through Lancaster Sound in the east and exiting through McClure Strait in the west.[30] Prior to the voyage, the State Department informed the Canadian government that it had no intention of staking a claim and was merely undertaking a feasibility study.[31] However, on September 10, 1969, while attempting to become the first vessel ever to make an east-to-west passage of McClure Strait, the SS *Manhattan* became trapped in the ice.[32] "She escaped only when steam was diverted from heating the living spaces to squeeze an additional 7,000 horsepower from her 43,000 horsepower turbines. Even then, it was only with the assistance of her constant companion, the Canadian icebreaker, 'John A. McDonald,' [sic] that she was able to escape."[33] The *John A. Macdonald* went on to free the SS *Manhattan* from the sea-ice on at least eleven further occasions during the trip.[34]

The ice conditions forced the super-tanker to retreat from McClure Strait and use the narrow Prince of Wales Strait instead, where, as Donat Pharand explains, "it had to go through the territorial waters of Canada because of the presence of the small Princess Royal Islands."[35] Arguably, the unanticipated character of the entrance into Canadian territorial waters, along with Canada's implicit granting of permission and the

provide aerial ice reconnaissance and assume responsibility for the coordination of such reconnaissance. The government has also selected and appointed an official Canadian government representative on board the S.S. *Manhattan* who will act as technical advisor and as co-ordinator of Canadian support for the operation." Parliament of Canada, House of Commons, Debates, 1st Session, 28th Parliament, 15 May 1969, pp. 8720–8721.

[29] Robert S. Reid, "The Canadian Claim to Sovereignty Over the Waters of the Arctic." (1974) 12 *Canadian Yearbook of International Law* 111 at 120.

[30] Ibid.

[31] Jay Walz, "Oil Stirs Concern Over Northwest Passage Jurisdiction," *New York Times*, March 15, 1969.

[32] Larry Gedney and Merritt Helfferich, "Voyage of the Manhattan," December 19, 1983, Alaska Science Forum Article No. 639, www.gi.alaska.edu/ScienceForum/ASF6/639. html.

[33] Ibid.

[34] W. D. Smith, "Tanker Manhattan Is Escorted Into Halifax Harbor," *New York Times*, November 9, 1969.

[35] Pharand, "The Arctic Waters and the Northwest Passage," n. 6, above, 38.

acceptance of considerable assistance from the Canadian Coast Guard, prevented the voyage of the SS *Manhattan* from contributing to the development of an international strait.

1.2 Voyage of the USCGC Polar Sea

The summer of 1985 saw a flurry of diplomatic notes concerning the Northwest Passage.

In May, the United States informed Canada that the US Coast Guard icebreaker *Polar Sea* would sail through the waterway "as an exercise of navigational rights and freedoms not requiring prior notification."[36] In June, the United States repeated its position, before stating the "transit, and the preparation for it, in no way prejudice the judicial position of either side regarding the Northwest Passage."[37] In July, Canada responded that, although the Passage constituted Canadian internal waters, it was "committed to facilitating navigation" through the waterway and was "prepared to work toward this objective."[38] It expressly agreed with the statement that the voyage would not prejudice the two countries' legal positions and then, unnecessarily and just a little provocatively, expressly provided the permission that Washington had refused to seek.[39] In September, Foreign Minister Joe Clark would say, correctly, that the voyage had left "no mark on Canada's Arctic sovereignty."[40] Yet it was the voyage of the *Polar Sea* that prompted Canada to articulate its internal waters position in clear terms, and to define the outer limits of those waters through the drawing of straight baselines.

A careful assessment thus reveals that there have, in fact, been no unequivocal challenges to Canada's legal position, and therefore no "international navigation" of the kind that could create an international strait. Nevertheless, some Canadian specialists have felt it necessary to argue that even two nonconsensual transits would be

---

[36] 1985 State Telegram 151842, May 17, 1985, quoted in Office of Ocean Affairs, *Limits in the Seas No. 112*, n. 24, above, at 73. The *Polar Sea* was returning to its homeport of Seattle after resupplying the US airbase at Thule, Greenland.

[37] State Department Note No. 222 of 24 June 1985, as quoted in Diplomatic Note No. 433, 31 July 1985, reprinted (in part) in Office of Ocean Affairs, *Limits in the Seas No. 112*, n. 24, above, p. 74.

[38] Diplomatic Note No. 433, 31 July 1985, reproduced fully only in the paper version of J. Ashley Roach and Robert W. Smith, *Excessive Maritime Claims*, 3rd edn. (Leiden: Martinus Nijhoff, 2012), 321.

[39] Ibid.

[40] Joe Clark, Secretary of State for External Affairs, Statement on Sovereignty, n. 15, above, p. 270.

insufficient to fulfill the "used by international navigation" criterion from the *Corfu Channel Case*.[41] Most non-Canadian academics agree that at least a moderate amount of traffic is necessary, with Richard Baxter writing in 1964 that "international waterways must be considered to be those rivers, canals, and straits which are used to a substantial extent by the commercial shipping or warships belonging to states other than the riparian nation or nations."[42] As for the criteria applied in the *Corfu Channel Case*, Baxter concluded that: "the test applied by the court lays more emphasis on the practices of shipping than on geographic necessities."[43]

Daniel O'Connell likewise emphasized the importance of the "actual use" criterion:

> When it is said, then, that a strait in law is a passage of territorial sea linking two areas of high sea this is not to be taken literally, but rather construed as meaning a passage which ordinarily carries the bulk of international traffic not destined for ports on the relevant coastlines. The test of what is a strait, unlike the test of what is a bay, is not so much geographical, therefore, as functional.[44]

Authors from the US military, uniquely, take the view that prospective use is sufficient[45] or even that geography is the only test.[46] However, these views are clearly inconsistent with the International Court of Justice decision in the *Corfu Channel Case* and the preponderance of expert opinion.

1.3 European Union and China

The US position on the Northwest Passage has received some support from the European Community (now Union), which in 1986 joined the State Department in protesting against Canada's drawing of straight baselines around the High Arctic islands:

---

[41] For instance, Donat Pharand argues that "proof must be adduced that it has a history as a useful route for international maritime traffic." Pharand, "The Arctic Waters and the Northwest Passage," 35.

[42] Richard R. Baxter, *The Law of International Waterways* (Cambridge, Mass.: Harvard University Press, 1964), 3.

[43] Ibid., at 9.

[44] Daniel P. O'Connell, *The International Law of the Sea*, vol. 1, ed. Ivan Shearer (Oxford: Clarendon Press, 1982), 497.

[45] Richard J. Grunawalt, "United States Policy on International Straits." (1987) 18 *Ocean Development and International Law* 445 at 456.

[46] James C. Kraska, "The Law of the Sea Convention and the Northwest Passage." (2007) 22 *International Journal of Marine and Coastal Law* 257 at 275.

The validity of the baselines with regard to other states depends upon the relevant principles of international law applicable in this case, including the principle that the drawing of baselines must not depart to any appreciable extent from the general direction of the coast. The Member States acknowledge that elements other than purely geographical ones may be relevant for purposes of drawing baselines in particular circumstances but are not satisfied that the present baselines are justified in general. Moreover, the Member States cannot recognize the validity of a historic title as justification for the baselines drawn in accordance with the order.[47]

The "general direction of the coast" requirement comes from the *Anglo-Norwegian Fisheries Case*.[48] Its application to Canada's High Arctic islands is complicated, however, by the widespread use of "Mercator" or "conic" projections which distort the size and shape of objects near the poles and thus make the coastal archipelago look like an appendage to the North American landmass rather than an integral part of it. A globe provides a much more accurate portrayal of the geography; it also provides more credibility to Canada's legal position. Pharand has determined that Canada's straight baseline system even meets the test formulated by the United States, namely "that the general trend of the most distant islands [does] not deviate more than 20° from coastline or its general direction."[49] He also notes that the US test is probably stricter than that required by international law.[50]

The European Community's protest also questions "the validity of a historic title as justification for the boundaries drawn in accordance with the order." However, this is not an objection to Canada's use of straight baselines per se, and might refer to the unusual length of several of the baselines.[51] In any event, it appears that the European protest has never been repeated. In 2009, the European Council of Ministers issued a statement on the Arctic that referred to a right of "transit passage," thus indicating a belief that at least one international

---

[47] British High Commission Note No. 90/86 of 9 July 1986, reprinted in Office of Ocean Affairs, *Limits in the Seas No. 112*, n. 24, above, 29–30. The United Kingdom was acting on behalf of all the members of the European Community, which in 1986 included Belgium, Denmark, France, Germany, Greece, Ireland, Italy, Luxemburg, the Netherlands, Portugal, Spain, and the United Kingdom.

[48] *Anglo-Norwegian Fisheries Case* (1951) ICJ Reports 116 at 133.

[49] Pharand, "The Arctic Waters and the Northwest Passage," n. 6, above, 19, quoting Office of Ocean Affairs, *Limits in the Seas No. 106: Developing Standard Guidelines for Evaluating Straight Baselines* (Washington, DC: US State Department), 16.

[50] Ibid.

[51] For a map of "Canadian Arctic Islands and Mainland Baselines," see https://www.acls-aatc.ca/files/english/books/6.10.jpg.

strait exists in the region.[52] But the reference was more likely directed at the Bering Strait between Alaska and the Russian Far East, which is an international strait and readily accepted as such by the United States and Russia.[53]

Finally, while journalists sometimes assume that China opposes Canada's legal position, the Chinese government has yet to take an official position on the status of either the Northwest Passage or the Northern Sea Route. Nor is it necessarily in China's interests to enter into disputes with the Arctic coastal states, since Canada and Russia are the only countries operationally positioned to provide adequate charts, navigation aids, ports of refuge, weather and ice forecasting, search and rescue, and a police presence for deterring and dealing with pirates, terrorists, and smugglers – all things that Chinese shipping companies will need.[54]

1.4 1988 Arctic Cooperation Agreement

The Northwest Passage dispute has not posed a problem for Canada or the United States since 1987, when US President Ronald Reagan visited Ottawa. Canadian Prime Minister Brian Mulroney, who presumably knew that globes favor Canada's legal position more than most flat maps, pointed out the Northwest Passage on a globe in his office.[55] Reagan responded by instructing his officials to negotiate a solution, which took the form of the 1988 Arctic Cooperation Agreement.[56] The Agreement dealt with the problematic issue of the time – US Coast Guard icebreakers sailing the Northwest Passage – by removing it from the legal dispute. The United States promised that "all navigation

---

[52] Council of the European Union, "Council Conclusions on Arctic Issues," December 8, 2009, available at www.consilium.europa.eu/uedocs/cms_Data/docs/pressdata/EN/foraff/111814.pdf.

[53] For more on Bering Strait, see below, pp. 157–159.

[54] See Michael Byers, "The Dragon Looks North," *Al Jazeera*, December 28, 2011, available at www.aljazeera.com/indepth/opinion/2011/12/20111226145144638282.html.

[55] Interview with Brian Mulroney, "Leveraging Canada–US Relations 'to Get Big Things Done,'" *Policy Options*, March 2011, pp. 12–18, available at www.irpp.org/po/archive/mar11/mulroney.pdf. According to Christopher Kirkey, the US president "said something to the effect that 'that looks a little different than the maps they showed me on the plane coming to Ottawa.'" Kirkey, "Smoothing Troubled Waters: The 1988 Canada–United States Arctic Co-operation Agreement." (1994–1995) 50 *International Journal* 401 at 409.

[56] "Agreement between the Government of Canada and the Government of the United States of America on Arctic Cooperation," Canada Treaty Series 1988, No. 29, available at www.lexum.com/ca_us/en/cts.1988.29.en.html.

by US icebreakers within waters claimed by Canada to be internal will be undertaken with the consent of the Government of Canada," while Canada promised to "facilitate navigation" by those vessels. The two countries also agreed that "[n]othing in this Agreement ... nor any practice thereunder affects the respective positions of the Governments of the United States and of Canada on the Law of the Sea in this or other maritime areas." In other words, the treaty was essentially an agreement to disagree.[57]

The Arctic Cooperation Agreement was designed to manage the Northwest Passage dispute indefinitely, since shipping at the time was restricted to icebreakers by the constant presence of thick, hard sea-ice. But, again, the ice is now thinning and receding and the volume of shipping is increasing. Many of the vessels now plying the waterway are foreign cruise ships and private yachts, which raise the risk of smugglers and illegal immigrants using the route to access North America. This poses a problem for the United States which, since 11 September 2001, has become concerned about the possibility of terrorists using the Northwest Passage to sneak into North America, or of "rogue states" transporting weapons of mass destruction via the continent's longest, mostly unguarded coastline. Some Americans have realized that these challenges are best addressed through a coastal state's domestic criminal, customs, and immigration laws, rather than the much weaker powers available under international law in an international strait. This conclusion is made easier by the fact that the state in question, Canada, is a close military and economic ally.

In October 2004, then-US ambassador Paul Cellucci said: "We are looking at everything through the terrorism prism. Our top priority is to stop the terrorists. So perhaps when this [the topic of the Northwest Passage] is brought to the table again, we may have to take another look."[58] Five months later, Cellucci revealed that he had asked the State Department to re-examine the United States' position in light of the

[57] In 2006, US Ambassador David Wilkins wrote that the agreement to seek Canadian permission was restricted to activities that are "not an exercise of the right of transit passage, such as marine scientific research," and that US icebreakers, "in the absence of marine scientific research, would not be required to seek Canadian consent before transiting the Northwest Passage." Letter from David Wilkins, Ambassador of the United States of America, to Peter Boehm, Assistant Deputy Minister, North America, Department of Foreign Affairs and International Trade, October 27, 2006, available at www.state.gov/documents/organization/98836.pdf.
[58] Greg Younger-Lewis, "US Might Be Safer if it Left Northwest Passage to Canada: US Ambassador," *Canadian Press Newswire (Toronto)*, October 7, 2004.

terrorist threat.[59] For some reason, however, the Canadian government failed to follow up on what was a clear if implicit invitation to negotiate. It was not until August 2007 that it stepped forward, abruptly and at the highest of levels, when Prime Minister Stephen Harper told President George W. Bush about Cellucci's views.[60] Without any preparatory diplomacy, the news fell on deaf ears.[61]

1.5 Concerns about a precedent

The US Navy, in particular, is concerned that recognizing Canada's legal position in the Northwest Passage could create a precedent for waterways elsewhere in the world that the United States claims are international straits. In January 2009, just before he left office, President George W. Bush signed a directive that included a reaffirmation of the United States' long-standing position that the Northwest Passage constitutes an international strait: "Freedom of the seas is a top national priority. ... Preserving the rights and duties relating to navigation and overflight in the Arctic region supports our ability to exercise these rights throughout the world, including through strategic straits."[62]

Yet Suzanne Lalonde and Frédéric Lasserre have analyzed seven cases "where the United States has protested respecting what it considers to be illegal inclusion of an international strait within a coastal State's internal waters, thus defending the principle of freedom of navigation."[63] In the first case, Japan has avoided any threat to US interests by limiting the breadth of its territorial sea in the La Pérouse/Soya, Osumi, Tsugaru, and Tsushima Straits, thus guaranteeing international

59 "North of Sixty: US Virtual Presence Posts in Canada," online dialogue with Ambassador Cellucci (March 9, 2005), available at http://web.archive.org/web/20080905100147/http://www.canadanorth.usvpp.gov/yukon/chat.asp.
60 See Tonda MacCharles and Bruce Campion-Smith, "Troops Out by '09, Bush Told," *Toronto Star*, August 21, 2007. At the same time, the by-then former ambassador made his personal views clear: "I think, in the age of terrorism, it's in our security interests that the Northwest Passage be considered part of Canada. That would enable the Canadian navy to intercept and board vessels in the Northwest Passage to make sure they're not trying to bring weapons of mass destruction into North America." Jim Brown, Canadian Press, "Ex-US envoy backs Canada's Arctic claim," *Toronto Star*, August 20, 2007, available at www.thestar.com/News/Canada/article/247881.
61 Several months later, in February 2008, Cellucci took part in a "model negotiation" between two teams of non-governmental experts. See discussion, below, p. 155.
62 National Security Presidential Directive 66 and Homeland Security Presidential Directive 25, January 9, 2009, available at www.fas.org/irp/offdocs/nspd/nspd-66.htm.
63 Suzanne Lalonde and Frédéric Lasserre, "The Position of the United States on the Northwest Passage: Is the Fear of Creating a Precedent Warranted?" (2012) 43 *Ocean Development and International Law* 28.

mobility despite claiming several less important waterways (Shimonoseki and Hoyo Straits and Bungo Channel) as internal waters. In three other cases – the Palk Strait between India and Sri Lanka, the Kerch Strait leading from the Black Sea to the Sea of Azov, and the Piombino Strait between the Italian mainland and Elba Island – the waterways are of little practical value to the United States because of shallow water, the lack of meaningful access provided, or the proximity of more advantageous routes.

Lalonde and Lasserre conclude that only the Northern Sea Route along the coast of Russia, the Qiongzhou Strait along the coast of China, and Head Harbour Passage, a short and narrow channel through Canadian waters close to the US state of Maine, "raise some of the same legal concerns" as the Northwest Passage and "present an undeniable and very real strategic interest for the United States."[64] They also specu-late that melting ice might actually diminish the importance of the Northern Sea Route by increasing access to the waters north of Russia's offshore islands, while "there may also be a tacit acknowledg-ment that China does exercise exclusive sovereignty over the Qiongzhou Strait and that this situation is not about to change."[65] As for Head Harbour Passage, "its importance is more local in character and thus unlikely to feature in any global strategic assessment."[66]

Lalonde and Lasserre also note that: "Other straits enclosed within the internal waters of particular States have not been the subject of US protests because they are governed by specific international treaties or agreements."[67] This important point will be returned to below, when we examine the options available to Canada and the United States as they seek to resolve the Northwest Passage dispute in the fundamen-tally changed circumstances of diminishing sea-ice.[68]

Finally, Lalonde and Lasserre point out that:

Most of the strategic straits [Gibraltar, Hormuz, Malacca, Singapore, Torres, etc.] referred to in the academic literature as potentially influenced by the Northwest Passage precedent, are simply not relevant. Such straits are not within the internal waters of the States bordering them and are therefore not subject to their exclusive control. More importantly, these major maritime highways are now unquestionably considered to be international straits to which the regime of transit passage applies. Their designation as international straits, and the

---

[64] Ibid. On the latter dispute, see Jon M. Van Dyke, "Canada's Authority to Prohibit LNG Vessels from Passing through Head Harbor Passage to US Ports." (2008–2009) 14 *Ocean and Coastal Law Journal* 45.
[65] Ibid.   [66] Ibid.   [67] Ibid.   [68] See discussion, below, pp. 154–157.

legal rights which flow from such a designation, can no longer be reasonably questioned, irrespective of the outcome of the Northwest Passage case.[69]

In short, the combination of narrowness (i.e., less than twenty-four-nautical-mile-wide chokepoints), absence of a specific treaty regime, paucity of nonconsensual foreign transits, presence of indigenous peoples and almost year-round sea-ice should make it possible legally to distinguish the Northwest Passage from all other potential or existing international straits – apart, that is, from the Russian Arctic straits that form part of the Northern Sea Route.

2 Northern Sea Route

The Northern Sea Route, which stretches along the top of Russia from the Atlantic to the Pacific, has become seasonally ice-free.[70] More than forty-six ships traversed the waterway in the summer and fall of 2012, most of them transporting natural resources from Russian ports to Asian markets.[71] South Korean shipyards are building ice-strengthened cargo vessels and tankers that will soon extend the shipping season further,[72] while the Russian government is building new icebreakers to escort convoys of commercial vessels.[73]

The Russian government is intent on turning the Northern Sea Route into a commercially viable alternative to the Suez Canal and the Strait of Malacca. In September 2011, Vladimir Putin said:

The shortest route between Europe's largest markets and the Asia-Pacific region lies across the Arctic. This route is almost a third shorter than the traditional southern one. I want to stress the importance of the Northern Sea Route as an international transport artery that will rival traditional trade lanes in service

---

[69] Ibid.   [70] For a map of the Northern Sea Route, see www.fni.no/insrop/nsrmap.jpg.

[71] "46 Vessels through Northern Sea Route," BarentsObserver.com, November 23, 2012, available at http://barentsobserver.com/en/arctic/2012/11/46-vessels-through-northern-sea-route-23-11. In 2011, thirty-four ships traversed the route, up from just four in 2010. Ibid.

[72] Steven Borowiec, "South Korea Angles for Influence on Arctic Policy," *World Politics Review*, September 25, 2012, available at www.worldpoliticsreview.com/articles/12366/south-korea-angles-for-influence-on-arctic-policy.

[73] Atle Staalesen, "Baltic Yard Wins Nuclear Icebreaker Contract," *Barents Observer*, August 6, 2012, available at http://barentsobserver.com/en/arctic/baltic-yard-wins-nuclear-icebreaker-contract-06-08.

fees, security and quality. States and private companies that choose the Arctic trade routes will undoubtedly reap economic advantages.[74]

There is, however, a diplomatic problem: the United States contests Russia's claim that portions of the Northern Sea Route – namely, the Vil'kitskii, Shokal'skii, Dmitrii Laptev, and Sannikov Straits – constitute Russian internal waters. Significantly, no other country has taken a side in the dispute, which began in 1963 when the US Coast Guard icebreaker *Northwind* surveyed the Laptev Sea; the next summer, the USS *Burton Island* did likewise in the East Siberian Sea. These voyages prompted the Soviet government to send an aide memoire to the US embassy in Moscow in July 1964 clearly setting out the position that the straits are internal waters:

The Northern seaway route is situated near the Arctic coast of the USSR. This route, quite distant from international seaways, has been used and is used only by ships belonging to the Soviet Union or chartered in the name of the Northern Seaways ... It should also be kept in mind that the northern seaway route at some points goes through Soviet territorial and internal waters. Specifically, this concerns all straits running west and east in the Karsky Sea. Inasmuch as they are overlapped twofold by Soviet territorial waters, as well as by the Dmitry, Laptev and Sannikov Straits, which unite the Laptev and Eastern Siberian Seas and belong historically to the Soviet Union. Not one of these stated straits, as is known, serves for international navigation. Thus over the waters of these straits the statute for the protection of the state borders of the USSR fully applies, in accordance with which foreign military ships will pass through territorial seas and enter internal waters of the USSR after advance permission of the Government of the USSR.[75]

In June 1965, the US government responded with a diplomatic note that summarized the Soviet internal waters claim solely in the language of "historic waters" and presented its own position, that the Russian Arctic straits are international straits, in a remarkably tautological manner:

So far as the Dmitry, Laptev and Sannikov Straits are concerned, the United States is not aware of any basis for a claim to these waters on historic grounds even assuming that the doctrine of historic waters in international law can be applied to international straits ... While the United States is sympathetic with efforts which have been made by the Soviet Union in developing the Northern Seaway Route and appreciates the importance of this waterway to Soviet

---

[74] Gleb Bryanski, "Russia's Putin Says Arctic Trade Route to Rival Suez," *Reuters*, September 22, 2011, available at http://ca.reuters.com/article/topNews/idCATRE78L5TC20110922.

[75] Reproduced in: Office of Ocean Affairs, *Limits in the Seas No. 112*, n. 24, above, p. 71 (emphasis added).

interests, nevertheless, it cannot admit that these factors have the effect of changing the status of the waters of the route under international law. With respect to the straits of the Karsky Sea described as overlapped by the Soviet territorial waters it must be pointed out that there is a right of innocent passage of all ships through straits used for international navigation between two parts of the high seas and that this right cannot be suspended. In the case of straits comprising high seas as well as territorial waters there is of course unlimited right of navigation in the high seas areas ... For the reasons indicated the United States must reaffirm its reservations of its rights and those of its nationals in the waters in question whose status it regards as dependent on the principle of international law and not decrees of the coastal state.[76]

By asserting that the waterways are international straits because they are international straits, the United States sought to sidestep the awkward fact that the waterways were not used for international shipping – which, again, is one of the criteria set out by the International Court of Justice in the *Corfu Channel Case*.[77]

2.1 Vil'Kitskii incidents

The Soviet–American dispute soon took on greater significance through what are referred to as the "Vil'Kitskii incidents." The Vil'Kitskii Straits are located between Bol'Shevik Island, located at the southern end of the Severnnaia Zemlia archipelago, and the Taimyr Peninsula, which is the northernmost portion of the Russian mainland. Their location at 78 degrees north latitude, about 800 nautical miles from the North Pole, makes them the most important chokepoint in the Northern Sea Route. In the summer of 1965, the USCGC *Northwind* approached the Vil'kitskii Straits from the west. Strong diplomatic pressure was applied by the Soviet Union; pressure that, according to one US Department of State spokesman, extended to a threat to "go all the way" if the American ship proceeded into the strait.[78] The US government responded by ordering the *Northwind* to turn round.[79]

---

[76] Ibid., pp. 21, 71–72 (emphasis added).   [77] See discussion, above, pp. 130 and 137.
[78] Richard Petrow, *Across the Top of Russia: The Cruise of the USCGC Northwind into the Polar Seas North of Siberia* (London: Hodder and Stoughton, 1968), p. 352, cited in Erik Franckx, *Maritime Claims in the Arctic: Canadian and Russian Perspectives* (Dordrecht: Martinus Nijhoff, 1993), 148.
[79] Franckx, *Maritime Claims in the Arctic*, at 148. Curiously, the State Department account of the incident is limited to a single sentence suggesting, incorrectly, that the vessel stayed the course: "The *Northwind* conducted its transit from July to September of 1965." Office of Ocean Affairs, *Limits in the Seas No. 112*, n. 24, above, p. 72.

In the summer of 1967, the US Coast Guard icebreakers *Edisto* and *Eastwind* set out to circumnavigate the Arctic Ocean. The plan, as communicated to the Soviet government, was for the vessels to sail north of Novaya Zemlya and Severnaya Zemlya "entirely in international waters."[80] Heavy ice conditions forced the ships to change course toward the Vil'Kitskii Straits. A diplomatic note was sent to Moscow that was carefully worded so as not to constitute a request for permission: "This squadron will ... make a peaceful and innocent passage through the straits of Vil'kitskii, adhering to the centerline as closely as possible, and making no deviation or delay."[81] The Soviet Union responded with an aide memoire the very same day – followed by an oral démarche four days later – reiterating that the straits were Soviet waters and that foreign vessels had to submit requests to enter thirty days in advance.[82] The US government aborted its plans of circumnavigation, while stating that it "strongly protests" the "unwarranted position that the proposed passage of the *Edisto* and *Eastwind* would be in violation by Soviet regulations, raising the possibility of action by the Soviet Government to detain the vessels or otherwise interfere with their movement."[83]

The Vil'Kitskii incidents are important from a legal perspective, again, because of the criteria for an international strait set out by the International Court of Justice, namely, that a strait must connect two areas of high seas and be "used for international navigation."[84] The latter functional criterion was clearly not met in the straits north of Russia. Moreover, as Donald Rothwell explains, since the incidents in the 1960s "there has been little further attempt by the United States or any other state actively to assert a right of freedom of navigation for its ships through the Russian Arctic straits."[85]

2.2 Opening of the Northern Sea Route

In 1985, the Soviet Union adopted straight baselines connecting the island groups of Novaya Zemlya, Severnaya Zemlya, and the New

---

[80] Office of Ocean Affairs, *Limits in the Seas No. 112*, n. 24, above, p. 72.

[81] Robert D. Wells, "The Icy Nyet." (1968) 94 (782) *US Naval Institute Proceedings* 73 at 77.

[82] Office of Ocean Affairs, *Limits in the Seas No. 112*, n. 24, above, p. 72.   [83] Ibid.

[84] See discussion, above, pp. 130 and 137.

[85] Donald R. Rothwell, *The Polar Regions and the Development of International Law* (Cambridge University Press, 1996), 205.

Siberian Islands to the mainland.[86] The move may have been prompted by the negotiation of the UN Convention on the Law of the Sea, which the Soviet Union had signed but not yet ratified, since the UNCLOS provisions on straight baselines are less favorable to coastal states than the pre-existing customary international law.[87] The opening of the Northern Sea Route to international shipping began shortly thereafter when, in 1987, Soviet General Secretary Mikhail Gorbachev said: "Across the Arctic runs the shortest sea route from Europe to the Far East, to the Pacific. I think that, depending on how the normalization of international relations goes, we could open the Northern Sea Route to foreign ships under our icebreaker escort."[88] Two years later, the USSR earned its first foreign currency from the Northern Sea Route when the *Tiksi*, a Soviet vessel, was chartered to carry goods from Germany to Japan.[89] In 1991, the French-flagged *Astrolabe* became the first non-Soviet vessel to traverse the Northern Sea Route.[90]

International interest in the Northern Sea Route led to the production of two major reports. The International Northern Sea Route Program (INSROP) was a Norwegian, Japanese, and Russian project that ran from 1993 to 1999 and focused on the viability of the waterway for international shipping. It concluded:

[A] substantial increase in international commercial shipping is feasible – in economic, technological and environmental terms. The largest and most obvious cargo potential is found in the huge oil and gas reserves in the Russian Arctic – both onshore and offshore – where marine export towards western markets is likely to start up early in the new Century. As for transit traffic, INSROP's survey of the main cargo-generating regions at the western and eastern ends of the NSR (NW Europe, NE Asia and the North American West Coast) identified a stable transit cargo potential, most notably for dry bulk.[91]

---

[86] Tullio Scovazzi, "New Developments Concerning Soviet Straight Baselines." (1988) 3 *International Journal of Estuarine and Coastal Law* 37; Vladimir Golitsyn, "The Arctic – On the Way to Regional Cooperation." (1989) 1 *Marine Policy Report* 91. For a discussion of the Canadian baselines, also adopted in 1985, see above, pp. 133–134 and 137–138.

[87] Pharand, "The Arctic Waters and the Northwest Passage," 15.

[88] Quoted in Rothwell, *The Polar Regions and the Development of International Law*, n. 85 above, p. 206.

[89] Erik Franckx, "The Legal Regime of Navigation in the Russian Arctic." (2009) 18 *Journal of Transnational Law and Policy* 327 at 329.

[90] Ibid.   [91] See International Northern Sea Route Program, at www.fni.no/insrop/.

The second report, the Arctic Operational Platform, was funded and organized by the European Commission between 2002 and 2006 and designed to help make the Northern Sea Route an environmentally and economically viable option for transporting oil and gas from the Russian Arctic. It concluded: "oil and gas transportation by the Northern Sea Route is technologically possible and economically feasible."[92]

In September 2009, with the thick, hard multi-year ice having disappeared from the Russian coast, two German container ships successfully navigated the Northern Sea Route on a voyage that began in Ulsan, South Korea, and ended in Rotterdam, Netherlands.[93] In November 2010, Norilsk Nickel, Russia's largest mining company, reported that one of its vessels had completed a round trip from Murmansk to Shanghai. The 9,836-nautical-mile trip took 41 days, compared to the 20,942 nautical miles and 84 days that it would have taken by way of the Suez Canal.[94] In August 2011, the *Vladimir Tikhonov*, a 300-meter-long super-tanker carrying natural gas condensate from Murmansk to Map Ta Phut, Thailand, became the largest vessel to complete the Northern Sea Route. It was able to do so because late-summer ice conditions now allow ships to sail northward of the New Siberia Islands, thus bypassing the shallow waters between those islands and the mainland. In August 2012, the Chinese research icebreaker *Xuelong* (Snow Dragon) transited the Northern Sea Route under the escort of the nuclear-powered Russian icebreaker *Vaygach*.[95] The presence of the *Vaygach* underlined an important point: despite the increase in shipping, none of these voyages can be taken to indicate that Russia believes the Northern Sea Route should be opened to unrestricted access.

3 Assessment of Canada's and Russia's legal positions

The Vil'kitskii, Shokal'skii, Dmitrii Laptev, and Sannikov Straits are almost certainly Russian internal waters, given the absence of any

---

[92] Arctic Operational Platform, at www.transport-research.info/web/projects/ project_details.cfm?id=38216.

[93] Tony Halpin, "Cargo Ships Navigate Northeast Passage for the First Time," *The Times*, September 14, 2009, p. 1.

[94] "DJ Norilsk Nickel Vessel Completes First Northern Sea Route Trip," *Waves Newsletter*, November 22, 2010, http://wavesnewsletter.com/?p=1475.

[95] Wang Qian, "Breaking the Ice," *China Daily*, September 30, 2012, available at www. chinadaily.com.cn/sunday/2012-09/30/content_15793745.htm.

nonconsensual transits by foreign surface vessels and the fact that only one country has expressly opposed the Russian position. Douglas Brubaker agrees with this assessment, even though he presumes (but does not substantiate) the existence of at least some nonconsensual transits as well as protests of the Russian position by countries other than the United States.[96] Rothwell writes: "Given the relative infrequency of foreign-flagged vessels passing through these straits, which seems even less frequent when compared to similar voyages through the Northwest Passage, it would seem to be difficult to classify any of the major straits in the Northeast Passage as 'international straits.'"[97] For their part, Robin Churchill and Vaughan Lowe write:

[A]part from some of the individual straits making up the [Northeast] Passage being enclosed by straight baselines drawn in 1985, there are doubts as to whether the straits can be said to be "used for international navigation", and thus attract a right of transit passage, in the light of the handful of sailings through the (often ice-bound) straits that have actually taken place.[98]

Cementing the Russian claim is the fact that the dispute's "critical date" – the point when the differing positions became clear and subsequent attempts to bolster them became inconsequential to the legal analysis – was 1964 or 1965.[99]

There is only one factor militating against the Russian legal position, namely, that the offshore Arctic islands enclosed by the straight baselines do not seem to lie in the "general direction of the coast."[100] However, Russia's internal waters position pre-dates the drawing of the straight baselines by several decades, and is therefore based on the long-standing acquiescence of other countries – including but not limited to the absence of nonconsensual transits.

The status of the Northwest Passage is less clear. There have been two surface transits where permission was not requested, though Canada provided considerable assistance to the SS *Manhattan* in 1969 and both granted permission and secured a statement of "without prejudice" with regard to the USCGC *Polar Sea* in 1985. Moreover, only the United

---

[96] R. Douglas Brubaker, *Russian Arctic Straits* (Dordrecht: Martinus Nijhoff, 2004), 41 and 189.

[97] Rothwell, *The Polar Regions and the Development of International Law*, n. 85, above, p. 206.

[98] Robin Churchill and Vaughan Lowe, *The Law of the Sea*, 3rd edn. (Manchester University Press, 1999), 106.

[99] On the critical date principle, see references, Chapter 1, n. 9, above.

[100] See discussion, above, p. 138.

States has consistently opposed Canada's legal position. The position is also bolstered by the support of the Canadian Inuit who have used and occupied the sea-ice of the Northwest Passage for thousands of years. And notwithstanding the unusual length of several of the Canadian baselines, the drawing of straight baselines around a coastal archipelago of 19,000 closely knit islands would seem consistent with the purpose of such lines as articulated in the *Anglo-Norwegian Fisheries Case*, namely, to subject to the regime of internal waters those sea areas which are "sufficiently closely linked to the land domain" – an idea which "should be liberally applied in the case of a coast, the geographical configuration of which is as unusual as that of Norway."[101]

Finally, the Northwest Passage dispute achieved its "critical date" in 1969, or perhaps in 1985, when Canada clearly articulated its internal waters position and adopted straight baselines. For this reason, even if a foreign ship were to sail through the Northwest Passage without Canada's permission today, it would not undermine Canada's legal claim (though it might well have political consequences). So we are left with just the two transits, where permission was not sought but was either implicitly or explicitly given, and where, in the latter instance, the two countries agreed that the voyage was without prejudice to the legal dispute. After engaging in a careful analysis of the "used for international navigation" requirement, Rothwell rightly concluded that, "without further judicial guidance on the question of international straits it is extremely difficult to determine conclusively whether the [Northwest] Passage is or is not an international strait."[102]

4 Canada–Russia cooperation

The similarities between the Northwest Passage and Northern Sea Route extend beyond the shared Russian and Canadian legal positions that their respective Arctic straits constitute internal waters. In 1982, Soviet and Canadian diplomats partnered in the negotiation of Article 234 of UNCLOS, which allows coastal states to exercise heightened regulatory powers over shipping in ice-prone areas for the prevention, reduction, and control of marine pollution out to 200 nautical miles

---

[101] *Fisheries Case (UK v. Norway)* (1951) ICJ Reports 116 at 133.
[102] Rothwell, The Polar Regions and the Development of International Law, n. 85, above, p. 200.

from shore.[103] Article 234 legitimated the 1970 Canadian Arctic Waters Pollution Prevention Act,[104] which was adopted following the voyage of the SS *Manhattan* and later provided a model for the Soviet Union's 1990 regulations on the Northern Sea Route.[105]

As was mentioned above, Canada and the Soviet Union both adopted straight baselines along their Arctic coastlines in 1985.[106] That same year, when the United States sent the USCGC *Polar Sea* through the Northwest Passage, Evgeni Pozdnyakov, a press attaché at the Soviet Embassy in Ottawa, publicly expressed support for Canada's legal position: "Whether it is the Northwest Passage or the Northeast Passage does not matter. Our position is based on provisions of international law. The waters around islands belonging to a country are the internal waters of that country."[107]

However, there is no evidence of any prior or subsequent statements of support by the Soviet Union or Russia for Canada's position, nor indeed evidence of Canadian statements in the reverse – which is curious, given the similarities in legal circumstances. The most logical explanation for this curiosity is political in character: Canada and the Soviet Union were on different sides of the Cold War. US opposition to Canada's claim has always been based on wider strategic concerns, namely, a felt need for maximum navigation rights worldwide. With Canadian and US security linked through NATO, NORAD, and the Five Eyes intelligence-sharing network, it would have been difficult enough for Canada to take an independent stance on the Northwest Passage issue. Taking the Soviet Union's side in the Northern Sea Route dispute was, in the event, simply not an option.

As for the Soviet Union's near-complete silence on the Northwest Passage, one can postulate that the Soviets decided not to disrupt the delicate balance that allowed Canada and the United States to "agree to disagree" on the issue. Had the Soviet Union come out strongly in favor of the Canadian position, the United States might have decided that Canada's independent stance was no longer tolerable – and then applied

---

[103] See discussion, below, pp. 164–165.
[104] Arctic Waters Pollution Prevention Act, 1969–70 Statutes of Canada, chap. 47, available at http://laws.justice.gc.ca/eng/acts/A-12/index.html.
[105] For a recent overview of the regulations, see Franckx, "The Legal Regime of Navigation in the Russian Arctic," 330–339.
[106] See discussions, above, pp. 131 and 146–147.
[107] Matthew Fisher, "Soviets Back Canada's Claim to Northwest Passage Waters," *Globe and Mail*, August 7, 1985.

the considerable pressures available to it as the dominant partner in a close but asymmetrical relationship. An alternative or additional explanation is that the Soviet Union was not concerned that any country would directly challenge its claim by overtly sailing through the Northern Sea Route. The risk of sparking a nuclear conflict would be too high, and the only US vessels capable of a surface voyage were lightly armed Coast Guard icebreakers that would be no match for their Northern Fleet.

Today, with the Cold War over and the sea-ice melting, environmental concerns and economic opportunities dominate the policy landscape. Russia is a member of the G8, G20, World Trade Organization (WTO), Council of Europe, Barents Euro-Arctic Council, and Arctic Council. Its largest trading partner is the European Union, made up mostly of NATO states. Russia's military power has also declined significantly: in 2011, its military spending was just one-tenth that of the United States ($71.9 bn. versus $711 bn.).[108]

In November 2007, Canadian Prime Minister Stephen Harper and then Russian Prime Minister Viktor Zubkov issued a joint statement on Canada–Russia economic cooperation.[109] In January 2010, according to WikiLeaks, Harper told NATO Secretary-General Anders Fogh Rasmussen that the military alliance had no role to play in the Arctic because Canada has a "good working relationship" with Russia with respect to the Arctic and "there is no likelihood of Arctic states going to war."[110] As for the Russian president, in September 2010, Vladimir Putin told a conference in Moscow: "If you stand alone you can't survive in the Arctic. Nature makes people and states to help each other."[111] As was explained above, Putin's comments came just a week after the Russian and Norwegian foreign ministers signed a maritime boundary

---

[108] "The 15 Countries with the Highest Military Expenditure in 2009," Stockholm International Peace Research Institute, 2010, available at www.sipri.org/research/armaments/milex/resultoutput/milex_15 (China: $143 bn. / France: $62.5 bn. / Germany: $46.7 bn. / Italy: $34.5 bn.).

[109] Joint Statement on Canada–Russia Economic Cooperation, November 28, 2007, available at www.cbern.ca/cms/One.aspx?portalId=625751andpageId=9815452.

[110] US State Department cable # VZCZCXR03302, January 20, 2010, available at http://aptn.ca/pages/news/2011/05/11/while-harper-talked-tough-with-nato-on-arctic-u-s-believed-pm-all-bark-no-bite/ (original cables are reproduced below the article).

[111] Luke Harding, "Vladimir Putin Calls for Arctic Claims to Be Resolved under UN Law," Guardian, September 23, 2010, available at www.guardian.co.uk/world/2010/sep/23/putin-arctic-claims-international-law.

treaty for the Barents Sea.[112] Then, in May 2011, Russia, Canada, the US, Denmark, Norway, Sweden, Finland, and Iceland signed a multilateral search-and-rescue treaty, the first legal instrument negotiated under the umbrella of the Arctic Council.[113]

All of this has consequences for the Northern Sea Route and Northwest Passage. In February 2009, Alan Kessel, the Legal Adviser to Canada's Minister of Foreign Affairs, met with his Russian counterpart, Roman Kolodkin, in Moscow. According to a Russian summary of the meeting:

Both sides noted a high degree of similarity in their position on the issue of international shipping in the Northwest Passage (Canada) and the Northern Sea Route (Russia) – the existing limitations that are being applied to those areas are necessary to preserve the fragile maritime environment and are in sync with the rights that UNCLOS concedes to coastal states in ice-covered areas. Both sides agreed to have more detailed consultations on this topic, including the issue of rights to historical waters in the context of the existing disputes over their status with the US.[114]

In the more than two decades since the Cold War ended, Russia and Canada have been integrated into the same global economy and become active participants in Arctic cooperation. But now, with the ice disappearing and foreign shippers looking north, it may only be a matter of time before other countries join the United States in overtly opposing Canada and/or Russia's legal positions on their Arctic straits (even if, as was suggested above, it might not actually be in their interest to do so). Given the high degree of similarity between the two situations, additional opposition to one claim could only serve to weaken the other. In these changed and challenging circumstances, the two countries would be wise to pursue a joint Russian-Canadian position on the legal status of the Northern Sea Route and Northwest Passage. Among other things, such issue-specific diplomatic cooperation would strengthen the leverage of both countries as they seek, singly or jointly, to negotiate some kind of long-term compromise with the United States.

---

[112] 2010 Treaty between the Kingdom of Norway and the Russian Federation concerning Maritime Delimitation and Cooperation in the Barents Sea and the Arctic Ocean, English translation available at www.regjeringen.no/upload/ud/vedlegg/folkerett/avtale_engelsk.pdf. See discussion, Chapter 2, above.

[113] Agreement on Aeronautical and Maritime Search and Rescue in the Arctic, May 12, 2011, available at http://arctic-council.npolar.no/en/meetings/2011-nuuk-ministerial/docs/. See discussion, Chapter 8, below.

[114] Russia–Canada consultations on the legal status of the Arctic, February 20, 2009, Moscow, available at http://byers.typepad.com/arctic/russiacanada-consultations-on-the-legal-status-of-the-arctic.html.

5 Canada–United States cooperation

It has always been difficult for Canada to discuss the Northwest Passage issue with the United States. A northern route from the Atlantic to the Pacific Ocean was the Holy Grail for explorers from Cabot to Hudson and Franklin, whose discoveries helped define the Canadian nation.[115] The Northwest Passage also constitutes Canada's most significant and enduring dispute with its more powerful neighbor; as such, it is a source of both pride and anxiety for many Canadians. Nevertheless, the two countries have managed to talk about the Northwest Passage when it has been necessary to do so. As mentioned above, Prime Minister Brian Mulroney addressed the challenge posed by US Coast Guard icebreakers by securing an agreement that such vessels would request permission from Canada before entering the waterway, and that their voyages would have no impact on the legal dispute.[116] The 1988 Arctic Cooperation Agreement would have resolved the matter, for all practical purposes, but for the dramatic melting of sea-ice now occurring.

The melting ice poses a fundamental challenge to the "agree to disagree" arrangement. Increased international shipping in the Northwest Passage will necessitate improvements in policing, search and rescue, oil spill response, and other basic services that only the coastal state is operationally positioned to provide. However, Canada's incentive to make those investments is reduced, so long as its jurisdiction to regulate shipping is contested.

Two further changes have combined to create an impetus for new Canada–United States negotiations. The terrorist attacks of 11 September 2001 shifted the focus of security concerns in the United States from state to non-state actors. In 2005, as mentioned above, US Ambassador Paul Cellucci revealed that he had asked the State Department to re-examine the United States' position on the Northwest Passage in light of the terrorist threat.[117] Cellucci's concern was that terrorists might take advantage of ice-free conditions to transport WMDs or enter North America. He went so far as to suggest publicly that Canada's legal position might now benefit the United States.

---

[115] See Pierre Berton, *The Arctic Grail: The Quest for the Northwest Passage and the North Pole, 1818–1909* (Toronto: McClelland and Stewart, 1988).
[116] See discussion, above, pp. 139–140.   [117] See discussion, above, pp. 140–141.

In 2008, Cellucci participated in a "Model Negotiation on Northern Shipping" between two teams of nongovernmental experts.[118] The goal of the two-day exercise was to discuss the issues, identify possible solutions, and make joint recommendations aimed at both governments. The teams agreed that the long history of United States–Canada cooperation in the Arctic indicates the potential for a new bilateral agreement, as does the history of cooperation on shipping through other waters under national jurisdiction such as the St. Lawrence Seaway. They made nine recommendations, including that the two countries collaborate in developing parallel rules and cooperative enforcement mechanisms for notification and interdiction in the waters north of Alaska and Canada, as well as on the establishment of shipping lanes, traffic management schemes, and oil spill response plans. They also recommended that the two countries make maximum use of the considerable legal powers they already possess over vessels, either those sailing to or from Canadian or American ports or those registered in either country.

A third change took place in 2009, when the new Obama administration adopted a highly cooperative approach to Arctic politics. It began with a "reset" of the relationship with Russia, the former Cold War rival. In April 2010, the "New START" treaty committed the two countries to reduce their stockpiles of nuclear weapons and submit to new verification measures.[119] It was a development of considerable importance for the Arctic, given that most of Russia's nuclear missile submarines are based north of the Arctic Circle. Parallel to this, the Obama administration took a series of Arctic-specific initiatives. It partnered with Russia in leading the negotiation of a multilateral search-and-rescue treaty,[120] and with Canada in mapping the continental shelf in the Beaufort Sea. As Chapter 3 explained, the two countries are now in the early stages of negotiating a maritime boundary in that area.

The Obama administration understood that Prime Minister Harper's sometimes quite assertive Arctic rhetoric was directed at Canadian

---

[118] See "Model Negotiation on Northern Waters," Annex II in Michael Byers, *Who Owns the Arctic? Understanding Sovereignty Disputes in the North* (Vancouver, BC and Berkeley, Calif.: Douglas & McIntyre, 2009); also available at http://byers.typepad.com/arctic/model-negotiation-on-northern-waters.html.

[119] Measures for the Further Reduction and Limitation of Strategic Offensive Arms (US–Russian Federation), April 8, 2010, available at www.state.gov/t/avc/newstart/index.htm.

[120] Agreement on Aeronautical and Maritime Search and Rescue in the Arctic, n. 113, above. See discussion, Chapter 8, below.

voters rather than foreign governments. As US Ambassador David Jacobson explained in a January 2010 cable released by WikiLeaks: "Conservatives make concern for 'The North' part of their political brand ... and it works."[121] In the same cable, the US envoy noted: "That the PM's public stance on the Arctic may not reflect his private, perhaps more pragmatic, priorities, however, was evident in the fact that during several hours together with Ambassador Jacobson on January 7 and 8, which featured long and wide-ranging conversations, the PM did not once mention the Arctic."

In these fundamentally changed circumstances, Canada and the United States should re-open discussions on the Northwest Passage. The US government is willing, as Jacobson's January 2010 cable made clear:

At this juncture, for Canada to advance its "sovereignty" interests there is a need to focus on bilateral and multilateral partnerships with its Arctic neighbors. Among the Arctic coastal states (and perhaps among all countries) Canada and the United States typically have the most closely aligned policy interests and generally share a common viewpoint on international law and common objectives in multilateral fora (such as the Arctic Council). From Canada's point of view, if the two countries can find bilateral common-ground on Arctic issues, the chance for Canadian success is much greater than going it alone against the interests of other countries or groups of countries.

In preparation for those discussions, Canada will have to consider the commitments – on access, policing, search and rescue, other services, and infrastructure – that the United States might reasonably request in exchange for recognizing the "internal waters" position. A new agreement could be concluded in the form of a bilateral treaty, which would then, ideally, be multilateralized through the conclusion of identical or at least similar bilateral treaties between Canada and other countries. This approach has already proven successful with the many nearly identical bilateral treaties concluded between the United States and Caribbean countries for drug-interdictions at sea, and the similar bilateral treaties concluded with "flag of convenience" states under the US-led Proliferation Security Initiative.[122] Such countries could usefully

---

[121] US State Department cable # VZCZCXYZ0001, January 21, 2010, available at http:// aptn.ca/pages/news/2011/05/11/while-harper-talked-tough-with-nato-on-arctic-u-s-believed-pm-all-bark-no-bite/ (original cables are reproduced below the article).

[122] See Michael Byers, "Policing the High Seas: The Proliferation Security Initiative." (2004) 98 *American Journal of International Law* 526 at 530 (on bilateral treaties concerning the interdiction of vessels suspected of carrying weapons of mass destruction) and

include Canada's other NATO partners as well as other allies of both Canada and the United States, such as South Korea, Japan, and the two major shipping registries of Liberia and Panama. Obviously, US support for such an approach would be essential.

Parallel to this, the United States and Russia could usefully negotiate a bilateral treaty with respect to the Northern Sea Route; a treaty which could also then be multilateralized through a process of replication with other countries. Alternatively, and more ambitiously, Canada, the United States and Russia might wish to open negotiations on a trilateral treaty on Arctic straits, a treaty that might also usefully address the Bering Strait between Alaska and the Russian Far East.

6 Bering Strait

Severe storms and frigid temperatures in combination with fog, ice, and remoteness make the Bering Strait a challenging location for navigators. Yet the Bering Strait is becoming an important shipping route because it connects the Pacific Ocean to both the Northwest Passage and the Northern Sea Route. The waterway has long been of strategic interest to Russia and the United States because of their close geographic proximity at that location. At the narrowest point, only forty-five nautical miles separate the mainland coasts of the two countries, with less than three nautical miles separating two islands in the middle of the strait: Big Diomede (Russia) and Little Diomede (United States).

Both Russia and the United States accept that the Bering Strait is an international strait through which foreign vessels may pass without their permission. The two coastal states already cooperate on search and rescue and the provision of aids to navigation, and are likely to increase that cooperation. According to a confidential US diplomatic cable released by WikiLeaks, the Russian Ministry of Foreign Affairs approached the US Embassy in Moscow in April 2009, "to request cooperation on a wide range of long-stalled Bering Strait initiatives, including nature protection, oil and gas exploration, and sea shipping and transport."[123]

538–540 (on bilateral treaties concerning the interdiction of vessels suspected of smuggling drugs).

[123] State Department reference # VZCZCXRO2637. Sent May 26, 2009, available at http://wikileaks.ch/cable/2009/05/09MOSCOW1346.html.

In the same cable, the US Embassy discussed the often-contradictory public statements on Arctic policy made by different Russian officials, and provided the following advice to the State Department:

The statements of the MFA [Ministry of Foreign Affairs] and President Medvedev indicate that moderates have focused on the Arctic as a zone of cooperation. Our continued support of the Arctic Council and bilateral engagement on the Arctic (included in the proposed U.S.–Russia Action Plan), can help bolster the moderates and give incentives to the GOR [Government of Russia] to continue cooperation. Increased scientific cooperation, particularly on climate change, could increase trust and build confidence. Under the framework of either multilateral or bilateral cooperation, we can also offer to jointly develop navigation aids and port facilities, continue developing and sharing sea current and meteorological data, promote social development for indigenous peoples, and cooperate on emergency response and oil spill remediation – all tasks that Medvedev charged the GOR with in his September 17, 2008 remarks, but will be difficult to fulfill without outside expertise.[124]

Exactly two years later, on the margins of a G8 summit in Deauville, France, Presidents Obama and Medvedev released a joint statement on cooperation in the Bering Strait region. The statement did not address shipping issues but instead focused on environmental cooperation, namely, "the expansion of interaction between the national agencies that are responsible for the specially protected natural territories/areas of both countries in the State of Alaska and the Chukotka Autonomous District."[125] However, in light of the WikiLeaks cable, it would not be surprising soon to see cooperation in other areas also.

In 1990, as was explained earlier, the United States and the Soviet Union negotiated a 1,600-nautical-mile maritime boundary in the Bering Strait, Bering Sea, and Chukchi Sea.[126] Although the Russian Duma has not yet ratified the treaty, the United States and Russia have agreed to treat it as provisionally binding as per Article 25 of the 1969 Vienna Convention on the Law of Treaties.[127]

[124] Ibid.

[125] US–Russia Statement on Cooperation in Bering Strait Region, May 26, 2011, available at http://iipdigital.usembassy.gov/st/english/texttrans/2011/05/20110526082231su0.7241262.html#axzz1SOGSoeUE.

[126] Agreement between the United States of America and the Union of Soviet Socialist Republics on the Maritime Boundary (1990) 29 ILM 941, available at www.state.gov/documents/organization/125431.pdf. See discussion, Chapter 2, above.

[127] Article 25 reads, in part: "A treaty or a part of a treaty is applied provisionally pending its entry into force if: the treaty itself so provides; or the negotiating States have in some other manner so agreed." 1969 Vienna Convention on the Law of Treaties,

Even if the boundary treaty were to unravel, the legal situation in the Bering Strait itself would remain unchanged. The opposition within Russia to the treaty concerns the location of the boundary in the Bering Sea a significant distance south of the Bering Strait. There is no disagreement as to the location of the boundary in the strait itself, including where it passes through the narrow and shallow channel between Big Diomede and Little Diomede. As a result of those islands, and the fact that they are each less than twenty-four nautical miles from the coastline on their side, any foreign vessels wishing to make the transit must pass through the territorial waters of either Russia or the United States. Again, they are entitled to do so because the waterway is accepted, by both coastal states, to be an international strait on both sides of the Diomedes. However, the status of the waterway also means that there are no shipping lane restrictions, or notification or pilotage requirements. Given the increase in ship traffic in this remote and often risky waterway, Russia and the United States would be well advised collaboratively to seek the approval of the International Maritime Organization for such measures – a process that is described in more detail in Chapter 6.

7 Unimak Pass

Since the Earth is a sphere, the shortest shipping route from the northwest United States and western Canada to China, Japan, and South Korea passes through Alaska's Aleutian Islands chain at a narrow strait called Unimak Pass.[128] Unimak Pass is just nine nautical miles wide. More than 5,000 ships already use it each year, many of them large container and bulk-cargo vessels.[129]

The tidal mixing of cold nutrient-rich waters in and around Unimak Pass supports a wealth of plankton, the basis of a rich food chain.[130] The area is part of the Alaska Maritime National Wildlife Refuge, which is home to 40 million seabirds. It is also home to an abundance of marine mammals, including endangered Steller sea lions, northern fur seals,

available at http://untreaty.un.org/ilc/texts/instruments/english/conventions/ 1_1_1969.pdf.

[128] See the map at www.nap.edu/openbook.php?record_id=12443&page=58.

[129] For the 2006-2007 numbers and a breakdown of vessel types, see *Risk of Vessel Accidents and Spills in the Aleutian Islands: Designing a Comprehensive Risk Assessment – Special Report 293* (Washington, DC: National Academies Press, 2009), 73-77, available at www.nap.edu/ catalog.php?record_id=12443.

[130] Ibid., pp. 59-63.

sea otters and a variety of whale species. This ecosystem has considerable economic value. The Bering Sea just north of Unimak Pass supports the largest commercial fishery in the United States, worth $2 billion annually.[131]

Severe weather and sea conditions are common in Unimak Pass, along with powerful tidal flows. In December 2004, the *Selendang Ayu*, a 225-meter-long Malaysian cargo ship, had just cleared the pass when it lost power in a storm.[132] The vessel was blown aground and broke apart, spilling 1.2 million liters of fuel oil. Almost none of the oil was recovered due to the remote location, bad weather, and the near-complete absence of oil spill clean-up equipment and personnel in the Aleutians. Complicating matters, the United States has long accepted that Unimak Pass is an international strait that foreign vessels can enter without permission or regulatory restriction.[133] As a result, there are also no shipping lanes, or notification or pilotage requirements.

Two decades after the *Exxon Valdez* spilled more than 80 million liters of oil into Prince William Sound,[134] a new threat looms over Unimak Pass – in the form of heavy oil exports from Canada to China. Two pipeline companies plan to dilute tar-like bitumen from Alberta with natural gas condensate so that it can be pumped west to the coast of British Columbia and shipped onward in tankers.[135] In 2012, US Coast Guard Commandant Robert Papp described Unimak Pass as a "key choke point" when explaining the United States' marine-security challenges to a Senate sub-committee: "There are literally thousands of ships that transit through there, carrying fuel and other things that were at risk for environmental disasters, sinkings and other things."[136]

---

[131] Ibid., p. 62.   [132] Ibid., p. 81.

[133] See *Annotated Supplement to the Commander's Handbook on the Law of Naval Operations* (Naval War College: Newport, Rhode Island, 1997), p. 2-86, Table A2-5, available at www.scribd.com/doc/36391405/US-Navy-Commander-s-Handbook-Annotated-Supplement-1997.

[134] See Art Davidson, *In the Wake of the Exxon Valdez* (San Francisco, Calif.: Sierra Club Books, 1990); Lila Guterman, "Exxon Valdez Turns 20" (March 20, 2009) 323(5921) *Science* 1558.

[135] See Jane Stevenson, "Enbridge Pushes Oil Tanker Safety Strategy," March 18, 2010, TheTyee.ca, available at http://thetyee.ca/News/2010/03/18/TankerSafety/; Mitchell Anderson, "Kinder Morgan's Grand Plan to Pipe Oil Sands Crude," June 2, 2011, TheTyee.ca, available at http://thetyee.ca/News/2011/06/02/KinderMorganGrandPlan/.

[136] US Coast Guard Commandant Robert Papp, Testimony before Senate Appropriations Subcommittee on Homeland Security, May 9, 2012, available at www.c-spanvideo.org/program/299429-1.

There are a few actions the US government could take. It could station a large rescue tug and several oil spill clean-up vessels at nearby Dutch Harbor. It could ask the International Maritime Organization to designate Unimak Pass as a "particularly sensitive sea area," which would enable the United States to require advance notification of passage and adherence to vessel traffic separation rules.[137] It could seek to persuade shipping companies voluntarily to route oil tankers south of the Aleutians, though this would increase both distance and cost. In the end, however, none of these steps is likely to prevent hundreds of oil tankers from transiting Unimak Pass each year. A more meaningful step would be for the United States to rethink its position on international straits, where historically it has pressed for maximum freedom of navigation, and to work with countries such as Canada and Russia to strengthen multilateral standards and coastal state powers.[138]

8 Nares Strait

Nares Strait is the narrow channel separating Greenland from Canada's Ellesmere Island and connecting Baffin Bay to the Lincoln Sea. It is also where the only contested land territory in the Arctic is located, in the form of tiny Hans Island.[139]

Nares Strait is more than 300 nautical miles long and at some points just twelve nautical miles wide. Substantial stretches therefore fall entirely within the territorial seas of either Denmark or Canada, with the delimitation between those zones (and beyond that the continental shelf) having been set by treaty in 1973.[140] Nares Strait is also relatively deep, with the shallowest stretch in the western Kane Basin providing 200 meters below a ship's keel. However, Nares Strait is an inhospitable place for surface vessels. In the winter and spring it is frozen solid; in the summer and fall it is populated by sea-ice flushed down from the Arctic Ocean and icebergs calved off the Petermann and Humboldt Glaciers on Greenland. Still, in recent years at least one and possibly more ice-breakers have penetrated Nares Strait from end to end.[141]

---

[137] See discussion, below, pp. 163–165.   [138] See discussion, below, pp. 163–167.
[139] For more on Hans Island, see Chapter 1, above.
[140] For more on the 1973 Canada–Denmark boundary treaty, see Chapter 2, above.
[141] The Greenpeace icebreaker *Arctic Sunrise* reportedly made the voyage in 2009. See Patrick Barkham, "The Sermilik Fjord in Greenland: A Chilling View of a Warming World," *Guardian*, September 1, 2009, available at www.guardian.co.uk/environment/2009/sep/01/sermilik-fjord-greenland-global-warming.

Canada and Denmark both take the view that Nares Strait is neither an international strait nor internal waters, but, because it passes through their territorial seas, they do accept that a right of "innocent passage" exists.[142] This view is evident from a treaty the two countries concluded in 1983 with respect to marine environment protection between Canada and Greenland.[143] The treaty fails to make any mention of an international strait. It also distinguishes between coastal state powers within and outside the territorial sea, and clearly assumes that each country has full powers to impose "vessel traffic management or ship reporting services" within its territorial sea.[144]

The United States almost certainly takes the position that Nares Strait is an international strait, since US Navy lawyers argue that the "used for international navigation" criterion for international straits is either non-existent or can be applied prospectively.[145] Moreover, submarines may sail submerged in international straits but not regular territorial waters, and US submarines often and sometimes overtly use Nares Strait. Submariners, who normally prefer to remain underwater for security reasons, would usually have no choice but to do so in Nares Strait because of the sea-ice and icebergs.

Nares Strait is unlikely ever to become an important shipping route. It does not offer the time- and distance-saving of the Northwest Passage for voyages between the Bering Strait and eastern North America, nor of Fram Strait on the east coast of Greenland for voyages between the

---

[142] The legal regime of innocent passage is set out in Articles 17–26 of UNCLOS, Chapter 4, n. 12, above. Essentially, foreign ships have a right of passage, provided that they do not threaten the security of the coastal state and that they abide by its laws concerning the safety of navigation, the preservation of the environment, the prevention of infringement of its customs, fiscal, immigration, or sanitary laws, etc.

[143] 1983 Agreement for Cooperation Relating to the Marine Environment (1984) 23(2) ILM 269, available at http://treaties.un.org/doc/Publication/UNTS/Volume%201348/volume-1348-I-22693-English.pdf.

[144] Ibid. Article 7 reads, in part: "1. The Parties shall cooperate and assist each other in their respective vessel traffic management or ship reporting services in relation to ships navigating in the area covered by this Agreement. 2. (i) The Parties shall cooperate in identifying, monitoring and reviewing as necessary appropriate routing areas for vessels in the area covered by this Agreement outside territorial waters with a view to avoiding harmful effects to the marine environment and to the economic and social conditions in the area covered by this Agreement."

[145] See discussion, above, p. 137. James C. Kraska of the US Naval War College has expressed the unusual view that Nares Strait is one of the routes of the Northwest Passage. Kraska, "The New Arctic Geography and US Strategy," in James C. Kraska (ed.), *Arctic Security in an Age of Climate Change* (New York: Cambridge University Press, 2011), 244 at 260.

Bering Strait and Europe. However, as the sea-ice melts it may be frequented by cruise ships and possibly fishing and oil exploration vessels en route to the central Arctic Ocean. If so, the status of the waterway might begin to matter, as Canada and Greenland seek to regulate access for environmental protection, safety, and national security purposes.

9 Multilateral mechanisms available to "strait states"

Alternatively, Canada and Russia could abandon their internal waters positions in the Northwest Passage and Northern Sea Route, in favor of the opportunities available to coastal states under international law to protect their interests in international straits. For instance, Article 39 of UNCLOS requires ships engaged in "transit passage" to "proceed without delay," "refrain from any threat or use of force against the sovereignty, territorial integrity or political independence of States bordering the strait" as well as "any activities other than those incidental to their normal modes of continuous and expeditious transit." It also requires such vessels to "comply with generally accepted international regulations, procedures and practices for safety at sea" as well as "generally accepted international regulations, procedures and practices for the prevention, reduction and control of pollution from ships."[146]

Article 40 of UNCLOS prohibits "any research or survey activities" in an international strait without the prior authorization of the coastal state or states. Article 41 foresees that a coastal state "may designate sea lanes and prescribe traffic separation schemes for navigation" in an international strait in concert with the "competent international organization," namely, the International Maritime Organization. Article 42 specifies that states bordering an international strait may regulate "the safety of navigation and the regulation of maritime traffic" as well as "the prevention, reduction and control of pollution, by giving effect to applicable international regulations regarding the discharge of oil, oily wastes and other noxious substances in the strait." According to Article 42, coastal states may also prohibit fishing as well as the "loading or unloading of any commodity, currency or person," provided that such laws and regulations do "not discriminate in form or in fact among

---

[146] Chapter 4, n. 12, above.

foreign ships or in their application have the practical effect of denying, hampering or impairing the right of transit passage."[147]

However, coastal states are extremely limited in the enforcement measures they may take in international straits to back up these regulatory powers. As Mary George observes, "it would be difficult for a strait State to give effect to the laws and regulations adopted under article 42(1) without infringing the limitations in article 42(2) against 'hampering or impairing the right of transit passage.'"[148] Stuart Kaye similarly concludes: "Coastal State rights applicable to transiting vessels are very limited."[149]

As was explained above, coastal states do have enhanced pollution prevention powers in ice-covered waters under Article 234 of UNCLOS:

Coastal States have the right to adopt and enforce non-discriminatory laws and regulations for the prevention, reduction and control of marine pollution from vessels in ice-covered areas within the limits of the exclusive economic zone, where particularly severe climatic conditions and the presence of ice covering such areas for most of the year create obstructions or exceptional hazards to navigation, and pollution of the marine environment could cause major harm to or irreversible disturbance of the ecological balance. Such laws and regulations shall have due regard to navigation and the protection and preservation of the marine environment based on the best available scientific evidence.[150]

The negotiation of Article 234 was prompted by Canada's adoption of the 1970 Arctic Waters Pollution Prevention Act.[151] However, it is unclear whether the provision would allow Canada or Russia to interdict noncompliant vessels in an international strait, at least until a pollution incident occurs. Hugh Caminos' analysis of the application of Article 233 (a provision which allows for a more limited degree of

---

[147] Ibid.

[148] Mary George, "The Regulation of Maritime Traffic in Straits Used for International Navigation," in Alex G. Oude Elferink and Donald R. Rothwell (eds.), Oceans Management in the 21st Century: Institutional Frameworks and Responses (Leiden: Martinus Nijhoff, 2004), 24.

[149] Stuart Kaye, "Regulation of Navigation in the Torres Strait: Law of the Sea Issues," in Donald R. Rothwell and Sam Bateman (eds.), Navigation Rights and Freedoms and the New Law of the Sea (Dordrecht: Kluwer, 2000), 119 at 123.

[150] Article 38, UNCLOS, Chapter 4, n. 12, above.

[151] Arctic Waters Pollution Prevention Act, n. 104, above, sec. 2. For a detailed account of the legal and diplomatic history, see Justin DeMowbray Nankivell, "Arctic Legal Tides: The Politics of International Law in the Northwest Passage," Ph.D. thesis, University of British Columbia, 2010, available at https://circle.ubc.ca/bitstream/handle/2429/26642/ubc_2010_fall_nankivell_justin.pdf?sequence=1.

pollution prevention jurisdiction in non-ice covered waters) to international straits illustrates the seriousness of the issue:

In order for a State bordering a strait to take any enforcement measures under Article 233, there must first be a direct nexus between the transiting vessels' violation of Article 42(1)(a) or (b), and the resulting major damage to the marine environment of the strait in question. The mere fact a State's laws and regulations enacted pursuant to Article 42 have been breached, does not ipso facto entitle that State to act under Article 233. If actual damage to the marine environment has already resulted, and it can be linked to a vessel's illegal actions, then the "States bordering the straits may take appropriate enforcement measures."[152]

It may also be questioned whether Article 234 will continue to apply to previously ice-covered waters as they become progressively ice-free. There is nothing in Article 234 to suggest that waters that are subject to greater pollution prevention jurisdiction, because they are covered with ice for most of the year, retain that status if and when the ice disappears for lengthy periods. The rights accorded under Article 234 are not vested in any particular maritime area on an indeterminable basis but flow from the character of the ocean's surface there.

As mentioned above, coastal states may request the International Maritime Organization to designate all or part of an international strait as a "Particularly Sensitive Sea Area," as Australia successfully did with Torres Strait in 2005.[153] However, it is unclear whether they acquire any new rights as a result. When Australia subsequently adopted a compulsory pilotage scheme, it was protested by the United States and Singapore as impermissible in an international strait.[154] Notwithstanding the protests, however, the adoption of compulsory pilotage has led to a 100 percent compliance rate, as compared to the previous rate of less than 50 percent under a voluntary scheme.[155] This suggests that an IMO designation is worth seeking.

---

[152] Hugo Caminos, "The Legal Régime of Straits in the 1982 United Nations Convention on the Law of the Sea." (1987) 205 *Recueil des cours* 128 at 172.

[153] "Designation of the Torres Strait as an Extension of the Great Barrier Reef Particularly Sensitive Sea Area," IMO Doc. MEPC 53/24/Add. 2, Annex 21, July 22, 2005, available at www.amsa.gov.au/marine_environment_protection/torres_strait/133-53.pdf.

[154] See Robert C. Beckman, "PSSAs and Transit Passage – Australia's Pilotage System in the Torres Strait Challenges the IMO and UNCLOS." (2007) 38 *Ocean Development and International Law* 325 at 326.

[155] See Sam Bateman and Michael White, "Compulsory Pilotage in the Torres Strait: Overcoming Unacceptable Risks to a Sensitive Marine Environment." (2009) 40 *Ocean Development and International Law* 184 at 191.

Nor would it seem necessary for Canada and Russia to concede their internal waters positions in order to seek International Maritime Organization designations of "Particularly Sensitive Sea Areas" and thus the Organization's approval for mandatory ship registration schemes, shipping lanes, and pilotage. Such designations might not determine the legality of the regulatory measures, but would at a minimum provide greater legitimacy for them. The designations could even be sought, and might well be granted, with the explicit acknowledgment that they are without prejudice to the legal disputes.

In 2010, Canada made mandatory its previously voluntary Arctic shipping registration system (NORDREG) without first engaging the International Maritime Organization.[156] Concerns were subsequently expressed within that organization, most of which focused on the lack of consultation that preceded the move to a mandatory system.[157] However, as McDorman points out: "The wording and negotiating history of Article 234 strongly supports the view that review or pre-approval by the IMO is not required for a measure that fits the wording of Article 234 and that a coastal State may rely on Article 234 for unilateral action involving standards and measures more stringent than the existing internationally accepted rules."[158]

It would also facilitate environmental protection and dispute resolution in all the Arctic straits if the IMO's 2009 "Guidelines on Ships Operating in Polar Waters" were made mandatory, as was originally intended.[159] Indeed, the Arctic Council has twice – in 2009 and 2011 – called for the IMO to transform the guidelines into a legally binding

---

[156] The new regulations (available at http://laws-lois.justice.gc.ca/eng/regulations/SOR-2010-127/page-1.html) came into force in 2010. See Ted L. McDorman, "National Measures for the Safety of Navigation in Arctic Waters: NORDREG, Article 234 and Canada," in Myron H. Nordquist, et al., The Law of the Sea Convention: US Accession and Globalization (Leiden: Martinus Nijhoff, 2012), 409.

[157] Singapore, for example, stated that "it is not apparent how the mandatory ship reporting and VTS system established under NORDREG ties in with the fundamental purpose of Article 234 of UNCLOS . . . which is to allow for the prevention, reduction and control of marine pollution. The need for such a mandatory system should be supported by best available evidence." Singapore, "Statement to MSC," in Annex 28 of IMO, "Report of the Maritime Safety Committee in its Eighty-Eighth Session," IMO Doc. MSC/88/26, December 15, 2010, para. 11.36.

[158] McDorman, "National Measures for the Safety of Navigation in Arctic Waters," n. 156, above.

[159] Guidelines for Ships Operating in Polar Waters, December 2, 2009, available at www.imo.org/blast/blastDataHelper.asp?data_id=29985&filename=A1024(26).pdf.

"Polar Code."[160] This would eliminate some of the disparities between the relatively clear and strict rules applied by Canada and Russia in the Northwest Passage and Northern Sea Route, and more ambiguous standards of international law such as Arctic 234. This, in turn, might make it easier for the United States and other countries to accept Canada's and Russia's legal positions.

10 Submarine voyages

Soviet submarines entered the Northwest Passage without permission during the Cold War.[161] However, they never threatened Canada's legal position there, because the whole purpose of submarines is to remain covert and only overt actions can undermine or create rights under international law.[162] Likewise, any NATO submarines that might have sailed through the straits north of the Soviet Union would have done so without any legal consequence for that country's claims.

The United States has not been so secretive with respect to its use of the Northwest Passage and, especially, Nares Strait. We know the USS *Seadragon* was the first American submarine to sail the Northwest Passage from east to west in 1960.[163] We also know the USS *Skate* sailed through Nares Strait from the Atlantic to the Arctic Ocean in 1962.[164] The USS *Hammerhead* sailed through the same waterway in 1970,[165] as did the

---

[160] See Tromso Declaration (2009) and Nuuk Declaration (2011), both available at www.arctic-council.org/index.php/en/about/documents/category/5-declarations; and discussion, Chapter 6, below.

[161] Bob Weber, "Soviet Subs Cruised Canadian Arctic Maps Suggest," *Canadian Press*, December 6, 2011, available at www.thestar.com/news/canada/article/1097530–soviet-subs-cruised-canadian-arctic-maps-suggest.

[162] See Anthony D'Amato, *The Concept of Custom in International Law* (Ithaca, NY: Cornell University Press, 1971), 469, where the author writes, with respect to the widespread use of torture by states, that the "objective evidence shows hiding, cover-up, minimization, and non-justification – all the things that betoken a violation of the law."

[163] Alfred S. McLaren, *Unknown Waters: A First-Hand Account of the Historic Under-Ice Survey of the Siberian Continental Shelf by USS Queenfish* (Tuscaloosa, Ala.: University of Alabama Press, 2008), 19. See also Donat Pharand and Leonard Legault, *The Northwest Passage: Arctic Straits* (Dordrecht: Martinus Nijhoff, 1984), 148.

[164] McLaren, *Unknown Waters*, p. 20. Pharand and Legault report on the return trip through the Northwest Passage but not the outbound trip through Nares Strait. See Pharand and Legault, *The Northwest Passage*, 148.

[165] Alfred S. McLaren, "The Evolution and Potential of the Arctic Submarine." (1985) 2 *POAC Conference Proceedings* (Danish Hydraulic Institute) 848 at 854, available at www.poac.com/Papers/POAC85_V2_all.pdf.

USS *Archerfish* in 1979.[166] Numerous other transits also likely occurred: in November 2005, the USS *Charlotte* surfaced at the North Pole, before submerging and heading to Halifax, Nova Scotia, for a port visit.[167] Although the US Navy would not give journalists details about the vessel's route, the shortest course would have been through Nares Strait.

In February 2009, the *Los Angeles Times* reported on Ice Exercise 2009, a classified mission described by the US Navy as the "testing of submarine operability and war-fighting capability" in the Arctic Ocean. Both the USS *Helena* and USS *Annapolis* were heading north to test their communications equipment in the waters around and below a research station on the sea-ice some 160 nautical miles north of Prudhoe Bay, Alaska. According to the report, the *Helena* had sailed from its homeport of San Diego. Although it was not clear when the other submarine had departed for the Arctic, the *Annapolis* is based in Groton, Connecticut, and the two shortest routes from there are through the Northwest Passage or Nares Strait. In March 2011, the USS *New Hampshire*, which is also based in Groton, participated in Ice Exercise 2011 in the same area north of Prudhoe Bay.[168]

What is not clear in these cases is whether Canada's permission had been sought and granted. Publicly, Canada has chosen to ignore the issue of submarine transits, and total ignorance would work in Canada's favor, again, because covert actions cannot make or change international law. However, it seems likely that Canada, a military ally of the United States in both NATO and NORAD, has known about at least some of the submarine activity and simply kept quiet. Such a combination of knowledge and passive acquiescence could prove fatal to Canada's legal position, were evidence of it made public, since this would establish actual nonconsensual usage of the Northwest Passage by international shipping.

It is just as likely that the US submarine traffic takes place with Canada's consent. In 1995, then Defence Minister David Collenette was asked in the House of Commons about submarines in the

---

[166] See "Research Guide to Submarine Arctic Operations," chap. 12, "US Submarine Arctic Operations – Historical Timeline," available at www.navsource.org/archives/08/pdf/08046001.pdf.

[167] "US Sub May Have Toured Canadian Arctic Zone," *National Post*, December 19, 2005, available at www.canada.com/nationalpost/story.html?id=fb21432a-1d28-415e-b323-ceb22d477732andk=69493.

[168] "Navy Announces ICEX 2011 Subs," *Navy News*, March 18, 2011, available at www.military.com/news/article/navy-news/navy-announces-icex-2011-subs.html.

Northwest Passage. He replied: "I believe we have a novel diplomatic arrangement with the United States under which they inform us of activities of their nuclear submarines under the ice, which enables us to at least say they are doing it with our acquiescence."[169] When an opposition Member of Parliament sought to verify the statement, Collenette corrected himself:

> There is no formal agreement covering the passage of any nation's submarines through Canadian Arctic waters. However, as a country that operates submarines, Canada does receive information on submarine activities from our Allies. This information is exchanged for operational and safety reasons with the emphasis on minimizing interference and the possibility of collisions between submerged submarines.[170]

A decade later, another defence minister referred to the arrangement as a "protocol." Bill Graham assured the *Globe and Mail* that the United States "would have told us" before any of their submarines transited Canadian waters.[171]

If a bilateral agreement on submarine voyages exists, it is likely modeled on the 1988 Arctic Cooperation Agreement, which specifies that voyages by US Coast Guard icebreakers are "without prejudice" to either country's legal claim.[172] If there is no such agreement, however, and if Canada is told about the voyages without being asked for permission, that combination of knowledge and acquiescence would undermine its legal position – if and when the situation was ever made public. Yet the issue of submarine voyages remains off the table, legally speaking, as long as both Canada and the United States continue to treat these activities as officially secret.

11 Summary

The United States take the view that both the Northern Sea Route and the Northwest Passage are "international straits" through which foreign vessels may pass without permission or much in the way of regulatory restraint. Russia and Canada take the opposite view: that the straits

---

[169] Terry Fenge, Letter to the Editor ("Submarines and Arctic Sovereignty"), *Globe and Mail*, February 10, 1996.
[170] Ibid.
[171] Jane Taber, "Harper Breaks Ice on Arctic Sovereignty," *Globe and Mail*, December 23, 2005.
[172] See discussion, above, pp. 139–140.

along their northern coastlines constitute "internal waters" where permission is always required and the full force of domestic law applies.

The rapid melting of Arctic sea-ice should prompt the United States to rethink its legal position on both waterways. The possibility that hundreds or even thousands of foreign ships could soon be sailing through the Canadian Arctic each year poses a challenge to US national security that can only adequately be addressed through coastal state powers which only Canada is operationally positioned to exercise. On the other side of the Arctic Ocean, Russia has deterred any direct challenge to its legal position in the Northern Sea Route and will continue to do so, meaning that the United States cannot hope to prevail there. It is also significant that the United States is itself becoming a "strait state" in both the Bering Strait and Unimak Pass, with all the security, environmental, and jurisdictional challenges that this entails. For all these reasons, negotiations are called for, with a view to concluding treaties on the various Arctic straits that address the unique challenges of the region and – by taking the straits out of the realm of customary international law – assuage US concerns about creating new precedents.

6 Environmental protection

One summer's day off Beechey Island, in Canada's High Arctic, I witnessed an awe-inspiring "feeding frenzy." The water was thick with life as millions of centimeter-long sea butterflies (a free-swimming mollusk that feeds on plankton) were forced to the surface by an enormous school of juvenile Arctic cod. A noisy assemblage of gulls, terns, fulmars, and other seabirds were feasting, along with a visibly joyous group of harp seals. A pod of beluga whales cruised by, their backs gently breaking the surface as they also fed. A young polar bear patiently watched the action from the shore; his fast would end when the sea-ice returned in the fall.

Most of the biomass in the Arctic exists in the ocean, which is why the potential for oil spills is of such great concern, and all the more so because oil degrades and disperses very slowly in cold water. Climate change, which is more apparent in the Arctic than anywhere else on Earth, is already imposing enormous stress on the region's highly specialized ecosystems. But while climate change and oil spills are the focus of environmental protection efforts in the Arctic today, one example of environmental cooperation pre-dates these concerns by more than a century.

1 Species protection

1.1 Northern fur seals

As a result of the Alaska Cession Convention of 1867,[1] the United States obtained sovereignty over the Pribilof Islands, which are four volcanic islands located about 180 nautical miles north of the Aleutian Islands

---

[1] Treaty concerning the Cession of the Russian Possessions in North America, Chapter 2, n. 21, above.

chain. The islands are the principal breeding ground of the northern fur seal, the pelts of which were in great demand. Foreign hunters, mostly Canadians, would wait beyond the three-nautical-mile territorial limit and kill the seals as they crossed onto the high seas. This practice of "pelagic sealing" (i.e., killing seals on the high seas) was decimating the population.

Between 1868 and 1873, the United States adopted several laws prohibiting the killing of seals on the Pribilof Islands and in adjoining waters.[2] The US Coast Guard began rigorously enforcing the ban in 1886, and it did so out to sixty nautical miles from shore, well beyond the territorial sea. Three "British" sealing vessels were arrested: "British" because the United Kingdom then still represented Canada in all matters of international affairs, including ship registration. The United Kingdom and the United States agreed to send the matter to arbitration and in 1893 the tribunal found in favor of the United Kingdom – while recommending that both states prohibit their nationals from engaging in pelagic sealing within sixty nautical miles of the Pribilof Islands.[3]

The arbitral decision led to one of the first international treaties aimed at conserving wildlife: the 1911 Convention Respecting Measures for the Preservation and Protection of Fur Seals in the North Pacific Ocean was concluded between the United States, Britain (on behalf of Canada), Japan, and Russia.[4] A successor treaty was adopted in 1957 but lapsed in 1984 when the US Senate failed to provide its "advice and consent" for the ratification of a protocol extending that treaty's application.[5] Fortunately, there is currently no market for northern fur seal pelts and the remaining population is unthreatened by hunting.

1.2 Polar bears

The iconic polar bear, which weighs up to 700 kilograms and stands more than three meters tall on its hind legs, is generally considered to

---

[2] See, generally, James Thomas Gay, *American Fur Seal Diplomacy: The Alaskan Fur Seal Controversy* (New York: Peter Lang, 1987); Natalia S. Mirovitskaya, Margaret Clark, and Ronald G. Purver, "North Pacific Fur Seals: Regime Formation as a Means of Resolving Conflict," in Oran Young and Gail Osherenko, *Polar Politics: Creating International Environmental Regimes* (Ithaca, NY: Cornell University Press, 1993), 22.

[3] *Bering Sea Fur Seals Arbitration* (1893) 1 *Moore International Arbitrations* 755, available at http://archive.org/details/fursealarbitrati03ber.

[4] 1911 Convention Respecting Measures for the Preservation and Protection of Fur Seals in the North Pacific Ocean, 214 *Canada Treaty Series* 80, available at http://archive.org/details/fursealsconventi00unit.

[5] 1957 Interim Convention on Conservation of North Pacific Fur Seals, 314 UNTS 105, available at http://sedac.ciesin.org/entri/texts/acrc/1957FS.txt.html.

be the world's largest land carnivore.[6] However, the polar bear's scientific name, *Ursus maritimus*, reflects the fact that it has evolved specifically to hunt on the frozen sea. Polar bears are found on the ice over the biologically productive shallow waters of northern Canada, Greenland, Norway, Russia, and Alaska. The pan-Arctic population of around 20,000–25,000 bears is divided into nineteen sub-populations, several of which are transboundary in nature, making their management and conservation a matter of international concern.[7]

In the mid-twentieth century, the use of icebreakers and aircraft to hunt polar bears led to concerns about the long-term survival of the species. In 1973, Canada, Denmark, Norway, the Soviet Union, and the United States signed the International Agreement on the Conservation of Polar Bears.[8] The so-called "Polar Bear Treaty" commits the five countries to "appropriate action to protect the ecosystems of which polar bears are a part" and to manage populations "in accordance with sound conservation practices based on the best available scientific data."[9] It also prohibits the use of "large motorized vessels" and aircraft for hunting polar bears.[10]

In 2000, the treaty was supplemented by a bilateral agreement between Russia and the United States.[11] The Agreement on the Conservation and Management of the Alaska–Chukotka Polar Bear Population introduced a new prohibition on the taking of "females with cubs, cubs less than one year of age, and bears in dens, including bears preparing to enter dens or who have just left dens."[12] It also established the United States–Russia Polar Bear Commission, made up of two representatives from each country, to determine "on the basis of reliable scientific data, including traditional knowledge of the native people, the polar bear population's annual sustainable harvest level" in the Chukchi, East Siberian, and Bering Seas.[13] Each country then has the right to one-half of the annual quota.

---

[6] See, generally, Ian Stirling, *Polar Bears: The Natural History of a Threatened Species* (Markham, Ont.: Fitzhenry and Whiteside, 2011).

[7] See "Population Status Reviews" on the website of the Polar Bear Specialist Group of the IUCN Species Survival Commission, at http://pbsg.npolar.no/en/status/.

[8] 1973 International Agreement on the Conservation of Polar Bears, available at http://pbsg.npolar.no/en/agreements/agreement1973.html.

[9] Ibid., Art. 2.   [10] Ibid., Art. 4.

[11] 2000 Agreement between the Government of the United States of America and the Government of the Russian Federation on the Conservation and Management of the Alaska–Chukotka Polar Bear Population, available at http://pbsg.npolar.no/en/agreements/US-Russia.html.

[12] Ibid., Art. 6(b).   [13] Ibid., Art. 8.

A similar agreement was also concluded between two indigenous groups: the Inuvialuit of Canada and the Inupiat of the United States.[14] Signed in 1988 and updated in 2000, the Inuvialuit–Inupiat Polar Bear Management Agreement establishes a joint commission made up of Inuvialuit and Inupiat to determine, again on the basis of scientific data, the annual sustainable harvest of polar bears in the southern Beaufort Sea and divide it between the two indigenous groups. Significantly, neither the national nor the state/territorial governments of the United States, Canada, Alaska, Yukon, or Northwest Territories is a signatory to this sub-state agreement – though all have acquiesced to it.

A third agreement was concluded between the governments of Canada, Nunavut, and Greenland in 2009.[15] It too creates a joint commission, made up primarily if not exclusively of Inuit, to make recommendations concerning the total allowable harvesting level of polar bears in Kane Basin and Baffin Bay as well as the allocation of quotas between Nunavut and Greenland. Denmark, while still responsible for Greenland's foreign relations, is not a party to the agreement, presumably because it concerns a natural resource and therefore falls under Greenland's jurisdiction.

Although these conservation agreements are significant, their long-term success is doubtful. Climate change, by lengthening the annual ice-free period, is forcing the bears onshore for increased lengths of time. Although the polar bear has evolved to store fat for extended periods, the longer ice-free summers are already stressing them, affecting their reproductive success and leading to higher mortality in some southern parts of their range.[16] The disappearance of the sea-ice also affects the rest of the ecosystem, including the Arctic cod and therefore the seals on which the bears prey. In 2007, the US Geological Survey predicted a two-thirds decline in the worldwide polar bear population by 2050.[17]

---

[14] 2000 Inuvialuit–Inupiat Polar Bear Management Agreement in the Southern Beaufort Sea, available at http://pbsg.npolar.no/en/agreements/USA-Canada.html.

[15] 2009 Memorandum of Understanding between the Government of Canada, the Government of Nunavut, and the Government of Greenland for the Conservation and Management of Polar Bear Populations, available at http://pbsg.npolar.no/export/sites/pbsg/en/docs/GN-MOU-PB.pdf.

[16] Ian Stirling and Andrew E. Derocher,"Effects of Climate Warming on Polar Bears: A Review of the Evidence." (2012) 18(9) *Global Change Biology* 2694; Ed Struzik, "Climate Change Threatens to Disrupt the Denning Habits of Polar Bears," *Edmonton Journal*, June 23, 2012, available at www.edmontonjournal.com/news/Climate+change+threatens +disrupt+denning+habits+polar/6831844/story.html.

[17] Steven C. Amstrup, *et al.*, "Forecasting the Range-Wide Status of Polar Bears at Selected Times in the 21st Century," US Geological Survey Administrative Report, 2007,

Within Canada, which is home to two-thirds of the world's polar bears, there is tension between scientists and Inuit over the abundance of the species.[18] Scientists claim that polar bear populations are decreasing and require further protection; Inuit claim that polar bear populations are increasing; the scientists respond that hungry bears are more likely to visit communities and therefore be seen by humans.[19]

In 2008, the US government listed the polar bear as a threatened species under the Endangered Species Act and banned the importation of polar bear hides into the United States.[20] The ban had an immediate impact on Inuit communities in Canada, where hunters have profited from selling their quotas to and from guiding American sport hunters. Now, unable to take proof of their kill home, fewer American hunters make the trip north. But hundreds of polar bear hides are still taken and exported each year, mostly to Europe.[21]

In 2010, the US government proposed that the polar bear be moved from Appendix II to Appendix I of the Convention on International Trade in Endangered Species (CITES), a step that would ban commercial trade of the animals worldwide.[22] The Canadian government, influenced by the Inuit view of the bear population, was able to enlist enough other countries to block the US proposal.[23] But the diplomatic struggle over the polar bear is not over: in June 2012, a coalition of environmental organizations and US legislators began pushing for the United States to renew its efforts to secure a CITES ban.[24]

available at www.usgs.gov/newsroom/special/polar_bears/docs/USGS_PolarBear_Amstrup_Forecast_lowres.pdf.

[18] Randy Boswell, "Inuit to Fight US Effort to Ban International Trade in Polar Bear Parts," *Postmedia News*, June 14, 2012, available at www.canada.com/business/Inuit+fight+effort+international+trade+polar+bear+parts/6782983/story.html#ixzz1yiwmbhmq.

[19] See, e.g., Ian Stirling and Claire Parkinson, "Possible Effects of Climate Warming on Selected Populations of Polar Bears (*Ursus maritimus*) in the Canadian Arctic." (2006) 59 *Arctic* 261.

[20] Felicity Barringer, "Polar Bear Is Made a Protected Species," *New York Times*, May 15, 2008, available at www.nytimes.com/2008/05/15/us/15polar.html.

[21] "CITES Turns Down Protections for Polar Bear, Bluefin Tuna," *Environmental News Service*, March 18, 2010, available at www.ens-newswire.com/ens/mar2010/2010-03-18-02.html.

[22] 1973 Convention on International Trade in Endangered Species of Wild Fauna and Flora, available at www.cites.org/.

[23] "CITES Turns Down Protections for Polar Bear, Bluefin Tuna," n. 21, above.

[24] Boswell, "Inuit to Fight US Effort," n. 18, above.

1.3 Whales

Bowhead whales are the largest of the purely Arctic or subarctic animals, growing to more than twenty meters in length and 130 tonnes in weight. Despite their bulk, bowheads eat some of the smallest animals in the Arctic: tiny crustaceans called "copepods" that the whales strain from the water column using sieve-like baleen plates. In some parts of the Arctic, the Inuit and before them the Thule relied on these gentle giants as a source of meat, blubber, and whalebone rafters for sod-covered winter homes. In the late nineteenth and early twentieth centuries, the slaughter of many thousands of bowheads by European and American whalers drove the species to the brink of extinction, with only 3,000 individuals estimated to have been alive in the 1920s.[25]

In 1946, the International Convention for the Regulation of Whaling was adopted. The Convention aimed "to provide for the proper conservation of whale stocks and thus make possible the orderly development of the whaling industry."[26] It also established the International Whaling Commission (IWC), which in 1982 adopted an indefinite moratorium on commercial whaling.

The success of the Convention and Commission is undeniable: today, more than 10,000 bowheads are found around the circumpolar Arctic. But several countries, notably Japan, Iceland, and Norway, oppose the moratorium, emphasizing that the Convention's goal was, again, to "make possible the orderly development of the whaling industry."[27] They question whether the scientific evidence supports a ban on the taking of all whale species and therefore permits a limited hunt – which Japan justifies as scientific research under Article 8(1) of the Convention, and which Iceland and Norway conduct by taking advantage of a mechanism, set out in Article 5, whereby states can exempt themselves from decisions taken by the Commission.[28]

Other countries operate entirely outside the IWC regime. The most significant of these is Canada, which banned commercial whaling in 1972 but withdrew from the Commission in 1982. It then guaranteed aboriginal whaling rights under land claims agreements with the

---

[25] NOAA Fisheries Service, Office of Protected Resources, "Bowhead Whale (*Balaena mysticetus*)," available at www.nmfs.noaa.gov/pr/species/mammals/cetaceans/bowheadwhale.htm.

[26] 1946 International Convention for the Regulation of Whaling, 161 UNTS 72, available at www.iwcoffice.org/cache/downloads/1r2jdhu5xtuswws0ocw04wgcw/convention.pdf.

[27] Ibid.   [28] Ibid.

Inuvialuit in 1984 and Inuit in 1993.[29] The IWC[30] and US President Bill Clinton condemned Canada's actions, with the latter writing:

Canada's conduct jeopardizes the international effort that has allowed whale stocks to begin to recover from the devastating effects of historic whaling ... International law, as reflected in the 1982 United Nations Convention on the Law of the Sea, obligates countries to work through the appropriate international organization for the conservation and management of whales. Canada has conducted whaling activities that diminish the effectiveness of a conservation program of the International Whaling Commission.[31]

The Clinton administration certified Canada under the Pelly Amendment, a provision of the Fishermen's Protection Act that grants the president the power to impose trade sanctions on the fisheries of any country that undermines the IWC whaling regime.[32] However, Clinton ultimately imposed no sanctions, apart from directing that no consideration be given to Canada's request for an exemption from a US trade ban on seal products.[33]

In recent years, the IWC has accepted a limited amount of "subsistence" whaling by the Inupiat of Alaska and Inuit of Greenland, and granted bowhead quotas for that purpose. This raises the question as to whether Canada should re-join the IWC regime.[34] At the same time, climate change is bringing new uncertainty to the future of the bowhead whale and other Arctic species such as the beluga and narwhal. As the ice melts, killer whales are moving north in significantly increased numbers, preying on other whales and seals that were previously able to hide in the narrow leads between ice floes.[35]

---

[29] See 1984 Inuvialuit Final Agreement (as amended), sec. 14(6), available at. www.daair. gov.nt.ca/_live/documents/documentManagerUpload/InuvialuitFinalAgreement1984. pdf; 1993 Nunavut Land Claims Agreement, sec. 5.6.1, available at http://nlca. tunngavik.com/.

[30] See, e.g., IWC Resolution 2000–2002 (Resolution on Whaling of Highly Endangered Bowhead Whales in the Eastern Canadian Arctic), available at iwcoffice.org/meetings/resolutions/resolution2000.htm#2.

[31] President William J. Clinton, "Message to the Congress on Canadian Whaling Activities," February 10, 1997, available at www.gpo.gov/fdsys/pkg/WCPD-1997-02-17/pdf/WCPD-1997-02-17-Pg175.pdf.

[32] Ibid.   [33] Ibid.

[34] For an excellent discussion of the issue, see Anthony Speca, "In the Belly of the Whaling Commission." Northern Public Affairs, June 18, 2012, available at www. northernpublicaffairs.ca/index/in-the-belly-of-the-whaling-commission/.

[35] Steven H. Ferguson, J. W. Higdon, and E. G. Chmelnitsky, "The Rise of the Killer Whales as a Major Arctic Predator," in Ferguson, et al., A Little Less Arctic: Top Predators in the World's Largest Northern Inland Sea, Hudson Bay (Dordrecht: Springer, 2010), 117.

2 Fisheries

Fishing in the Arctic Ocean has been limited by an absence of commercially attractive species and the near-constant presence of sea-ice. But with the ocean warming and the ice melting, sockeye salmon, Atlantic cod, pollock, and other commercially attractive species may soon move northward. In addition, species indigenous to the Arctic Ocean could be deemed commercially attractive once they become accessible: Arctic cod, for instance, could be the subject of a reduction fishery for fishmeal.

Within 200 nautical miles from shore, jurisdiction to regulate fishing falls exclusively to the coastal state. However, stocks that live in the high seas beyond the EEZ, or move between the high seas and the EEZ, are vulnerable to over-exploitation by the long-range fishing fleets of non-Arctic countries. In the face of scientific uncertainty as to how fish populations will respond to changing water temperatures and ice conditions, an international agreement on fisheries protection and management for the central Arctic Ocean (i.e., beyond 200 nautical miles from shore) is needed. Ideally, such an agreement would be negotiated and implemented before commercial fishing commences and the interests of non-Arctic fishing nations become vested in this uncertain and inherently fragile fisheries frontier.

Such an agreement has strong and compelling precedents, in the form of existing treaties concerning high seas fisheries in the Barents Sea (as discussed in Chapter 2) and Bering Sea, as well as the 1995 UN Agreement on Straddling and Highly Migratory Fish Stocks, the North Atlantic Fisheries Organization, and the North East Atlantic Fisheries Commission.

2.1 Bering Sea "donut hole"

The Bering Sea is approximately 670,000 square nautical miles in area. Within that, the "donut hole" is a 36,000-square-nautical-mile oval-shaped enclave of high seas surrounded and defined by the seaward limits of the Russian and US EEZs.

In the 1980s, fishing boats from China, Japan, Poland, South Korea, and elsewhere began fishing in the donut hole for pollock, which move between international waters and the EEZs of both Russia and the United States. The fishing quickly progressed to overfishing and, in 1992, the pollock stocks collapsed. The Russian and US governments responded by negotiating the 1994 Convention on the Conservation and

Management of the Pollock Resources in the Central Bering Sea.[36] Significantly, the treaty was also signed by China, Japan, Poland, and South Korea.

The treaty established a temporary moratorium on pollock fishing in the donut hole and a scientific and technical committee charged with assessing the biomass of the species on an on-going basis. An annual conference of the parties uses those assessments to establish an allowable harvest level for the following year. If the biomass is less than 1.67 million metric tonnes, the allowable harvest level is zero – and no directed fishing for pollock in the donut hole is permitted. The Convention also commits the parties to enforcement measures that include a mandatory observer program, as well as allowing the boarding and inspection of their vessels by officials from other parties. The Convention also requires the parties to make violations of its provisions offenses, albeit ones that can be tried and punished only in the flag state of the offending vessel. But, impressive as it is, the Convention came too late for the pollock stocks, which to this day have not reached the minimum level required to permit any fishing.

2.2 Arctic Ocean Fisheries Organization

In view of the increased potential and interest for commercial fishing in the central Arctic Ocean, the Pew Environment Group released an open letter in 2012 that was signed by more than 2,000 scientists from sixty-seven countries.[37] The scientists advised that in the absence of adequate scientifically informed management, the central Arctic Ocean is at risk of damage, including but not limited to overfishing. They called for the creation of an international fisheries agreement to protect the central Arctic Ocean through catch quotas "based on sound scientific and precautionary principles, and starting with a catch level of zero as a reflection of the state of understanding of the fisheries ecology of the region."[38] The scientists also pointed out that, in contrast to the situation of the pollock in the Bering Sea, there still exists an opportunity to

---

[36] 1994 Convention on the Conservation and Management of Pollock Resources in the Central Bering Sea, 34 ILM 67, available at www.afsc.noaa.gov/REFM/CBS/Docs/Convention%20on%20Conservation%20of%20Pollock%20in%20Central%20Bering%20Sea.pdf.

[37] Pew Environment Group, "More than 2,000 Scientists Worldwide Urge Protection of Central Arctic Ocean Fisheries." available at www.oceansnorth.org/arctic-fisheries-letter.

[38] Ibid.

obtain data and create management prior to high levels of fishing and "before precautionary management is no longer an option."[39]

Some individual countries are also concerned. In 2008, Senators Ted Stevens and Lisa Murkowski of Alaska co-sponsored a Senate resolution that directed the US executive branch to "negotiate an agreement or agreements for managing migratory, trans-boundary, and straddling fish stocks in the Arctic Ocean and establishing a new international fisheries management organization or organizations for the region." The resolution further directed that this agreement or agreements "should conform to the requirements of the United Nations Fish Stocks Agreement" and that in the meantime the United States should "support international efforts to halt the expansion of commercial fishing activities in the high seas of the Arctic Ocean."[40] The resolution was passed unanimously and signed into law by President George W. Bush.

In 2009, the Obama administration followed the direction set by Congress and banned commercial fishing in US federal waters north of Alaska.[41] Announcing the ban, Commerce Secretary Gary Locke said:

As Arctic sea ice recedes due to climate change, there is increasing interest in commercial fishing in Arctic waters. We are in a position to plan for sustainable fishing that does not damage the overall health of this fragile ecosystem. This plan takes a precautionary approach to any development of commercial fishing in an area where there has been none in the past.[42]

The ban on fishing in US Arctic waters caused some controversy in Canada because it purported to include the 6,250-square-nautical-mile disputed zone in the Beaufort Sea.[43] The Canadian government also expressed the view that a moratorium was "only one tool for addressing

---

[39] "An Open Letter from International Scientists," (2012), available at www.oceansnorth.org/arctic-fisheries-letter.

[40] SJ Res. 17 [110th], "A joint resolution directing the United States to initiate international discussions and take necessary steps with other Nations to negotiate an agreement for managing migratory and transboundary fish stocks in the Arctic Ocean," available at www.govtrack.us/congress/billtext.xpd?bill=sj110-17.

[41] Allison Winter, "US Bans Commercial Fishing in Warming Arctic," *New York Times*, August 21, 2010, www.nytimes.com/gwire/2009/08/21/21greenwire-us-bans-commercial-fishing-in-warming-arctic-33236.html.

[42] Ibid.; Randy Boswell, *PostMedia News*, "Advocates Push for Temporary Ban on Arctic Fishing," May 1, 2011, available at www.nunatsiaqonline.ca/stories/article/185776_advocates_push_for_temporary_ban_on_arctic_fishing/.

[43] Randy Boswell, "Canada Protests US Arctic Fishing Ban," *CanWest News Service*, September 4, 2009, available at www2.canada.com/nanaimodailynews/news/nation/story.html?id=b8757b5b-0b10-4769-9696-cdf9c315a754.

sustainability risks. Other tools, such as exploratory fisheries protocols, area closures, etc., are risk-based yet compatible with sustainable use."[44] However, if Canada does not adopt a complete ban, and if commercial fishing commences at some point on the Canadian side of the Beaufort Sea, difficult negotiations between Canada and the US will be required – since allowing fishing on one side of the boundary while a ban exists on the other would be tantamount to opening a drain on one side of a shared swimming pool.

The same risk exists along the United States–Russia boundary in the Chukchi Sea, to the north of the Bering Strait and outside the area dealt with in the Bering Sea Fisheries Agreement. Fortunately, such shared stock arrangements are relatively standard practice between states with adjacent or opposing EEZs. The more intriguing prospect, as foreseen in the US Congressional resolution, is a regional fisheries organization for the central Arctic Ocean, one that would operate within the framework of the UN Agreement on Straddling Fish Stocks and Highly Migratory Fish Stocks that was concluded in 1995 and came into force six years later.[45]

Much like the fur seals of the nineteenth century, straddling stocks are comprised of fish species that migrate between the EEZ of a coastal state and the high seas. Again, this has traditionally posed a problem for fisheries management because any conservation measures undertaken by the coastal state could be rendered ineffective by unregulated fishing just outside its EEZ. The 1995 Straddling Stocks Agreement enables coastal

---

[44] Randy Boswell, "Canada, US May Be at Odds over Conservation; Beaufort Sea Policy," *National Post*, August 26, 2009. In April 2011, the Canadian government and the Inuvialuit Regional Corporation signed a memorandum of understanding acknowledging that current scientific information is insufficient to start a commercial fishery in the Beaufort Sea and pledging jointly to develop a precautionary fisheries plan. "Beaufort Sea Commercial Fishing Banned," *CBC News*, April 15, 2011, available at www.cbc.ca/news/canada/north/story/2011/04/15/beaufort-sea-commercial-fishing-ban. html. In April 2012, the Canadian government accepted that "any possible future commercial fishery in the high seas of the central Arctic Ocean must be governed by effective management and conservation measures that are based on sound scientific advice, in consultation with Northerners and are agreed upon internationally." It also stated: "To that end, Canada continues to engage in discussions with the other four Arctic Ocean coastal states, including the United States, to address all relevant issues." Joint Statement by Keith Ashfield, Minister of Fisheries and Oceans and Leona Aglukkaq, Minister of Health and Minister of the Canadian Northern Economic Development Agency, April 25, 2012, available at www.dfo-mpo.gc.ca/media/statement-declarations/2012/20120425-eng.htm.

[45] 1995 UN Agreement on Straddling Fish Stocks and Highly Migratory Fish Stocks, available at www.un.org/Depts/los/convention_agreements/convention_overview_fish_stocks.htm.

states to create a regional fisheries organization to manage straddling and highly migratory stocks in the areas beyond 200 nautical miles from shore, by setting quotas as well as other means. However, any such organization must be open, on a non-discriminatory basis, to states from outside the region. Any state wanting to fish within the region must join the organization, but on doing so it is able to participate fully, and this includes participating in the setting of quotas. The Northwest Atlantic Fisheries Organization (NAFO), for instance, counts Japan and South Korea among its members, even though the NAFO Convention applies only to the waters immediately offshore the EEZs in the northeast United States, eastern Canada, and southwest Greenland.[46]

To the east of the NAFO Convention Area, the North East Atlantic Fisheries Commission (NEAFC) has a massive regulatory area, divided into three parts that include the central portions of the Norwegian and Barents Seas – areas that fall squarely within the Arctic.[47] NEAFC was established by the 1980 Convention on Future Multilateral Cooperation in North East Atlantic Fisheries, which counts among its members Iceland, Norway, Russia, the European Union, and Denmark on behalf of Greenland and the Faroe Islands.[48] The Commission deals with the difficult issue of regulating non-member fishing while respecting the freedom of the seas. If vessels flagged by non-member countries fish in the NEAFC area in a manner that "undermines the effectiveness" of the Commission's regulations, they can be prohibited from landing fish or taking on fuel or supplies in NEAFC member states.[49] They can also be placed on a list of vessels presumed to be engaged in "illegal, unreported and unregulated fishing;" a list that is transmitted to other regional fisheries organizations, the member states of which can then choose also to deny access to their ports.

Establishing an Arctic Ocean Fisheries Organization would therefore likely require the participation of some non-Arctic states, since those

[46] For a useful map, see www.nafo.int/about/frames/about.html.
[47] For a useful map, see www.neafc.org/page/27.
[48] 1980 Convention on Future Multilateral Co-operation in the North East Atlantic Fisheries, *Official Journal of the European Communities*, available at www.jus.uio.no/english/services/library/treaties/08/8-02/northeast-atlantic-fisheries.xml. The NEAFC adopted amendments to the Convention in 2004 and 2006 that the parties have accepted on a provisional basis, pending ratification. See www.neafc.org/system/files/london-declaration_and_new_convention.pdf.
[49] See "NEAFC Scheme of Control and Enforcement," especially chap. 7 (Measures to Promote Compliance by Non-Contracting Party Fishing Vessels), available at www.neafc.org/scheme/chapter7.

states would necessarily be allowed to join if they wished. These countries would then have access to the fisheries beyond 200 nautical miles, if and when science-based consensus on quotas was achieved. However, there is no need to hold off on negotiations while waiting to see which non-Arctic states demonstrate an interest in Arctic Ocean fisheries. The coastal states already have an interest and, under Article 8 of the Straddling Stocks Agreement, are perfectly entitled to establish a regional fisheries organization on their own – provided it remains open to other states with "a real interest in the fisheries concerned."[50]

Moreover, it can sometimes be easier to find the political will to conclude a treaty before competing interests arise and public opinion is engaged. Political will in support of an Arctic Ocean Fisheries Organization clearly exists on the part of the United States, which, despite its frequent caution with respect to international organizations, is taking the initiative here. Other Arctic states would be wise to consider whether this is an opportunity that they can afford to miss. The high seas north of the Bering Strait are already ice-free in late summer, and located closer to South Korea, Japan, and China than many of the areas where those countries' long-range fishing boats currently operate.

However, it would not be wise to negotiate and manage an Arctic Ocean Fisheries Organization within the Arctic Council, since non-members of the Council would need to be directly involved in the decision-making. Significantly, the 2001 Arctic Search and Rescue Agreement was not negotiated within – or adopted by – the Arctic Council either. Rather, a task force was established by the member states that operated separately from the Arctic Council, and the treaty was signed by those states rather than adopted by the Council. In other words, the treaty was adopted under the umbrella of the Arctic Council but not within the Council itself.

Using the same approach for an Arctic Ocean Fisheries Organization would address another concern about involving the Arctic Council, namely that Denmark, Sweden, and Finland are members of the European Union and do not control their own fisheries policies. As a result, the European Commission would have to negotiate on behalf of those three countries.[51] But there is no reason why the European

---

[50] UN Agreement on Straddling Fish Stocks and Highly Migratory Fish Stocks, n. 45, above.

[51] The European Commission would not have to negotiate on behalf of Greenland, for, while Denmark is a member of the EU, Greenland is not – a decision, implemented in

Commission could not participate as a full member in a task force established under the umbrella of the Arctic Council.

Including the European Union in fisheries negotiations under the Arctic Council would offer other benefits. First, in order for an Arctic Ocean Fisheries Organization to succeed, the European Union will have to join at some point, because of the size and geographic proximity of long-range fishing fleets in European Union member states such as Spain, Portugal, and the United Kingdom. To secure the full and timely participation of the European Union, it might be considered advantageous to include it from the outset. Second, the European Union has already expressed its strong support for science-based cooperative management of Arctic Ocean fisheries. In 2009, the European Union's Council of Ministers accepted "the need to promote a precautionary approach to new fishing activity in Arctic high seas, as well as measures for protecting marine biodiversity in areas beyond national jurisdiction."[52] It expressed "its readiness to consider a proposal to put in place a regulatory framework for the part of the seas not yet covered by an international conservation system by extending the mandate of relevant Regional Fisheries Management Organisations or any other proposal to that effect agreed by the relevant parties." It also expressed its support for "a temporary ban on new fisheries in those waters."

Third, the inclusion of the European Union as a partner in fisheries negotiations under the umbrella of the Arctic Council might usefully be linked to the European Union's application for permanent observer status at the Council.[53] Arguably, a regional organization gains rather than loses by involving powerful non-regional actors in consultative and supporting roles, which is why Canada and the United States have been accorded observer status at the Council of Europe. Admitting the European Union as a permanent observer and including it in fisheries negotiations could quickly result in an Arctic Oceans Fisheries Organization that had widespread and enthusiastic support. Obviously, the same argument applies vis-à-vis China, its application for permanent observer status at the Arctic Council, and its interests and influence as a long-range fishing state.

1985, that was rooted in a desire to manage its own fishery. See "Greenland Out of EEC," Chapter 1, n. 47, above.

[52] Council of the European Union, "Council Conclusions on Arctic Issues," December 8, 2009, available at oceansnorth.org/resources/council-european-union-conclusions-arctic-issues.

[53] See discussion, below, pp. 236–237.

3 Shipping

In July 2010, the M/V *Lyubov Orvlova*, a Russian-owned ice-strengthened cruise ship destined for the Canadian Arctic, was delayed in Newfoundland after Transport Canada inspectors identified problems with its plumbing system.[54] The ship was granted a permit after its owner promised to fix the problems following the summer sailing season. I spent two weeks on the *Lyubov Orvlova* that August, and was struck by its battered and rusting condition, and especially the open lifeboats that would have been next to useless in an Arctic storm. The ship was arrested on its return to Newfoundland in September 2010, at the request of the Inuit-owned company that had chartered the vessel and lent $250,000 to its owner. When it emerged that the owner also owed the crew five months in back wages, he abandoned the vessel.[55]

3.1 Ship safety

The fact that unsafe ships are able to enter Arctic waters is not due to any lack of jurisdiction on the part of the coastal states. Even if the Northwest Passage and the chokepoints of the Northern Sea Route were considered "international straits," Canada and Russia would still have some regulatory powers in these waterways.[56]

After the SS *Manhattan* sailed through the Northwest Passage in 1969, the Canadian government adopted the 1970 Arctic Waters Pollution Prevention Act (AWPPA).[57] The legislation imposed strict safety and environmental requirements on all shipping within 100 nautical miles of Canada's Arctic coast. The AWPPA was, at the time, contrary to international law, which did not recognize coastal state rights beyond twelve nautical miles (i.e., the outer limit allowable for a territorial sea). But it prompted the negotiation and adoption of Article 234

---

[54] Chris Windeyer, "Transport Canada Raps Cruise North for Safety Issues," *Nunatsiaq News*, July 20, 2012, available at www.nunatsiaqonline.ca/stories/article/ 200710_Transport_Canada_raps_Cruise_North_for_safety_issues/.

[55] "Deteriorating Russian Cruise Ship's Future Unclear," *CBC News*, April 11, 2012, available at www.cbc.ca/news/canada/newfoundland-labrador/story/2012/04/11/nl-orlova-update-411.html.

[56] On the disputes over the legal status of the Northwest Passage and the Northern Sea Route, see Chapter 5, above.

[57] Arctic Waters Pollution Prevention Act, Chapter 3, n. 46, above. In June 2009, Canada took full advantage of Article 234 by extending the reach of the AWPPA to 200 nautical miles. See An Act to Amend the Arctic Waters Pollution Prevention Act, SC 2009, c. 11, available at http://laws-lois.justice.gc.ca/eng/AnnualStatutes/2009_11/page-1.html.

of the 1982 UN Convention on the Law of the Sea, which allows coastal states to enact laws against maritime pollution out to 200 nautical miles when almost year-round ice creates exceptional navigational hazards:

Coastal States have the right to adopt and enforce non-discriminatory laws and regulations for the prevention, reduction and control of marine pollution from vessels in ice-covered areas within the limits of the exclusive economic zone, where particularly severe climatic conditions and the presence of the ice covering such areas for most of the year create obstructions or exceptional hazards to navigation, and pollution of the marine environment could cause major harm to or irreversible disturbance of the ecological balance. Such laws and regulations shall have due regard to navigation and the protection and preservation of the marine environment based on the best available scientific evidence.[58]

The adoption of Article 234 also contributed to the development of a parallel rule of customary international law. By 1985, this outcome had enabled Canada to rescind a reservation to its acceptance of the compulsory jurisdiction of the International Court of Justice; a reservation that it had entered when adopting the AWWPA in 1970.[59] In 1990, Russia adopted regulations on shipping in the Northern Sea Route that closely mirror those set out in the Canadian legislation.[60]

The Arctic Marine Shipping Assessment was produced by the Arctic Council's Working Group on the Protection of the Arctic Marine Environment and approved at the Council's 2009 ministerial meeting.[61] The Assessment found that "The most significant threat from ships to the Arctic marine environment is the release of oil through accidental or illegal discharge. Additional potential impacts of Arctic ships include ship strikes on marine mammals, the introduction of alien species, disruption of migratory patterns of marine mammals and anthropogenic noise produced from marine shipping activity."[62] It also found that "There are no uniform, international standards for ice navigators and for Arctic safety and survival for seafarers in polar conditions. And,

---

[58] UNCLOS, Introduction, n. 15, above.
[59] The reservation was withdrawn nine years before UNCLOS came into force, and a full eighteen years before Canada ratified the treaty. See (1985–1986) 40 *International Court of Justice Yearbook* 64.
[60] See Erik Franckx, "The Legal Regime of Navigation in the Russian Arctic." (2009) 18 *Journal of Transnational Law and Policy* 327 at 330–339.
[61] 2009 Arctic Marine Shipping Assessment, available at www.arctic.noaa.gov/detect/documents/AMSA_2009_Report_2nd_print.pdf.
[62] Ibid., p. 5.

there are no specifically tailored, mandatory environmental standards developed by IMO for vessels operating in Arctic waters."[63] The Assessment recommended that the Arctic countries, "in recognition of the unique environmental and navigational conditions in the Arctic ... cooperatively support efforts at the International Maritime Organization to strengthen, harmonize and regularly update international standards for vessels operating in the Arctic" including through the mandatory application of an updated version of the IMO's 2009 Guidelines for Ships Operating in Arctic Ice-Covered Waters.[64] The Guidelines emphasize the importance of ice-strengthened hulls for vessels operating in Arctic waters, that tankers carrying potential pollutants into Arctic waters should have double hulls, and that all vessel, navigation, and communications equipment should be appropriate for remote and challenging Arctic conditions. The Arctic Council's ministers agreed with the Assessment's recommendation, and have on two occasions called for the IMO to transform the Guidelines into a legally binding "Polar Code."[65]

The IMO's Sub-Committee on Ship Design and Equipment is currently negotiating that instrument, which would set out detailed rules concerning the certification, design, construction, equipping, and operation of Arctic vessels, with particular attention being paid to environmental protection.[66] Good progress is apparently being made, with the United States playing a prominent role in the negotiations. However, a difficult issue has arisen as to the means by which the rules will become binding on states. The IMO's Marine Environment Protection Committee has recommended a new treaty that would need to be ratified by states, even though this would delay the entry into force of the rules and perhaps preclude US ratification. The United States is pushing for the Polar Code to be treated as a series of amendments to the 1974 Convention for the Safety of Life at

---

[63] Ibid., p. 4.
[64] Ibid., p. 6. International Maritime Organization, "Guidelines for Ships Operating in Polar Waters," A26/Res. 1024, adopted December 2, 2009, available at www.imo.org/blast/blastDataHelper.asp?data_id=29985&filename=A1024(26).pdf.
[65] See Tromso Declaration (2009) and Nuuk Declaration (2011), both available at www.arctic-council.org/index.php/en/about/documents/category/5-declarations.
[66] See, e.g., Turid Stemre, "Background and Status of the IMO Initiative to Develop a Mandatory Polar Code," IMO Workshop, Cambridge, September 27–30, 2011, available: www.imo.org/MediaCentre/HotTopics/polar/Documents/Polarkoden%20Cambridge-clean%20session%201-1.pdf.

Sea[67] which has long used a "tacit acceptance procedure" to update its obligations, sometimes in quite substantial ways.[68] The former approach offers greater legitimacy, the latter greater efficacy, and it remains to be seen which approach will ultimately be chosen for the Polar Code.

3.2 Ballast water

Lightly loaded cargo ships carry large amounts of water in their ballast tanks to provide stability on the open sea. Ballast water is usually taken on at the last port of call, and released either at the next port of call or en route in shallower water or calmer seas. Thousands of species have been transported around the world by ballast water and some have become established as invasive species in new ecosystems, often to the detriment of indigenous species. A few have caused considerable economic damage, as has been the case with zebra mussels introduced by ballast water into the Great Lakes of the United States and Canada.[69]

In 2004, the International Maritime Organization adopted the Convention for the Control and Management of Ships' Ballast Water and Sediments.[70] The "BWM Convention" requires that new vessels be built with ballast water treatment systems, and that existing vessels be retrofitted with such systems. The retrofitting requirement is to be phased in over time, with deadlines depending on the age of the vessel and the size of its ballast tanks. As an intermediate measure, the BWM Convention requires that ships flush their ballast water at least fifty nautical miles from shore in waters that are at least 200 meters deep.[71] However, the BWM Convention will not come into force until it has been ratified by at least thirty countries representing 35 percent of the world's shipping tonnage. As of November 2012, thirty-six countries had ratified, including Canada, Norway, Sweden, Russia, and – most significantly – Liberia, but the combined tonnage was still only 29

---

[67]   1974 International Convention for the Safety of Life at Sea, consolidated 2004 version available at library.arcticportal.org/1696/1/SOLAS_consolidated_edition2004.pdf.

[68]   See Lei Shi, "Successful Use of the Tacit Acceptance Procedure to Effectuate Progress in International Maritime Law." (1998–1999) 11 *University of San Francisco Maritime Law Journal* 299.

[69]   Among other things, zebra mussels clog the intake pipes of water treatment and power plants. See, generally, Great Lakes Information Network, "Zebra Mussels in the Great Lakes Region." www.great-lakes.net/envt/flora-fauna/invasive/zebra.html.

[70]   2004 International Convention for the Control and Management of Ships' Ballast Water and Sediments. www.cep.unep.org/meetings-events/11th-igm/bw-convention-final-text.

[71]   Ibid., Annex, Regulation B-4.

percent.[72] In the meantime, the US Coast Guard and Environmental Protection Agency have adopted their own rules, aimed primarily at protecting the Great Lakes, which will take effect in US waters by 2021.[73] Unfortunately, the release of ballast water in the Arctic is still largely unregulated and poses real risks. Since Arctic ports are used mostly to export raw materials, ships generally arrive with little cargo and full ballast tanks.[74] Ships entering the relatively shallow and protected waters of the Northwest Passage and Northern Sea Route also release ballast water in order to reduce their draft. As an interim measure of protection, designated locations for flushing ballast water could be established in deep water where invasive species are less likely to survive.[75] Yet deepwater flushing has its own hazards: In 2006, a 200-meter-long automobile-carrying vessel, the *Cougar Ace*, rolled onto its side while transferring ballast water off Alaska.[76] Although the ship was successfully salvaged, the 4,812 new vehicles on board were damaged and later scrapped.

In the circumstances, it is important that the BWM Convention comes into force, through ratifications from countries representing another 6 percent of the world's shipping tonnage. Panama, with 22 percent of the tonnage, would make the difference on its own.

4 Nuclear accidents

Despite the enormity of the oceans, nuclear submarines have a tendency to collide, probably because they spend so much time shadowing one another. In 1992, the USS *Baton Rouge* hit a Russian submarine near Murmansk. In 1993, the USS *Grayling* crashed into a Russian submarine further out in the Barents Sea. In 2009, a British submarine and a French submarine managed to hit each other in the middle of the Atlantic

[72] See International Maritime Organization, "Status of Conventions," at www.imo.org/About/Conventions/StatusOfConventions/Pages/Default.aspx.

[73] Felicity Barringer, "New Rules Seek to Prevent Invasive Stowaways," *New York Times*, April 7, 2012, available at www.nytimes.com/2012/04/08/science/earth/invasive-species-target-of-new-ballast-water-rule.html.

[74] See Arthur J. Niimi, "Environmental and Economic Factors Can Increase the Risk of Exotic Species Introductions to the Arctic Region through Increased Ballast Water Discharge." (2004) 33 *Environmental Management* 712.

[75] Paul Brodie, "Ballast Water Rules Are Long Overdue." *Chronicle Herald*, October 17, 2010, D3, available at byers.typepad.com/arctic/2010/10/ballast-water-rules-are-long-overdue.html.

[76] Rachel D'Oro, "Insufficient Stability Is Blamed for Turning Ship." *Associated Press*, July 27, 2006, available at juneauempire.com/stories/072706/sta_20060727006.shtml.

Ocean.[77] Other nuclear submarines have run aground, caught fire, or suffered other serious accidents, with the most famous being the *Kursk*, a Russian cruise missile submarine that sank in the Barents Sea in 2000. At least eight nuclear submarines – two of them American, six of them Soviet or Russian – have been lost worldwide.[78] Given the importance of the Arctic Ocean for the Russian submarine fleet, and therefore for the US fleet, the risk of accidents is particularly high there.

An international safety protocol for communicating and coordinating submarine traffic is clearly required, one that builds on the 1972 Agreement between the United States and Soviet Union on the Prevention of Incidents on and over the High Seas, which primarily addressed surface vessels.[79] Such a protocol should include the NATO countries, Russia, and probably India and China. It would ideally be global in scope, but could usefully begin with the Arctic Ocean.

Nuclear accidents could also occur in the Arctic because of the presence of reactors on other vessels, most notably some of the icebreakers operated by Russia.[80] In addition, the first floating nuclear power plant in the world, the *Akademik Lomonosov*, was deployed to the Kamchatka region in Russia's Far East in 2012.[81]

After the 1986 meltdown at Chernobyl, two treaties were quickly adopted under the umbrella of the International Atomic Energy Agency. The first, the 1986 Convention on Early Notification of a Nuclear Accident, established a notification system for accidents having the potential to result in significant transboundary releases of radiation.[82] The second, the 1986 Convention on Assistance in the Case of a Nuclear Accident or Radiological Emergency, provides a framework for rapid communication and collaboration between countries in the event of a nuclear accident, even in the absence of a transboundary

---

[77] "Nuclear Subs Collide in Atlantic," *BBC News*, February 16, 2009. news.bbc.co.uk/2/hi/7892294.stm.

[78] Christopher Tingle, "Submarine Accidents: A 60-Year Statistical Assessment." (2009) *Professional Safety: Journal of the American Society of Safety Engineers* 31.

[79] 1972 Agreement between the Government of the United States of America and the Government of the Union of Soviet Socialist Republics on the Prevention of Incidents On and Over the High Seas, available at www.fas.org/nuke/control/sea/text/sea1.htm.

[80] See Bellona Foundation, "Nuclear Icebreakers," available at www.bellona.org/english_import_area/international/russia/civilian_nuclear_vessels/icebreakers/30107.

[81] "Akademik Lomonosov: The World's First Floating Nuclear Plant," *Marine Insight News Network*, October 12, 2011, available at www.marineinsight.com/marine/marine-news/featured/akademik-lomonosov-the-worlds-first-floating-nuclear-plant/.

[82] 1986 Convention on Early Notification of a Nuclear Accident, available at www.iaea.org/Publications/Documents/Infcircs/Others/infcirc335.shtml.

radiation risk.[83] However, treaties on their own can only facilitate and not compel compliance. Japan is a party to the 1986 Conventions, yet showed a disturbing lack of transparency or openness to outside assistance after its 2011 tsunami-precipitated nuclear crisis.[84]

5 Deep-sea mining

The International Seabed Authority (ISA) was established under the 1982 UN Convention on the Law of the Sea.[85] Based in Kingston, Jamaica, it is charged with organizing and controlling all mineral-related activities on the seabed in the so-called "Area" – essentially, all those portions of the ocean floor that fall beyond the limits of national jurisdiction. The ISA enters into contracts with public and private corporations, authorizing them to explore and exploit designated areas. Under the terms of UNCLOS, the ISA is also supposed to have its own mining entity, called the "Enterprise', but no moves have yet been made to create this.

Even the United States, which has not yet acceded to UNCLOS, accepts the legitimacy of the ISA. In the early 1990s, Washington used its post-Cold War predominant influence to secure modifications to the deep-sea mining provisions of UNCLOS; modifications that enable private industry, including United States-based companies, to gain access to this new resource frontier.[86]

The ISA initially focused on the potential mining of manganese nodules: apple-sized lumps of manganese, nickel, copper, and cobalt that in some places cover large areas of the abyssal plain. In 2000, it adopted

---

[83] 1986 Convention on Assistance in the Case of a Nuclear Accident or Radiological Emergency, available at www.iaea.org/Publications/Documents/Infcircs/Others/infcirc336.shtml.

[84] See, e.g., Chico Harlan, "Report Blasts Japan's Preparation for, Response to Fukushima Disaster," *Washington Post*, July 5, 2012, available at www.washingtonpost.com/world/new-report-blasts-japans-preparation-for-response-to-fukushima-disaster/2012/07/05/gJQAN1OEPW_story.html. On the status of the 1986 Conventions, see www.iaea.org/Publications/Documents/Conventions/cenna_status.pdf and www.iaea.org/Publications/Documents/Conventions/cacnare_status.pdf.

[85] See the ISA website at www.isa.org.jm/.

[86] See Christopher Joyner, "The United States and the New Law of the Sea." (1996) 27 *Ocean Development and International Law* 41. The new provisions on deep seabed mining, along with the opportunity to secure widely recognized rights over extended continental shelves, constitute significant incentives for US accession.

regulations on the exploration for such nodules.[87] Beginning in 2001, it entered into a series of fifteen-year contracts with corporations from Bulgaria, China, Cuba, the Czech Republic, France, Germany, India, Japan, Korea, Poland, Russia, and Slovakia.[88] The current areas of exploration are in the Pacific and Indian Oceans, but no mining has yet taken place. Fields of manganese nodules are known to exist in the Arctic Ocean – indeed, the first discovery of such nodules was in the Kara Sea off Siberia in 1868[89] – and they may some day attract commercial interest.

After six years of negotiations, the ISA adopted a second set of regulations on polymetallic sulfides in 2012.[90] These sulfur-bearing minerals, which are found around underwater geysers called "hydrothermal vents," often contain economic concentrations of strategic minerals, including copper, nickel, cobalt, and rare-earth elements. Hungry for strategic minerals to support its burgeoning high-tech economy, China has moved quickly to take advantage. Within days of the new regulations being adopted, the state-owned China Ocean Minerals Research and Development Association filed an application with the ISA to extract ore from an underwater ridge in the Indian Ocean.[91] But China's foray into deep-sea mining is not a serious threat to other countries, since they can file their own applications.

The deep-sea mining regime is not perfect. UNCLOS requires that countries ensure "effective protection" for the environment during deep-sea mining but provides no guidance as to what effective protection entails. The recently adopted regulations on polymetallic sulfides state that the ISA shall "establish and keep under periodic review environmental rules, regulations and procedures to ensure effective protection for the marine environment from harmful effects," and that such rules should reflect a "precautionary approach."[92] Such an approach could involve the outright prohibition of mining around

[87] Regulations on Prospecting and Exploration for Polymetallic Nodules in the Area, adopted 13 July 2000, available at www.isa.org.jm/en/documents/mcode.

[88] For information on the contractors, see www.isa.org.jm/en/scientific/exploration/contractors.

[89] International Seabed Authority, "Polymetallic Nodules," available at www.isa.org.jm/files/documents/EN/Brochures/ENG7.pdf.

[90] Regulations on Prospecting and Exploration for Polymetallic Sulphides, May 7, 2010, available at www.isa.org.jm/files/documents/EN/Regs/PolymetallicSulphides.pdf.

[91] "Comra Applies for Approval of Plan of Work for Exploration for Polymetallic Sulphides," International Seabed Authority Press Release, May 25, 2010, available at www.isa.org.jm/en/node/518.

[92] Regulations on Prospecting and Exploration for Polymetallic Sulphides, n. 90, above.

hydrothermal vents, because stirring up the seabed spreads toxic sulfides and disturbs the highly specialized ecosystems that flourish in the hot, mineral-laden water.

In 2003, Canada was the first to apply the precautionary approach to deep-sea mining when it designated the Endeavour Hydrothermal Vents as a "marine protected area."[93] Located southwest of Vancouver Island in more than 2,000 meters of water, the vents fall within Canada's 200-nautical-mile EEZ. Prohibiting mining there might eventually offer unforeseen commercial benefits, because the ecosystems around hydrothermal vents are based on unique, heat-tolerant organisms. In the complete darkness that exists at great depths, they convert chemical energy into organic material by chemosynthesis, much like plants convert solar energy by photosynthesis. Enzymes from some of the highly specialized organisms at the Endeavour vents are already being studied for industrial and medical applications.

In other instances, a balance might be sought between the extraction of minerals and the protection of ecosystems. A Canadian company, Nautilus Minerals, is currently conducting the engineering phase of a sulfide-mining project in the Bismarck Sea, within the territorial waters of Papua New Guinea.[94] As part of an environmental impact assessment required by the Papua New Guinea government, the company committed to reducing sediment plumes and long-term damage to the seabed ecosystem – including leaving some of the area around the vent undisturbed so the endemic organisms there can recolonize the mine site. As the ISA establishes detailed regulations and vets mining applications, it should ensure that practices beyond 200 nautical miles follow at least some version of this model.

At some point, the protection and exploitation of hydrothermal vents could become an issue in the Arctic. More than a dozen such vents have been discovered along the Gakkel Ridge between Greenland and Norway, complete with large mounds of sulfide minerals. Other vents may exist along other Arctic Ocean ridges, either within or beyond the jurisdiction of coastal states.

The continental shelves of the Arctic Ocean also contain vast stores of methane hydrates: natural gas compressed and frozen into an ice-like

---

[93] Fisheries and Oceans Canada, "Endeavour Hydrothermal Vents," at www.dfo-mpo.gc. ca/oceans/marineareas-zonesmarines/mpa-zpm/pacific-pacifique/endeavour-eng.htm.
[94] Nautilus Minerals, "Solwara 1 Project – High Grade Copper and Gold," available at www.nautilusminerals.com/s/Projects-Solwara.asp.

form by high pressure and low temperature. The technology required commercially to capture these hydrates does not yet exist, and when it does the costs may well be prohibitive. Methane hydrates might also exist on the deep seabed beyond the jurisdiction of coastal states, and this may eventually attract attention from non-Arctic countries. But like manganese nodules and polymetallic sulfides, these resources will be subject to the organization and control of the ISA, precluding an unregulated race for riches. Moreover, the risks and costs associated with mining deep below the remote, often dark, cold and stormy Arctic Ocean will always be substantial. It might be decades, even centuries, before any deep-sea mining takes place in the Arctic Ocean.

6 Air-borne pollution

6.1 Persistent organic pollutants

Persistent organic pollutants are toxic chemicals, including DDT and PCBs, which were mostly produced and used in the industrialized countries. Significant amounts of these toxins were, and still are, being carried to the Arctic by a process of global distillation involving volatilization at low latitudes and condensation at high latitudes that is sometimes referred to as the "grasshopper effect." After being deposited in the Arctic, the toxins move up the food chain, accumulating in the fatty tissues of predators such as seals, bears, and ultimately humans. Multinational negotiations on the problem led to the adoption of the 2001 Stockholm Convention on Persistent Organic Pollutants, which requires states to take specific steps to reduce or eliminate the production of persistent organic pollutants and to dispose safely of existing stocks.[95] So far, 178 countries have ratified the convention, including Canada, China, the European Union, India and Japan.[96] In 2009, the Convention was amended to include nine new chemicals, some of which are still widely used as pesticides and flame-retardants and will now be phased out. Two years later, the crop pesticide endosulfan was added to the list.[97]

---

[95] 2001 Stockholm Convention on Persistent Organic Pollutants, available at chm.pops. int/Convention/tabid/54/Default.aspx.

[96] See Status of Ratifications, available at chm.pops.int/Countries/StatusofRatifications/ tabid/252/Default.aspx.

[97] See "The New POPs under the Stockholm Convention," available at http://chm.pops.int/ Convention/ThePOPs/TheNewPOPs/tabid/2511/Default.aspx.

The Arctic dimension of the problem played a decisive role in the negotiation of the Stockholm Convention.[98] The Inuit Circumpolar Council was represented at the talks by Sheila Watt-Cloutier, who was later nominated (jointly with former US vice-president Al Gore) for the Nobel Peace Prize for her work on climate change. Watt-Cloutier emphasized that the Inuit are the world's most vulnerable victims of persistent organic pollutants, to the point where women must think twice about breastfeeding their babies. At one particularly critical stage, she presented a soapstone carving of an Inuit woman and infant to Klaus Toepfer, the executive director of the United Nations Environment Programme.[99] The carving was placed at the head of the negotiating table, where it remained for the duration of the talks.

6.2 Arctic haze

The term "Arctic haze" first appeared in a 1956 paper published by J. Murray Mitchell, Jr., who described visible atmospheric layers of undetermined origin.[100] Mitchell was involved in the "Ptarmigan flights," which were conducted by the US Air Force between 1948 and 1967 to record meteorological conditions in the Arctic.[101] But it was not until the late 1970s that other researchers established that Arctic haze was caused by human activities,[102] and not until the mid-1980s that Mitchell's paper was used to understand the phenomenon better. One of the findings concerned the "greater frequency of occurrences in later winter" due to the lower rate of particle and gas removal during the "cold, dark, and rather stable system" that prevails in the Arctic during

---

[98] David Downie and Terry Fenge, *Northern Lights Against POPs: Combating Toxic Threats in the Arctic* (Montreal and Kingston: McGill–Queen's University Press, 2003); Bruce E. Johansen, "The Inuit's Struggle with Dioxins and Other Organic Pollutants." (2002) 26 *American Indian Law Quarterly* 479.

[99] Marla Cone, *Silent Snow: The Slow Poisoning of the Arctic* (New York: Grove Press, 2005), 200.

[100] J. M. Mitchell, Jr., "Visual Range in the Polar Regions with Particular Reference to the Alaskan Arctic." (1956) *Journal of Atmospheric and Terrestrial Physics* 195.

[101] Ken Wilkening, "Science and International Environmental Nonregimes: The Case of Arctic Haze." (2011) 28 *Review of Policy Research* 131, available at www.highbeam.com/doc/1G1-253536411.html.

[102] Arctic Monitoring and Assessment Programme, "AMAP Assessment 2006: Acidifying Pollutants, Arctic Haze, and Acidification in the Arctic," 1, available at amap.no/documents/index.cfm?dirsub=%2FAMAP%20Assessment%202006%20-%20Acidifying%20Pollutants%2C%20Arctic%20Haze%20and%20Acidification%20in%20the%20Arcticandsort=default.

that season.[103] Researchers have also learned that only a small percentage of Arctic haze originates in the Arctic.[104] For the most part, it is "long-range transported air pollution"[105] composed primarily of sulfate with varying amounts of "particulate organic matter, nitrogen compounds, dust and black carbon, as well as trace elements such as heavy metals and other contaminants."[106] The sulfate originates from a number of sources, including power plants, oil and gas production, smelters, and pulp and paper mills, while nitrogen compounds come mostly from oxidation of vehicle exhausts.[107]

Arctic haze has both direct and indirect effects on the environment and climate. It changes the "radiation balance" in the Arctic by creating a "layer of light-absorbing material" over otherwise light-reflecting ice and snow surfaces.[108] The aerosols in the haze may even affect the properties of clouds, especially their "emissivity" – the rate at which the clouds emit radiation. Arctic haze increases the amount of solar radiation retained at the Earth's surface, leading to an increase in the rate of ice- and snowmelt, especially during the spring.

In 1979, the UN Economic Commission for Europe adopted the Convention on Long-Range Transboundary Air Pollution.[109] The Convention provides a framework for scientific collaboration and policy coordination that has been filled in by eight protocols setting out specific measures for reducing emissions. One of the protocols – the 1999 Gothenburg Protocol to Abate Acidification, Eutrophication and Ground-Level Ozone[110] – has been identified by the Arctic Council's Arctic Monitoring and Assessment Program (AMAP) as having particular importance for the reduction of Arctic haze.[111] The Gothenburg Protocol sets

---

[103] See Glen E. Shaw, "The Arctic Haze Phenomenon," (August 16, 1995) 76 *Bulletin of the American Meteorological Society* 2403, available at http://journals.ametsoc.org/doi/pdf/10.1175/1520-0477(1995)076%3C2403%3ATAHP%3E2.0.CO%3B2; and Arctic Monitoring and Assessment Programme, "AMAP Assessment 2006," ibid., p. ix.

[104] Arctic Monitoring and Assessment Programme, "AMAP Assessment 2006," ibid.

[105] Ibid.   [106] Shaw, n. 103, above, p. 2405.

[107] Arctic Monitoring and Assessment Programme, "AMAP Assessment 2006," n. 102, above, p. 1.

[108] Ibid., p. 38.

[109] United Nations Economic Commission for Europe, 1979 Convention on Long-Range Transboundary Air Pollution, available at www.unece.org/env/lrtap/lrtap_h1.html.

[110] Protocol to Abate Acidification, Eutrophication, and Ground-Level Ozone, available at www.unece.org/fileadmin/DAM/env/lrtap/full%20text/1999%20Multi.E.Amended.2005.pdf.

[111] Arctic Monitoring and Assessment Programme, "AMAP Assessment 2006," n. 102, above, p. ix.

emission ceilings for sulfates, nitric oxides, volatile organic compounds, and ammonia. It also establishes strict levels for particular emission sources such as power plants and vehicles, and requires that the best available methods be implemented to reduce emissions.[112] The United States, Finland, Sweden, Norway, and Denmark have ratified the Gothenburg Protocol; Russia, Canada, and Iceland have yet to do so.[113]

AMAP has also recommended the establishment of more monitoring stations for air and precipitation chemistry in the US, Canadian, and Russian Arctic.[114] These stations would help scientists develop a better understanding of how Arctic haze operates and changes over time.[115] Unfortunately, Canada took the opposite track in 2012, shutting down its Polar Environment Atmospheric Research Laboratory (PEARL) in Eureka, Nunavut, at 80 degrees north.[116]

6.3 Black carbon

Black carbon is particulate matter produced during the combustion of hydrocarbon fuels when there is insufficient oxygen present for the fuel to be completely converted to carbon dioxide and water.[117] It is sometimes referred to as "soot" – a general term that includes various types of carbon-based particulates.[118] In developed countries, the main source of black carbon is the exhaust from diesel engines. In developing countries, black carbon commonly originates from the burning of biomass – including wood, vegetable oil, and animal dung – for fuel.[119]

When black carbon is deposited onto snow and ice, it dramatically reduces the "albedo," or reflectivity.[120] This causes the snow and ice to

---

[112] Protocol to Abate Acidification, Eutrophication, and Ground-Level Ozone, n. 110, above.

[113] United Nations Economic Commission for Europe, "Status of Ratification of the 1999 Gothenburg Protocol to Abate Acidification, Eutrophication and Ground-Level Ozone as of 24 May 2012," at www.unece.org/env/lrtap/status/99multi_st.html.

[114] Ibid., p. 97.   [115] Ibid., p. 98.

[116] "High Arctic Research Station Forced to Close: PEARL Played a Key Role in Ozone Measurements, International Collaborations." *CBC News*, February 28, 2012, available at www.cbc.ca/news/politics/story/2012/02/28/science-pearl-arctic-research.html.

[117] P. K. Quinn, et al., *The Impact of Black Carbon on the Arctic Climate* (Oslo: Arctic Monitoring and Assessment Programme, 2011), 4, available at www.amap.no/documents/.

[118] James Hansen and Larissa Nazarenko, "Soot Climate Forcing Via Snow and Ice Albedos." (2004) 101(2) *Proceedings of the National Academy of Sciences* 423, available at www.pnas.org/content/101/2/423.full.pdf+html.

[119] Cath O'Driscoll. "Soot Warming Significant." (2011) 17 *Chemistry and Industry* 10.

[120] See Arctic Council Task Force on Short-Lived Climate Forcers, "Technical Report: An Assessment of Emissions and Mitigation Options for Black Carbon for the Arctic

melt more quickly, and as the melting progresses the particles become more concentrated on the surface, which accelerates the melting further. Even when carbon particles remain in the air column they can still increase the rate of melting by absorbing solar energy and warming the surrounding air.[121]

Until recently, the contributions of black carbon and other "short-lived climate pollutants" (SLCPs) to climate change were largely overlooked. Although black carbon particles remain in the atmosphere for only a few weeks (whereas carbon dioxide molecules persist for years), recent research suggests that black carbon may be responsible for "25 percent of observed global warming over the past century."[122] There is little doubt that black carbon is a significant factor in the melting of Arctic sea-ice, glaciers, and permafrost.[123]

The short lifespan of black carbon in the atmosphere means that reducing these emissions might be the quickest way to slow global warming. According to Mark Jacobson, the director of Stanford University's Atmosphere/Energy Program, it "may be the only method of saving Arctic ice."[124] In 2009, the Arctic Council established a task force to identify the primary sources of black carbon and recommend "immediate actions."[125] Although reducing black carbon emissions anywhere on the planet would have positive consequences in the Arctic, the task force reported that reducing sources in or near the Arctic would have more of an impact there.[126] It found that the greatest sources of black carbon in the Arctic are diesel vehicles, agricultural and prescribed forest burning, wildfires, and residential heating. It identified marine shipping as "a potentially significant source, especially in the Arctic due to its projected increase over time and its proximity to snow and ice."[127]

Council," May 2, 2011, p. 2, available at arctic-council.npolar.no/accms/export/sites/default/en/meetings/2011-nuuk-ministerial/docs/3_1_ACTF_Report_02May2011_v2.pdf.

[121] See National Aeronautics and Space Administration, "Black Soot and Snow: A Warmer Combination," December 22, 2003, available at www.nasa.gov/centers/goddard/news/topstory/2003/1223blacksoot.html.

[122] Ibid.   [123] Ibid.   [124] O'Driscoll, n. 119, above, p. 10.

[125] Alister Doyle, "Arctic Nations Plan Soot Crackdown," *Boston Globe*, April 30, 2009, available at www.boston.com/news/world/europe/articles/2009/04/30/arctic_nations_plan_soot_crackdown/.

[126] Arctic Council Task Force on Short-Lived Climate Forcers, "Technical Report," n. 120, above, p. 2.

[127] Arctic Council Task Force on Short-Lived Climate Forcers, "Progress Report and Recommendations for Ministers," May 2, 2011, p. 3, available at arctic-council.npolar.

In the lead-up to the 2011 meeting of Arctic Council ministers, US Deputy Secretary of State Jim Steinberg indicated that a specific treaty on black carbon would not be negotiated; instead, there would be a "coordinated focus" on taking "strong actions domestically."[128] Most Arctic countries do not yet have measures in place that address black carbon specifically, though they do have programs that restrict SLCP emissions and therefore indirectly black carbon.[129] In 2011, the US Environmental Protection Agency (EPA) solicited proposals for research on mitigating diesel sources of black carbon in the Russian Arctic, research that will then be applicable in other Arctic countries.[130]

In addition, the United States is leading efforts to reduce black carbon emissions beyond the Arctic. In February 2012, the United States, Canada, Bangladesh, Ghana, Mexico, Sweden, and the United Nations Environment Programme (UNEP) announced the creation of a "Climate and Clean Air Coalition to Reduce Short-Lived Climate Pollutants."[131] The coalition is a voluntary initiative meant to promote measures that reduce SLCPs such as black carbon, with the areas identified for "immediate action" including "heavy duty diesel vehicles and engines" and "oil and gas production."[132] In May 2012, the rest of the G8 countries (France, Germany, Italy, Japan, Russia, and the United Kingdom) agreed to join the coalition.[133]

no/accms/export/sites/default/en/meetings/2011-nuuk-ministerial/docs/3-0a_TF_SPM_recommendations_2May11_final.pdf.

[128] Joby Warrick and Juliet Eilperin, "Arctic Council to Address Role of Soot in Global Warming," *Washington Post*, May 11, 2011, available at www.washingtonpost.com/national/arctic-council-to-address-role-of-soot-in-global-warming/2011/05/11/AFourXsG_story.html.

[129] For an overview of each Arctic country's pollution measures that may affect black carbon emissions, see Arctic Council Task Force on Short-Lived Climate Forcers, "Technical Report," n. 120, above, sec. 5, pp. 34–51.

[130] Environmental Protection Agency, Request for Proposals: "Arctic Black Carbon: Reduction of Black Carbon from Diesel Sources," 2011, pp. 1–2, available at www.epa.gov/international/grants/Arctic-Black-Carbon-ModifiedRFP.pdf.

[131] United Nations Environment Programme, "New Climate and Clean Air Coalition Expands to 13 Members: New Initiatives Assessed for Fast and Scaled-Up Action on Black Carbon, Methane, and HFCs," April 24, 2012, available at www.unep.org/newscentre/default.aspx?DocumentID=2678andArticleID=9116. The coalition website is located at www.unep.org/ccac/Home/tabid/101612/Default.aspx.

[132] Climate and Clean Air Coalition to Reduce Short-Lived Climate Pollutants, "Focal Areas," available at www.unep.org/ccac/FocalAreas/tabid/102153/Default.aspx.

[133] UNEP News Centre, "All G8 Countries Back Action on Black Carbon, Methane and Other Short Lived Climate Pollutants," May 22, 2012, available at www.unep.org/newscentre/default.aspx?DocumentID=2683andArticleID=9134.

7 Oil spills

The world was reminded of the great risks posed by oil spills when the *Deepwater Horizon*, a drilling rig leased by BP, exploded and sank 35 nautical miles off the Louisiana coast in April 2010. The ruptured wellhead spewed at least 800 million liters before it could be capped three months later. Immeasurable, intergenerational damage was caused to the environment of the Gulf of Mexico, and to the fishing and tourism industries of at least four US states.[134]

The risks posed by oil spills are even greater in the Arctic. As mentioned above, oil disperses and degrades very slowly at cold temperatures.[135] More than two decades after the *Exxon Valdez* spilled more than 80 million liters into Prince William Sound on Alaska's southern coast, oil from that accident persists in the ecosystem.[136] Distance, sea-ice, seasonal darkness, rough weather, and a lack of coastal infrastructure and population centers render the prospects for a successful clean-up even more remote further north. The highly specialized species that make up Arctic marine ecosystems are particularly sensitive to disruption and already badly stressed by warming water temperatures and disappearing sea-ice. Last, but not least, many indigenous inhabitants of the Arctic are still dependent on fish and marine mammals for food.

7.1 United States

The pace of Arctic oil and gas development varies from country to country. In the United States, successive administrations have supported offshore exploration on the continental shelf north of Alaska as part of an effort to reduce the country's reliance on foreign sources of energy. In the 1980s, Shell drilled 16 exploratory wells; in 2005, it bid $44 million for exploration leases in the Beaufort Sea and, in 2008, another $2.2 billion for leases in the

---

[134] See, e.g., National Oceanic and Atmospheric Administration, "Natural Resource Damage Assessment, Status Update for the *Deepwater Horizon* Oil Spill." (April 2012), available at www.gulfspillrestoration.noaa.gov/wp-content/uploads/ FINAL_NRDA_StatusUpdate_April2012.pdf.

[135] See Pew Environment Group, "Oil Spill Prevention and Response in the US Arctic Ocean: Unexamined Risks, Unacceptable Consequences." (November 2010), available at www.pewtrusts.org/uploadedFiles/wwwpewtrustsorg/Reports/ Protecting_ocean_life/PEW-1010_ARTIC_Report.pdf.

[136] See Lila Guterman, "Exxon Valdez Turns 20" (March 20, 2009) 323(5921) *Science* 1558. See also Art Davidson, *In the Wake of the Exxon Valdez* (San Francisco, Calif.: Sierra Club Books, 1990).

Chukchi Sea.[137] In 2010, both Shell and BP drilled offshore wells on the US side of the Beaufort Sea. Then, in response to the *Deepwater Horizon* blowout, the Obama administration suspended sales of offshore oil leases. In 2011, US Coast Guard Commandant Robert Papp warned Congress that the United States was unprepared to respond to a major oil spill in the Arctic.[138]

The oil companies responded that their Alaskan offshore projects take place from artificial islands or platforms anchored to the seabed in waters less than 70 meters deep. This, the companies claimed, made the Arctic drilling categorically different from deep-water drilling from floating platforms in the Gulf of Mexico.[139] The Obama administration accepted this argument and, in 2012, Shell deployed two drill ships and twenty additional vessels to US waters north of Alaska.[140] Although Shell ultimately failed to complete a well that summer, due to equipment problems and drifting sea-ice,[141] the deployment of two drill ships was required by the US government to provide the capability of drilling a "relief well" during the same drilling season as any primary well. When a blowout occurs, drilling an adjacent intercepting well can reduce the pressure from the escaping oil, allowing the primary well to be capped.

7.2 Canada

During the 1970s and 1980s, ninety-three wells were drilled in the Canadian portion of the Beaufort Sea while another forty wells were

[137] John M. Broder and Clifford Krauss, "New and Frozen Frontier Awaits Offshore Oil Drilling," *New York Times*, May 23, 2012, available at www.nytimes.com/2012/05/24/science/earth/shell-arctic-ocean-drilling-stands-to-open-new-oil-frontier.html.

[138] "Testimony of Commandant Admiral Robert Papp Jr., US Coast Guard, before the Senate Committee on Commerce, Science, and Transportation, Subcommittee on Oceans, Atmosphere, Fisheries, and Coast Guard," August 12, 2011, available at www.dhs.gov/ynews/testimony/20110812-papp-keeping-coast-guard-ready-alaska.shtm.

[139] Broder and Krauss, n. 137, above. In 2010, the World Wildlife Fund responded: "[T]he risk of a blowout is not related to depth, per se. Last year's blowout in the Timor Sea, which took 74 days to cap, occurred in 261 feet of water. The IXTOC I, the worst accidental spill in history until the *Deepwater Horizon* disaster, took place in only 160 feet of water. Both of these catastrophes occurred in depths and pressures comparable to those found in the Beaufort and Chukchi seas." World Wildlife Fund, "Drilling for Oil in the Arctic: Too Soon, Too Risky," December 1, 2010, p. 18, available at www.worldwildlife.org/what/wherewework/arctic/WWFBinaryitem18711.pdf.

[140] Broder and Krauss, n. 137, above.

[141] Kim Murphy, "Drill Rigs Wind Up Operations in Arctic Alaska Seas," *Los Angeles Times*, October 31, 2012, available at www.latimes.com/news/nation/nationnow/la-na-nn-arctic-drill-alaska-20121031,0,6809964.story.

drilled in offshore areas near Canada's High Arctic islands.[142] At the time, Canada led the world in providing a regulatory regime for Arctic offshore drilling, including a requirement – introduced in 1976 – that oil companies have the capability to drill a same-season relief well.

During the 1990s, government subsidies for Arctic oil and gas exploration were eliminated and no offshore drilling took place. However, as oil prices have risen, oil companies have returned to the Beaufort Sea, purchasing large exploration leases from the Canadian government.[143] Some of these leases have been for deep-water areas where drilling a well, whether an initial well or a relief well, would necessarily be a multi-year exercise.[144] For this reason, some of those leaseholders began lobbying Canada's National Energy Board (NEB), the federal body responsible for regulating offshore drilling in the Canadian Arctic, for a relaxation of the same-season relief well requirement.[145] After the *Deepwater Horizon* blowout, the companies themselves called for a pause, so that any regulatory changes could be informed by the incident.[146]

In 2011, the NEB issued a report into Arctic offshore drilling in which it retained the same-season relief well requirement, while adding an important potential loophole:

The intended outcome of the Same Season Relief Well Policy is to kill an out-of-control well in the same season in order to minimize harmful impacts on the environment. We will continue to require that any company applying for an offshore drilling authorization provides us with specific details as to how they will meet this policy. An applicant wishing to depart from our policy would have to demonstrate how they would meet or exceed the intended outcome of our policy. It would be up to us to determine, on a case-by-case basis, which tools are appropriate for meeting or exceeding the intended outcome of the Same Season Relief Well Policy. ... We acknowledge that there is a continual evolution of

---

[142]   National Energy Board, "Review of Offshore Drilling in the Canadian Arctic," December 2011, p. 3, available at www.neb-one.gc.ca/clf-nsi/rthnb/pplctnsbfrthnb/ rctcffshrdrllngrvw/fnlrprt2011/fnlrprt2011-eng.pdf.

[143]   See discussion, Chapter 3, above.

[144]   Oceans North Canada, "Becoming Arctic-Ready: Policy Recommendations for Reforming Canada's Approach to Licensing and Regulating Offshore Arctic Oil and Gas." (September 2011), Fig. 1, p. 1, available at oceansnorth.org/becoming-arctic-ready.

[145]   National Energy Board, n. 142, above, p. 5.

[146]   Shawn McCarthy, "Oil Giants Contest Arctic Relief Well Requirement," *Globe and Mail*, April 5, 2011, available at www.theglobeandmail.com/report-on-business/industry-news/energy-and-resources/oil-giants-contest-arctic-relief-well-requirement/ article582755/.

technology worldwide, including the technology needed to kill an out-of-control well. We are open to changing and evolving technology.[147]

At the same time, the NEB introduced a new set of Filing Requirements for Offshore Drilling in the Canadian Arctic.[148] Any company applying for regulatory approval must now identify any animals that would be "particularly sensitive to a major oil spill," explain how its drill plan addresses "marine protected areas and seasonal movements of marine animals," and how "environmental factors in the Arctic, including extreme temperatures, darkness, polynyas [i.e. localized areas of open water in winter], ice cover, ice movement, sea state, currents, shoreline features, and seafloor features, could potentially affect the project."[149] The companies are also required to describe "the worst-case scenario, including the estimated flow rate, total volumes of fluids, oil properties, and maximum duration of a potential blowout" and "the measures available to regain well control through same-well intervention, and by drilling a relief well."[150]

In 2012, the Canadian government opened an additional 2,638 square nautical miles of the Beaufort Sea for exploration bids.[151] The new area was divided into six parcels, four of which are located in the southern Beaufort Sea, and two of which are in the eastern Beaufort just off Banks Island.[152] When reporting on the auction, the *Globe and Mail* observed that: "The return of Beaufort interest may be evidence that oil companies are comfortable with new rules the National Energy Board released last year that allow companies to depart from a rule that requires, in a disaster, that an emergency well be completed before winter – if they can show other means that provide equivalent safety measures."[153] The *Globe and Mail* was wrong, at least with respect to the level of interest in the Beaufort Sea. Only one company entered bids:

---

[147] National Energy Board, n. 142, above, p. 40.
[148] National Energy Board, "Filing Requirements for Offshore Drilling in the Canadian Arctic," December 2011, available at www.neb-one.gc.ca/clf-nsi/rthnb/pplctnsbfrthnb/rctcffshrdrllngrvw/rctcrvwflngrqrmnt/rctcrvwflngrqmnt-eng.pdf.
[149] Ibid., p. 9.   [150] Ibid., p. 21.
[151] Nathan Valderklippe, "Reviving Arctic Oil Rush, Ottawa to Auction Rights in Massive Area," *Globe and Mail*, May 16, 2012, available at www.theglobeandmail.com/news/politics/reviving-arctic-oil-rush-ottawa-to-auction-rights-in-massive-area/article2435284/.
[152] See the map on p. 3 of the "Call for Bids," April 28, 2012, available at www.aadnc-aandc.gc.ca/DAM/DAM-INTER-HQ/STAGING/texte-text/nog_rm_ri_bsm_bsm12_bid_1334948912303_eng.pdf.
[153] Ibid.

tiny, British-based Franklin Petroleum, which secured all of the new leases by promising just $7.5 million of spending on exploration.[154] But the fact remains that Canada has backed away slightly from the same-season relief well requirement.

7.3 Norway

Norwegian oil companies have considerable experience with offshore drilling in the North Sea and, increasingly, the Norwegian Sea: that part of the North Atlantic Ocean between the North Sea, the Barents Sea, Greenland, and the west coast of Norway. In the face of declining oil production in the North Sea, and therefore declining government royalties, most Norwegians had accepted the necessity of opening the Norwegian Arctic to offshore drilling. However, that consensus fragmented after the *Deepwater Horizon* blowout, with plans to tap resources around the Lofoten Islands coming under particular scrutiny. The 200-kilometer-long chain of islands lies offshore the Norwegian mainland north of the Arctic Circle. The archipelago is famous for its jagged mountains, which rise straight out of the sea, as well as its cold-water reefs and a large cod fishery.[155] A compromise was reached in 2011, protecting the Lofoten Islands but allowing offshore drilling further north.[156] Shortly thereafter, a massive field containing at least 500 million barrels of high-quality oil was discovered further south, near Bergen, which might have been expected to slow the rush toward the more northerly waters.[157] But, in 2012, the Norwegian government announced that it was opening bids on seventy-two new exploration blocks in the Barents Sea and a further fourteen in the Norwegian Sea.[158]

[154] "Low-Ball Arctic Oil Lease Earns Opposition Scorn," *Canadian Press*, September 21, 2012, available at www.cbc.ca/news/canada/north/story/2012/09/20/beaufort-franklin-ndp.html.

[155] In 2002, Norway included the Lofoten Islands in its "tentative list," the first stage in the acquisition of "World Heritage Site" status at UNESCO. See whc.unesco.org/en/tentativelists/1751/.

[156] Bjoern H. Amland, Associated Press, "Norway Blocks Oil Drilling in Fish-Spawning Area," March 11, 2011, available at seattletimes.nwsource.com/html/businesstechnology/2014465947_apeunorwayoildrilling.html.

[157] Bjoern H. Amland, Associated Press, "Statoil Announces Huge North Sea Oil Discovery," August 16, 2011, available at abcnews.go.com/Business/wireStory?id=14313838#.T-pFPI7O5UQ.

[158] "Norway Offers Exploration Licenses in Arctic Waters," *Reuters*, June 26, 2012, available at www.reuters.com/article/2012/06/26/norway-licences-idUSL6E8HQ3FW20120626.

Fortunately, Norway has some of the highest safety standards for offshore drilling of any country in the world, including a long-standing requirement for the capability to initiate a relief well within twelve days of a blowout.[159] Its Arctic expertise and technology is sought around the world, including in Greenland and Russia.

7.4 Greenland

The government of Greenland sees oil and gas development as a crucial element in its move toward financial and political independence from Denmark and has been keen to issue offshore exploration licenses. The licenses have been snapped up by multinational oil companies, attracted by geological indications of considerable oil and gas potential off Greenland's west and northeastern coasts.

Davis Strait is located between Greenland and Canada's Baffin Island. It is sometimes referred to as "iceberg alley" due to the thousands of icebergs that calve off the glaciers of western Greenland and are carried south to the North Atlantic by ocean currents. Davis Strait experiences intense storms, is located 800 nautical miles from any significant port or population center, and is in complete darkness for several months each year. The strait is also home to several endangered species of whales as well as a commercial shrimp and turbot fishery.

Greenland has adopted Norway's high standards for offshore drilling. When Cairn Energy, a Scottish oil company, drilled a number of wells in Davis Strait in 2010 and 2011, two drill ships were required to be in the area at all times, leaving one available to drill a relief well if a blowout occurred.[160] Several "ice-management vessels" were also kept on standby to tow threatening icebergs away.[161] Despite the standards, and despite knowing that the media and environmental groups were following its activities closely, Cairn Energy took risks that were later deemed unacceptable. Specifically, the company used more than 160 tonnes of Ultrahib, a drilling lubricant that is "red-listed" under European regulations because it breaks down very slowly in the environment. Although the Danish National Environmental Research

---

[159] "Norsok Standard D-010 Rev. 3 (Well Integrity in Drilling and Well Operations)," August 2004, sec. 4.8.2, available at www.standard.no/PageFiles/1315/D-010r3.pdf.

[160] See "Media Backgrounder: Cairn's Prevention and Response Capabilities Offshore Greenland," available at www.cairnenergy.com/files/pdf/greenland/PreventionandResponseCapabilities.pdf.

[161] Ibid.

Institute gave Cairn permission to use Ultrahib in 2011, it later said the amount used was "unacceptable" and "in violation of international resolutions."[162]

Since pollution does not respect international boundaries, any release of oil or drilling lubricants on the Greenland side of Davis Strait could easily end up in Canadian waters. In 2010, then Canadian Environment Minister Jim Prentice told the House of Commons that officials had discussed the planned drilling with Greenland's government and that "Canadians can be assured that the environment will be protected."[163] At the same time, however, a spokesperson for the Department of Foreign Affairs told the Canadian Press that officials from Canada and Greenland did not know if a 1983 agreement with Denmark on pollution prevention and reduction in the marine environment still applied, now that Greenland had jurisdiction over its own natural resources.[164] The Department has since expressed the view that Greenland is the successor to Denmark's obligations under the agreement.[165] Those obligations include a 1991 amendment to the 1983 agreement that deals with spill preparedness and response, foresees the sharing of equipment and personnel, and explicitly includes hydrocarbons.[166]

Cairn Energy failed to discover oil or gas off Greenland and wrote off $1 billion in losses.[167] However, the government of Greenland continues to issue exploration licenses off the west coast of the island,

---

[162] Ray Weaver, "Oil Company Criticized for Release of Hazardous Chemical," *Copenhagen Post*, May 23, 2012, available at www.cphpost.dk/business/oil-company-criticised-release-hazardous-chemical.

[163] "Drilling Plans Near Greenland Spark Concern," *Canadian Press*, April 30, 2010, available at www.ctvnews.ca/drilling-plans-near-greenland-spark-concern-1.507833.

[164] Ibid. See also 1983 Agreement for Cooperation relating to the Marine Environment (Canada and Denmark) (1984) 23(2) ILM 269, available at treaties.un.org/doc/Publication/UNTS/Volume%201348/volume-1348-I-22693-English.pdf.

[165] See the website of the Canadian Department of Foreign Affairs and International Trade, "Denmark (Faroe Islands/Greenland)," Chapter 1, n. 50, above.

[166] 1991 Exchange of Notes Constituting an Agreement to Amend Annex B of the 1983 Agreement for Cooperation Relating to the Marine Environment (Canada and Denmark), available at treaties.un.org/doc/Publication/UNTS/Volume%201853/volume-1853-I-22693-English.pdf.

[167] "Davis Strait Oil Well Comes Up Dry Again," *CBC News*, September 13, 2011, available at www.cbc.ca/news/canada/north/story/2011/09/13/north-cairn-davis-strait-oil-wells-dry.html; Terry Macalister, "City Investors Are Getting Cold Feet about Arctic Oil Prospecting," *Guardian*, June 21, 2012, available at www.guardian.co.uk/environment/2012/jun/21/investment-arctic-oil-drilling.

including some close to Canada's Lancaster Sound, a marine area so biologically rich that it is sometimes referred to as the "Serengeti of the Arctic."[168]

7.5 Russia

Russia is the world's largest producer of oil, with most of the production occurring onshore in western Siberia. Russian offshore production is dominated by natural gas, with the enormous Shtokman field in the Barents Sea commanding much of the attention. Natural gas is less of a hazard to the environment than oil, because any gas that leaks either evaporates or explodes, with potentially severe but localized consequences. However, Exxon currently plans to invest $3 billion in oil exploration in the Kara Sea, in partnership the Russian state-owned company Rosneft. Russian Deputy Prime Minister Igor Sechin predicts that oil projects in the Kara Sea will attract between $200 billion and $300 billion in direct investment over the next decade,[169] though, as Charles Emmerson and Glada Lahn have noted, "this figure is highly speculative."[170]

Russia's environmental protection record leaves much to be desired. In 2011, Oleg Kuznetsov, an official from the Russian Emergencies Ministry, revealed the existence of almost 25,000 objects containing solid radioactive waste in Russian waters, many of them off the northern coast, including reactors from old nuclear submarines scuttled near the Novaya Zemlya archipelago.[171] In addition, nuclear waste deposited onshore is now leaking into the Arctic Ocean.[172] As for oil spills, Russia loses at least 1 percent of its annual oil production through leaks and

---

[168] See Government of Greenland, Bureau of Mines and Petroleum, "Current Licenses," at www.bmp.gl/petroleum/current-licences. On Lancaster Sound, see Gloria Galloway, "Ottawa Moves to Protect Serengeti of the Arctic," Globe and Mail, December 6, 2010, available at www.theglobeandmail.com/news/politics/ottawa-moves-to-protect-serengeti-of-the-arctic/article4081939/.

[169] Isabel Gorst, Charles Clover, and Ed Crooks, "Exxon and Rosneft Sign Arctic Deal," Financial Times, August 30, 2011. Sechin is quoted as saying: "One ice-proof platform costs $15bn minimum. For the Kara Sea, we require at least 10 platforms."

[170] Charles Emmerson and Glada Lahn, Arctic Opening: Opportunity and Risk in the High North (London: Lloyd's, 2012), p. 25 (Box 3), available at www.chathamhouse.org/publications/papers/view/182839.

[171] "Russia Reports 25,000 Undersea Radioactive Waste Sites," RIA Novosti, December 26, 2011, available at en.rian.ru/Environment/20111226/170500108.html.

[172] Jorn Madslien, "Nuclear Waste Poses Arctic Threat," BBC News, October 19, 2006, available at news.bbc.co.uk/2/hi/6058302.stm.

spills.[173] Approximately 10 percent of that production – around 500,000 tons – escapes into rivers that flow into the Arctic Ocean.[174] Depending on the density of the oil, 500,000 tons is around 550 million liters, or more than half the amount spilled in the *Deepwater Horizon* disaster. This dismal record raises serious questions about Russia's ability to engage in safe offshore oil exploration, production, and transport. In 2011, a floating oil platform capsized and sank while being towed in the Sea of Okhotsk, in Russia's Far East just north of Japan.[175] Fifty-three people died. The rig was owned by Gazprom, which just a few months earlier had announced that it was sending another floating platform to engage in exploratory drilling in the Pechora Sea in the Russian Arctic. This second rig, designed to operate in remote locations, can store up to 130 million liters of oil between visits from tankers.[176]

Russia has treaties with its neighbors concerning cooperation in the event of an oil spill. In 1989, the Soviet Union and the United States concluded an Agreement concerning Cooperation in Combating Pollution in the Bering and Chukchi Seas in Emergency Situations.[177] Under the agreement, the two countries "undertake to render assistance to each other in combatting pollution incidents ... regardless of where such incidents may occur," to develop a "Joint Contingency Plan," and "periodically [to] conduct joint pollution response exercises and meetings in accordance with the provisions of the Plan." In 1994, Russia and Norway signed an agreement on oil spill response in the Barents Sea. The agreement requires the two countries also to develop a joint contingency plan and to notify each other in the event of a spill.[178]

---

[173] Nataliya Vasilyeva, "Russia Oil Spills Wreak Devastation," *Associated Press*, December 17, 2011, available at www.boston.com/business/articles/2011/12/17/ap_enterprise_russia_oil_spills_wreak_devastation/.

[174] Ibid.

[175] Nataliya Vasilyeva, "Kolskaya Oil Rig Sinking Sparks Doubt Over Arctic Plan," *Associated Press*, December 23, 2001, available at www.huffingtonpost.com/2011/12/23/kolskaya-oil-rig-sinking-arctic_n_1167103.html.

[176] Ibid.

[177] 1989 Agreement between the Government of the United States of America and the Government of the Union of Soviet Socialist Republics concerning Cooperation in Combating Pollution in the Bering and Chukchi Seas in Emergency Situations, 2190 UNTS 180, available at www.akrrt.org/mou/Kp-US_USSR_89.pdf.

[178] "Overenskomst mellom Norge og Russland angående samarbeid om bekjempelse av oljeforurensning i Barentshavet, 28 April 1994," in *Overenskomster med fremmede makter* (Oslo: Norwegian Ministry of Foreign Affairs, 1996), pp. 94–98, cited in Olav Schram Stokke, "Sub-regional Cooperation and Protection of the Arctic Marine Environment: The Barents Sea," in Davor Vidas (ed.), *Protecting the Polar Marine Environment: Law and Policy for Pollution Prevention* (Cambridge University Press, 2000), 124 at 138.

7.6 Liability for oil spills

A number of treaties govern liability for pollution from oil tankers, beginning with the 1969 International Convention on Civil Liability for Oil Pollution Damage (CLC Convention) and the 1971 International Convention on the Establishment of an International Fund for Compensation for Oil Pollution Damage (Fund Convention).[179] Negotiated and managed under the umbrella of the International Maritime Organization, these treaties operate on the basis of strict liability for ship owners (i.e., liability even in the absence of fault) and create a system of compulsory liability insurance. In return, ship owners benefit from liability caps that are based on the tonnage of the vessels, with damages above the caps being compensated – up to set limits – from a fund that is supported by levies on oil shipments. In 1992, the treaties were augmented by two protocols that raised the liability limit under the CLC Convention to $139 million, and the compensation limit under the Fund Convention to $315 million.[180] In 2000, the limits were raised by another 50 percent, and in 2003 a further protocol created an optional "Supplementary Fund" that raised the compensation limit to $1.2 billion for states choosing to ratify it.[181]

The United States has not ratified any of these treaties, choosing to deal with the matter of liability entirely under domestic law. This could cause serious legal problems in the event of a spill from a foreign-flagged tanker close to the US coast or, especially, in either of the two international straits passing through US territorial waters, namely the Bering Strait and Unimak Pass.[182] All the other Arctic countries have ratified the updated CLC and Fund Conventions, as have Liberia and Panama, the world's two largest shipping registries.[183] In addition, five of the Arctic countries – Canada, Denmark, Norway, Sweden, and Finland – have joined the Supplementary Fund.[184]

As cargo ships have become larger and longer-range, oil tankers are no longer the only vessels able to cause substantial oil spills. As

---

[179] See International Oil Pollution Compensation Funds, Liability and Compensation for Oil Pollution Damage: Texts of the 1992 Civil Liability Convention, the 1992 Fund Convention and the Supplementary Fund Protocol (2011 edn.), available at www.iopcfunds.org/uploads/tx_iopcpublications/Text_of_Conventions_e.pdf.

[180] Ibid.   [181] Ibid.   [182] See discussion, Chapter 5, above.

[183] For list of the States Parties to the 1992 CLC, 1992 Fund Convention, and 2003 Supplementary Fund, see www.iopcfunds.org/about-us/legal-framework/1992-fund-convention-and-supplementary-fund-protocol/.

[184] Ibid.

mentioned above, a Malaysian cargo ship broke apart and spilled 1.2 million liters of fuel oil ("bunker oil") while transiting Unimak Pass in 2004; almost none of the oil was recovered, due to the remote location, bad weather, and the near-complete absence of oil spill clean-up equipment in the Aleutian Islands.[185] Another treaty, the 2001 International Convention on Civil Liability for Bunker Oil Pollution Damage, requires that ship owners carry insurance against this risk. However, Article 6 of the so-called "Bunker Convention" preserves the right of ship owners and insurers to limit their liability "under any applicable national or international regime, such as the Convention on Limitation of Liability for Maritime Claims, 1976, as amended."[186] That 1976 Convention sets liability limits that are significantly lower than the damages that could potentially result from a large spill of fuel oil in the Arctic.[187]

No treaty has yet been concluded to deal with liability and compensation for pollution caused by offshore oil rigs, pipelines, or sub-sea wellhead production systems. As governments struggle to address the unique challenges of regulating offshore drilling in the Arctic, one particularly important issue concerns liability caps set out in domestic laws. BP has estimated its total costs from the *Deepwater Horizon* blowout at approximately $41 billion, including compensation for environmental and economic damage.[188] These costs eclipsed the liability limits under US law, with the 1990 Oil Pollution Act setting a limit of just $75 million for natural resource and economic damages.[189] However, the limit does not apply in cases of fault or gross negligence, and BP, rather than contesting the point, chose to waive the limit from the outset. In May 2010, Senator Lisa Murkowski of Alaska blocked a bill that would have raised the cap under the Oil Pollution Act to $10 billion.[190]

---

[185] See discussion, Chapter 5, above.

[186] For the text of the "Bunker Convention," see www.gard.no/ikbViewer/Content/ 3210767/Bunkers%20Convention%20and%20ratifications%20March%202012.pdf.

[187] See 1976 Convention on Limitation of Liability for Maritime Claims, as amended by the 1996 Protocol, available at www.emsa.europa.eu/main/enforcement-eu-legislation/ topics-a-instruments/download/974/595/23.html.

[188] Jonathan L. Ramseur, "Liability and Compensation Issues Raised by the 2010 Gulf Oil Spill," Congressional Research Service, March 11, 2011, available at http://assets. opencrs.com/rpts/R41679_20110311.pdf.

[189] PL 101-380, primarily codified at 33 USC § 2701, *et seq.* For a useful summary of the issues, see Ramseur, "Liability and Compensation Issues," ibid.

[190] Jake Sherman, "Murkowski Blocks Oil Liability Bill," *Politico*, May 13, 2010, available at www.politico.com/news/stories/0510/37207.html.

In the Canadian Arctic, liability for an offshore oil spill is limited to just $40 million by regulations adopted under the 1970 Arctic Waters Pollution Prevention Act.[191] However, the matter is complicated by the fact that the 1984 Inuvialuit Final Agreement provides: "Where it is established that actual wildlife harvest loss or future harvest loss was caused by development, the liability of the developer shall be absolute and he shall be liable without proof of fault or negligence for compensation to the Inuvialuit and for the cost of mitigative and remedial measures."[192] The Inuvialuit Final Agreement applies in the Inuvialuit Settlement Area, which includes most of the Canadian portion of the Beaufort Sea.[193] Nathan Vanderklippe of the *Globe and Mail* has written that: "the extent of liability under the Inuvialuit agreement is questionable. It applies to costs related to "harvest loss" and "future harvest loss" – and it's unclear whether all spill costs would be covered."[194] But while the full extent of liability is unclear, a major oil spill would clearly cause damage to the marine ecosystem on which the Inuvialuit rely, on a scale that is magnitudes greater than $40 million.

A good argument can be made for eliminating the liability caps on Arctic oil exploration, development, and shipping. The existing limits are a form of public subsidy to the oil industry, since potential costs above the limits need not be factored into insurance costs, and therefore also not into any assessment of the economic viability of a potential project. Liability caps prevent the full internalization of costs, and can thus promote activities that do not make economic sense from a comprehensive perspective. Greenland has been showing some leadership on this issue, demanding that oil companies provide a $2 billion guarantee in advance of exploratory drilling. Smaller companies are required to

---

[191] Arctic Waters Pollution Prevention Regulations, CRC, c. 354, s. 8 ("For the purposes of section 6 of the Act, the maximum amount of liability of an operator in respect of each deposit of waste is as follows: ... (f) in the case of an operation engaged in exploring for, developing or exploiting oil and gas, $40 million").

[192] Inuvialuit Final Agreement (as amended), Art. 13(15), available at www.daair.gov.nt.ca/_live/documents/documentManagerUpload/InuvialuitFinalAgreement1984.pdf.

[193] See discussion, above, pp. 80–82.

[194] Nathan Vanderklippe, "Oil Drillers Willing to Accept Liability for Accidents in Arctic," *Globe and Mail*, September 13, 2011, available at www.theglobeandmail.com/report-on-business/industry-news/energy-and-resources/oil-drillers-willing-to-accept-liability-for-accidents-in-arctic/article4199962/.

provide the money up front, with the "bond" being designated specifically for meeting the clean-up costs resulting from any spill.[195]

7.7 Agreement on oil spill preparedness and response

All eight Arctic Council states have ratified the 1990 Convention on Oil Pollution Preparedness, Response and Cooperation (OPRC), a treaty negotiated within the framework of the International Maritime Organization.[196] Parties to OPRC are required to establish measures for dealing with pollution incidents; these include the stockpiling of oil spill equipment, the development of clean-up plans, and the holding of exercises. They are also required to cooperate in the event of a spill; this may include providing equipment when requested by another party. OPRC also promotes the development of bilateral and multilateral agreements for oil pollution preparedness and response on a regional basis.

In 1997, the Arctic Council adopted a set of "Arctic offshore oil and gas guidelines," which it updated in 2002 and again in 2009.[197] Although the guidelines included both general principles as well as some more detailed recommendations, they fell short in two respects. First, they were non-binding, with all the compliance problems this can entail. Second, they avoided some of the more difficult and important issues, such as whether oil companies should be required to maintain a same-season relief well capability.[198]

In 2011, the Arctic Council created a task force to negotiate a treaty on Marine Oil Pollution Preparedness and Response.[199] The task force, co-chaired by Norway, Russia, and the United States, will present a finished treaty in 2013, one that is modeled on the 2011 Arctic Search and Rescue Agreement and therefore focuses on improving communication and coordination when accidents occur.[200] In terms of substantive obligations, the new treaty is unlikely to go beyond the 1990 OPRC to address difficult issues such

---

[195] Tim Webb, "Greenland Wants $2bn Bond from Oil Firms Keen to Drill in its Arctic Waters," *Guardian*, November 12, 2010, available at www.guardian.co.uk/business/2010/nov/12/greenland-oil-drilling-bond.

[196] 1990 International Convention on Oil Pollution Preparedness, Response and Co-operation, available at www.ifrc.org/docs/idrl/I245EN.pdf.

[197] For the 2009 version, see http://arctic-council.org/filearchive/Arctic%20Offshore%20Oil%20and%20Gas%20Guidelines%202009.pdf.

[198] See discussion, above, pp. 201–205.

[199] See Task Force on Arctic Marine Oil Pollution Preparedness and Response, at www.arctic-council.org/index.php/en/about-us/task-forces/280-oil-spill-task-force.

[200] See discussion, below, pp. 277–279.

as same-season relief well capability, minimal requirements for the positioning and deployment of equipment and personnel, or the raising or lifting of liability caps. To the degree that the treaty will fill a gap, it is likely to be in terms of promoting regional consultations, coordination, and cooperation, since there is currently no legally binding, multilateral marine oil pollution response instrument specific to the Arctic.

Although improved communication and coordination can help, managing the risks associated with Arctic oil will remain a formidable task. The crux of the matter was set out in a 2010 World Wildlife Fund report: "Mounting an effective response to a major oil spill in the Arctic is presently not possible due to enormous environmental challenges, a lack of capacity and the severe limitations of current response methods in ice-covered waters."[201] The same report identified a so-called "response gap" whereby: "Due to the Arctic's remoteness and extreme weather, there is also a high percentage of time when no response, however ineffective, could even be attempted."[202] In the circumstances, what is really needed is an Arctic-wide treaty that focuses on oil spill prevention, and this might involve forcing companies to internalize the full costs of offshore drilling in the region. Oil companies will develop and implement the enhanced safety measures needed in the Arctic, but only if they are forced to bear the full risk and cost of the damage caused by spills.

8 Ecosystem-based management

Ecosystem-based management involves dealing with all the sources of environmental stress as a package, for instance both pollution *and* overfishing. This approach has been taken in other regional contexts, including the Mediterranean Sea, the Baltic Sea, and the Northeast Atlantic Ocean – a sizeable portion of which falls within the Arctic.[203] Ecosystem-based management has also been applied in the Barents Sea. In 1993, the Nordic countries, Russia, and the European Commission adopted the Declaration on Cooperation in the Barents Euro-Arctic

[201] World Wildlife Fund, "Drilling for Oil in the Arctic," n. 139, above.   [202] Ibid.
[203] See, e.g., Peter M. Haas, *Saving the Mediterranean: The Politics of International Environmental Cooperation* (New York: Columbia University Press, 1990); Martin Lindegren, *et al.*, "Preventing the Collapse of the Baltic Cod Stock through an Ecosystem-Based Management Approach." (2009) 106 *Proceedings of the National Academy of Science of the United States of America* 14722; Chris Frid, *et al.*, "Ecosystem-Based Fisheries Management: Progress in the NE Atlantic." (2005) 29 *Marine Policy* 461.

Region – the so-called "Kirkenes Declaration," after the town in northern Norway where it was signed.[204] The declaration focused on developing regional cooperation on sustainable development and, to that end, established an intergovernmental forum called the Barents Euro-Arctic Council (BEAC).[205] At the same time, a collection of provincial governments and indigenous peoples established a parallel forum called the Barents Regional Council (BRC).[206]

The Arctic Ocean coastal states are working toward such an approach for the central Arctic Ocean, although so far they have done so through a series of complementary arrangements within the Arctic Council (Arctic Marine Shipping Assessment; the forthcoming treaty on Oil Spill Preparedness and Response), the International Maritime Organization (Guidelines on Arctic Shipping; the forthcoming Polar Code), and the United Nations (Framework Convention on Climate Change), rather than in a single instrument or institution.

One Arctic-specific proposal was made in a 2008 paper written for the World Wildlife Fund by Rob Huebert and Brooks Yeager. They call for the establishment of a regional fisheries organization or a regional sea agreement under UNCLOS and usefully identify the Convention for the Protection of the Marine Environment of the North-East Atlantic ("OSPAR Convention") as one possible model.[207] The idea of a regional fisheries organization has already been discussed earlier in this chapter. As for a regional sea agreement, this is certainly possible under the UN Environmental Program's "Regional Seas Program."[208] But, while regional seas have become focal points for multilateral environmental cooperation elsewhere in the world, it may be questioned whether the mere existence of a regional sea creates legal obligations.[209]

---

[204] "Declaration on Cooperation in the Barents Euro-Arctic Region," Kirkenes. Norway, January 11, 1993, available at www.unep.org/dewa/giwa/areas/kirkenes.htm.

[205] See the website of the Barents Euro-Arctic Council at www.beac.st/in_English/Barents_Euro-Arctic_Council.iw3.

[206] See the website of the Barents Regional Council at www.beac.st/in_English/Barents_Euro-Arctic_Council/Barents_Regional_Council.iw3.

[207] Rob Huebert and Brooks Yeager, "A New Sea: The Need for a Regional Agreement on Management and Conservation of the Arctic Marine Environment." (World Wildlife Fund, 2008), available at http://awsassets.panda.org/downloads/a_new_sea_jan08_final_11jan08.pdf.

[208] United Nations Environmental Programme, "Regional Seas Program," at www.unep.org/regionalseas/default.asp.

[209] Ibid.

Huebert and Yeager stretch a bit further in claiming that the Arctic Ocean is an "enclosed" or "semi-enclosed sea" under Article 122 of UNCLOS, a status that would provide the coastal states with enhanced regulatory powers. But, as J. Enno Harders points out, "[Article 122] requires 'a narrow outlet' to another sea or ocean ... The open sea spaces of the Greenland Sea, the Norwegian Sea and the Bering Strait clearly contradict the status of the Arctic Ocean as semi-enclosed, both from the geographical and from the legal point of view."[210] That said, it is clearly desirable that the Arctic Ocean coastal states increase their efforts to protect the environment of the central Arctic Ocean in a holistic manner, including but not limited to oil spill prevention, preparedness and response, fisheries management, and shipping safety.

9 Summary

Just like the Arctic marine ecosystem that I witnessed on glorious display off Beechey Island, all of the necessary elements in Arctic environmental protection are closely interconnected. International environmental law has a long history in the Arctic, beginning in the nineteenth century with efforts to preserve the northern fur seal, and continuing during the Cold War with protections for whales and polar bears. Today, the principal environmental challenges arise out of melting sea-ice and rising oil prices, two factors that – in tragic and ironic combination – are rapidly drawing shipping and resource development northwards. The Arctic states are only just beginning to respond with new law-making initiatives on shipping safety, oil spill preparedness and response, and it is hoped a regional fisheries organization. More cooperation is needed, and quickly, on regional standards for oil spill prevention, the raising or lifting of oil spill liability caps, and reducing the emissions of climate forcers such as Arctic haze and black carbon. The region's historic, fragile balance between ice and water makes it uniquely vulnerable to climate change, and utterly essential to the global climate. In this sense, international cooperation on the environment now begins, and ends, in the Arctic.

---

[210] J. Enno Harders, "In Quest of an Arctic Legal Regime: Marine Regionalism – A Concept of International Law Evaluated." (1987) 11 *Marine Policy* 285 at 295–296. See, similarly, Erik Molenaar, "Current and Prospective Roles of the Arctic Council System within the Context of the Law of the Sea." (2012) 27 *International Journal of Marine and Coastal Law* 553 at 563. Harders goes on to argue that the Arctic Ocean's status as a "regional sea" creates legal obligations for the coastal states to manage cooperatively the environment under both UNCLOS and general principles of international environmental law. Ibid.

7   Indigenous peoples

For millennia, humans have lived along the coastlines of the Arctic Ocean. Their presence preceded the origin of states, the concept of title to territory, and the arrival of European explorers and settlers, who treated the homelands of indigenous peoples as *terra nullius* – land belonging to no one. Consequently, several Arctic indigenous peoples now straddle national borders and boundaries. The Inuit live in four states: Canada, Denmark, Russia, and the United States. The Saami (also spelled Sami or Sámi) also live in four states: Norway, Sweden, Finland, and Russia. The Athabaskans and Gwich'in live in both Canada and the United States while the Aleut live on the Aleutian Island chain in both Alaska and (in small part) Russia.[1] In the Arctic, the relationship between indigenous peoples and international law is similar to that same relationship elsewhere in the world. Most indigenous peoples do not seek self-determination in the sense of independent statehood, but instead strive for "internal self-determination," that is to say, for human rights and self-government within the borders of existing states.[2]

The indigenous peoples of the Arctic came into contact with Europeans at quite different times. The Saami have co-existed with non-Saami people for thousands of years and are integrated into the economies, education systems, and governance structures of Norway,

---

[1] For a useful map, see Winfried K. Dallmann, "Indigenous Peoples of the Arctic Countries," Norwegian Polar Institute, at www.arctic-council.org/images/maps/indig_peoples.pdf.

[2] See, generally, S. James Anaya, *Indigenous Peoples in International Law*, 2nd edn. (Oxford University Press, 2004); Joshua Castellino and Niamh Walsh (eds.), *International Law and Indigenous Peoples* (Dordrecht: Martinus Nijhoff, 2004).

Sweden, and Finland.[3] They have also benefited from having their rights protected within domestic and international law as far back as 1751 when the delineation of the border between Sweden and Denmark–Norway by the Strömstad Treaty created a potential impediment to the movement of the Saami and their reindeer herds. The problem was solved by an attachment to the Strömstad Treaty called the "Lapp Codicil," which states in part:

> The Sami need the land of both states. Therefore, they shall, in accordance with tradition, be permitted both in autumn and spring to move their reindeer herds across the border into the other state. And hereafter, as before, they shall, like the state's own subjects, be allowed to use land and share for themselves and their animals, except in the places stated below, and they shall be met with friendliness, protected and aided.[4]

The Lapp Codicil, which is still in force, is sometimes referred to as the "Saami Magna Carta."

The Inuit of Greenland came into contact with Viking settlers as early as the twelfth century. In contrast, the Inuit of Canada and Alaska practiced their traditional way of life without significant interruption until the twentieth century and even then the contact mostly involved sporadic visitation by fur traders, whalers, missionaries, and police, rather than settlement. More recently, the establishment of radar stations during the Cold War and an initial search for petroleum resources during the 1960s and 70s led to an influx of military personnel and oil workers. The indigenous peoples of Russia faced particular challenges as a result of attempts to collectivize reindeer herding, as well as Joseph Stalin's efforts to develop the Arctic by moving millions of workers and prisoners there. The pressures have continued, with the oil and gas industry in Russia's Arctic now accounting for around 20 percent of the country's GDP.[5]

There are approximately 70,000 Saami in Norway, Sweden, Finland, and Russia, 155,000 Inuit in Alaska, Canada, Greenland, and Russia, 55,000 Athabaskans and Gwich'in in Alaska and Canada, 15,000 Aleut

---

[3] Galdu, the Resource Centre for the Rights of Indigenous Peoples, has published numerous reports on Saami political representation, resource management, and cultural and educational self-determination. See www.galdu.org.

[4] Lennard Sillanpää, *Impact of International Law on Indigenous Rights in Northern Europe* (Ottawa: Indian and Northern Affairs Canada, 1992), 6.

[5] Timothy Bancroft-Hinchey, "Climate Change, the Arctic and Russia's National Security," *Pravda*, March 25, 2010, available at http://english.pravda.ru/russia/politics/25-03-2010/112732-climate_russia-0/.

in Alaska and Russia, and 250,000 members of other indigenous groups in northern Russia. In terms of education, housing, health care, and wage employment, the Saami of the Nordic countries are the best off, followed by the Inuit of Greenland. The situation elsewhere can only be described as poor. To give just one example, the suicide rate among Inuit youth in Canada is thirty times the national average.[6] Poor economic conditions play a role here, along with a loss of traditional culture and a shortage of opportunities for meaningful political participation.[7]

1 Political participation and self-determination

The right to self-determination is mentioned in many treaties, including the UN Charter, and is widely considered to be part of customary international law.[8] The 1966 International Covenant on Civil and Political Rights and the 1966 International Covenant on Economic, Social and Cultural Rights include the identical first article: "All peoples have the right of self-determination. By virtue of that right they freely determine their political status and freely pursue their economic, social and cultural development."[9]

Although the right of indigenous peoples to self-determination is not generally considered to include a right to independent statehood, states are required to accord meaningful opportunities for political participation and local decision-making – often referred to as "self-government" – to indigenous peoples within their territories.[10] The Saami were the first Arctic indigenous people to be afforded significant opportunities for political participation, as Shayna Plaut explains:

The Saami Council was created in 1956 in the wake of a post World War II wave of liberalism, human rights and social justice that swept Northern Europe. It fed off the Nordic countries' desire to be seen as leaders in equality and human

---

[6] Helen Branswell, "Death, Suicide Rates among Inuit Kids Soar over Rest of Canada," *Globe and Mail*, July 18, 2012, available at www.theglobeandmail.com/news/national/death-suicide-rates-among-inuit-kids-soar-over-rest-of-canada/article4426600/.

[7] For an equally dark picture of the situation in Alaska, and some explanations, see William Yardley, "In Native Alaskan Villages, a Culture of Sorrow," *New York Times*, May 14, 2007, available at www.nytimes.com/2007/05/14/us/14alaska.html.

[8] Article 1(2) of the UN Charter refers to "the principle of equal rights and self-determination of peoples." See www.un.org/en/documents/charter/chapter1.shtml.

[9] International Covenant on Civil and Political Rights, available at www2.ohchr.org/english/law/ccpr.htm. International Covenant on Economic, Social and Cultural Rights, available at www2.ohchr.org/english/law/cescr.htm.

[10] See, e.g., Anaya, *Indigenous Peoples in International Law*, n. 2, above, pp. 153–184.

rights, and consequently the proponents of the Saami Council were able to secure governmental support in establishing a Saami Parliament that grew in administrative and economic strength in each Nordic country. Its primary goal was to reverse the policies of linguistic and cultural assimilation that had become domestic policy and prevented Saami from being able to enjoy their collective rights as a people.[11]

The popularly elected Saami Parliaments were established in Norway in 1989, Sweden in 1993, and Finland in 1996. Although they have limited legislative capacity, these institutions fulfill an important consultative role by ensuring that Saami views and interests are integrated into decision-making at the national level.[12] They also administer funds for Saami language and education programs.

Since 2001, the three parliaments have met annually as the Saami Parliamentary Conference. In 2005, the Saami Parliamentary Conference presented the "Draft Nordic Saami Convention" to the governments of Norway, Sweden, and Finland.[13] Five years later, the Draft Convention was accepted as a basis for negotiation by the three national governments, and formal talks have been underway since 2011. The Draft Convention affirms that the Saami are an indigenous people with "a particular need to develop its society across national borders," and that the three states "have a national as well as an international responsibility to provide adequate conditions for the Saami culture and society." These conditions include a substantial degree of self-government, as Article 3 of the Draft Convention makes clear:

As a people, the Saami has the right of self-determination in accordance with the rules and provisions of international law and of this Convention. In so far as it follows from these rules and provisions, the Saami people has the right to determine its own economic, social and cultural development and to dispose, to their own benefit, over its own natural resources.[14]

As was explained in Chapter 1, the Inuit of Greenland have achieved extensive powers of self-government as a result of a 2008 referendum that gave responsibility for judicial affairs, policing, and natural

---

[11] Shayna Plaut, "'Cooperation Is the Story' – Best Practices of Transnational Indigenous Activism in the North." (2012) 16 *International Journal of Human Rights* 193 at 197.

[12] Else Grete Broderstad, "Political Autonomy and Integration of Authority: The Understanding of Saami Self-Determination." (2001) 8 *International Journal on Minority and Group Rights* 151.

[13] For the text of the initial draft, see www.regjeringen.no/Upload/AID/temadokumenter/sami/sami_samekonv_engelsk.pdf.

[14] Ibid.

resources to the government of Greenland. Since the government is democratic, and Inuit make up 88 percent of the population, the world's largest island is well on its way to becoming the first Inuit-governed state.

The 1971 Alaska Native Claims Settlement Act was adopted by the US Congress to provide greater certainty for the oil industry as well as a degree of self-government for the indigenous peoples of that US state.[15] The legislation provided nearly $1 billion in cash payments and created twelve regional for-profit corporations with surface and mineral rights for 180,000 square kilometers of land. A combination of investments and oil industry activity has provided considerable on-going revenue for some groups, most notably the 11,000 Inupiat represented by the Arctic Slope Regional Corporation (ASRC).[16] The ASRC is now the largest Alaskan-owned company with approximately 10,000 employees world-wide.[17] In addition, the incorporation of the North Slope Borough has enabled the Inupiat-controlled government of the borough to levy property taxes on oil and gas facilities, and to become the sole provider of services (and the largest employer by far) in an area that is nearly as large as the United Kingdom.[18] However, the Alaska Native Claims Settlement Act has provided relatively little protection for indigenous rights – including subsistence hunting and fishing rights – in the other nine-tenths of the largest US state.

Canada's Inuit have acquired a degree of self-government as the result of a series of land claims agreements that stretch from the Inuvialuit Settlement Region in the Yukon and Northwest Territories to Nunatsiavut in Labrador. Most significantly, the Inuit of the High Arctic islands and west coast of Hudson Bay have acquired their own political entity within Canada's federal structure. The territory of Nunavut, with an 85 percent indigenous population, has a majoritarian government system that in practice provides Inuit self-government. But while the government of Nunavut has considerable autonomy over social services, education, health care, and the administration of justice, the government of Canada maintains a tight grip on resource revenue. This leaves the territory almost entirely dependent on fiscal transfers, which are not increasing in line with population growth – in part

[15] 1971 Alaska Native Claims Settlement Act, 43 USC Chapter 33, available at www.law.cornell.edu/uscode/text/43/chapter-33.
[16] See the ASRC website at www.asrc.com.   [17] Ibid.
[18] See North Slope Borough Corporation, at www.co.north-slope.ak.us/.

because Nunavut has a birth rate that is twice the national average.[19] Control over resource revenue has become a key issue for the government of Nunavut, which believes that fiscal autonomy along with the further development of extractive industries would enable it to improve education, health care, and living conditions. Not surprisingly, resource revenue is the sticking point in devolution talks between the Canadian and Nunavut governments.[20]

Inuit self-determination has taken different forms in other parts of northern Canada. In 2005, the Labrador Inuit Land Claims Agreement was concluded between the Inuit of Labrador, the federal government, and the provincial government of Newfoundland and Labrador.[21] Although Nunatsiavut remains part of Newfoundland and Labrador, its newly created government is responsible for health, education, and cultural affairs. Similar powers are now being sought by the Inuit of Nunavik, who live within Quebec and settled their land claims with the federal and provincial governments in 1975.[22]

Russia's northern indigenous peoples have almost no opportunities for meaningful political participation, partly as a result of being minority populations within their traditional homelands, and partly as a result of the centralized and autocratic nature of Soviet, and now Russian, politics. That said, the Russian Saami do consult with the Saami Council and the Saami Parliamentary Conference. In addition, they and other indigenous peoples are represented at the Arctic Council by the Russian Association of Indigenous Peoples of the North, Siberia and Far East (RAIPON) – a collection of thirty-four regional and ethnic organizations created in 1990 and originally called the Association of Peoples of the North of the USSR.[23]

However, RAIPON itself complains on its website that

In many regions, strong opposition by the authorities is manifested in complete disregard for indigenous peoples and violation of their lawful rights and

---

[19] "Nunavut Still Canada's Youngest, Fastest Growing Jurisdiction: Statistics Canada," *Nunatsiaq News*, July 20, 2011, available at www.nunatsiaqonline.ca/stories/article/206678_nunavut_is_canadas_youngest_fastest_growing_place_stats_can_report/.
[20] See Anthony Speca, "Nunavut, Greenland and the Politics of Resource Revenues." (May 2012) *Policy Options* 62, available at www.irpp.org/po/archive/may12/speca.pdf.
[21] 2005 Labrador and Inuit Land Claims Agreement, available at www.exec.gov.nl.ca/exec/igas/land_claims/agreement.html.
[22] See Makivik Corporation, "Nunavik Government," at www.makivik.org/building-nunavik/nunavik-government/.
[23] See RAIPON at www.raipon.info/en/.

interests. Government representatives are trying to continue policies of paternalism toward and control over indigenous peoples; often they do not know or acknowledge international standards for human and aboriginal rights and they do not understand the goals of the movement.[24]

In November 2012, the Russian Ministry of Justice ordered RAIPON to suspend operations for six months, ostensibly due to a lack of compliance with Russian law. The move prompted the "Senior Arctic Officials" of the Arctic Council member states, along with the other indigenous "permanent participants," to issue a statement of concern – a statement that was, significantly, supported by Russian Arctic Ambassador Anton Vasiliev.[25] This suggests that the Ministry of Justice may have been acting without the support of the rest of the Russian government. But regardless of how this particular controversy plays out, the situation for Russian indigenous peoples will likely only grow worse in the years ahead, as resource extraction companies dramatically expand their activities in Russia's Arctic, further pushing aside indigenous peoples and their traditional way of life.[26]

At the level of implementation, self-determination remains a work in progress for Arctic indigenous peoples. Nevertheless, the as-yet-unperfected character of the indigenous rights of Arctic peoples has not prevented several Arctic states from invoking the historic presence of those same peoples in support of their own, state-centric sovereignty claims.

2 Indigenous rights and state claims

It is generally accepted that a "continuous and peaceful display of sovereignty" can provide a basis for title to territory.[27] It has also been recognized, most notably by the International Court of Justice in the *Western Sahara Case*, that rights acquired by an indigenous people can

---

[24] Section on "Social" at RAIPON website: www.raipon.info/en/history/social.html.

[25] See Jane George, "Arctic Council Officials Call for Reinstatement of Russian Indigenous Org," *Nunatsiaq News*, November 15, 2012, available at www.nunatsiaqonline.ca/stories/article/65674arctic_council_calls_for_russian_indigenous_orgs_return/.

[26] See, e.g., Lucy Ash, "Yamal reindeer herders hemmed in by gas fields and pipelines," *BBC News*, May 10, 2012, available at www.bbc.co.uk/news/magazine-17956108.

[27] *Island of Palmas Case (Netherlands v. USA)* (1928) 2 Reports of International Arbitral Awards 829 at 869 (Max Huber, arbitrator), available at http://untreaty.un.org/cod/riaa/cases/vol_II/829-871.pdf.

contribute to a state's title to territory.[28] For this reason, both Canada and Denmark have sometimes invoked traditional "use and occupancy" of land and ice by Arctic indigenous peoples as an element of their sovereignty claims.

In 1930, during an exchange of notes concerning title over the Sverdrup Islands, located north of the Northwest Passage, the Norwegian chargé d'affaires in London recognized Canadian sovereignty and only then requested that access be provided to Norwegian nationals for commercial activities there.[29] As was explained in Chapter 1, the British chargé d'affaires in Oslo denied the request on the basis that the Canadian government had designated "the Arctic areas as hunting and trapping preserves for the sole use of the aboriginal population of the Northwest Territories, in order to avert the danger of want and starvation through the exploitation of the wild life by white hunters and traders."[30]

Two decades later, in 1953 and 1955, the Canadian government relocated seventeen Inuit families from northern Quebec to Resolute Bay and Grise Fiord, creating Canada's two most northerly permanent communities. The Inuit were essentially being treated as flagpoles. As Shelagh Grant has explained, the relocations were motivated by a desire to demonstrate Canadian use and occupancy of the High Arctic islands in the face of a greatly increased US military presence during the Second World War and Cold War, as well as reports of Greenland Inuit visiting Ellesmere Island.[31] The Inuit, who had never lived that far north, called the hamlets "Qausuittuq" (the place where the sun never sets) and "Auyuittuq" (the place where the ice never melts).

In 1984, the Canadian government and the Inuvialuit of the western Arctic concluded the Inuvialuit Final Agreement, which, among other things, set the western boundary of the Inuvialuit Settlement Area in the Beaufort Sea at the 141°W meridian.[32] As was explained in Chapter

---

[28] Western Sahara, Advisory Opinion (1975) ICJ Reports 12 at 38–39, paras. 79–80. See discussion, above, pp. 132–133.

[29] See discussion, Chapter 1, above.

[30] Letter from the British chargé d'affaires in Oslo to the Norwegian Minister for Foreign Affairs, November 5, 1930, in Exchange of Notes Regarding the Recognition by the Norwegian Government of the Sovereignty of His Majesty over the Sverdrup Islands, Canada Treaty Series 1930, No. 17, available at http://byers.typepad.com/arctic/1930.html.

[31] Shelagh D. Grant, "A Case of Compounded Error: The Inuit Resettlement Project, 1953, and the Government Response, 1990." (1991) 19(1) Northern Perspectives (Canadian Arctic Resources Committee) 3.

[32] 1984 Inuvialuit Final Agreement (as amended), available at www.daair.gov.nt.ca/_live/documents/documentManagerUpload/InuvialuitFinalAgreement1984.pdf.

3, the meridian, which on land serves as the border between Alaska and the Yukon, is also the line favored by Canada in a maritime boundary dispute with the United States. Using the contested line in the Final Agreement might therefore have been designed to bolster Canada's claim internationally. If so, it was a misjudged effort. The "critical date" for the boundary dispute preceded the Final Agreement by more than a decade, thus denying legal relevance to subsequent actions aimed at strengthening either side's position.[33] Moreover, any rights over the disputed offshore sector that might be held by the Inuvialuit under international law would have been shared with the Inupiat of Alaska. Since the Inuvialuit and Inupiat are essentially the same people, this makes it difficult to convert the indigenous rights of the former into a fixed boundary line. Yet, notwithstanding the Final Agreement's lack of relevance at the level of international law, it does provides a significant domestic lever for the Inuvialuit vis-à-vis the government of Canada with respect to any state-to-state boundary negotiations, since the rights of the Inuvialuit are constitutionally protected under Canadian law.[34]

In 1985, Canadian Foreign Minister Joe Clark referenced the historic presence of the Inuit when he set out Canada's legal position on the Northwest Passage: "From time immemorial Canada's Inuit people have used and occupied the ice as they have used and occupied the land."[35] In 1993, the Nunavut Land Claims Agreement affirmed the intention of the Inuit of the Canadian High Arctic to transfer to the federal government "all their aboriginal claims, rights, title and interests, if any, in and to lands and waters anywhere within Canada and adjacent offshore areas within the sovereignty or jurisdiction of Canada."[36] A further provision of the Nunavut Land Claims Agreement made clear the intention of the Inuit to strengthen Canada's position in international law: "Canada's sovereignty over the waters of the Arctic Archipelago is supported by Inuit use and occupancy."[37] Unfortunately, this mutually beneficial arrangement has since come under stress: in 2006, the Inuit land claims

---

[33] On the critical date principle, see Chapter 1, n. 9, above.
[34] See discussion, Chapter 3, above.
[35] Joe Clark, Secretary of State for External Affairs, Statement on Sovereignty, Chapter 5, n. 15, above, p. 270.
[36] 1993 Nunavut Land Claims Agreement, Chapter 5, n. 16, above, sec. 2.7.1(a).
[37] Ibid., sec. 15.1.1(c).

organization Nunavut Tunngavik Incorporated launched a lawsuit against the Canadian government alleging that its commitments under the land claims agreement had not been fulfilled.[38]

Finally, in 2005, Tom Høyem, a former Danish minister for Greenland, invoked Inuit usage as a component of Denmark's claim to Hans Island:

Hans Island has been used for centuries by Greenlandic Inuit as an ideal vantage point to get an overview of the ice situation and of the hunting prospects, especially for polar bears and seals. The Canadian Inuit have never used the island. . . . Hans Island is, in fact, an integrated part of the Thule–Inuit hunting area. They even gave it its local name, Tartupaluk, which means kidney.[39]

As was explained in Chapter 1, this reference to the Greenlandic Inuit is not decisive because the same Inuit often traveled to Ellesmere Island, which is now universally regarded as Canadian territory. Invoking the historic use and occupancy of indigenous peoples might matter in some situations, such as the Northwest Passage.[40] In other situations, it might only imply a moral and political obligation on the part of the invoking government to support indigenous interests. Whatever the case, Arctic indigenous peoples have not been content to wait for national governments to deliver. Instead, they have cooperated closely and strategically with each other in an on-going effort to influence state-based diplomacy and international law-making.

3 Indigenous transnationalism and international law-making

The transnational nature of Arctic indigenous peoples has created unique opportunities for them to influence and engage in international law-making, by cooperating with the same indigenous group on the other side of a border, by reaching out to indigenous peoples elsewhere and, in the following example, by simply bypassing states.

---

[38] See Terry Fenge, "Inuit and the Nunavut Land Claims Agreement: Supporting Canada's Arctic Sovereignty." (December 2007–January 2008) *Policy Options* 84, available at www.irpp.org/po/archive/dec07/fenge.pdf. In June 2012, the Nunavut Court of Justice granted a summary judgment on the first aspect of the case, namely the failure of the Canadian government to create a Nunavut General Monitoring Plan, and awarded $14.8 million in damages to the land claims organization. See Nunavut Tunngavik Inc., "Historic Ruling from the Nunavut Court of Justice Upholding Inuit Rights," June 28, 2012, available at www.tunngavik.com/blog/2012/06/28/historic-ruling-from-the-nunavut-court-of-justice-upholding-inuit-rights/.

[39] Tom Høyem, "Mr. Graham, You Should Have Told Us You Were Coming," *Globe and Mail*, July 29, 2005.

[40] See discussion, Chapter 5, above.

As mentioned above, the Inuvialuit of Canada's western Arctic and the Inupiat of Alaska are largely the same people, divided by a virtually imperceptible and rarely enforced international land border and a contested international maritime boundary. It is therefore not surprising that they would wish to cooperate on matters of common concern, including the protection and management of a species integral to their culture, namely the polar bear. As was explained in Chapter 6, the Inuvialuit–Inupiat Polar Bear Management Agreement was concluded in 1988.[41] It establishes a joint commission composed of Inuvialuit and Inupiat representatives to determine and divide the annual sustainable harvest of polar bears in the southern Beaufort Sea. Neither the federal nor the state or territorial governments of the United States, Canada, Alaska, the Yukon or Northwest Territories are signatories to this sub-state agreement – though all have acquiesced to it, thereby providing tacit consent.

More often, Arctic indigenous peoples have cooperated with the intention of influencing the international law-making engaged in by states. As Timo Koivurova and Leena Heinämäki explain:

Indigenous peoples regularly regard international law as a very important tool for the advancement of their political goals. This is most likely because in many states their opportunities for influencing political development are rather limited. In this light, it would seem to be a worthwhile strategy for them to try to influence the development of international law, which has the authority to impose legal obligations on all states (customary law) or states party to an international treaty. As many of the problems of today can be solved only at the global or regional level, indigenous peoples are also quite naturally interested in gaining access to the international treaty-making processes.[42]

The first step in the search for law-making influence involved unifying the voices and pooling the organizational capacities of the different national components of a single indigenous people located in two or more states. The Inuit Circumpolar Council (ICC), for instance, is a nongovernmental organization that draws the Inuit of Alaska, Canada, Greenland, and Russia together into a single political force. Created in 1977 as the Inuit Circumpolar Conference, the ICC is decentralized and highly democratic, with four national branches that work

---

[41] Inuvialuit–Inupiat Polar Bear Management Agreement in the Southern Beaufort Sea, as updated in 2000, available at http://pbsg.npolar.no/en/agreements/USA-Canada.html.

[42] Timo Koivurova and Leena Heinämäki, "The Participation of Indigenous Peoples in International Norm-making in the Arctic." (2006) 42 *Polar Record* 101.

closely with other national Inuit groups such as Canada's Inuit Tapiriit Kanatami.[43] Together, the four national branches form a supranational body that elects a chairperson, strikes committees, and represents the Inuit at both the Arctic Council and the UN Permanent Forum on Indigenous Issues – an advisory body to the UN Economic and Social Council (ECOSOC).[44]

The ICC played a role in Greenland's achievement of home rule in 1979 and its withdrawal from the European Economic Community six years later.[45] But the most significant influence exercised by the transnational Inuit organization has been with respect to international environmental issues. As was explained in Chapter 6, the Inuit Circumpolar Council played a role in the negotiation and adoption of the Stockholm Convention on Persistent Organic Pollutants. The Convention requires that states stop the production of these toxins, which are carried atmospherically to the Arctic where they accumulate in the fatty tissues of predators such as seals, bears, and ultimately humans.

The Inuit have also made progress in alerting the rest of humanity to the scale and immediacy of climate change, which affects them directly and profoundly as snow and ice conditions become less predictable and populations of their food animals decline. In 2005, Sheila Watt-Cloutier and sixty-two other Inuit from Canada and Alaska filed a petition with the Inter-American Commission on Human Rights in Washington, DC.[46] They argued that the United States, by failing to reduce its considerable emissions of carbon dioxide and other greenhouse gases, has violated the cultural and environmental rights of the Inuit. In 2006, the Commission declined to hear the petition, writing, "the information provided does not enable us to determine whether the alleged facts would tend to characterize a violation of rights protected by the American Declaration."[47] However, the Commission subsequently

---

[43] See, generally, Gary N. Wilson, "Inuit Diplomacy in the Circumpolar North." (2007) 13 *Canadian Foreign Policy Journal* 65.

[44] See UN Permanent Forum on Indigenous Peoples at http://social.un.org/index/IndigenousPeoples.aspx.

[45] Wilson, n. 43, above, p. 67.

[46] Inuit Circumpolar Council Canada, "Inuit Petition Inter-American Commission on Human Rights to Oppose Climate Change Caused by the United States of America," December 7, 2005, available at www.inuitcircumpolar.com/index.php?Lang=En&ID=316.

[47] Jane George, "ICC Climate Change Petition Rejected," *Nunatsiaq News*, December 15, 2006, available at www.nunatsiaqonline.ca/archives/61215/news/nunavut/61215_02.html.

conducted a general hearing – its first ever – to investigate the relationship between climate change and human rights.[48] This development, and indeed the entire effort around the petition, contributed to raising media and public awareness about climate change in the United States. As mentioned in Chapter 6, Watt-Cloutier was nominated for the Nobel Peace Prize in 2007 in recognition of her work on international environmental issues.[49]

The Inuit have also reached out to the "Small Island Developing States," a group of low-lying Pacific Island countries that cooperate among themselves to raise awareness and push for international action on climate change. As Watt-Cloutier has explained: "As we melt, the small developing island states sink."[50] The alliance is called "Many Strong Voices," and since 2005 it has focused on influencing interstate negotiations at conferences of the parties to the UN Framework Convention on Climate Change.[51]

Created in 1956, the Saami Council represents the Saami of Norway, Sweden, Finland, and Russia.[52] The main goals of the Saami Council have been to reverse a history of linguistic assimilation and to promote cultural rights and transboundary freedom of movement, which is especially important for a semi-nomadic reindeer-herding people spread across four states.[53] The Saami Council was originally the voice for Saami on the state and regional (Nordic) levels, but much of that work has been taken over by the Saami parliaments. The Saami Council now focuses on representing Saami at the international level, and on connecting with other indigenous peoples and organizations. From the outset, the Saami Council's work has been supported by the national governments of Norway, Sweden, and Finland – countries that have long been at the forefront of the human rights movement, both domestically and internationally.

The Inuit and Saami, as Plaut explains, "have spent generations building and maintaining a relationship of cooperation and collaboration."[54]

---

[48] Jessica Gordon, "Inter-American Commission on Human Rights to Hold Hearing After Rejecting Inuit Climate Change Petition." (2007) 7 *Sustainable Development Law and Policy* 55.

[49] "Gore Nominated for Nobel Peace Prize," *Environmental News Service*, February 1, 2007, available at www.ens-newswire.com/ens/feb2007/2007-02-01-09.html.

[50] Quoted at www.manystrongvoices.org/media.aspx.

[51] See Many Strong Voices at www.manystrongvoices.org/.

[52] See Saami Council at www.saamicouncil.net/?deptid=1116.

[53] Plaut, n. 11, above, p. 197.   [54] Ibid., p. 194.

They "take turns representing the Arctic at the United Nations Permanent Forum on Indigenous Issues ... in addition to attending each other's executive meetings."[55] In 1996, the Inuit and Saami were able to exercise influence during the creation of the Arctic Council, including by securing a meaningful status of "permanent participant" for themselves and other Arctic indigenous peoples.[56] This outcome was, as David Scrivener explains, not easily obtained:

Canada and the ICC were quick to notice the extent to which early US drafts of the rules of procedure, while correctly emphasising the intergovernmental nature of the Council, intentionally clawed back the advantages of the permanent participants relative to ... observers, in essence equating the former with the latter. With the exception of Russia, the other Arctic states supported Canada in re-asserting the "specialness" of the permanent participants and their right to be fully consulted before the member governments reach collective decisions.[57]

Permanent participant status is very significant for the indigenous peoples who are represented by six groups at Arctic Council meetings: the Aleut International Association, Arctic Athabaskan Council, Gwich'in Council International, Inuit Circumpolar Council, Saami Council, and Russian Association of Indigenous Peoples of the North.[58] Together, the Inuit Circumpolar Council and the Saami Council also pushed for a consensus approach to decision-making at the Arctic Council, understanding that this would reduce their disadvantage – as permanent participants rather than members – of not having voting power.[59] As Olav Mathias Eira of the Saami Council explained to Plaut, the requirement for universal consent means that individual member states can sometimes be enlisted to block consensus on behalf of indigenous peoples:

---

[55] Ibid.
[56] See, generally, Frances Abele and Thierry Rodon, "Inuit Diplomacy in the Global Era: The Strengths of Multilateral Internationalism." (2007) 13(3) *Canadian Foreign Policy* 46.
[57] David Scrivener, "Arctic Environmental Cooperation in Transition." (1999) 35(192) *Polar Record* 51 at 56.
[58] See www.arcticpeoples.org/index.php?option=com_k2&view=item&layout=item&id= 237&Itemid=6. The permanent participants are supported administratively by an Indigenous Peoples' Secretariat, though this body suffers from not having a permanent funding mechanism.
[59] Evan T. Bloom, "Establishment of the Arctic Council." (1999) 93 *American Journal of International Law* 712 at 716.

"Permanent Participant Status is much better than observer status [which is what we have with the UN]. All the decisions of the Arctic Council have to be reached by consensus. Although we do not have a vote, we can block a vote." Eira paused to laugh. "We can ask Iceland to help or something, to say 'No!' See, we Saami have almost the same power as the US; we just lack the money."[60]

As Article 2 of the Ottawa Declaration on the Establishment of the Arctic Council makes clear: "The category of Permanent Participation is created to provide for active participation and full consultation with the Arctic indigenous representatives within the Arctic Council."[61] The use of consensus decision-making, though not required by the Ottawa Declaration, is entirely consistent with its goals.

4 Circumpolar Inuit Declaration on Sovereignty

Obtaining permanent participant status in the Arctic Council was not an unqualified victory for northern indigenous peoples. An asterisk in the 1996 Ottawa Declaration on the Establishment of the Arctic Council leads to one of just two footnotes, which specifies that "The use of the term 'peoples' in this declaration shall not be construed as having any implications as regard the rights which may attach to the term under international law."[62] The debate over "people" versus "peoples," and the right of self-determination implied by the second term, has been more or less settled as a result of the adoption in 2007 of the UN Declaration on the Rights of Indigenous Peoples – which includes the "s" throughout.[63] But, to the chagrin of the northern indigenous peoples, their status as Arctic Council permanent participants has not ensured them places at the table during every negotiation concerning the region. In May 2008, the six permanent participants, along with

---

[60] Olav Mathias Eira, personal communication quoted in Plaut, n. 11, above, p. 203. Ironically, as Plaut explains, "The Saami Council and the ICC found a strange friend and advocate for the consensus model in America's historical reluctance to join formal, contentious driven, political bodies." Plaut, n. 11, above, citing Bloom, n. 59, above.

[61] Declaration on the Establishment of the Arctic Council, Ottawa, September 19, 1996 (1996) 35 ILM 1387, available at www.arctic-council.org/index.php/en/about/documents/category/5-declarations.

[62] Ibid.

[63] 2007 UN Declaration on the Rights of Indigenous Peoples, available at www.un.org/esa/socdev/unpfii/documents/DRIPS_en.pdf. For a contrary view, see Karen Engle, "On Fragile Architecture: The UN Declaration on the Rights of Indigenous Peoples in the Context of Human Rights." (2011) 22 *European Journal of International Law* 141.

Iceland, Sweden, and Finland, were not invited to a meeting of the five Arctic Ocean coastal states hosted by Denmark at Ilulissat, Greenland. The Inuit Circumpolar Council responded by issuing a "Circumpolar Inuit Declaration on Sovereignty in the Arctic" that included specific reference to the exclusion from the Ilulissat meeting:

In spite of a recognition by the five coastal Arctic states (Norway, Denmark, Canada, USA and Russia) of the need to use international mechanisms and international law to resolve sovereignty disputes (see 2008 Ilulissat Declaration), these states, in their discussions of Arctic sovereignty, have not referenced existing international instruments that promote and protect the rights of indigenous peoples. They have also neglected to include Inuit in Arctic sovereignty discussions in a manner comparable to Arctic Council deliberations.[64]

The Circumpolar Inuit Declaration on Sovereignty is essentially an extended argument for including the Inuit in any future Arctic decision-making. It is a declaration "on" sovereignty rather than "of" sovereignty and does not claim sovereignty in the sense of statehood. The document begins by asserting that the Inuit, as a people, "enjoy the rights of all peoples" including the rights recognized in international instruments such as the UN Charter and the two international covenants on human rights. In this context, it advances a robust form of "internal" self-determination:

Central to our rights as a people is the right to self-determination. It is our right to freely determine our political status, freely pursue our economic, social, cultural and linguistic development, and freely dispose of our natural wealth and resources. States are obligated to respect and promote the realization of our right to self-determination.[65]

The document then catalogues a series of rights that flow from the Inuit's status as an indigenous people:

Our rights as an indigenous people include the following rights recognized in the *United Nations Declaration on the Rights of Indigenous Peoples (UNDRIP)*, all of which are relevant to sovereignty and sovereign rights in the Arctic: the right to self-determination, to freely determine our political status and to freely pursue our economic, social and cultural, including linguistic, development (Art. 3); the right to internal autonomy or self-government (Art. 4); the right to

---

[64] "A Circumpolar Inuit Declaration on Sovereignty in the Arctic," April 2009, sec. 2.6, available at https://www.itk.ca/publication/circumpolar-declaration-sovereignty-arctic (emphasis in original).

[65] Ibid., sec. 1.4.

recognition, observance and enforcement of treaties, agreements and other constructive arrangements concluded with states (Art. 37); the right to maintain and strengthen our distinct political, legal, economic, social and cultural institutions, while retaining the right to participate fully in the political, economic, social and cultural life of states (Art. 5); the right to participate in decision-making in matters which would affect our rights and to maintain and develop our own indigenous decision-making institutions (Art. 18); the right to own, use, develop and control our lands, territories and resources and the right to ensure that no project affecting our lands, territories or resources will proceed without our free and informed consent (Art. 25–32); the right to peace and security (Art. 7); and the right to conservation and protection of our environment (Art. 29).[66]

Like the UN Declaration on the Rights of Indigenous Peoples, the Circumpolar Inuit Declaration seeks both to consolidate *and* to develop international law. For this reason, it omits to mention that UN General Assembly resolutions such as the UN Declaration are not legally binding instruments. In addition, the customary international law status of some of the UN Declaration's provisions remains contested, especially the stipulation that governments must consult with indigenous peoples "in order to obtain their free, prior and informed consent before adopting and implementing legislative or administrative measures that may affect them."[67] That said, new norms of international law often take the form of "soft law" on their way to acquiring binding "hard law" status, and that may well be happening here.[68]

The Circumpolar Inuit Declaration on Sovereignty in the Arctic then moves on to address directly the topic identified in its title:

---

[66] Ibid. (emphasis in original).

[67] See S. James Anaya, "Indigenous Peoples' Participatory Rights in Relation to Decisions about Natural Resource Extraction: The More Fundamental Issue of What Rights Indigenous Peoples Have in Lands and Resources." (2005) 22 *Arizona Journal of International and Comparative Law* 7. Canada has expressed the view that "the Declaration is a non-legally binding document that does not reflect customary international law" ("Canada's Statement of Support on the United Nations Declaration on the Rights of Indigenous Peoples," November 12, 2010, available at www.ainc-inac.gc.ca/ap/ia/dcl/stmt-eng.asp). The United States has similarly stated that "While the Declaration is not legally binding, it carries considerable moral and political force" ("Announcement of US Support for the United Nations Declaration on the Rights of Indigenous Peoples," December 16, 2010, available at www.state.gov/r/pa/prs/ps/2010/12/153027.htm).

[68] See Mauro Barelli, "The Role of Soft Law in the International Legal System: The Case of the United Nations Declaration on the Rights of Indigenous Peoples." (2009) 58 *International and Comparative Law Quarterly* 957. On soft law generally, see Christine Chinkin, "The Challenge of Soft Law: Development and Change in International Law." (1989) 38 *International and Comparative Law Quarterly* 850.

"Sovereignty" is a term that has often been used to refer to the absolute and independent authority of a community or nation both internally and externally. Sovereignty is a contested concept, however, and does not have a fixed meaning. Old ideas of sovereignty are breaking down as different governance models, such as the European Union, evolve. Sovereignties overlap and are frequently divided within federations in creative ways to recognize the right of peoples. For Inuit living within the states of Russia, Canada, the USA and Denmark/ Greenland, issues of sovereignty and sovereign rights must be examined and assessed in the context of our long history of struggle to gain recognition and respect as an Arctic indigenous people having the right to exercise self-determination over our lives, territories, cultures and languages.[69]

The divisibility of sovereignty certainly makes it easier for national governments to satisfy the self-determination rights of indigenous peoples. But, contrary to the view expressed in the Circumpolar Inuit Declaration, it can be argued that when strands of sovereignty are shared out between states and international organizations or sub-national governments this is done with the consent of the national government that originally held all of the sovereign rights. To the degree that sovereignty is transferred to indigenous governments through land claims agreements in Canada or the United States, or devolution in Greenland, this too occurs with consent. As a result, to continue the argument to its logical conclusion, there is nothing in state practice that supports the right of an indigenous people to obtain sovereign rights from a national government without that government's consent.

Even if the argument advanced in the Circumpolar Inuit Declaration fails to convince on legal grounds, it still leads to a clear and morally powerful conclusion: "The inextricable linkages between issues of sovereignty and sovereign rights in the Arctic and Inuit self-determination and other rights require states to accept the presence and role of Inuit as partners in the conduct of international relations in the Arctic."[70] Moreover, this conclusion was strategically deployed with real political purpose, as part of a lobbying effort that included among its targets the US Secretary of State.

In March 2010, the Canadian government decided to hold a follow-up to the Ilulissat meeting, this time in Chelsea, Quebec. As Denmark had done two years earlier, Canada chose to invite only the four other Arctic Ocean coastal states and not the indigenous permanent participants,

---

[69] "A Circumpolar Inuit Declaration on Sovereignty in the Arctic," n. 64, above, sec. 2.1.
[70] Ibid., sec. 3.3.

nor Iceland, Sweden, or Finland.[71] Secretary of State Hillary Clinton, who said she had been contacted by representatives of the excluded indigenous groups, publicly chastised her hosts for that decision: "Significant international discussions on Arctic issues should include those who have legitimate interests in the region. And I hope the Arctic will always showcase our ability to work together, not create new divisions."[72] In another apparent measure of her displeasure, Clinton skipped the news conference the Canadian government had arranged for the foreign ministers at the end of the meeting.[73] As a result, no further "Arctic-5" meetings have taken place and, to this degree, the Inuit Circumpolar Declaration on Sovereignty in the Arctic has already proven quite successful.

5 Does sovereignty "begin at home"?

In 2007, Stephen Harper said: "Canada has a choice when it comes to defending our sovereignty in the Arctic: either we use it or we lose it."[74] In the same speech, the prime minister promised up to eight ice-strengthened ships and an Arctic refueling station for the Canadian Navy. Inuit leaders replied that they had been "using" the Arctic for millennia, and then built on that point to argue that healthy communities are as important to Canada's Arctic sovereignty as military equipment and personnel. Moreover, as Mary Simon of Inuit Tapiriit Kanatami explained, healthy communities – and therefore sovereignty – could only be achieved through collaboration with the Inuit:

Arctic sovereignty must mean that our government recognizes that Inuit stand ready to be active partners in collaborative strategies to improve the health and education and infrastructure in our Arctic communities. Arctic policies must be based on a respectful and permanent partnership with the Inuit of Canada.[75]

The same argument was advanced by the Inuit Circumpolar Council, which, in its Circumpolar Inuit Declaration on Sovereignty in the Arctic, stated: "The foundation, projection and enjoyment of

---

[71] Rob Gillies, "Clinton Rebukes Canada on Arctic Meeting," *Associated Press*, March 29, 2010, available at www.guardian.co.uk/world/feedarticle/9009648.
[72] Ibid.   [73] Ibid.
[74] "Harper on Arctic: 'Use it or Lose it'," *Victoria Times Colonist*, July 10, 2007, available at www.canada.com/topics/news/story.html?id=7ca93d97-3b26-4dd1-8d92-8568f9b7cc2a.
[75] Mary Simon, "Inuit and the Canadian Arctic: Sovereignty Begins at Home." (2009) 43 *Journal of Canadian Studies* 250 at 259.

Arctic sovereignty and sovereign rights all require healthy and sustainable communities in the Arctic. In this sense, 'sovereignty begins at home.'"[76]

But, as earlier chapters of this book have explained, the only disputed territory in the entire circumpolar Arctic is Hans Island, which is uninhabited. The only unresolved Arctic maritime boundary dispute is in the Beaufort Sea, where the historic presence of the Inuvialuit has little bearing on the international law arguments. As for the legal issues concerning extended continental shelves in the central Arctic Ocean, they too are separate from Inuit "use and occupancy" – in part because the Inuit never ventured that far north. This leaves the Northwest Passage, where Inuit "use and occupancy" is indeed relevant, but only insofar as it preceded the dispute's "critical date" of 1969 or 1985.

Although the contemporary presence of indigenous peoples does not strengthen the legal positions of states, a collaborative relationship with indigenous groups can strengthen the moral and political authority and therefore influence of states when they advance policies, such as environmental protection, that benefit Arctic indigenous peoples. In 2007, Canada's three territorial governments presented a more nuanced and compelling vision of indigenous peoples in the twenty-first century, as "stewards of sovereignty" deserving of gratitude and support from national governments:

The North is defined not by lines or dots on a map, but by our people. Canada's sovereignty over northern lands, internal waters and waters covered by ice is rooted in history, international law and the occupancy and use of Aboriginal people. Northerners are the embodiment – the human dimension – of Canada's Arctic sovereignty.

But in order for Northerners to continue to act as stewards of Canadian sovereignty, the North needs sustainable communities. Northerners must be supported in building communities where we can live healthy lives; where opportunities for employment, education and training exist; where we can raise our families in adequate, suitable and affordable homes; where health and social services exist that are comparable to the rest of Canada; and where we can build a future for ourselves and our children.[77]

---

[76] "A Circumpolar Inuit Declaration on Sovereignty," n. 64, above, sec. 3.1.2.
[77] The Yukon, Northwest Territories, and Nunavut, "A Northern Vision: A Stronger North and a Better Canada," 2007, p. 7, available at www.anorthernvision.ca/documents/newvision_english.pdf.

6 Seal product exports

The most difficult relationship for the Inuit in recent years has been with non-Arctic states, specifically the European Union. In response to widespread public concern about cruelty associated with seal hunting, the European Commission (the executive branch of the European Union) banned the import of seal products in 2009.[78] Seal hunting is an integral part of Inuit culture and an important source of food for them, with the sale of seal pelts also contributing much needed income. However, seal hunting is also conducted on a much larger scale by non-Inuit hunters in Atlantic Canada, with the non-Inuit hunt accounting for more than 95 percent of Canada's seal product exports. To be fair, the European Commission did include an exemption for "seal products which result from hunts traditionally conducted by Inuit and other indigenous communities and which contribute to their subsistence."[79] But, somewhat counter-intuitively, the impact of the ban has been to destroy the market for seal products within the European Union for non-Inuit and Inuit hunters alike.

The European Commission's introduction of the import ban was poorly timed, for it came just as the Arctic Council member states were considering an application from the European Union for permanent observer status. The Canadian government, at the encouragement of Inuit organizations and the Nunavut government, used the veto that is inherent in consensus decision-making to block consideration of the application.[80] Then, in 2011, the Arctic Council adopted criteria for determining the "general suitability" of an applicant for observer status that include "the extent to which observers ... [r]espect the values, interests, culture and traditions of Arctic indigenous peoples and other Arctic inhabitants."[81] The adoption of the criteria could make it easier for Canada to justify blocking applications from the European Union in the future, though ultimately the decision to exclude or admit

---

[78] The import ban is set out in Regulation (EC) No. 1007/2009, available at http://eur-lex. europa.eu/LexUriServ/LexUriServ.do?uri=OJ:L:2009:286:0036:0039:EN:PDF. On the politics and policy development leading to the ban, see Njord Wegge, "Politics between Science, Law and Sentiments: Explaining the European Union's Ban on Trade in Seal Products." (2012) 6 *Environmental Politics* 1.

[79] Ibid.

[80] "Canada against EU Entry to Arctic Council because of Seal Trade Ban," *CBC News*, April 29, 2009, available at www.cbc.ca/news/world/story/2009/04/29/cda-eu-arctic-seal.html.

[81] See "Observers" at www.arctic-council.org/index.php/en/about-us/partners-links.

will be based on political considerations rather than the (deliberately) ambiguous standards.

In 2010, Inuit Tapiriit Kanatami, the national Inuit organization of Canada, brought a case before the European General Court challenging the European Commission's import ban.[82] It argued that the ban causes "serious and irreparable harm" by preventing Inuit from exporting seal products to the European Union, thus interfering with the social fabric of their communities. In particular, it argued that the ban violates the right of Inuit to respect for private and family life under Article 8 of the European Convention on Human Rights. In September 2011, the Court ruled the case inadmissible, though it provided no reasons for this.[83] In November 2011, the Inuit organization appealed that decision to the European Court of Justice.[84] A second case, also brought by Inuit Tapiritt Kanatami, contests the validity of the so-called "Inuit exemption," and does so because an invalid exemption would render the entire ban void. At the time of writing, the European General Court has yet to render judgment on this second case.

In 2009, Canada and Norway (which is not a member of the European Union) both requested "consultations" with the European Commission on the seal product ban, the first step in a dispute settlement process at the World Trade Organization (WTO).[85] In 2011, the WTO established a single dispute settlement panel to hear both complaints,[86] and in 2012, Canada and Norway took the next step of requesting the appointment of panelists.[87] Canada and Norway claim the import ban contravenes the principle of non-discrimination within the "national treatment"

[82] *Inuit Tapiriit Kanatami and Others* v. *Parliament and Council*, Case T-8/10, [2010] OJ C 100/41, available at http://eur-lex.europa.eu/LexUriServ/LexUriServ.do?uri=OJ:C:2010:100:0041:0041:EN:PDF.

[83] Order of the General Court of 6 September 2011 – *Inuit Tapiritt Kanatami and Others* v. *Parliament and Council* (Case T-18/10), available at http://eur-lex.europa.eu/LexUriServ/LexUriServ.do?uri=OJ%3AC%3A2011%3A319%3A0020%3A0021%3Aen%3APDF.

[84] See (February 25, 2012) *Official Journal of the European Union* C58/3, available at http://eur-lex.europa.eu/LexUriServ/LexUriServ.do?uri=OJ:C:2012:058:0003:0003:EN:PDF.

[85] See Simon Lester, "The WTO Seal Products Dispute: A Preview of the Key Legal Issues." 14(2) *ASIL Insight*, January 13, 2010, available at www.asil.org/insights100113.cfm.

[86] WTO Dispute Settlement Board, decision of April 21, 2011, available at www.wto.org/english/news_e/news11_e/dsb_21apr11_e.htm. For the current status of the case, see *European Communities – Measures Prohibiting the Importation and Marketing of Seal Products*, Dispute DS400, at www.wto.org/english/tratop_e/dispu_e/cases_e/ds400_e.htm.

[87] "Canada Calls for WTO Action on Seal Ban Dispute," *Nunatsiaq News*, September 24, 2012, available at www.nunatsiaqonline.ca/stories/article/65674canada_calls_for_wto_action_on_seal_ban_dispute/.

and "most-favored nation" provisions of the General Agreement on Tariffs and Trade (GATT) and Technical Barriers to Trade (TBT) Agreement. They also claim the ban violates Article 2 of the TBT Agreement because it is not "necessary to achieve a legitimate objective" and constitutes an "unnecessary obstacle to trade."[88] The European Commission claims the ban is justified on the grounds of "public morals," in this instance the moral revulsion that many Europeans feel about the killing of seals. The WTO has accepted similar arguments in one previous case,[89] and rejected them in another.[90]

Regardless of what the WTO panel and subsequently the WTO Appellate Body decide, the dispute over seal products is unlikely to disappear given the domestic political pressures felt by the governments on both sides. Moreover, the only potentially effective trade remedy – opening the European common market to all seal products regardless of origin – is disproportionate to the economic harm suffered by a relatively small number of Inuit. It can also be questioned whether the WTO should be the final arbiter on an issue such as the human rights of an indigenous people, that can only tangentially be addressed under international trade law.[91]

7 Indigenous peoples and human rights

By any standard, the 1953 and 1955 relocations of seventeen families to Resolute Bay and Grise Fiord violated the human rights of the people who were moved. For the Inuit originally from northern Quebec, the

---

[88] For two papers that explain the legal arguments in depth and predict entirely different results, see Xinjie Luan and Julien Chaisse, "Preliminary Comments on the WTO Seals Products Dispute: Traditional Hunting, Public Morals and Technical Barriers to Trade." (2011) 22 *Colorado Journal of International Environmental Law and Policy* 79, available at www.colorado.edu/law/sites/default/files/Vol.22.1.pdf and Robert Howse and Joanna Langille, "Permitting Pluralism: The *Seal Products* Dispute and Why the WTO Should Accept Trade Restrictions Justified by Noninstrumental Moral Values." (2012) 37 *Yale Journal of International Law* 367, available at www.yjil.org/docs/pub/37-2-howse-langille-permitting-pluralism.pdf.

[89] *United States – Measures Affecting the Cross-Border Supply of Gambling and Betting Services*, Dispute DS285, available at https://www.wto.org/english/tratop_e/dispu_e/cases_e/ds285_e.htm.

[90] *China – Measures Affecting Trading Rights and Distribution Services for Certain Publications and Audiovisual Entertainment Products*, Dispute DS363, available at https://www.wto.org/english/tratop_e/dispu_e/cases_e/ds363_e.htm.

[91] See Kamrul Hossain, "The EU Ban on the Import of Seal Products and the WTO Regulations: Neglected Human Rights of the Arctic Indigenous Peoples?" (2013) 49 *Polar Record* 154.

1,600 kilometer move northwards was like a trip to the moon. Their traditional knowledge and hunting techniques were out of place, there was not enough snow to build igloos, and the total darkness from November to February was both unfamiliar and disabling. For more than half a century, a debate has raged in Canada over whether the relocations were coerced or voluntary. At the very least, a substantial degree of misrepresentation was involved, with the Inuit having been promised better hunting and living conditions.[92] The ensuing debate, however, postponed the provision of compensation for more than four decades. It was not until 1996 that the Canadian government agreed to a $10 million package, and even then the government ignored the recommendations of three different bodies – the House of Commons Standing Committee on Aboriginal Affairs and Northern Development, the Canadian Human Rights Commission, and the Royal Commission on Aboriginal Peoples – by refusing to apologize. Although the compensation agreement recognized Inuit "pain, suffering and hardship" it also stated "government officials of the time were acting with honourable intentions in what was perceived to be the best interests of the Inuit."[93]

A similar relocation of Inuit took place in Greenland, also in 1953, when an entire community of 116 people was moved 150 kilometers from Thule to Qaanaaq so that the US Air Force could expand its base at the former location.[94] The "Hingitaq 53" (Hingitaq means "the deported" and 53 refers to the year of the relocation) later sued the government of Denmark. In 1999, the Danish Court of Appeals found that rights of the Hingitaq 53 had indeed been violated and awarded them 17,000 kroner (about $3,000) each as well as a collective indemnity of 500,000 kroner (about $90,000).[95] However, it denied their right to return. The Danish Supreme Court upheld that decision in 2003, and

---

[92] For the different sides of the debate, see Frank Tester and Peter Kulchyski, *Tammarniit (Mistakes): Inuit Relocation in the Eastern Arctic, 1939–63* (Vancouver: University of British Columbia Press, 1994); Gerard Kenney, *Arctic Smoke and Mirrors* (Prescott, Ontario: Voyageur Publishing, 1994).

[93] Jim Bell, "What Are the Exiles Signing?" *Nunatsiaq News*, March 15, 1996, available at www.nunatsiaqonline.ca/archives/back-issues/week/60315.html#1.

[94] See Jean Malaurie, *The Last Kings of Thule: With the Polar Eskimos, as They Face their Destiny* (trans. Adrienne Foulke) (London: Jonathan Cape, 1982); Stephen Fottrell, "Inuit Survival Battle against US Base," *BBC News*, May 27, 2004, available at http://news.bbc.co.uk/1/hi/world/europe/3753677.stm.

[95] Fottrell, "Inuit Survival Battle," ibid.

a subsequent appeal to the European Court of Human Rights was dismissed on jurisdictional grounds.[96]

The current social and economic conditions of northern indigenous peoples, especially in Canada and Russia, clearly violate some of the rights set out in the International Covenant on Economic, Social and Cultural Rights, including the rights to "adequate food, clothing and housing" (Art. 11), "the enjoyment of the highest attainable standard of physical and mental health" (Art. 12), and education (Art. 13).[97] But, while both Canada and Russia have ratified the Covenant, neither has ratified its Optional Protocol[98] nor agreed to any other enforcement mechanism.

In the Nordic countries, the economic and social rights of the Saami are relatively well protected. Their principal concerns now relate to the need for a fuller implementation of the right to self-determination, of the rights to land, water, and natural resources (especially in the face of oil and gas development, logging, and climate change), and to the protection of their language as well as the provision of culturally appropriate education.[99]

8 Indigenous peoples and whaling

Being able to practice their traditional way of life is of central concern to indigenous peoples. But, as was explained in Chapter 6, the hunting of whales by Arctic indigenous peoples has been a source of considerable controversy. After the International Whaling Commission (IWC) introduced a worldwide ban on whaling in 1982, Canada withdrew from the IWC regime and guaranteed whaling rights to the Inuvialuit and Inuit in land claims agreements concluded in 1984 and 1993.[100]

---

[96] See *HINGITAQ 53* v. *Denmark*, Application No. 18584/04, decision from the European Court of Human Rights on admissibility, available at https://www.elaw.org/node/3834.

[97] 1966 International Covenant on Economic, Social and Cultural Rights, available at www2.ohchr.org/english/law/cescr.htm.

[98] 2008 Optional Protocol to the International Covenant on Economic, Social and Cultural Rights, UN General Assembly Resolution A/RES/63/117, available at www2. ohchr.org/english/law/docs/a.RES.63.117_en.pdf.

[99] See James Anaya, UN Special Rapporteur on the Rights of Indigenous Peoples, "The Situation of the Sami People in the Sápmi Region of Norway, Sweden and Finland," June 6, 2011, UN Doc. A/HRC/18/35/Add.2, available at http://unsr.jamesanaya.org/country-reports/the-situation-of-the-sami-people-in-the-sapmi-region-of-norway-sweden-and-finland-2011.

[100] See Inuvialuit Final Agreement, n. 32, above, sec. 14(6); 1993 Nunavut Land Claims Agreement, sec. 5.6.1, available at http://nlca.tunngavik.com/.

Although the IWC has accepted a limited amount of "subsistence" whaling by the Inupiat of Alaska and the Inuit of Greenland, the Canadian government – and therefore the Canadian Inuit – remain outside the regime.[101]

To their credit, the Inuit are pushing for the protection of key bowhead whale habitat. The community of Clyde River on the east coast of Baffin Island has persuaded the Canadian government to designate Isabella Bay and the adjoining territorial waters as a "national wildlife area."[102] Hundreds of bowheads spend their summers in Isabella Bay feasting on an abundance of copepods. Under Canadian law, national wildlife areas are off-limits to commercial activities unless specific permits are obtained.

Seven hundred kilometers to the north, Lancaster Sound constitutes the principal eastern entrance to the Northwest Passage. It is also home to bowhead whales, most of the world's narwhals, and one-third of North America's beluga whales, as well as walrus, polar bears, ringed, bearded, and harp seals and millions of seabirds. For more than two decades, Canada and the United Nations Educational, Scientific and Cultural Organization (UNESCO) considered designating Lancaster Sound as a World Heritage Site.[103] Such a designation could have facilitated the introduction of shipping lanes in order to reduce the impact of ship noise on marine mammals. To some degree, it might also have supported Canada's position that the Northwest Passage constitutes

---

[101] For an excellent discussion of the issue, see Anthony Speca, "In the Belly of the Whaling Commission," *Northern Public Affairs*, June 18, 2012, available at www.northernpublicaffairs.ca/index/in-the-belly-of-the-whaling-commission/.

[102] "Canada Preserves Arctic Wilderness for Whales, Bears, Birds," *Environmental News*, September 4, 2008, available at www.ens-newswire.com/ens/sep2008/2008-09-04-01.html.

[103] As a party to the 1972 Convention Concerning the Protection of the World Cultural and Natural Heritage, Canada is required to identify the natural sites of outstanding universal value on its territory (Art. 3, available at http://whc.unesco.org/archive/convention-en.pdf). However, nominations to the World Heritage List are not considered unless the nominated property has previously been included on the state party's "tentative list" of the properties it intends to consider for nomination in subsequent years. Parties are encouraged to re-examine and re-submit their tentative list at least once every decade. Under Canada's original tentative list of world heritage sites (1980), Lancaster Sound was included as part of Sirmilik National Park. However, the proposal was subsequently abandoned and Lancaster Sound does not currently appear on Canada's updated tentative list (2004). UNESCO World Heritage Centre, Tentative Lists: Canada, http://whc.unesco.org/en/tentativelists/state=ca. There are at present no marine World Heritage Sites in the Arctic. See UNESCO World Heritage Lists at http://whc.unesco.org.

"internal waters" fully subject to its regulation and control. But successive Canadian governments have failed to pursue the UNESCO process to completion, perhaps because of a concern that this might provoke a challenge from the United States, which opposes Canada's Northwest Passage position.[104]

The less controversial domestic step of designating Lancaster Sound as a "national marine conservation area" (the equivalent of a national park) has also been held up for decades, with Inuit concerns about possible limitations on hunting rights contributing to the delay.[105] In 2009, the Canadian government announced that it would spend $5 million to study whether such a conservation area would be "a practical approach to sustainable management in Lancaster Sound."[106] The answer is not obvious, however, since without the international recognition that comes with a World Heritage Site designation, foreign ships might pay less attention to domestic regulations. Canada's creation of a national marine conservation area could usefully be coupled with a renewed effort to secure UNESCO designation, thus linking the domestic designation to an international designation in a mutually supportive way.

At the same time the announcement about Lancaster Sound was made, a memorandum of understanding on Inuit participation in the feasibility study was signed between the Canadian government, the Nunavut government, and the local Inuit association. Yet little cooperation has been apparent since then.[107] In 2010, the Canadian government chartered the German research icebreaker *Polarstern* to conduct seismic testing of the area. The Inuit, concerned about the impact of seismic waves on marine mammals, and seeing a contradiction in the

---

[104] See discussion, Chapter 5, above.

[105] According to Parks Canada, a proposal for a national marine conservation area was prepared in 1987, but the feasibility assessment was suspended at the request of the local Inuit. Parks Canada, "Canada's National Marine Conservation Areas System Plan: Lancaster Sound," available at www.pc.gc.ca/progs/amnc-nmca/systemplan/itm1-/arc6_E.asp.

[106] See Gloria Galloway, "Ottawa Moves to Protect Serengeti of the Arctic," *Globe and Mail*, December 6, 2010, available at www.theglobeandmail.com/news/politics/ottawa-moves-to-protect-serengeti-of-the-arctic/article4081939/; and "Health of the Oceans Initiatives – A Listing by Lead Department or Agency," available at www.dfo-mpo.gc.ca/oceans/management-gestion/healthyoceans-santedesoceans/initiatives-eng.htm.

[107] "Ottawa Proposes Boundaries for Lancaster Sound Marine Conservation Area: Promised Steering Committee Yet to Be Created," *Nunatsiaq News*, December 6, 2010, available at www.nunatsiaqonline.ca/stories/article/987678_ottawa_proposes_boundaries_for_lancaster/.

Canadian government arranging for seismic studies in an area designated to be off-limits for oil and gas development, sought and received an injunction from the Nunavut Supreme Court.[108] The German icebreaker, which had already crossed the Atlantic en route to Lancaster Sound, had little choice but to turn around.

9 Indigenous peoples and nuclear weapons

In 1968, an American B-52 bomber crashed into the sea near the US base at Thule, Greenland, resulting in the loss of one unexploded nuclear bomb under the ice.[109] Around the same time, it became apparent that US and Soviet nuclear submarines were frequenting the waters around Greenland and Canada's High Arctic islands.[110] These developments were of concern to the Inuit, who were also aware that atmospheric nuclear weapons tests by the United States, Britain, and France in the South Pacific had directly affected and prompted a coordinated response from the indigenous peoples there. The indigenous Pacific islanders were instrumental in the initiation of the inter-state negotiations that led to the 1985 South Pacific Nuclear Free Zone Treaty. That instrument, usually referred to as the "Treaty of Rarotonga," has been ratified by Australia, the Cook Islands, Fiji, Kiribati, Nauru, New Zealand, Niue, Papua New Guinea, the Solomon Islands, Tonga, Tuvalu, Vanuatu, and Western Samoa.[111] In a parallel effort, the Inuit Circumpolar Council adopted a resolution in 1983 that called for "no nuclear testing or nuclear devices in the arctic or sub-arctic."[112]

---

[108] Josh Wingrove, "Lancaster Sound: A Seismic Victory for the Inuit," *Globe and Mail*, August 13, 2010, available at www.theglobeandmail.com/news/politics/lancaster-sound-a-seismic-victory-for-the-inuit/article1377067/.

[109] Gordon Corera, "Mystery of Lost US Nuclear Bomb," *BBC News*, November 10, 2008, available at http://news.bbc.co.uk/1/hi/7720049.stm.

[110] For more on submarines, see Chapter 5, above, as well as the first paragraph of Chapter 8, below.

[111] For more information on the Treaty of Rarotonga, see www.nti.org/treaties-and-regimes/south-pacific-nuclear-free-zone-spnfz-treaty-rarotonga/. For the text of the treaty, see http://cns.miis.edu/inventory/pdfs/aptspnfz.pdf.

[112] ICC, "Resolution on a Nuclear Free Zone," available at http://web.archive.org/web/20110826020556/http://www.arcticnwfz.ca/documents/I%20N%20U%20I%20T%20CIRCUMPOLAR%20RES%20ON%20nwfz%201983.pdf. A similar statement had been made six years earlier, though not in the form of a resolution. See Russel Barsh, "Demilitarizing the Arctic as an Exercise of Indigenous Self-Determination." (1986) 55 *Nordic Journal of International Law* 208.

Although the resolution did not lead to an inter-state agreement, the end of the Cold War and the more recent increase in circumpolar cooperation could – as discussed in Chapter 8 – make a similar effort more promising today.

10 Summary

The historic presence of Arctic indigenous peoples has been invoked in support of state claims to title over territory and, in the case of the Northwest Passage, to the "internal waters" status of straits and channels within groups of islands. Arctic indigenous peoples have also participated in processes of international law-making, by cooperating across borders within and between ethnic groups in strategic and sometimes remarkably successful efforts to influence state decision-making. One such success concerns the status of indigenous peoples as "permanent participants" within the Arctic Council, which gives them places at the table alongside the member states. Another success concerns the consensus approach to decision-making used in the Arctic Council, which effectively eliminates the permanent participants' disadvantage of not having votes. A third success concerns the termination of the practice of the Arctic Ocean coastal states meeting separately from the Arctic Council – and therefore from the permanent participants – as the so-called "Arctic-5." Although the influence of Arctic indigenous peoples is reflective of a more general, worldwide opening-up of international law-making processes to non-state actors, such developments seem to proceed more quickly and easily in regions where inter-state cooperation is still relatively novel, where patterns of diplomacy are not yet set, and where regional organizations are only just being formed.

8 Security

The Arctic is not only the Arctic Ocean, but also the northern tips of three continents: Europe, Asia and America. It is the place where the Euroasian, North American and Asian Pacific regions meet, where the frontiers come close to one another and the interests of states belonging to mutually opposed military blocs and nonaligned ones cross.

Mikhail Gorbachev[1]

The USS *Nautilus* sailed under the North Pole in 1958; one year later, the USS *Skate* surfaced there. As platforms for missiles, nuclear-powered submarines offered better concealment, range, and mobility than either launch sites on land or long-range bomber aircraft. Their ability to stay submerged for months on end also meant that they could operate year-round under the Arctic sea-ice. By 1980, there were forty-six submarines armed with nuclear missiles in the Soviet Union's Northern Fleet.[2] Some of those vessels would not have left the Arctic Ocean; others would have entered the Atlantic through the "Greenland–Iceland–United Kingdom Gap." Some would have traversed the Northwest Passage or Nares Strait, the ice-choked channel between Canada and Greenland. In 2011, on board the Russian Academy of Science's research vessel *Akademik Ioffe*, I was able to compare the old Soviet charts for those waters with Canada's newest ones. The former had significantly more depth soundings than the latter, especially in the

---

[1] Mikhail Gorbachev, "Presentation of the Order of Lenin and the Gold Star to the City of Murmansk," October 1, 1987, available at www.barentsinfo.org/?DeptID=3473.
[2] John Kristen Skogan, "The Evolution of the Four Soviet Fleets 1968-1987," in John Kristen Skogan and Arne Olav Brundtland, *Soviet Seapower in Northern Waters: Facts, Motivation, Impact and Responses* (London: Pinter, 1990), 18.

approaches to the US airbase at Thule, Greenland and the Canadian airbase at Resolute Bay.[3]

The Soviets also used the Arctic as a site for nuclear testing, with the largest weapon ever tested – the fifty megaton Tsar Bomba – being detonated in the air above Novaya Zemlya in 1961. In total, more than 200 nuclear tests took place on or above that archipelago on the eastern side of the Barents Sea, leaving a legacy of radioactive fallout that will persist for centuries.[4]

During the early stages of the Cold War, long-range bombers provided the principal means for delivering nuclear weapons. American B-52s circled over Canada's High Arctic, waiting for the signal to enter the Soviet Union's airspace with their deadly payloads. On the other side of the Arctic Ocean, Tupolev Tu-95 "Bear" bombers engaged in the same macabre ritual. In 1968, a B-52 crashed on the ice near Thule with four hydrogen bombs on board. Although the high explosives used to trigger the nuclear warheads went off, the warheads themselves did not – since the crew had not armed them. A massive recovery operation was launched, at considerable risk to the Americans, Danes, and local Inuit involved.[5] Three of the warheads were recovered; the fourth remains somewhere under the ice, containing plutonium with a half-life of 24,000 years.[6]

NATO even shared a 200-kilometer-long Arctic land border with the Soviet Union: in northern Norway, alongside the heavily militarized Kola Peninsula and a lengthy and disputed boundary offshore in the Barents Sea.[7] There was a second, similarly disputed maritime boundary between Alaska and the Soviet Far East – with just forty-five nautical miles separating the two mainland coasts in the Bering Strait, and just

---

[3] See Bob Weber, "Russian Maps Suggest Soviet Subs Cruised Canadian Arctic," *Canadian Press*, December 6, 2011, available at www.theglobeandmail.com/news/national/russian-maps-suggest-soviet-subs-cruised-canadian-arctic/article2261379/. The soundings were also in slightly different locations, with different measurements, which confirm the Soviet charts were not compiled from Canadian charts.

[4] International Atomic Energy Agency, *Nuclear Explosions in the USSR: The North Test Site Reference Material* (Vienna: Division of Nuclear Safety and Security, 2004), 5 and 29, available at www-ns.iaea.org/downloads/rw/waste-safety/north-test-site-final.pdf.

[5] Stephen Mulvey, "Denmark Challenged over B52 Crash," *BBC News*, May 11, 2007, available at http://news.bbc.co.uk/2/hi/europe/6647421.stm.

[6] Gordon Corera, "Mystery of Lost US Nuclear Bomb," *BBC News*, November 10, 2008, available at http://news.bbc.co.uk/2/hi/europe/7720049.stm.

[7] For more on the Barents Sea boundary, see Chapter 2, above.

three nautical miles separating the Soviet island of Big Diomede and the US island of Little Diomede in the middle of that waterway.[8]

During the Cold War, international law played a small but significant role in Arctic security. Article 5 of the 1949 North Atlantic Treaty set out the collective defense obligation of NATO countries, which included Iceland, Norway, Denmark, Canada, and the United States, and therefore encompassed Greenland, Canada's High Arctic islands, and Alaska.[9] In 1958, Canada and the United States concluded the North American Aerospace Defense Command (NORAD) Agreement, which centralized continental air defense in a bi-national command structure. The NORAD Agreement has been renewed ten times while the mandate of the joint command has been expanded twice, first to include aerospace defense and then the sharing of maritime surveillance.[10]

In 1941, Denmark and the United States signed an Agreement Relating to the Defense of Greenland whereby the latter country took over responsibility for the island until the end of the Second World War.[11] A new agreement in 1951 allowed the United States to expand the airbase at Thule and exercise exclusive jurisdiction there.[12] In 2004, despite the concerns of local Inuit, a further agreement was concluded to allow for the upgrading of the radar systems at Thule as a component of US ballistic missile defense.[13]

Many of the arms control agreements concluded between the United States and the Soviet Union were also of relevance to the Arctic,

---

[8] For more on the Bering Sea boundary, see Chapter 2, above.

[9] 1949 North Atlantic Treaty, available at www.nato.int/cps/en/natolive/official_texts_17120.htm. Article 5 reads, in part: "The Parties agree that an armed attack against one or more of them in Europe or North America shall be considered an attack against them all and consequently they agree that, if such an armed attack occurs, each of them, in exercise of the right of individual or collective self-defense recognised by Article 51 of the Charter of the United Nations, will assist the Party or Parties so attacked by taking forthwith, individually and in concert with the other Parties, such action as it deems necessary, including the use of armed force, to restore and maintain the security of the North Atlantic area."

[10] The most recent, 2006, version of the NORAD Agreement is available at www.state.gov/documents/organization/69727.pdf.

[11] 1941 Agreement Relating to the Defense of Greenland (1941) 35(3) *American Journal of International Law Supplement* 129.

[12] 1951 Agreement on the Defense of Greenland, available at http://avalon.law.yale.edu/20th_century/den001.asp.

[13] "US Expands Greenland Relations in Support of Missile Defense," *Environment News Service*, August 9, 2004, available at www.ens-newswire.com/ens/aug2004/2004-08-09-02.asp.

including the 1963 Partial Test Ban Treaty,[14] the 1971 Seabed Treaty,[15] the 1972 Strategic Arms Limitation Treaty (SALT I),[16] and the 1972 Anti-Ballistic Missile Treaty[17] – from which the George W. Bush administration formally withdrew the United States in 2001, before deploying ballistic missile defense interceptors to Fort Greely, Alaska.[18]

1 De-escalating the Pole

Two decades after the end of the Cold War, the risk of conflict is dramatically reduced in the Arctic. As mentioned above, Russia is a member of the G20, WTO, Council of Europe, Barents Euro-Arctic Council, and Arctic Council. Its largest trading partner is the European Union, made up mostly of NATO states. Russia's military power has also declined significantly: in 2011, its military spending at $72 billion was just one-tenth that of the United States ($711 bn.).[19]

The leaders of the Arctic countries agree that there is little risk of conflict in the region. As mentioned above, in January 2010, Canadian Prime Minister Stephen Harper told the Secretary General of NATO that Canada had a good working relationship with Russia with respect to the Arctic, that a NATO presence could backfire by exacerbating tensions, and that there was no likelihood of Arctic states going to war.[20] Nine months later, Russian Prime Minister (now President) Vladimir Putin

---

[14] 1963 Treaty Banning Nuclear Weapon Tests in the Atmosphere, in Outer Space and Under Water, 480(1) UNTS 6964, available at http://treaties.un.org/doc/Publication/UNTS/Volume%20480/volume-480-I-6964-English.pdf.

[15] 1971 Treaty on the Prohibition of the Emplacement of Nuclear Weapons and Other Weapons of Mass Destruction on the Sea-Bed and the Ocean Floor and in the Subsoil Thereof, 955 UNTS 115, available at http://disarmament.un.org/treaties/t/sea_bed/text.

[16] 1972 Interim Agreement between the United States of America and the Union of Soviet Socialist Republics on Certain Measures with respect to the Limitation of Strategic Offensive Arms (SALT I), available at http://cns.miis.edu/inventory/pdfs/aptsaltI.pdf.

[17] 1972 Treaty between the United States of America and the Union of Soviet Socialist Republics on the Limitation of Anti-Ballistic Missile Systems (ABM Treaty), available at www.nti.org/media/pdfs/aptabm.pdf?_=1316631917and_=1316631917.

[18] "Statement by the Press Secretary: Announcement of Withdrawal from the ABM Treaty," December 13, 2001, available at http://georgewbush-whitehouse.archives.gov/news/releases/2001/12/20011213-2.html.

[19] "The 15 Countries with the Highest Military Expenditure in 2009," Stockholm International Peace Research Institute, 2010, available at www.sipri.org/research/armaments/milex/resultoutput/milex_15 (China: $143 bn. / US: $711 bn. / France: $62.5 bn. / Germany: $46.7 bn. / Italy: $34.5 bn.).

[20] US State Department cable # VZCZCXR03302, Chapter 5, n. 110, above.

made his speech about trying to stand alone and surviving in the Arctic and how nature makes people and states help each other.[21] Senior members of the Canadian and US militaries have confirmed these views. In 2009, Canada's chief soldier, General Walter Natynczyk, said: "If someone were to invade the Canadian Arctic, my first task would be to rescue them."[22] In 2010, the US Chief of Naval Operations, Admiral Gary Roughead, issued a memorandum on "Navy Strategic Objectives for the Arctic" that stated, "the potential for conflict in the Arctic is low."[23]

Nevertheless, all of the Arctic countries have taken steps to improve their military capabilities in the North. The Canadian government has promised to build up to eight ice-strengthened patrol ships for its navy, although (as of January 2013) no contracts have been signed.[24] It also promised to establish a deep-water naval port on northern Baffin Island, though that plan has been scaled back substantially.[25] The size of the Canadian Rangers, a reserve unit made up of part-time volunteers from Northern communities, has been increased slightly from 4,100 to 4,700.[26]

Denmark, which has four frigates that can operate in up to eighty centimeters of first-year ice, put two additional smaller ice-strengthened patrol ships into service in 2008 and 2009. Several of these ships and their helicopters are deployed around Greenland, as far north as ice conditions allow.[27]

---

[21] Luke Harding, "Vladimir Putin Calls for Arctic Claims to Be Resolved under UN Law," *Guardian*, September 23, 2010, available at www.guardian.co.uk/world/2010/sep/23/putin-arctic-claims-international-law.

[22] Pierre-Henry Deshayes, "Arctic Threats and Challenges from Climate Change," *Agence France-Presse*, December 6, 2009, available at www.google.com/hostednews/afp/article/ALeqM5iESW9KN4XHyuP2QpnDqDf5wGxJVg.

[23] US Chief of Naval Operations, "Navy Strategic Objectives for the Arctic," May 21, 2010, p. 3, available at http://greenfleet.dodlive.mil/files/2010/09/US-Navy-Arctic-Strategic-Objectives-21-May-2010.pdf.

[24] Lee Berthiaume, "Armed Arctic Vessels Face Delay in Latest Procurement Setback," *Postmedia News*, May 8, 2012, available at www.nunatsiaqonline.ca/stories/article/65674armed_arctic_vessels_face_delay_in_latest_procurement_setback/.

[25] Bob Weber, "Ottawa Scraps Big Plans for Arctic Naval Facility," *Canadian Press*, March 23, 2012, available at http://thechronicleherald.ca/canada/76576-ottawa-scraps-big-plans-arctic-naval-facility.

[26] David Pugliese, "Canadian Rangers Increase in Size. Ranks are at around 4,700," *Ottawa Citizen*, July 25, 2011, available at http://blogs.ottawacitizen.com/2011/07/25/canadian-rangers-increase-in-size-ranks-are-at-around-4700/.

[27] See quotation from Danish Rear-Admiral Henrik Kudsk, n. 135, below, pp. 272–273.

For a country of only five million people, Norway has a superbly equipped military. It operates five Aeigis-class frigates, six diesel-electric submarines, and a 104-meter ice-strengthened patrol ship called the NoCGV *Svalbard*. Norway also has F-16 fighter jets and is moving, albeit with some hesitation, toward replacing them with F-35s.[28] In 2010, the Norwegian Armed Forces raised some eyebrows internationally when they moved their joint operational headquarters to a Cold War-era underground complex north of the Arctic Circle.[29] The new location is, in fact, at the approximate midpoint of a narrow, elongated country.

In 2011, Russian Defense Minister Anatoly Serdyukov announced that two army brigades would be created to protect his country's Arctic resources, though he declined to give any details of the plan.[30] In 2012, Russia's *RT News* reported on another plan to establish twenty border posts in the Arctic, including along the Northern Sea Route, with fifteen to twenty guards stationed at each.[31] Neither plan seems to be directed at other countries; instead, they appear to address the non-state threats that will accompany increased commercial activity in and around Russia's northern regions, such as smuggling, illegal immigration, and terrorism.[32]

Other Russian military plans have been met with skepticism from some quarters, as the following passage from a 2012 report published by the Center for Climate and Energy Solutions shows:

The 2007–2015 Russian State Armament Programme emphasizes the rebuilding of their northern naval capabilities. Under this program the Russians will build new nuclear-powered submarines, including both fast attack (SSNs) and nuclear missile-carrying submarines (SSBNs). The Russian geographic reality means that these vessels will be based in northern waters. The head of the Russian Navy has stated that the Russians also plan to build five or six carrier battle-groups, which would be primarily based at their northern bases. ... The Russians have also resumed a significant military presence in the Arctic. In August 2007 they

---

[28] Andrea Shalal-Esa, "Lockheed Welcomes Norway Backing of F-35 Fighter," *Reuters*, March 23, 2012, available at http://uk.reuters.com/article/2012/03/23/us-lockheed-fighter-norway-idUKBRE82M1CQ20120323.

[29] "Inside Norway's Underground Military HQ," *BBC News*, September 22, 2010, available at www.bbc.co.uk/news/world-europe-11386699.

[30] Thomas Grove, "Russia Creates Two Brigades of Arctic Troops," *Reuters*, July 1, 2011, available at http://uk.reuters.com/article/2011/07/01/russia-arctic-troops-idUKLDE76017D20110701.

[31] "Russia to Set Up Arctic Frontier Posts," *RT News*, April 16, 2012, available at http://rt.com/politics/arctic-border-posts-russia-132/.

[32] On non-state threats, see discussion below.

restarted long-range bomber patrols. In the same year they also resumed north-ern patrols of naval surface units. They have been careful to remain within international airspace, but in some instances have approached the borders of Canada, Norway, and the United States.[33]

Assessing the Russian government's statements and actions regarding the Arctic is always challenging, not least because the country's princi-pal naval ports are by necessity located along the southwest coast of the Barents Sea. Murmansk and other ice-free Arctic ports became even more important after the dissolution of the Soviet Union, which resulted in Russia losing access to its naval installations in the Baltic States, and in Kaliningrad's separation from the rest of Russia by the newly independent countries of Belarus and Lithuania. These factors make it difficult to distinguish between Arctic-specific deployments and investments, and those aimed at maintaining Russia's capabilities elsewhere.[34]

Both Russia and the United States continue to deploy nuclear sub-marines in the Arctic Ocean and fly military aircraft there. Sometimes, these maneuvers cause undue excitement in neighboring countries. After one exercise in 2009, when two Bear bombers were intercepted more than ninety nautical miles from the Canadian coast over the Beaufort Sea, Canadian Defence Minister Peter MacKay called a press conference. He pointed out that the incident had occurred just one day before US President Barack Obama visited Ottawa, and stated: "I am not going to stand here and accuse the Russians of having deliberately done this during the presidential visit, but it was a strong coincidence."[35] Later, when Prime Minister Stephen Harper was asked about the matter, he suggested that the Russian planes had actually entered Canadian airspace – which, like the territorial sea, extends just twelve nautical miles offshore. "This is a real concern to us," he said. "I have expressed at various times the deep concern our government has with increas-ingly aggressive Russian actions around the globe and Russian

[33] Rob Huebert, *et al.*, "Climate Change and International Security: The Arctic as a Bellwether." 2012, Center for Climate and Energy Solutions, p. 18, available at www.c2es.org/publications/climate-change-international-arctic-security/.

[34] Rob Huebert, "The Newly Emerging Arctic Security Environment," Canadian Defence and Foreign Affairs Institute, March 2010, p. 16, available at www.cdfai.org/PDF/The%20Newly%20Emerging%20Arctic%20Security%20Environment.pdf.

[35] Steven Chase, "Ottawa Rebukes Russia for Military Flights in Arctic," *Globe and Mail*, February 28, 2009, available at www.theglobeandmail.com/news/politics/ottawa-rebukes-russia-for-military-flights-in-arctic/article1149408/.

intrusions into our airspace." Harper promised to "respond every time the Russians make any kind of intrusion on the sovereignty of Canada's Arctic."[36]

American and Russian responses to the Canadian comments were more informative about the actual security situation in the Arctic. The four-star US general in charge of NORAD assured journalists that the Russians had "conducted themselves professionally" and not entered Canadian or US airspace, while a Russian diplomat explained that NORAD had been notified of the flights in advance, in accordance with a long-standing agreement between Washington and Moscow.[37]

As Charles Emmerson usefully reminds us, "the force projection capability of modern Russia does not approach that of the Soviet Union" and "the domestic legitimacy of the Putin–Medvedev regime depends on economic prosperity more than military might."[38] Siemon Wezeman described the situation accurately in a paper published by the Stockholm International Peace Research Institute in 2012:

> While some media, politicians and researchers have portrayed the changes in the capabilities of the Arctic littoral states as significant military build-ups and potential threats to security, the overall picture is one of limited modernization and increases or changes in equipment, force levels and force structure. Some of these changes – for example, the strengthening of the Canadian Rangers, the move of the main Norwegian land units to the north of Norway or the new Russian Arctic units – have little or nothing to do with power projection into the areas of the Arctic with unclear ownership; rather they are for the patrolling and protecting of recognized national territories that are becoming more accessible, including for illegal activities.[39]

In addition, a number of steps have been taken to reduce the militarization of the Arctic, including the US withdrawal from the Keflavík airbase on Iceland in 2006, and Russia's acceptance of Western assistance with the decommissioning and clean-up of Soviet-era nuclear submarines and warheads along Russia's Arctic coast. Then, in 2011,

---

[36] Ibid.

[37] Ibid.; and testimony of Dmitry Trofimov before Canadian House of Commons Standing Committee on National Defence, March 23, 2009, available at www.parl.gc.ca/HousePublications/Publication.aspx?DocId=3760417&Language=E&Mode=1.

[38] Charles Emmerson, *The Future History of the Arctic* (New York: Public Affairs, 2010), p. 121.

[39] Siemon T. Wezeman, "Military Capabilities in the Arctic." SIPRI Background Paper, Stockholm, March 2012, pp. 13–14, available at http://books.sipri.org/product_info?c_product_id=442.

the "New START" entered into force between the United States and Russia.[40] Part of Barack Obama's effort to "reset" the relationship between the two countries, the treaty requires a 50 percent reduction in the number of strategic nuclear missile launchers.

All of which raises the question as to whether NATO has any continuing relevance for the Arctic.[41] For the foreseeable future, the answer is probably "no" – at least in terms of NATO's traditional collective defense mandate under the North Atlantic Treaty. However, NATO has progressively sought to expand its mandate, most significantly through a new "Strategic Concept" adopted by NATO ministers in 2010.[42] In that document, NATO tasks itself, not just with collective defense but also crisis management and "cooperative security" – including the on-going protection of trade routes, energy supplies, and pipelines. Although the Strategic Concept does not mention the Arctic, it is likely that NATO's expanded mandate will take it northwards and that coordination and cooperation with other organizations, most notably the Arctic Council, will be required when it does.

To date, the Arctic Council has shied away from security issues because of a footnote in the 1996 Ottawa Declaration that reads: "The Arctic Council should not deal with matters related to military security."[43] The footnote was included at the insistence of the United States, which was presumably concerned about the new intergovernmental forum's potential effect on the delicate US–Russian nuclear balance in the region.[44] Today, in quite different circumstances that include a track record of modest successes on the part of the Arctic Council, the member states would be well advised to revisit that decision. Nor is there any impediment to their so doing, as Erik Molenaar has cogently pointed out:

---

[40] New START Treaty, Chapter 2, n. 71, above.

[41] See, e.g., Helga Haftendorn, "NATO and the Arctic: Is the Atlantic Alliance a Cold War Relic in a Peaceful Region Now Faced with Non-Military Challenges?" (2011) 20 *European Security* 337; Sven G. Holtsmark, "Towards Cooperation or Confrontation? Security in the High North." Research Paper No. 45, NATO Defense College, February 2009, available at www.ndc.nato.int/research/series.php?icode=1.

[42] "Strategic Concept for the Defence and Security of the Members of the North Atlantic Treaty Organization," available at www.nato.int/lisbon2010/strategic-concept-2010-eng.pdf.

[43] Declaration on the Establishment of the Arctic Council, Chapter 7, n. 61, above.

[44] Rob Huebert, "New Directions in Circumpolar Cooperation: Canada, the Arctic Environmental Protection Strategy and the Arctic Council." (1998) 5 *Canadian Foreign Policy* 37 at 54.

The use of the voluntary term "should" – which is appropriate for a non-legally binding instrument – nevertheless indicates that the Council could deal with such matters anyway, provided there is consensus to do so. In fact, as the Ottawa Declaration is not legally binding, it does not pose much of an obstacle to the Members if they would wish to go even beyond the already very broad mandate of the Council.[45]

2 China

China does not pose a military threat in the Arctic, which is remote from its shores. As the world's largest trading nation, China is a member of the G20 and the WTO and has an on-going interest in maintaining good relations with Arctic states. Although China's military budget is growing rapidly, in 2011, its defense expenditures were still just one-fifth of those of the United States, or around the same as France, Germany, and Italy combined.[46]

China has long been engaged in Arctic science, especially with regard to climate change. According to Linda Jakobson, China has organized twenty-six expeditions and established three research stations in the Arctic since 1984.[47] One of those stations is located on the Norwegian archipelago of Svalbard. China also operates a 163-meter research ice-breaker, the *Snow Dragon*, and is building a second, smaller research icebreaker.

The Chinese government is fully aware of the enormous potential for offshore oil and natural gas development in the Arctic, but it also knows that most of that oil and gas is in the sedimentary rocks of the continental shelves, and that, under the law of the sea, coastal countries have exclusive rights to any natural resource within 200 nautical miles of their shores.[48] The Chinese are also aware that coastal states may have jurisdiction over seabed resources even further out – if they can demonstrate scientifically that the shape and geology of the ocean floor constitute a "natural prolongation" of their land mass.[49] China does

---

[45] Erik Molenaar, "Current and Prospective Roles of the Arctic Council System within the Context of the Law of the Sea." (2012) 27 *International Journal of Marine and Coastal Law* 553 at 570.

[46] "The 15 Countries with the Highest Military Expenditure in 2011," n. 19, above.

[47] "China's Perspective on Arctic Matters." (2009) 55(15) *Shijie Zhishi*, translated in Linda Jakobson, "China Prepares for an Ice-Free Arctic." SIPRI Insights on Peace and Security, No. 2010/2, March 2010, p. 3, available at http://books.sipri.org/files/insight/SIPRIInsight1002.pdf.

[48] See discussion, Chapter 4, above.   [49] Ibid.

not contest these rights. It has ratified the UN Convention on the Law of the Sea and, in the East China Sea, is using the same provisions of that treaty as Arctic countries are using to assert sovereign rights over an extended continental shelf.[50] At the same time, China has made clear that it expects Arctic countries to respect international law with regard to the outer limits of extended continental shelves, and the rights of all countries to access resources in the internationalized "Area" beyond that.[51]

Nor is there any need for China to challenge the claims of the Arctic countries. Offshore oil and gas are expensive to find, extract, and transport, especially in an extremely remote and physically inhospitable region. To access these riches, Arctic countries will need strong markets and vast amounts of capital, both of which China is well positioned to provide. As for Arctic Ocean fisheries, China already works well with several regional fisheries organizations – in return for being allotted science-based quotas.[52]

China's law-abiding approach to the Arctic has, however, been shaken by the postponement of its application for permanent observer status at the Arctic Council. Unfortunately, the Chinese request came at the same time as the European Union request – and the European Commission's import ban on seal products – and was collaterally suspended.[53] Then, in 2011, when the Arctic Council adopted new criteria for permanent observers, it included the condition that they recognize "the Arctic States' right to administer the Arctic Ocean under the Convention on the Law of the Sea."[54] China is unlikely to accept this condition, which as currently worded implies that Arctic states have the right to administer the entire Arctic Ocean. In actual fact, China and other non-Arctic countries are fully entitled to navigate freely beyond twelve nautical miles from shore, to fish beyond 200 nautical miles from shore, and to exploit seabed resources that lie beyond the continental shelf.

The Arctic Council member states made a mistake by failing to acknowledge explicitly that their own rights, while extensive, are not

---

[50] See Alexander M. Peterson, "Sino–Japanese Cooperation in the East China Sea: A Lasting Arrangement?" (2009) 42 *Cornell International Law Journal* 441. China's disputes in the South China Sea revolve around quite different issues of title to land territory, in the form of islands and shoals, and the entitlements of such features to maritime zones.
[51] See discussion, Chapter 4, above.   [52] See discussion, Chapter 6, above.
[53] See discussion, Chapter 7, above.
[54] See "Observers," at www.arctic-council.org/index.php/en/about-us/partners-links.

unlimited. As it stands, they could hardly have devised a better strategy for stoking Chinese fears about their intentions in the North. Chinese officials interviewed by Linda Jakobson and Jingchao Peng in 2012 "privately expressed displeasure with some of the criteria: the stipulations that an applicant must have demonstrated the 'political willingness and financial ability to contribute to the work of the Permanent Participants' and 'recognize Arctic states' sovereignty, sovereign rights and jurisdiction in the Arctic.'"[55] Jakobson and Peng also report that Chinese academics have criticized the criteria for raising "the political threshold in order to stop non-Arctic states interfering" in Arctic affairs; that "Arctic states are announcing to the world: the Arctic belongs to the Arctic states," and that "If many countries were to be excluded from the Arctic Council, the power of the council would be weakened and it would be difficult for it to remain the primary institution to negotiate Arctic affairs."[56]

China is respecting international law and has legitimate interests in the Arctic. Its request for permanent observer status should be granted forthwith.

3 Arctic nuclear-weapon-free zones

In 1982, while NATO and the Soviet Union were still locked in the Cold War, the Inuit Circumpolar Council adopted a resolution against the presence or testing of nuclear weapons in the Arctic.[57] With the Arctic Ocean being a major theatre of operation for nuclear submarines, the Inuit initiative was destined to fail. But now, in fundamentally changed circumstances, it may be time to return to the idea of a nuclear-weapon-free zone in the Arctic.

Already two treaties have, for decades, prohibited nuclear weapons in certain parts of the Arctic. In 1920, the Svalbard Treaty effectively demilitarized the Norwegian archipelago by prohibiting the establishment of any "naval base" or "fortification" and stating that the islands

---

[55] Linda Jakobson and Jingchao Peng, "China's Arctic Ambitions." SIPRI Policy Paper 34, November 2012, available at http://books.sipri.org/product_info?c_product_id=449.

[56] Ibid., citing and translating Y. Qian, "How Far Is China from the Arctic." (2011) 29 *Liaowang Dongfang Zhoukan*, available at www.lwdf.cn/wwwroot/dfzk/Focuseast/252093. shtml; and Peiqing Guo, "Making Preparations against an Arctic Monroe Doctrine." (2011) 42 *Liaowang* 71–72.

[57] See discussion, Chapter 7, above.

"may never be used for warlike purposes."[58] Forty countries have ratified the Svalbard Treaty, including all the Arctic states.[59] In 1971, the Seabed Treaty, which applies to all the world's oceans, prohibited the deployment of nuclear weapons on the seabed beyond twelve nautical miles from shore.[60] Ninety-four countries have ratified the Seabed Treaty, including all the Arctic states and all the declared nuclear weapon states apart from France.[61] It is also possible to argue that coastal states are entitled, as the result of a more recently developed rule of customary international law, to prohibit shipments of ultra-hazardous nuclear cargoes through their exclusive economic zones.[62] Yet most proponents of a nuclear-weapon-free zone in the Arctic envisage a comprehensive, region-wide arrangement similar to the 1959 Antarctic Treaty, which requires that the entire Antarctic remain demilitarized.[63]

The possibility of nuclear-weapon-free zones was encouraged by the 1968 Non-Proliferation Treaty, Article VII of which states: "Nothing in this Treaty affects the right of any group of States to conclude regional treaties in order to assure the total absence of nuclear weapons in their respective territories."[64] In 1975, the UN General Assembly added more detail to the concept, defining a nuclear-weapon-free zone as:

any zone, recognized as such by the General Assembly of the United Nations, which any group of States, in the free exercises of their sovereignty, has established by virtue of a treaty or convention whereby:

---

[58] Treaty concerning the Archipelago of Spitsbergen, Chapter 1, n. 24, above, Art. 9.

[59] See "Traktat angående Spitsbergen (Svalbardtraktaten)," available at www.lovdata.no/cgi-bin/udoffles?doc=tra-1920-02-09-001.txt&.

[60] 1971 Treaty on the Prohibition of the Emplacement of Nuclear Weapons and Other Weapons of Mass Destruction on the Sea-Bed and the Ocean Floor and in the Subsoil Thereof, 955 UNTS 115, available at http://disarmament.un.org/treaties/t/sea_bed/text. See, generally, Jozef Goldblat, "The Seabed Treaty and Arms Control," in Richard Fieldhouse (ed.), Security at Sea: Naval Forces and Arms Control (Oxford University Press and Stockholm International Peace Research Institute, 1990), 187.

[61] See "Status of the Treaty," at http://disarmament.un.org/treaties/t/sea_bed.

[62] See Jon M. Van Dyke, "The Disappearing Right to Navigational Freedom in the Exclusive Economic Zone." (2005) 29 Marine Policy 107 at 110–112.

[63] 1959 Antarctic Treaty, 402 UNTS 71, available at www.ats.aq/documents/ats/treaty_original.pdf. Article 1(1) reads: "Antarctica shall be used for peaceful purposes only. There shall be prohibited, inter alia, any measure of a military nature, such as the establishment of military bases and fortifications, the carrying out of military manoeuvres, as well as the testing of any type of weapons."

[64] 1968 Treaty on the Non-Proliferation of Nuclear Weapons, 729 UNTS 161, available at www.iaea.org/Publications/Documents/Infcircs/Others/infcirc140.pdf.

(a) The statute of total absence of nuclear weapons to which the zone shall be subject, including the procedure for the delimitation of the zone, is defined;

(b) An international system of verification and control is established to guarantee compliance with the obligations deriving from that statute.[65]

There are five nuclear-weapon-free zones in existence today: in Latin America,[66] the South Pacific,[67] Southeast Asia,[68] Africa,[69] and Central Asia.[70]

In the same 1975 resolution, the UN General Assembly attempted to create an obligation on the part of the declared nuclear weapon states – China, France, Russia, the United Kingdom, and the United States – to ratify protocols or otherwise commit to "respect in all its parts the statute of total absence of nuclear weapons" in the zones and to "refrain from using or threatening to use nuclear weapons against the States included."[71] However, the General Assembly has no power to impose legal obligations and these so-called "negative security assurances" have not always been forthcoming. The United States has only provided one assurance, to the Latin American nuclear-weapon-free zone.[72] Russia has provided two, to the Latin American[73] and South Pacific zones.[74]

The most successful nuclear-weapon-free zones have been created in areas where nuclear weapons had not yet been deployed. That factual circumstance probably explains the success of the Svalbard, Antarctic, and Seabed treaties. The Arctic represents a quite different reality, having been home for decades to thousands of nuclear warheads and delivery systems, including missiles, bombers, and submarines. Given

---

[65] UNGA Res. 3472 B (1975), available at www.opanal.org/Docs/UN/UNAG30res3472i.pdf.

[66] 1967 Treaty for the Prohibition of Nuclear Weapons in Latin America and the Caribbean (Treaty of Tlatelolco), available at http://disarmament.un.org/treaties/t/tlatelolco/text.

[67] 1985 South Pacific Nuclear Free Zone Treaty (Treaty of Rarotonga), available at http://disarmament.un.org/treaties/t/rarotonga/text.

[68] 1995 Treaty on the Southeast Asia Nuclear Weapon-Free Zone (Treaty of Bangkok), available at http://disarmament.un.org/treaties/t/bangkok/text.

[69] 1996 African Nuclear Weapon Free Zone Treaty (Treaty of Pelindaba), available at http://disarmament.un.org/treaties/t/pelindaba/text.

[70] 2006 Treaty on a Nuclear-Weapon-Free Zone in Central Asia (Treaty of Semipalatinsk), available at http://disarmament.un.org/treaties/t/canwfz/text.

[71] UNGA Res. 3472 B (1975), n. 65, above.

[72] The negative security assurance is set out in Additional Protocol II to the Treaty of Tlatelolco, available at http://disarmament.un.org/treaties/t/tlateloco_p2/text. On US ratification, see http://disarmament.un.org/treaties/t/tlateloco_p2.

[73] Ibid.

[74] "Status of the Protocol," available at http://disarmament.un.org/treaties/t/rarotonga_p2.

the continued importance of the Arctic Ocean as a deployment area for both Russian and NATO nuclear missile submarines, a comprehensive Arctic nuclear-weapon-free zone seems unlikely – that is, until global nuclear disarmament is achieved. That said, UN Security Council Resolution 1887, which was drafted by the United States and adopted unanimously in 2009, expressly supports the creation of nuclear-weapon-free zones as an effective way of preventing nuclear proliferation. The preamble to the resolution reads, in part:

> The Security Council ... Welcoming and supporting the steps taken to conclude nuclear-weapon-free zone treaties and reaffirming the conviction that the establishment of internationally recognized nuclear-weapon-free zones on the basis of arrangements freely arrived at among the States of the region concerned, and in accordance with the 1999 United Nations Disarmament Commission guidelines, enhances global and regional peace and security, strengthens the nuclear non-proliferation regime, and contributes toward realizing the objectives of nuclear disarmament.[75]

In another sign of the changing attitudes of the nuclear weapon states, the Obama administration announced in 2011 that it would submit two protocols on negative security assurances to the US Senate for its advice and consent to ratification, namely, the protocols to the South Pacific and African nuclear-weapon-free zones.[76]

In the Arctic, there are a number of incremental steps that might usefully be taken on the path toward a region-wide nuclear-weapon-free zone. One option is for one or more of the six Arctic non-nuclear-weapon states simply to declare themselves nuclear-weapon-free zones, as Mongolia did in 1992.[77] After the five nuclear weapon states issued a joint statement providing security assurances to Mongolia in connection with its nuclear-weapon-free status, the UN General Assembly formally recognized that status in 2001.[78]

---

[75] S/RES/1887 (2009), adopted September 24, 2009, available at www.europarl.europa.eu/meetdocs/2009_2014/documents/sede/dv/sede301109unscr1887_/sede301109 unscr1887_en.pdf.

[76] Alfred Nurja, "Obama Submits NWFZ Protocols to Senate," *Arms Control Today*, June 2011, available at www.armscontrol.org/act/2011_06/NWFZ.

[77] "Nuclear-Weapon-Free Status of Mongolia," available at http://cns.miis.edu/inventory/pdfs/mongol.pdf.

[78] UNGA Res. 55/33/S, November 20, 2000, available at www.un.org/depts/dhl/resguide/r55.htm.

Although their actions would not be binding on states, there is nothing to stop sub-state units such as Nunavut and Greenland from making similar declarations – as hundreds of cities around the world have done.[79] It is difficult to see how declarations that simply recognized the non-existence of nuclear weapons in Nunavut or Greenland would infringe on the powers of the Canadian and Danish governments over defense and foreign affairs.

More ambitiously, two or more of the six Arctic non-nuclear-weapon states could negotiate a nuclear-weapon-free zone among themselves, without seeking to involve Russia and the United States except in terms of subsequent negative security assurances. Indeed, the possibility of a Nordic nuclear-weapon-free zone has been discussed for more than half a century.[80] Arguably, any such treaty could run up against the commitments of Canada, Denmark, Iceland, or Norway under NATO, to allow nuclear weapons to be deployed on their territory in wartime.[81] But these countries could avoid any legal conflict by withdrawing from NATO's Nuclear Planning Group, membership of which is neither required under the alliance, nor as important as it was during the Cold War.

The most promising, immediately available, opportunity was identified more than three decades ago, when Franklyn Griffiths proposed a multilateral treaty to demilitarize the surface water and sea-ice of the central Arctic Ocean.[82] By focusing on maintaining the demilitarized condition of an area that was not yet militarized, the proposal followed the model of the Seabed Treaty. At the time, the surface of the central

---

[79] See Nigel Young, "Peace Movements in History: Perspectives from Social Movements," in S. Mendlovitz and R.B. Walker (eds.), *Towards a Just World Peace* (London: Butterworths, 1987), 137 at 154–157.

[80] Ingemar Lindahl, *The Soviet Union and the Nordic Nuclear-Weapons-Free-Zone Proposal* (London: Macmillan, 1988); Clive Archer, "Plans for a Nordic Nuclear-Weapon Free Zone." (2004) 34 *Kosmopolis* 201 (supplement), available at https://helda.helsinki.fi/bitstream/handle/10224/3635/archer201-207.pdf.

[81] See Douglas Roche and Ernie Regehr, "Canada, NATO and Nuclear Weapons." Project Ploughshares Working Paper 01-3 (2001), available at www.ploughshares.ca/content/canada-nato-and-nuclear-weapons.

[82] Franklyn Griffiths, "A Northern Foreign Policy." (1979) 7 *Wellesley Papers* (Toronto: Canadian Institute of International Affairs), 61. In 2010, Griffiths raised the idea again, at a NATO-related workshop, where he reports: "It was right away shot down as unrealistic and as undesirable in proposing to alter the high-seas regime in international law." Griffiths, "Arctic Security: The Indirect Approach," in James Kraska (ed.), *Arctic Security in an Age of Climate Change* (New York: Cambridge University Press, 2011), 3 at 5 n. 2.

Arctic Ocean was at little risk of being militarized, and the main benefit of such a treaty would therefore have been in fostering cooperation between the United States and the Soviet Union. Now, with the Arctic sea-ice disappearing, the risk of surface naval vessels deploying to the Arctic Ocean (beyond the historically ice-free areas of the Barents and Norwegian seas) is increasing every year, and Griffiths' proposal therefore deserves serious consideration.

An incidental but strategic benefit of Griffiths' proposal is that, by preventing ships equipped for surface anti-submarine warfare from being deployed to the Arctic Ocean, it would protect and stabilize the deterrent provided by nuclear submarines. This, of course, is something the sea-ice historically did. Obviously, exceptions would have to be included in the treaty for peaceful military operations such as search and rescue, as well as the surfacing of submarines in emergencies.

A treaty to demilitarize the surface water and sea-ice of the central Arctic Ocean would be relatively easy to negotiate, implement, and verify – and could therefore be the first topic related to "military security" to be undertaken by the Arctic Council, if and when the member states choose to move beyond the anachronistic recommendation within the Ottawa Declaration.[83]

4 Non-state actors

Today, the most significant security threats in the Arctic are found along its southern fringes, in the Northwest Passage, Northern Sea Route, and along the coasts of the Barents, Bering, Beaufort, and Norwegian Seas. These threats involve non-state actors such as drug-smugglers, illegal immigrants, and even terrorists who might take advantage of ice-free waters to move contraband, people, or WMDs into North America or Europe, or between the Pacific and Atlantic Oceans. That said, great distances, challenging weather, and small populations (among which it is difficult for outsiders to remain unnoticed) combine to keep the threat levels far below those that exist in more southerly regions. Moreover, the opening of Arctic shipping routes could have the effect of mitigating at least one serious security threat from non-state actors elsewhere, by enabling some cargo vessels to avoid the pirate-infested

---

[83] See discussion, above, p. 253.

waters of the Indian Ocean and Strait of Malacca. Piracy costs the international shipping industry as much as $8 billion each year.[84]

4.1 Drug-smuggling

Illegal drugs are readily available in most Arctic communities, which raises the possibility that the same routes used to transport drugs northwards could be employed in reverse as entryways to Europe or North America. In 2007, Canadian authorities arrested a Norwegian-flagged private yacht – the *Berserk II* – at Cambridge Bay, Nunavut. On board were several individuals with criminal backgrounds, including drug-smuggling.[85] Although the voyage was probably just an amateurish attempt to challenge Canada's Northwest Passage claim, it might have also been a scouting mission. Four years later, during an Arctic eco-cruise, I went ashore at Franklin Bay, 600 kilometers to the west of where the *Berserk II* was arrested. Franklin Bay is the site of a long-abandoned Cold War radar station, and down the middle of the old gravel runway were a fresh trio of airplane tracks. There are hundreds of similar airstrips at other abandoned military, prospecting, and scientific research sites along the Northwest Passage, all within easy reach of a passing cruise ship, cargo vessel, or private yacht.

Drug-smuggling in the Arctic raises few issues of international law, because countries have undisputed jurisdiction over criminal activities within their territory and territorial sea as well as in adjoining international straits.[86] Additionally, it is widely accepted that coastal states may exercise jurisdiction over drug-smuggling within a "contiguous zone" located between twelve and twenty-four nautical miles offshore.[87] It is sometimes argued that action may also be taken against

---

[84] See Geopolicity, "The Economics of Piracy." May 2011, available at www.geopolicity. com/upload/content/pub_1305229189_regular.pdf.

[85] See Testimony of Philip Whitehorne, Canada Border Services Agency, to the Senate Committee on Fisheries and Oceans, November 5, 2009, available at www.parl.gc.ca/ Content/SEN/Committee/402/fish/13evb-e.htm?Language=EandParl=40andSes=2and comm_id=7.

[86] Article 42(1) of the UNCLOS reads, in part: "Subject to the provisions of this section, States bordering straits may adopt laws and regulations relating to transit passage through straits, in respect of all or any of the following: ... (d) the loading or unloading of any commodity, currency or person in contravention of the customs, fiscal, immigration or sanitary laws and regulations of States bordering straits," Introduction, n. 15, above.

[87] Article 33(1) of UNCLOS reads, in part: "In a zone contiguous to its territorial sea, described as the contiguous zone, the coastal State may exercise the control necessary to ... prevent infringement of its customs, fiscal, immigration or sanitary laws and regulations within its territory or territorial sea," ibid.

drug-smugglers on the high seas, based on the principles of "protective jurisdiction" or "universal jurisdiction."[88] However, when properly registered vessels are involved, the primacy of flag-state jurisdiction makes this argument difficult to sustain.[89] More often, drug-smuggling is addressed through "ship-rider" agreements that allow a vessel from one state to interdict a vessel from another state, or indeed any vessel seeking to flee into that second state's territorial sea. The term "ship-rider" refers to the fact that a law-enforcement officer from the second state is typically deployed on the interdicting ship during such operations. Canada and the United States have an agreement of this kind, designed for their East and West coasts as well as the Great Lakes, which could be used for cooperative law enforcement in the Beaufort Sea.[90] In the future, similar agreements might usefully be concluded between Canada and Denmark for the waters separating Canada and Greenland, between Norway and Russia for the Barents Sea, and between Russia and the United States for the Chukchi Sea, Bering Strait, and Bering Sea. Although a ship-rider agreement with Russia might seem unlikely, Russia and the United States have been using the equivalent of ship-riders since 1994 for the purpose of cooperative fisheries management in the Bering Sea.[91]

4.2 Illegal immigration

Illegal immigration is an issue of growing concern around the Arctic, including along Russia's land borders with Finland and Norway. As Charles Emmerson explains:

In the Cold War, the standing policy of the Norwegian government was that anyone who made it across the border would not be repatriated to the Soviet Union. On average, only one or two people were successful each year. These days, the numbers are much greater and the motivations tend to be economic

---

[88] See, e.g., Christina Sorensen, "Drug Trafficking on the High Seas: A Move Toward Universal Jurisdiction under International Law." (1990) 4 *Emory International Law Review* 207.

[89] For a brief but useful discussion, see Robin Churchill and Vaughan Lowe, *The Law of the Sea*, 3rd edn. (Manchester University Press, 1999), 217–218.

[90] "Framework Agreement on Integrated Cross-Border Maritime Law Enforcement Operations between the Government of Canada and the Government of the United States of America," May 2009, available at www.publicsafety.gc.ca/prg/le/_fl/int-cross-brdr-martime-eng.pdf.

[91] Convention on the Conservation and Management of Pollock Resources, Chapter 6, n. 36, above. See discussion, Chapter 6, above.

rather than political. Norway's fear of mass emigration from Russia in the early 1990s has been replaced by apprehension over the possibility of organized criminals trying to ferry illegal immigrants into Norway, part of Europe's open Schengen area. . . . The Russians, for their part, worry about infiltration of "terrorists."[92]

Some attempts at illegal immigration have also occurred elsewhere in the Arctic. In September 2006, a Romanian man sailed a six-meter motorboat from Greenland to Grise Fiord on Canada's Ellesmere Island.[93] The next month, two Turkish sailors jumped ship at Churchill, Manitoba, and bought train tickets to Winnipeg.[94] Although incidents like these do not raise issues of international law that are different from those in more southern regions, they do suggest that border surveillance will need to be improved in the Arctic.

The most significant challenge comes from increased shipping, including but not limited to cruise ships, which already offload hundreds of foreign nationals into small northern communities that lack any border controls but have scheduled air services to the south. National authorities have only begun to recognize the challenge. In Canada, regulations adopted under the Marine Transportation Security Act require mariners to provide ninety-six hours' notice and "a general description of the cargo" before entering Canadian territorial waters.[95] A mandatory Arctic shipping registration system (NORDREG) requires them to notify officials of the numbers of persons on board, and to provide daily updates on the location of the vessel.[96] Finally, anyone wishing to set foot on Canadian soil must notify both the Canadian Border Services Agency and the Department of Citizenship and Immigration; for this reason, Arctic cruise operators will often arrange for inspectors to be present at their first Canadian port of call.

---

[92] Emmerson, *The Future History of the Arctic*, n. 38, above, p. 104.

[93] "Romanian Who Boated to High Arctic Fesses Up," *CBC News*, November 15, 2006, available at www.cbc.ca/news/canada/north/story/2006/11/14/grise-romanian.html.

[94] Michel Comte, "Turkish Sailors Jump Ship in Canada Arctic, Prompt Security Review," *Agence France-Presse*, October 30, 2006, available at http://dl1.yukoncollege.yk.ca/agraham/discuss/msgReader$3341?mode=topicandy=2006andm=11andd=2.

[95] Marine Transportation Security Regulations, SOR/2004-144, Section 221(1), available at http://laws-lois.justice.gc.ca/eng/regulations/SOR-2004-144/index.html.

[96] Northern Canada Vessel Traffic Services Zone Regulations, SOR/2010-127, available at http://laws-lois.justice.gc.ca/eng/regulations/SOR-2010-127/page-1.html. See also McDorman, "National Measures for the Safety of Navigation in Arctic Waters," Chapter 5, n. 156, above.

None of these measures is contentious, apart from Canada's failure to consult with other countries before making NORDREG mandatory.[97] But neither are they likely to prevent professional criminals or terrorists from infiltrating North America without being detected. Further measures may be called for, such as requiring full crew and passenger manifests for all ships planning to use the Northwest Passage, or physically inspecting ships during the course of those voyages. Such measures will raise all the difficult issues concerning the status of the waterway and the extent of coastal state powers that were discussed in Chapter 5.

Lastly, it is likely that illegal immigration will increase in the Arctic, not just because of the improved accessibility provided by the loss of sea-ice, but because the same general process of climate change will force hundreds of millions of people to leave their homes in the developing world. Canada, the United States, and European countries already face influxes of migrants fleeing poverty, persecution, and conflict, but their numbers can be expected to increase exponentially at the very same time that melting sea-ice provides new entry points in the North.

4.3 Trafficking of weapons of mass destruction

In 2007, Paul Cellucci said: "I think, in the age of terrorism, it's in our security interests that the Northwest Passage be considered part of Canada. That would enable the Canadian navy to intercept and board vessels in the Northwest Passage to make sure they're not trying to bring weapons of mass destruction into North America."[98] The former US ambassador to Canada was right: a coastal state does have more jurisdictional powers within "internal waters" than in an "international strait." But, as mentioned in Chapter 5, coastal states are hardly powerless in international straits, especially where matters of national security are concerned.[99] For instance, Article 39(1) of UNCLOS states, in part:

Ships and aircraft, while exercising the right of transit passage, shall: (a) proceed without delay through or over the strait; (b) refrain from any threat or use of force against the sovereignty, territorial integrity or political independence of States bordering the strait, or in any other manner in violation of the principles

---

[97] See discussion, above, p. 166.
[98] Jim Brown, Canadian Press, "Ex-US Envoy Backs Canada's Arctic Claim," Chapter 5, n. 60, above.
[99] See discussion, above, pp. 163–167.

of international law embodied in the Charter of the United Nations; (c) refrain from any activities other than those incident to their normal modes of continuous and expeditious transit unless rendered necessary by force majeure or by distress.[100]

In addition, Article 42(1) of UNCLOS reads, in part:

States bordering straits may adopt laws and regulations relating to transit passage through straits, in respect of all or any of the following: ... (d) the loading or unloading of any commodity, currency or person in contravention of the customs, fiscal, immigration or sanitary laws and regulations of States bordering straits.[101]

Coastal states also have a right of self-defense under Article 51 of the UN Charter and customary international law that trumps the inviolability of foreign-registered vessels as notional extensions of their flag state's territory.[102] This right may be exercised in the collective self-defense of allies, as reflected in Article 5 of the North Atlantic Treaty.[103] And, within constraints – the details of which have been subject to contestation and at least some change since 11 September 2001 – the right of self-defense may be exercised pre-emptively.[104]

The right of self-defense will not be available in all instances, and is a justification that responsible countries use only as a last resort. Recognizing this, the US-led Proliferation Security Initiative (PSI) has been used to promote widespread international cooperation on combating air and maritime trafficking of weapons of mass destruction, by using the existing jurisdiction of coastal, port, and flag states rather than seeking new rights under international law.[105] For instance, a ship that passes through the Bering Strait while flying the flag of Liberia or Panama may be interdicted by the US Navy or Coast Guard – as a result of some of those countries' flag-state powers having been consensually delegated to the United States via bilateral treaties concluded as part of

---

[100] Introduction, n. 15, above.   [101] Ibid.
[102] Article 51 reads, in part: "Nothing in the present Charter shall impair the inherent right of individual or collective self-defense if an armed attack occurs against a Member of the United Nations, until the Security Council has taken measures necessary to maintain international peace and security." 1945 UN Charter, available at www.un.org/en/documents/charter/index.shtml.
[103] See discussion, above, p. 247.
[104] See Tom Ruys, *"Armed Attack" and Article 51 of the UN Charter: Evolutions in Customary Law and Practice* (Cambridge University Press, 2010).
[105] Byers, "Policing the High Seas," Chapter 5, n. 122, above.

the PSI. There is nothing to stop, and everything to commend, the conclusion of similar treaties between Canada or Russia and both Liberia and Panama, which are the world's two largest shipping registries.

Lastly, there are opportunities available for Canada–United States cooperation in managing security and other shared concerns notwithstanding the on-going dispute over the status of the Northwest Passage. As mentioned above, in May 2006 the North American Aerospace Defense Command (NORAD) Agreement was expanded to include the sharing of surveillance over maritime approaches and "internal waterways."[106] Canada's defense minister at the time, Gordon O'Connor, later confirmed that this includes the Northwest Passage.[107]

4.4 Terrorist attacks on aircraft

Over three successive summers, from 2010 to 2012, military personnel from the United States, Russia, and Canada participated in joint exercises designed to test their response to the hijacking of commercial flights in the airspace between and over Alaska and the Russian Far East.[108] Reportedly, a news release from the North American Aerospace Defense Command said the exercises, code-named Vigilant Eagle, "continue to foster the development of cooperation between the Russian Federation Air Force and NORAD in preventing possible threats of air terrorism."[109]

Terrorist attacks on aircraft have been the subject of several UN Security Council resolutions and treaties. In 1970, Security Council Resolution 286 called on states to "take all possible legal steps" to prevent "hijackings or any other interference with international civil air travel."[110] In 1971, the Montreal Convention on the Suppression of

---

[106] The most recent, 2006, version of the NORAD Agreement is available at www.state.gov/documents/organization/69727.pdf.

[107] Parliament of Canada, House of Commons, Debates, 1st Session, 39th Parliament, 8 May 2006, 15:00. For other ways in which the US and Canada could cooperate, see "Model Negotiation on Northern Waters," Chapter 5, n. 118, above.

[108] See "Norad Tests Hijacked Jetliner Response," CBC News, August 10, 2010, available at www.cbc.ca/news/canada/story/2010/08/10/norad-russia-terrorist-hijacking.html; David Pugliese, "Russia, Canada and the US to Launch Vigilant Eagle Exercise Aimed at Preventing Air Terrorism," Ottawa Citizen, August 10, 2012, available at http://blogs. ottawacitizen.com/2012/08/10/russia-canada-and-the-u-s-to-launch-vigilant-eagle-exercise-aimed-at-preventing-air-terrorism/.

[109] Pugliese, "Russia, Canada and the US," ibid.

[110] UN Security Council Resolution 286 (1970), available at www.un.org/documents/sc/res/1970/scres70.htm.

Unlawful Acts against the Safety of Civil Aviation required that "Contracting States shall, in accordance with international and national law, endeavour to take all practicable measures" to prevent acts of violence against aircraft.[111] In 2005, Security Council Resolution 1624 called on states "to strengthen the security of their international borders, including by combating fraudulent travel documents and, to the extent attainable, by enhancing terrorist screening and passenger security procedures."[112]

Although none of these instruments is specific to the Arctic, it can be questioned whether they are being fully implemented there. In Canada, for example, flights remaining north of 60 degrees latitude are not subject to security screening. This includes fully fueled Boeing 737s with sufficient range to reach major cities in the United States. The same planes are also excused from screening when used on charter flights to and from southern Canadian cities such as Ottawa and Edmonton. The failure to require security screening is particularly troublesome when it occurs at airports where the necessary staff and equipment are already present, and where screening is therefore both "practicable" and "attainable."

4.5 Protests against oil and gas infrastructure

Twenty-two Greenpeace activists were arrested in 2011 when they boarded an oil rig off Greenland and interrupted drilling for twelve hours.[113] Three months later, a threat assessment prepared by the Royal Canadian Mounted Police identified Greenpeace as part of a "growing radicalized environmentalist faction" that "is opposed to the development of Canada's Arctic region, as well as Canada's offshore petroleum industry."[114] The Greenpeace actions off Greenland, the threat assessment continued, "highlight the need to be prepared for potential threats to the safety and security of offshore oil and gas platforms." In 2012, Greenpeace activists suspended themselves from the

---

[111] 1971 Montreal Convention for the Suppression of Unlawful Acts against the Safety of Civil Aviation, Art. 10, available at http://treaties.un.org/untc//Pages//doc/Publication/UNTS/Volume%20974/volume-974-I-14118-English.pdf.

[112] UN Security Council Resolution 1624 (2005), available at www.un.org/Docs/sc/unsc_resolutions05.htm.

[113] "Greenpeace Head Naidoo Held in Cairn Oil Rig Protest," BBC News, June 17, 2011, available at www.bbc.co.uk/news/uk-scotland-13814009.

[114] Jim Bronskill, "Radical Environmentalism Growing, Warns New Report," Canadian Press, July 30, 2012, available at www2.canada.com/nanaimodailynews/news/story.html?id=37448c64-168c-4192-82f0-a9a01d1c2310.

side of an offshore oil rig in Russia's Pechora Sea for fifteen hours, this time without interrupting the drilling.[115] Also in 2012, part of the rationale for the deployment of additional US Coast Guard resources to northern Alaska was the potential for direct action by environmentalists against oil rigs.[116] At the same time, the US government adopted a regulation that created a 500-meter exclusion zone around Shell's *Noble Discoverer* platform.[117]

Protests by activist groups can certainly be costly to oil companies and governments, including in terms of public opinion. Yet there is an important distinction between peaceful acts of civil disobedience and violence, which if politically motivated can constitute terrorism. Again, terrorism is unlikely in the Arctic because of the great distances, challenging weather conditions, and small local populations.[118]

5 Search and rescue

The World, the largest privately owned yacht on the planet, took advantage of the fast-receding sea-ice to transit the Northwest Passage in August 2012.[119] The 200-meter Bahamian-flagged vessel is actually a luxury condo complex, with some of the 165 units valued at more than $10 million.[120] Dozens of much larger cruise ships already sail the waters around Greenland and Svalbard, including the 3,780-passenger *Costa Pacifica*, the sister ship of the *Costa Concordia* which ran onto rocks off Italy in January 2012.[121]

---

[115] Andrew E. Kramer, "Greenpeace Activists Climb Russian Oil Rig," *New York Times*, August 24, 2012, available at www.nytimes.com/2012/08/25/world/europe/greenpeace-activists-climb-russian-oil-rig-in-arctic-ocean.html.

[116] Kirk Johnson, "For Coast Guard Patrol North of Alaska, Much to Learn in a Remote New Place," *New York Times*, July 21, 2012, available at www.nytimes.com/2012/07/22/us/coast-guard-strengthens-presence-north-of-alaska.html.

[117] See FR Doc. No. 2012-15950, Federal Register, vol. 77, no. 126, June 29, 2012, pp. 38718–38723, available at http://cryptome.org/2012/06/uscg062912.htm.

[118] See Mary Pemberton, "Officials: Alaska Pipeline Not That Vulnerable," *Associated Press*, December 2, 2006, available at www.usatoday.com/news/nation/2006-02-12-pipeline-threats_x.htm.

[119] Jane George, "The World Gets Green Light to Transit Northwest Passage," *Nunatsiaq News*, August 31, 2012, available at www.nunatsiaqonline.ca/stories/article/65674the_world_gets_the_green_light_to_transit_the_northwest_passage/.

[120] See, e.g., "A Place on the World – For $17.5 Million," *Wall Street Journal*, March 6, 2009, available at http://online.wsj.com/article/SB123629449070245501.html.

[121] See "Terror at Sea: The Sinking of the Concordia," Channel 4 television documentary, broadcast January 31, 2012, available at www.channel4.com/programmes/terror-at-sea-the-sinking-of-the-concordia/4od.

Voyages by smaller, ice-strengthened "expedition" cruise ships have already revealed the dangers of navigating the Arctic, including small chunks of icebergs called "growlers" that are exceptionally hard and float low in the water, making them difficult to spot. In 2007, the Liberian-flagged MS *Explorer* sank during an Antarctic voyage after striking a growler. Fortunately, the sea was calm at the time and all the passengers were rescued.[122]

A second danger is running aground, especially within the relatively shallow Northwest Passage and Northern Sea Route. In 1996, the Bahamian-flagged MS *Hanseatic* went aground on a sand bar near Gjoa Haven, Nunavut; fortunately, the weather was good and a Russian ship rescued the passengers within a week.[123] In 2010, the Bahamian-flagged M/V *Clipper Adventurer* (since renamed the M/V *Sea Adventurer*) ran onto an underwater ledge near Kugluktuk, Nunavut.[124] The weather was once again good, and the Canadian Coast Guard icebreaker *Amundsen* was only two days' sailing-distance away.

In Canada's Arctic, the risk of striking bottom is increased by the absence of good navigation charts. In 2010, John Falkingham told the *Nunatsiaq News* that inadequate charts are the "single biggest issue in the Arctic."[125] Falkingham, who spent three decades in the Canadian Ice Service, explained that only one-tenth of Canada's Arctic waters are charted to modern standards, and that the job will – at the current rate – take centuries to complete.

A third danger is the unpredictable and often extreme Arctic weather. Even in summer, gale-force winds and seven-meter swells are common. Although winds and waves like this are not normally a problem for a well-manned ship, they can tear a grounded vessel apart – leaving the passengers with no choice but to abandon ship. Cold weather storms can also lead to "icing," which occurs when ocean spray freezes on the

---

[122] Bureau of Maritime Affairs, Liberia, "Report of Investigation in the Matter of Sinking of Passenger Vessel EXPLORER (O.N. 8495)," available at www.photobits.com/dl/Explorer %20-%20Final%20Report.PDF.

[123] Transportation Safety Board, "Marine Investigation Report M96H0016, Grounding – Passenger Vessel 'HANSEATIC'," available at www.tsb.gc.ca/eng/rapports-reports/ marine/1996/m96h0016/m96h0016.asp.

[124] Transportation Safety Board, "Marine Investigation Report M10H0006, Grounding – Passenger Vessel *Clipper Adventurer*," available at www.tsb.gc.ca/eng/rapports-reports/ marine/2010/m10h0006/m10h0006.asp.

[125] Jane George, "Expert Sounds Alarm about Dangerous Arctic Waters," *Nunatsiaq News*, August 30, 2010, available at www.nunatsiaqonline.ca/stories/article/ 300810_Expert_sounds_alarm_about_dangerous_Arctic_waters/.

superstructure of a ship and causes it to become top-heavy and subject to capsizing.[126]

Search-and-rescue capability is also needed to respond to aircraft accidents. In 1991, a Canadian C-130 Hercules crashed twenty kilometers from the Canadian military post at Alert on Ellesmere Island, killing five of the eighteen passengers and crew. The thirteen survivors waited more than a day in a raging blizzard before rescuers could reach them.[127] In 1996, a Tupolev Tu-154M airliner crashed into a mountain on Svalbard killing all 141 people on board.[128] In 2011, a Boeing 737 crashed into a hillside while attempting a landing at Resolute Bay, in the middle of Canada's High Arctic: twelve people died on impact, while the three survivors were assisted by the remarkable coincidence that hundreds of Canadian soldiers were just three kilometers away conducting a search-and-rescue exercise based on an air crash scenario.[129]

Tens of thousands of commercial flights take "trans-polar" or "high latitude" routes over the Arctic each year, and while modern jetliners are remarkably reliable, accidents – such as the crash of Air France Flight 447 into the South Atlantic in 2009 – can still occur. During the long Arctic winter, frigid temperatures require that rescuers reach any crash survivors within hours, despite the often-great distances involved. Retired Colonel Pierre Leblanc has told me that the prospect of a commercial airline accident was the one thing that kept him awake at night during his many years commanding Canadian Forces Northern Area (since renamed Joint Task Force North). When I asked Leblanc's successor, Colonel Norm Couturier, what would happen if a large jet crash-landed on Ellesmere Island in winter, his response was emphatic: "We could not get there."

Canada's search-and-rescue capabilities in the Arctic are surprisingly limited. The Canadian Forces have some long-range search-and-rescue

---

[126] See Lasse Makkonen, *Atmospheric Icing on Sea Structures* (Hanover, NH: US Army Cold Regions Research and Engineering Laboratory, Monograph 84-2, 1984), available at www.boemre.gov/tarprojects/056/056AC.PDF.

[127] Clyde H. Farnsworth, "After a Plane Crash, 30 Deadly Hours in the Arctic," *New York Times*, November 5, 1991, available at www.nytimes.com/1991/11/05/world/after-a-plane-crash-30-deadly-hours-in-the-arctic.html?src=pm.

[128] Aircraft Accident Investigation Board, Norway, "Report on the Accident to Vnukovo Airline's Tupolev TU-154M RA 85621," Report 07/99, available at www.aibn.no/ra-85621-pdf.

[129] Transportation Safety Board, "First Air Accident, Resolute Bay, Nunavut, 20 August 2011," available at www.tsb.gc.ca/eng/medias-media/majeures-major/aviation/A11H0002/MI-A11H0002.asp.

helicopters, but they are based 3,000 kilometers from the Northwest Passage and have to refuel several times on the way. C-130 Hercules planes are also used for search and rescue, but they too are based in southern Canada, and unlike helicopters cannot hoist people on board. The Canadian Coast Guard's icebreakers are growing old, while the Canadian Navy lacks ice-capable vessels altogether – and has seen plans for new Arctic/Offshore Patrol Ships repeatedly delayed.[130]

In contrast, Russia has significant search-and-rescue capabilities in the Arctic, mostly due to the militarization of the region that occurred during the Cold War. It is now taking steps to maintain that capability: in November 2011, Moscow allocated 910 million rubles (approximately $28 million) to the creation of ten search-and-rescue centers along the Northern Sea Route.[131]

In Alaska, search and rescue is provided by the US Coast Guard which operates six C-130 Hercules planes and twelve long-range helicopters from two locations on the southern coast of the state. The Coast Guard is backed up by the US Army, which has Chinook helicopters based at Fort Wainwright,[132] and the Alaska National Guard, which also flies helicopters and Hercules.[133] In response to increased activity along the Arctic Ocean coastline, the Coast Guard recently began positioning two helicopters in Barrow during the summer months.[134]

Search and rescue around Greenland is provided by the Danish military, which has a substantial naval presence, as Rear-Admiral Henrik Kudsk has explained:

For designated use in the Arctic we have a total of seven ships. We have four frigate-sized ships (three and a half thousand tonnes) – they operate helicopters and are ice capable. We normally keep one permanently stationed around Greenland and the other permanently stationed around the Faroe Islands. In addition to these four, we have two medium sized patrol ships (a little less than

---

[130] Lee Berthiaume, "Armed Arctic Vessels Face Delay in Latest Procurement Setback," *Postmedia News*, May 8, 2012, available at www.nunatsiaqonline.ca/stories/article/65674armed_arctic_vessels_face_delay_in_latest_procurement_setback/.

[131] Trude Pettersen, "Russia to Have Ten Arctic Rescue Centers by 2015," *Barents Observer*, November 18, 2011, available at http://barentsobserver.com/en/topics/russia-have-ten-arctic-rescue-centers-2015 (note: the article mistranslates "МЛН" as "billion" rather than "million").

[132] Staff Sgt. Patricia McMurphy, "Fort Wainwright Receives New Chinook CH-47F Helicopters," US Army Alaska Public Affairs, July 23, 2012, available at www.usarak.army.mil/main/Stories_Archives/July-23-27-2012/120723_FS3.asp.

[133] See Alaska National Guard website at www.akguard.com/.

[134] Johnson, "For Coast Guard Patrol North of Alaska," n. 116, above.

two thousand tonnes). And then we have one remaining small cutter, *Tulugaq* – which means Raven in the local Inuit language – with a 13-man crew, but still ice capable. In terms of our naval capacities, these ships are spread around. In the summer we deploy two of them in a permanent station to the very far North – [this is] east of your [Canadian] Northwest Passage, east of Resolute Bay, but on our side. Up around the Thule area, we hold a ship permanently, whenever the ice permits. So as soon as the ice thaws, we have a ship up there. And we have the same on the northeast coast of Greenland, on the other side.[135]

Norway, for its part, operates long-range helicopters off its five frigates.[136] It also maintains two land-based search-and-rescue helicopters in the Arctic: one on Svalbard, the other at Banak on the mainland just south of the Barents Sea.[137] The Norwegian government is in the process of procuring sixteen new search-and-rescue helicopters, with deliveries due to begin in 2016.[138]

The Arctic, however, is an immense region where accidents can occur thousands of kilometers away from the nearest search-and-rescue assets. Fortunately, the need to respond quickly and effectively to save lives in peril has long been one of the easiest things on which countries can agree. The sinking of the *Titanic* prompted the negotiation of the International Convention for the Safety of Life at Sea, which was adopted in 1914. As mentioned in Chapter 6, the fifth version of the so-called "SOLAS Convention," adopted in 1974, initiated a "tacit acceptance procedure" whereby proposed amendments to the Convention enter into force unless a set number of objections are received from parties before a specified date.[139] Since the beginning, the SOLAS Convention

---

[135] Jane Kokan, "Greenland: Canada's Arctic Neighbour." (January/February 2012) 9(1) *FrontLine Defence* 23 at 24, available at www.frontline-canada.com/downloads/12-1_RAdmKudsk.pdf.

[136] See "Nansen Class Anti-Submarine Warfare Frigates, Norway," at www.naval-technology.com/projects/nansen/.

[137] Anne Holm Gundersen, "Search and Rescue Cooperation in the Arctic – Experiences and Future Challenges," presentation to the 2012 Arctic Dialogue, Bodø, Norway, available at www.uin.no/Documents/Om%20UiN/Fakulteter/HHB/Arctic%20Dialogue/Presentations%202012/Norwegian%20research%20and%20rescue_Anne_Holm_Gundersen.pdf.

[138] "NO-Sola: Search and Rescue Helicopters, 2011/S 207-337613, Contract Notice," available at http://ted.europa.eu/udl?uri=TED:NOTICE:337613-2011:TEXT:EN:HTML. Iceland is taking part in the Norwegian procurement and intends to purchase one helicopter with the option of acquiring two more.

[139] Lei Shi, "Successful Use of the Tacit Acceptance Procedure to Effectuate Progress in International Maritime Law." (1998–1999) 11 *University of San Francisco Maritime Law Journal* 299.

has required each party "to ensure that any necessary arrangements are made for coast watching and for the rescue of persons in distress at sea round its coasts."[140]

Annex 12 to the 1944 Convention on International Civil Aviation ("Chicago Convention") also deals with search and rescue. It was adopted in 1951 and has been updated repeatedly since then.[141] Parties are required to provide assistance to survivors of accidents regardless of nationality (Art. 2.1.2). They are also required to "arrange for the establishment and provision of search-and-rescue services within their territories" (Art. 2.1.1) as well as on the high seas or "in areas of undetermined sovereignty" – with zones of responsibility in those latter areas being determined by regional air navigation agreements (Art. 2.1.1.1). Annex 12 also requires neighboring states to coordinate their search-and-rescue organizations and, "[s]ubject to such conditions as may be prescribed by its own authorities," each party "shall permit immediate entry into its territory of rescue units of other States for the purpose of searching for the site of aircraft accidents and rescuing survivors of such accidents" (Art. 3.1.3).

The 1979 International Convention on Maritime Search and Rescue ("SAR Convention") requires states parties, individually or cooperatively, to "participate in the development of search-and-rescue services to ensure that assistance is rendered to any person in distress at sea" (Para. 2.1.1) and to develop "search-and-rescue regions" which are "sufficient" and "contiguous" but, where practical, not overlapping (Para. 2.1.3).[142] Paragraph 2.1.7 also makes clear that: "The delimitation of search-and-rescue regions is not related to and shall not prejudice the delimitation of any boundary between States."

The 1979 SAR Convention places a heavy emphasis on cooperation, with a mix of requirements and recommendations. Paragraph 3.1.1 requires states parties to coordinate their search-and-rescue organizations and recommends that they coordinate specific search-and-rescue operations.

---

[140] 1974 International Convention for the Safety of Life at Sea, chap. 5, Regulation 15, 1184 UNTS 278, available at www.austlii.edu.au/au/other/dfat/treaties/1983/22.html. The many amendments are listed at www.tc.gc.ca/eng/marinesafety/rsqa-imo-solas-546.htm.

[141] 1944 Convention on International Civil Aviation, Annex 12, 7th edn., 2001, available at www.scribd.com/doc/18191224/Anexo-12-Search-and-Rescue.

[142] 1979 International Convention on Maritime Search and Rescue, 1405 UNTS 119, as amended in 1998 and 2004, available at http://cil.nus.edu.sg/rp/il/pdf/1979%20International%20Convention%20on%20Maritime%20Search%20and%20Rescue-pdf.

Paragraph 3.1.2 recommends that each state party "authorize, subject to applicable national laws, rules and regulations, immediate entry into or over its territorial sea or territory of rescue units of other Parties solely for the purpose of searching for the position of maritime casualties and rescuing the survivors of such casualties." Relatedly, Paragraph 3.1.3 requires that any party wishing access to another state's territory for a search-and-rescue operation "transmit a request, giving full details of the projected mission and the need for it." Paragraph 3.1.4 requires that the requested party "immediately acknowledge the receipt of such a request" and "as soon as possible indicate the conditions, if any, under which the projected mission may be undertaken." In short, cooperation is required except insofar as access to territory is concerned, with the parties retaining the sovereign right to deny access for any reason.

In 1982, the UN Convention on the Law of the Sea reinforced these earlier treaties, stating: "Every coastal State shall promote the establishment, operation and maintenance of an adequate and effective search-and-rescue service regarding safety on and over the sea and, where circumstances so require, by way of mutual regional arrangements cooperate with neighbouring States for this purpose."[143]

A number of states did just that, including the Soviet Union and the United States. In 1988, the two Cold War rivals concluded a bilateral treaty on maritime search and rescue, though, as one might expect, the agreement was hardly far-reaching.[144] It defined respective search-and-rescue areas using the boundary between the countries and required that the parties "cooperate and coordinate their operations as appropriate" (Art. 3.1). However, the agreement also stated: "Search-and-rescue operations on or over the territorial seas, internal waters, and land of either Party shall be conducted, as a rule, by the rescue units of that Party" (Art. 3.2).

As far back as 1949, the United States and Canada concluded an exchange of notes enabling any of their aircraft engaged in collaborative search and rescue to bypass the normal entry procedures.[145] In

---

[143] UNCLOS, Art. 98(2) Introduction, n. 15, above.

[144] 1988 Agreement between the Government of the United States of America and the Government of the Union of Soviet Socialist Republics on Maritime Search and Rescue, 2191 UNTS 115, available at http://treaties.un.org/doc/Publication/UNTS/Volume%202191/v2191.pdf.

[145] 1949 Exchange of Notes between Canada and the United States of America Constituting an Agreement Relating to Air Search and Rescue Operations along the Common Boundary of the Two Countries, Canada Treaty Series 1949/2, available at www.lexum.com/ca_us/en/cts.1949.02.en.html.

1999, the United States, Canada, and the United Kingdom concluded a three-way memorandum of understanding on air and maritime search and rescue that enables personnel and equipment from one country to enter onto or over the territory of another country without its knowledge, so long as they are engaged in an emergency rescue and provide notification of entry "as soon as practicable."[146]

In 2003, Russia and NATO signed an agreement on submarine rescues.[147] Developed in response to the loss of the Russian nuclear-attack submarine *Kursk* three years earlier, the agreement specified that NATO and Russia would work toward common search-and-rescue procedures, collaboration in the development of equipment, the exchange of relevant information, and even joint exercises. Russia took part in NATO search-and-rescue exercises in 2005 and 2008[148] and hosted its own international exercise in 2009 with participation from Finland, Norway, and Sweden.[149] In 2005, a British submersible was used to free seven Russian sailors whose mini-submarine became tangled up in a fishing net 190 meters below the surface of the Pacific Ocean off the Kamchatka Peninsula.[150]

In 2008, the members of BEAR (the "Barents Euro-Arctic Region" made up of Norway, Sweden, Finland, and Russia) signed an "Agreement between the Governments in the Barents Euro-Arctic Region on Cooperation within the Field of Emergency Prevention, Preparedness and Response."[151] The treaty prescribes a number of steps to facilitate the transboundary deployment of search-and-rescue equipment and personnel, whenever such assistance is requested by one country of another.

---

[146] See US Department of Homeland Security and Public Safety Canada, "Compendium of US–Canada Emergency Management Assistance Mechanisms," June 2012, p. 9, available at www.dhs.gov/xlibrary/assets/policy/btb-compendium-of-United States-Canada-emergency-management-assistance-mechanisms.pdf.

[147] "NATO and Russia Sign Submarine Rescue Agreement," NATO Update, February 8, 2003, available at www.nato.int/docu/update/2003/02-february/e0208a.htm.

[148] "NRC Practical Cooperation Factsheet," at www.nato-russia-council.info/HTM/EN/news_41.shtm.

[149] "Barents Rescue-2009," August 26, 2009, at http://barentsobserver.com/en/murmansk-obl/barents-rescue-2009.

[150] "Russians Saved in Deep-Sea Rescue," BBC News, August 7, 2005, at http://news.bbc.co.uk/1/hi/world/europe/4128614.stm.

[151] "Agreement between the Governments in the Barents Euro-Arctic Region on Cooperation within the Field of Emergency Prevention, Preparedness and Response," December 11, 2008, available at www.barentsinfo.fi/beac/docs/Agreement_Emergency_Prevention_Preparedness_and_Response_English.pdf.

As a result of all this international law-making, the ground was already well prepared when, in April 2009, the Arctic Council approved "the establishment of a task force to develop and complete negotiation by the next Ministerial meeting in 2011 of an international instrument on cooperation on search-and-rescue operations in the Arctic."[152] The task force was co-chaired by the United States and Russia.

The subsequent Agreement on Cooperation on Aeronautical and Maritime Search and Rescue in the Arctic ("Arctic SAR Agreement") was signed at the Arctic Council ministerial in May 2011.[153] It was trumpeted as a major development, but, as the preamble to the agreement notes, all eight Arctic countries were already parties to the 1944 Chicago Convention and the 1979 SAR Convention. Article 7(1) goes on to state that those two conventions "shall be used as the basis for conducting search-and-rescue operations under this Agreement," and, indeed, the provisions of the Arctic SAR Agreement closely track the Chicago and SAR Conventions.

The Arctic SAR Agreement delimits aeronautical and maritime search-and-rescue regions ("SRRs") for the eight Arctic states (Art. 1 as well as Para. 1 of the Annex) and states that "Each Party shall promote the establishment, operation and maintenance of an adequate and effective search and rescue capability" within their area of geographic responsibility (Art. 3(3)).[154] It specifies that when a party requests search-and-rescue assistance from another party, the second party "shall promptly decide on and inform the requesting Party whether or not it is in a position to render the assistance requested and shall promptly indicate the scope and the terms of the assistance that can

---

[152] Tromso Declaration, April 29, 2009, Section on "Arctic Marine Environment," available at http://arctic-council.org/filearchive/Tromsoe%20Declaration-1.pdf.

[153] Agreement on Cooperation on Aeronautical and Maritime Search and Rescue in the Arctic, May 12, 2011, available at www.arctic-council.org/index.php/en/about/documents/category/20-main-documents-from-nuuk.

[154] Like the 1979 SAR Convention, Art. 3(2) of the Arctic SAR Convention states: "The delimitation of search and rescue regions is not related to and shall not prejudice the delimitation of any boundary between States or their sovereignty, sovereign rights or jurisdiction." It does so for a reason, namely, that the lines do not necessarily track agreed boundaries. For instance, in the Beaufort Sea the 141°W meridian is used to divide the Canadian and American SSRs all the way to the North Pole, notwithstanding the on-going dispute between the two countries as to the location of the maritime boundary, while the remote and nearly unpopulated Norwegian island of Jan Mayen is placed entirely within the Icelandic SRR. For a visual depiction of the SRRs, see (2011) Arctic Search and Rescue Delimitation Map, available at http://library.arcticportal.org/1500/.

be rendered" (Art. 7(3e)). However, when a party requests permission to enter the territory of another party for search-and-rescue purposes, including refueling, the requested party is not required to give permission; instead, it "shall advise as soon as possible as to whether entry into its territory has been permitted and the conditions, if any, under which the mission may be undertaken" (Art. 8(1) and (2)).

Again, the legal obligations set out in the Arctic SAR Agreement add nothing to the rules that are already binding on the Arctic countries as a result of the 1944 Chicago Convention and the 1979 SAR Convention. Nor does the agreement create any "new operational or resource requirements" with respect, for instance, to the positioning of equipment or the response times expected of personnel.[155] Where the agreement does add something new is with respect to the other cooperative steps it encourages but does not require of states. These include the sharing of information services as well as procedures, techniques, equipment, and facilities; joint research and development initiatives; reciprocal visits by experts; and joint search-and-rescue exercises. All this is important, not least because many of the people involved in these interactions will be military personnel. As a result, the communication and cooperation occurring under the Arctic SAR Agreement can be expected to build trust and reduce tensions between the armed forces of the various Arctic states, including between NATO and Russia.

The first joint exercise took place in October 2011, just five months after the adoption of the Arctic SAR Agreement. Hosted by the Canadian military in a hotel in Whitehorse, Yukon, and attended by delegates from all the Arctic Council member states, the meeting focused on operational aspects of search and rescue.[156] Then, in April 2012, senior military leaders from the eight Arctic countries met in Goose Bay, Labrador, to discuss cooperation on search and rescue, disaster relief, and situational awareness.[157] The generals and admirals agreed to meet again on an annual basis.[158]

---

[155] Canada Command, "Search and Rescue (SAR) Overview, Arctic Caucus Meeting, 17–19 August 2011," available at www.pnwer.org/Portals/18/Arctic%20Caucus%20SAR% 20Overview%20Presentation.pdf.

[156] "Whitehorse Table-Top Exercise Brings Arctic SAR Experts Together," *Nunatsiaq News*, October 10, 2011, available at www.nunatsiaqonline.ca/stories/article/ 65674whitehorse_table-top_exercise_brings_arctic_sar_experts_together/.

[157] *Reuters*, "Arctic Generals Agree on Closer Ties," April 13, 2012, available at www. thestar.com/news/canada/politics/article/1161369–arctic-generals-agree-on-closer-ties.

[158] Ibid.

It is also significant that the Arctic SAR Agreement was the first legally binding instrument negotiated within the framework of the Arctic Council. From a purely pragmatic, short-term perspective, a simple declaration by the Arctic Council ministers of their countries' continued commitment to the 1944 Chicago and 1979 SAR conventions would have sufficed. But the member states were clearly seeking to do more, namely, to contribute to the cooperative momentum within Arctic diplomacy, and specifically to develop the Arctic Council into a regional organization under which international law-making can take place. In this context, it is significant that, concurrent with the adoption of the Arctic SAR Agreement, the member states agreed to create a permanent secretariat for the Arctic Council.[159] One can see in these moves an effort to reinforce the position of the Arctic states as the principal decision-makers with respect to the region.

6 Summary

Although the Arctic Ocean was on the frontlines of the Cold War, the region's transformation into a zone of inter-state cooperation increasingly includes cooperation on security issues. Russia is now a member of the WTO whose largest trading partner is the European Union, an organization made up mostly of NATO states. As the sea-ice melts, all of the Arctic countries have taken steps to improve their military capabilities in the North, but the focus has been firmly on non-state threats such as drug-smuggling and illegal immigration. The new circumstances have led to the negotiation of an Arctic Search and Rescue Agreement among the eight Arctic Council member states, and other initiatives now seem possible – including a treaty to keep the surface water and sea-ice of the central Arctic Ocean demilitarized. Concerns about non-state security threats also have the potential to provide an impetus for Canada–United States negotiations on the status of the Northwest Passage.

---

[159] Nuuk Declaration, 7th Ministerial Meeting of the Arctic Council, May 12, 2011, available at http://arctic-council.org/filearchive/nuuk_declaration_2011_signed_copy-1.pdf.

Conclusion

In Moscow, a map produced by the Canadian Department of Natural Resources has pride of place in Arctic Ambassador Anton Vasiliev's office in the Stalinist-era skyscraper that houses the Russian Ministry of Foreign Affairs. The choice of wall covering reflects several key aspects of the contemporary Arctic.

First, although the global influence of Russia and Canada is diminishing, the world's two geographically largest countries remain predominately influential in the Arctic. That influence is shared by the United States, which although a reluctant Arctic power is still a global superpower. Second, rising demand for natural resources has in combination with climate change propelled the Arctic into the mainstream of international diplomacy. Vasiliev is one of Russia's most capable diplomats and a fluent English speaker. Perhaps as significantly, he also speaks Mandarin and has considerable experience in China, a rising superpower and the most likely market for Russia's vast Arctic riches. The arrival of the Arctic in mainstream diplomacy has also been signaled by the attendance of the US Secretary of State at Arctic Council meetings, as well as by applications for permanent observer status from the European Union and China, the world's largest and third-largest economies.

This rapid repositioning of the Arctic has caught many journalists unprepared and ill-equipped to explain and analyze the situation. As a result, reporting about the Arctic has placed too much emphasis on the remote possibility of inter-state conflict, and not nearly enough emphasis on the trend toward cooperation that is actually taking place. This unbalanced approach has contributed to further misunderstandings among the recipients of that reporting, including the general public and at least some politicians. Yet, as this book demonstrates, there is a considerable amount of cooperation in the Arctic. Some of that cooperation is manifested through a growth of international law, more and more of which is specific to the Arctic, and these rules are helping countries to avoid and resolve what might otherwise be difficult disputes.

Most of the cooperation in the Arctic is based on clearly defined rights over land, adjoining waters, and the resources of the continental shelf. These rights are core components of a global international legal system that has been constructed through centuries of contestation and coordination, as states worked out how to define the boundaries between their respective jurisdictions and cooperate in the pursuit of common goals. The maturity of this process is manifest in the fact that tiny Hans Island is the only disputed land territory in the entire circumpolar Arctic.

Around the world, the outward extension of coastal state rights in the twentieth century created a potential for conflict that was quickly dispelled, as states rejected the option of acquiring maritime rights by conquest and turned instead to a developing body of rules on maritime boundary delimitation. Again, the maturity of the legalization process is evident in the fact that only one maritime boundary dispute remains in the Arctic, in the Beaufort Sea north of Canada and Alaska. Even in the central Arctic Ocean, where oil, gas, and other resources may exist on the extended continental shelf beyond 200 nautical miles from shore, and where disputes over overlapping coastal state rights are notionally still possible, all five coastal states have accepted that the extent of their jurisdiction will be determined on the basis of existing legal rules and scientific facts. Arctic governments clearly understand the value of well-defined limits, within which they can go about the business of licensing the extraction of natural resources, protecting the environment, and providing essential services such as ice-forecasting and search and rescue.

To some degree, this cooperative dynamic existed even during the Cold War. The 1973 Polar Bear Treaty was a first step in multilateral environmental protection that was made possible by the iconic status of this animal in the cultures of Arctic nations. More significantly, the subsequent UN Conference on the Law of the Sea provided an opportunity for cooperation between the Soviet Union and the United States during one of the most strained periods of their superpower confrontation. With a Canadian as the chair of the drafting committee, the two delegations negotiated provisions of the 1982 United Nations

Convention on the Law of the Sea that have direct implications for the Arctic. These include Article 234, the so-called "Arctic exception" concerning pollution prevention in ice-covered waters, as well as Arctic 76 on extended continental shelves.

By providing a mechanism for structuring cooperation across and beyond the limits of national jurisdiction, international law can be particularly useful in respect to large, remote, inhospitable, and sparsely populated regions. For this reason, Arctic countries have embarked on a number of law-making initiatives that were initially of a non-binding "soft-law" character, such as the Ottawa Declaration that created the Arctic Council and the International Maritime Organization's Guidelines on Arctic Shipping. Now, Arctic law-making is evolving toward "hard-law" treaties such as the Stockholm Convention on Persistent Organic Pollutants and the Arctic Search and Rescue (SAR) Agreement. The latter instrument is particularly interesting because it does not create any obligations additional to those set out in existing, non-Arctic-specific treaties. Instead of adding new law, the Arctic SAR Agreement is simply creating a new meeting space for Arctic governments and especially Arctic militaries, within which communities of shared understandings, interests, and identities will likely form. The Arctic SAR Agreement may well open the way to cooperation on other Arctic security issues such as smuggling and illegal immigration, across the old Cold War divide, and notwithstanding the now anachronistic footnote to the Ottawa Declaration that has so far discouraged the Arctic Council from addressing matters of "military security."

Arctic indigenous peoples have begun to play a significant and increasing role in regional diplomacy and international law-making by organizing themselves in transboundary groups that transcend state borders and ethnic divisions. The inclusion of the Arctic indigenous peoples as permanent participants in the Arctic Council, and their successful effort to stop the practice of the Arctic Ocean coastal states (the "Arctic-5") meeting without them has put paid to the traditional view that indigenous peoples lack both "legal personality" and influence in international relations. In the twenty-first century, indigenous peoples have rights in international law, including a right of inclusion in decision-making about the areas in which they live.

The shift from Cold War confrontation to Arctic cooperation is difficult to explain from the "positivist" and "realist" theoretical perspectives that dominated the disciplines of international law and international relations during the twentieth century. "Constructivist" perspectives would seem to provide more explanatory leverage now, though they cannot explain all. Within the security context, especially, significant elements of power politics remain, as is apparent in the continued presence of substantial nuclear arsenals in the region, and the continuing absolutism of the United States on their legal characterization of the Northern Sea Route and Northwest Passage as "international straits."

Arguably, the co-existence of realist and non-realist explanations reflects a geopolitical situation in flux, as the end of the Cold War, a dramatic intensification of international trade and investment, and other opportunities for repeated interactions at venues such as the Arctic Council enable diplomats, politicians, as well as industry, indigenous and civil society leaders to develop shared interests and identities that might, over time, build a level of trust that enables more demilitarization in the region. In this regard, the shared northern sensibilities of Arctic nations will help, as might the growing interest of non-Arctic countries in the region – since external challenges can lead to a greater sense of commonality among the members of a group.

Although a more detailed theoretical analysis of Arctic politics will have to wait for another book, it is possible to hypothesize that even regions dominated by security concerns and realist thinking are susceptible to "creeping cooperation": a momentum-generating process of institutionalization and legalization, as trust develops and the benefits of working together across issues become ever more apparent. In this sense, the Arctic, with its unique combination of security, environmental, and indigenous politics, is an excellent laboratory for students of twenty-first-century international relations.

Bibliography

Abele, Frances, and Thierry Rodon, "Inuit Diplomacy in the Global Era: The Strengths of Multilateral Internationalism." (2007) 13(3) *Canadian Foreign Policy* 45.

Adams, Marie, Kathryn J. Frostz, and Lois A. Harwood, "Alaska and Inuvialuit Beluga Whale Committee (AIBWC) – An Initiative in At Home Management." (1993) 46 *Arctic* 134.

Amstrup, Steven C., *et al.*, "Forecasting the Range-Wide Status of Polar Bears at Selected Times in the 21st Century," US Geological Survey Administrative Report, 2007, available at www.usgs.gov/newsroom/special/polar_bears/docs/USGS_PolarBear_Amstrup_Forecast_lowres.pdf.

Anaya, S. James, *Indigenous Peoples in International Law*, 2nd edn. (Oxford University Press, 2004).

"Indigenous Peoples' Participatory Rights in Relation to Decisions about Natural Resource Extraction: The More Fundamental Issue of What Rights Indigenous Peoples Have in Lands and Resources." (2005) 22 *Arizona Journal of International and Comparative Law* 7.

"The Situation of the Sami People in the Sápmi Region of Norway, Sweden and Finland." June 6, 2011, UN Doc. A/HRC/18/35/Add. 2, available at http://unsr.jamesanaya.org/country-reports/the-situation-of-the-sami-people-in-the-sapmi-region-of-norway-sweden-and-finland-2011.

Anderson, David H., "The Status under International Law of the Maritime Areas around Svalbard." (2009) 40(4) *Ocean Development and International Law* 373.

Antinori, Camille M., "The Bering Sea: A Maritime Delimitation Dispute Between the United States and the Soviet Union." (1987) 18 *Ocean Development and International Law* 1.

Archer, Clive, "Plans for a Nordic Nuclear-Weapon-Free Zone." (2004) 34 *Kosmopolis* 201 (supplement), available at https://helda.helsinki.fi/bitstream/handle/10224/3635/archer201-207.pdf.

Ballantyne, Joe, *Sovereignty and Development in the Arctic: Selected Exploration Programs in the 1980s* (Whitehorse: self-published, 2009).

Barelli, Mauro, "The Role of Soft Law in the International Legal System: The Case of the United Nations Declaration on the Rights of Indigenous Peoples." (2009) 58 *International and Comparative Law Quarterly* 957.

Barsh, Russel, "Demilitarizing the Arctic as an Exercise of Indigenous Self-Determination." (1986) 55 *Nordic Journal of International Law* 208.

Bateman, Sam, and Clive Schofield, "State Practice Regarding Straight Baselines in East Asia – Legal, Technical and Political Issues in a Changing Environment." Paper prepared for a conference at the International Hydrographic Bureau, Monaco, October 16–17, 2008, available at www.gmat.unsw.edu.au/ablos/ABLOS08Folder/Session7-Paper1-Bateman.pdf.

Bateman, Sam, and Michael White, "Compulsory Pilotage in the Torres Strait: Overcoming Unacceptable Risks to a Sensitive Marine Environment." (2009) 40 *Ocean Development and International Law* 184.

Baxter, Richard R., *The Law of International Waterways* (Cambridge, Mass.: Harvard University Press, 1964).

Beckman, Robert C., "PSSAs and Transit Passage – Australia's Pilotage System in the Torres Strait Challenges the IMO and UNCLOS." (2007) 38 *Ocean Development and International Law* 325.

Berton, Pierre, *The Arctic Grail: The Quest for the Northwest Passage and the North Pole, 1818–1909* (Toronto: McClelland and Stewart, 1988).

Bloom, Evan T., "Establishment of the Arctic Council." (1999) 93 *American Journal of International Law* 712.

Borgerson, Scott G., "Arctic Meltdown: The Economic and Security Implications of Climate Change." (2008) 87(2) *Foreign Affairs* 63.

Bourne, Charles B., and Donald M. McRae, "Maritime Jurisdiction in the Dixon Entrance: The Alaska Boundary Re-examined." (1976) 14 *Canadian Yearbook of International Law* 183.

Boyd, Susan B., "The Legal Status of the Arctic Sea Ice: A Comparative Study and a Proposal." (1984) 22 *Canadian Yearbook of International Law* 98.

Broderstad, Else Grete, "Political Autonomy and Integration of Authority: The Understanding of Saami Self-Determination." (2001) 8 *International Journal on Minority and Group Rights* 151.

Brubaker, R. Douglas, *Russian Arctic Straits* (Dordrecht: Martinus Nijhoff, 2004).

Brunnée, Jutta, and Stephen Toope, *Legitimacy and Legality in International Law* (Cambridge University Press, 2010).

Byers, Michael, *Custom, Power and the Power of Rules* (Cambridge University Press, 1999).

"Policing the High Seas: The Proliferation Security Initiative." (2004) 98 *American Journal of International Law* 526.

Who Owns the Arctic? Understanding Sovereignty Disputes in the North (Vancouver, BC and Berkeley, Calif.: Douglas & McIntyre, 2009).

Caminos, Hugo, "The Legal Régime of Straits in the 1982 United Nations Convention on the Law of the Sea." (1987) 205 *Recueil des cours* 128.

Careaga, Luis, "Un condominium franco-espagnol: L'île des faisans ou de la conférence," thesis, Faculté de droit et des sciences politiques, University of Strasbourg, 1932.

Carnaghan, Matthew, and Allison Goody, "Canadian Arctic Sovereignty." (January 26, 2006), Parliamentary Information and Research Service (PRB

05-61E), Library of Parliament, available at www.parl.gc.ca/Content/LOP/
researchpublications/prb0561-e.htm.

Castellino, Joshua, and Niamh Walsh (eds.), *International Law and Indigenous
Peoples* (Dordrecht: Martinus Nijhoff, 2004).

Charney, Jonathan I., "Rocks that Cannot Sustain Human Habitation." (1999) 93
American Journal of International Law 863.

Charney, Jonathan I., and Lewis Alexander (eds.), *International Maritime
Boundaries*, vol. 1 (Dordrecht: American Society of International Law/
Martinus Nijhoff, 1993).

Chen, Zhuoheng, *et al.*, "Petroleum Potential in Western Sverdrup Basin,
Canadian Arctic Archipelago." (December 2000) 48(4) *Bulletin of Canadian
Petroleum Geology* 323.

Chinkin, Christine, "The Challenge of Soft Law: Development and Change in
International Law." (1989) 38 *International and Comparative Law Quarterly* 850.

Churchill, Robin, and Vaughan Lowe, *The Law of the Sea*, 3rd edn. (Manchester
University Press, 1999).

Churchill, Robin, and Geir Ulfstein, *Marine Management in Disputed Areas: The Case
of the Barents Sea* (London: Routledge, 1992).

Colson, David, "The Delimitation of the Outer Continental Shelf between
Neighboring States." (2003) 97 *American Journal of International Law* 91.

Cone, Marla, *Silent Snow: The Slow Poisoning of the Arctic* (New York: Grove Press,
2005).

Crawford, James, *The Creation of States in International Law*, 2nd edn. (Oxford
University Press, 2006).

D'Amato, Anthony, *The Concept of Custom in International Law* (Ithaca, NY: Cornell
University Press, 1971).

Davidson, Art, *In the Wake of the Exxon Valdez* (San Francisco, Calif.: Sierra Club
Books, 1990).

Downie, David, and Terry Fenge, *Northern Lights Against POPs: Combating Toxic
Threats in the Arctic* (Montreal and Kingston: McGill–Queen's University
Press, 2003).

Duffy, Helen, *The "War on Terror" and the Framework of International Law*
(Cambridge University Press, 2005).

Elliot-Meisel, Elizabeth B., *Arctic Diplomacy: Canada and the United States in the
Northwest Passage* (New York: Peter Lang, 1998).

Emmerson, Charles, *The Future History of the Arctic* (New York: Public Affairs,
2010).

Emmerson, Charles, and Glada Lahn, *Arctic Opening: Opportunity and Risk in the
High North* (London: Lloyd's, 2012), available at www.chathamhouse.org/
publications/papers/view/182839.

Engle, Karen, "On Fragile Architecture: The UN Declaration on the Rights of
Indigenous Peoples in the Context of Human Rights." (2011) 22 *European
Journal of International Law* 141.

Feldman, Mark B., and David Colson, "The Maritime Boundaries of the United
States." (1981) 75 *American Journal of International Law* 729.

Fenge, Terry, "Inuit and the Nunavut Land Claims Agreement: Supporting Canada's Arctic Sovereignty." (December 2007–January 2008) 29(1) *Policy Options* 84.

Ferguson, Steven H., J. W. Higdon, and E. G. Chmelnitsky, "The Rise of the Killer Whales as a Major Arctic Predator," in Steven H. Ferguson, *et al.*, *A Little Less Arctic: Top Predators in the World's Largest Northern Inland Sea, Hudson Bay* (Dordrecht: Springer, 2010).

Finlay, Brian D., "Russian Roulette: Canada's Role in the Race to Secure Loose Nuclear, Biological, and Chemical Weapons." (2006) 61 *International Journal* 411.

Fitzmaurice, Gerald, *The Law and Procedure of the International Court of Justice*, vol. 1 (Cambridge University Press, 1995).

Fox, Hazel, Paul McDade, Derek Rankin Reid, Anastasia Strati, and Peter Huey, *Joint Development of Offshore Oil and Gas: A Model Agreement for States for Joint Development with Explanatory Commentary* (London: British Institute of International and Comparative Law, 1989).

Franckx, Erik, *Maritime Claims in the Arctic: Canadian and Russian Perspectives* (Dordrecht: Martinus Nijhoff, 1993).

"The Legal Regime of Navigation in the Russian Arctic." (2009) 18 *Journal of Transnational Law and Policy* 327.

Frid, Chris, *et al.*, "Ecosystem-Based Fisheries Management: Progress in the NE Atlantic." (2005) 29 *Marine Policy* 461.

Gautier, Donald L., *et al.*, "Assessment of Undiscovered Oil and Gas in the Arctic." (May 2009) 324 (5931) *Science* 1175.

Gay, James Thomas, *American Fur Seal Diplomacy: The Alaskan Fur Seal Controversy* (New York: Peter Lang, 1987).

Gedney, Larry, and Merritt Helfferich, "Voyage of the Manhattan," December 19, 1983, Alaska Science Forum Article No. 639, available at http://web.archive.org/web/20120429124511/http://www2.gi.alaska.edu/ScienceForum/ASF6/639.html.

Geopolicity, "The Economics of Piracy." May 2011, available at www.geopolicity.com/upload/content/pub_1305229189_regular.pdf.

George, Mary, "The Regulation of Maritime Traffic in Straits Used for International Navigation," in Alex G. Oude Elferink and Donald R. Rothwell (eds.), *Oceans Management in the 21st Century: Institutional Frameworks and Responses* (Leiden: Martin Nijhoff, 2004).

Goldblat, Jozef, "The Seabed Treaty and Arms Control," in Richard Fieldhouse (ed.), *Security at Sea: Naval Forces and Arms Control* (Oxford University Press and Stockholm International Peace Research Institute, 1990).

Goldie, L. F. E., "The Critical Date." (1963) 12 *International and Comparative Law Quarterly* 1251.

Golitsyn, Vladimir, "The Arctic – On the Way to Regional Cooperation." (1989) 1 *Marine Policy Report* 91.

Gordon, Jessica, "Inter-American Commission on Human Rights to Hold Hearing After Rejecting Inuit Climate Change Petition." (2007) 7 *Sustainable Development Law and Policy* 55.

Grant, Shelagh D., "A Case of Compounded Error: The Inuit Resettlement Project, 1953, and the Government Response, 1990." (1991) 19(1) *Northern Perspectives* (Canadian Arctic Resources Committee) 3.

Gray, David H., "Canada's Unresolved Maritime Boundaries." (1997) 5(3) *IBRU Boundary and Security Bulletin* 61, available at www.dur.ac.uk/resources/ibru/publications/full/bsb5-3_gray.pdf.

Griffiths, Franklyn, "A Northern Foreign Policy." (1979) 7 *Wellesley Papers* (Toronto: Canadian Institute of International Affairs), 61.

(ed.), *Politics of the Northwest Passage* (Kingston and Montreal: McGill–Queen's University Press, 1987).

"Arctic Security: The Indirect Approach," in James Kraska (ed.), *Arctic Security in an Age of Climate Change* (New York: Cambridge University Press, 2011).

Grunawalt, Richard J., "United States Policy on International Straits." (1987) 18 *Ocean Development and International Law* 445.

Guo, Peiqing, "Making Preparations against an Arctic Monroe Doctrine." (2011) 42 *Liaowang* 71–72.

Haas, Peter M., *Saving the Mediterranean: The Politics of International Environmental Cooperation* (New York: Columbia University Press, 1990).

Haftendorn, Helga, "NATO and the Arctic: Is the Atlantic Alliance a Cold War Relic in a Peaceful Region Now Faced with Non-Military Challenges?" (2011) 20 *European Security* 337.

Hansen, James, and Larissa Nazarenko, "Soot Climate Forcing Via Snow and Ice Albedos." (2004) 101(2) *Proceedings of the National Academy of Sciences* 423, available at www.pnas.org/content/101/2/423.full.pdf+html.

Harders, J. Enno, "In Quest of an Arctic Legal Regime: Marine Regionalism – A Concept of International Law Evaluated." (1987) 11 *Marine Policy* 285.

Hass, Peter M., *Saving the Mediterranean: The Politics of International Environmental Cooperation* (New York: Columbia University Press, 1990).

Head, Ivan L., "Canadian Claims to Territorial Sovereignty in the Arctic Regions." (1963) 9 *McGill Law Journal* 200.

Henriksen, Tore, and Geir Ulfstein, "Maritime Delimitation in the Arctic: The Barents Sea Treaty." (2011) 42 *Ocean Development and International Law* 1.

Holtsmark, Sven G., "Towards Cooperation or Confrontation? Security in the High North." Research Paper No. 45, NATO Defense College, February 2009, available at www.ndc.nato.int/research/series.php?icode=1.

Hossain, Kamrul, "The EU Ban on the Import of Seal Products and the WTO Regulations: Neglected Human Rights of the Arctic Indigenous Peoples?" (2013) 49 *Polar Record* 154.

Howse, Robert, and Joanna Langille, "Permitting Pluralism: The Seal Products Dispute and Why the WTO Should Accept Trade Restrictions Justified by Noninstrumental Moral Values." (2012) 37 *Yale Journal of International Law*

367, available at www.yjil.org/docs/pub/37-2-howse-langille-permitting-pluralism.pdf.

Huebert, Rob, "Steel, Ice and Decision-Making: The Voyage of the *Polar Sea* and its Aftermath," Ph.D. thesis, Dalhousie University, 1994.

"New Directions in Circumpolar Cooperation: Canada, the Arctic Environmental Protection Strategy and the Arctic Council." (1998) 5 *Canadian Foreign Policy* 37.

"The Newly Emerging Arctic Security Environment," Canadian Defence and Foreign Affairs Institute, March 2010, available at www.cdfai.org/PDF/The%20Newly%20Emerging%20Arctic%20Security%20Environment.pdf.

Huebert, Rob, and Brooks Yeager, "A New Sea: The Need for a Regional Agreement on Management and Conservation of the Arctic Marine Environment." (World Wildlife Fund, 2008), available at http://awsassets.panda.org/downloads/a_new_sea_jan08_final_11jan08.pdf.

Huebert, Rob, *et al.*, "Climate Change and International Security: The Arctic as a Bellwether." 2012, Center for Climate and Energy Solutions, available at www.c2es.org/publications/climate-change-international-arctic-security/.

Jakobson, Linda, "China Prepares for an Ice-Free Arctic." SIPRI Insights on Peace and Security, No. 2010/2, March 2010, available at http://books.sipri.org/files/insight/SIPRIInsight1002.pdf.

Jakobson, Linda, and Jingchao Peng, "China's Arctic Ambitions." SIPRI Policy Paper 34, November 2012, available at http://books.sipri.org/product_info?c_product_id=449.

Jennings, Robert, and Arthur Watts, *Oppenheim's International Law*, 9th edn. (London: Longman, 1992).

Johansen, Bruce E., "The Inuit's Struggle with Dioxins and Other Organic Pollutants." (2002) 26 *American Indian Law Quarterly* 479.

Joyner, Christopher, "The United States and the New Law of the Sea." (1996) 27 *Ocean Development and International Law* 41.

Kaczynski, Vlad M., "US–Russian Bering Sea Marine Border Dispute: Conflict over Strategic Assets, Fisheries and Energy Resources." (May 2007) 20 *Russian Analytical Digest* 2.

Kaye, Stuart, "Regulation of Navigation in the Torres Strait: Law of the Sea Issues," in Donald R. Rothwell and Sam Bateman (eds.), *Navigation Rights and Freedoms and the New Law of the Sea* (Dordrecht: Kluwer, 2000).

Keating, Bern, *The Northwest Passage: From the Mathew to the Manhattan, 1497–1969* (Chicago: Rand McNally and Company, 1970).

Kenney, Gerard, *Arctic Smoke and Mirrors* (Prescott, Ont.: Voyageur Publishing, 1994).

Keyuan, Zou, "The Sino–Vietnamese Agreement on Maritime Boundary Delimitation in the Gulf of Tonkin." (2005) 36 *Ocean Development and International Law* 13.

Kirkey, Christopher, "Smoothing Troubled Waters: The 1988 Canada–United States Arctic Co-operation Agreement." (1994–1995) 50 *International Journal* 401.

"Delineating Maritime Boundaries: The 1977–1978 Canada–US Beaufort Sea Continental Shelf Delimitation Boundary Negotiations." (1995) 25 *Canadian Review of American Studies* 49.

Klein, Natalie, *Dispute Settlement in the UN Convention on the Law of the Sea* (Cambridge University Press, 2004).

Kohen, Marcelo, *Possession contestée et souveraineté territorial* (Paris: Presses universitaires de France, 1997).

Koivurova, Timo, "Alternatives for an Arctic Treaty – Evaluation and a New Proposal." (2008) 17 *Review of European Community and International Environmental Law* 14, available at http://onlinelibrary.wiley.com/doi/10.1111/j.1467-9388.2008.00580.x/full.

Koivurova, Timo, and Leena Heinämäki, "The Participation of Indigenous Peoples in International Norm-Making in the Arctic." (2006) 42 *Polar Record* 101.

Kokan, Jane, "Greenland: Canada's Arctic Neighbour." (January/February 2012) 9(1) *FrontLine Defence* 23, available at www.frontline-canada.com/downloads/12-1_RAdmKudsk.pdf.

Kovalev, Aleksandr Antonovich, *Contemporary Issues of the Law of the Sea: Modern Russian Approaches* (trans. W. E. Butler) (Utrecht: Eleven International Publishing, 2004).

Kraska, James C., "The Law of the Sea Convention and the Northwest Passage." (2007) 22 *International Journal of Marine and Coastal Law* 257.

(ed.), *Arctic Security in an Age of Climate Change* (New York: Cambridge University Press, 2011).

Kunoy, Bjørn, "Disputed Areas and the 10-Year Time Frame: A Legal Lacuna?" (2010) 41 *Ocean Development and International Law* 112.

"The Terms of Reference of the Commission on the Limits of the Continental Shelf: A Creeping Legal Mandate." (2012) 25 *Leiden Journal of International Law* 109.

Lalonde, Suzanne, and Frédéric Lasserre, "The Position of the United States on the Northwest Passage: Is the Fear of Creating a Precedent Warranted?" (2012) 43 *Ocean Development and International Law* 28.

Lathrop, Coalter, "Continental Shelf Delimitation Beyond 200 Nautical Miles: Approaches Taken by Coastal States Before the Commission on the Limits of the Continental Shelf," in David A. Colson and Robert W. Smith (eds.), *International Maritime Boundaries* (Leiden: American Society of International Law/Martinus Nijhoff, 2011), 4139.

Lawson, Karin L., "Delimiting Continental Shelf Boundaries in the Arctic: The United States–Canada Beaufort Sea Boundary." (1981) 22 *Virginia Journal of International Law* 221.

Leitzell, Katherine, "When Will the Arctic Lose its Sea Ice?" National Snow and Ice Data Center, May 3, 2011, available at http://nsidc.org/icelights/2011/05/03/when-will-the-arctic-lose-its-sea-ice/.

Lester, Simon, "The WTO Seal Products Dispute: A Preview of the Key Legal Issues." 14(2) *ASIL Insight*, January 13, 2010, available at www.asil.org/insights100113.cfm.

Lilje-Jensen, Jorgen, and Milan Thamborg, "The Role of Natural Prolongation in Relation to Shelf Delimitation Beyond 200 Nautical Miles." (1995) 64 *Nordic Journal of International Law* 619.

Lindahl, Ingemar, *The Soviet Union and the Nordic Nuclear-Weapons-Free-Zone Proposal* (London: Macmillan, 1988).

Lindegren, Martin, *et al.*, "Preventing the Collapse of the Baltic Cod Stock through an Ecosystem-Based Management Approach." (2009) 106 *Proceedings of the National Academy of Science of the United States of America* 14722.

Loukacheva, Natalia, *The Arctic Promise: Legal and Political Autonomy of Greenland and Nunavut* (University of Toronto Press, 2007).

Luan, Xinjie, and Julien Chaisse, "Preliminary Comments on the WTO Seals Products Dispute: Traditional Hunting, Public Morals and Technical Barriers to Trade." (2011) 22 *Colorado Journal of International Environmental Law and Policy* 79.

McDorman, Ted L., "The Role of the Commission on the Limits of the Continental Shelf: A Technical Body in a Political World." (2002) 17 *International Journal of Marine and Coastal Law* 301.

"The Continental Shelf beyond 200 nm: Law and Politics in the Arctic Ocean." (2009) 18 *Journal of Transnational Law and Policy* 155.

Salt Water Neighbors: International Ocean Law Relations between the United States and Canada (New York: Oxford University Press, 2009).

"National Measures for the Safety of Navigation in Arctic Waters: NORDREG, Article 234 and Canada," in Myron H. Nordquist, *et al.*, *The Law of the Sea Convention: US Accession and Globalization* (Leiden: Martinus Nijhoff, 2012).

McLaren, Alfred S., "The Evolution and Potential of the Arctic Submarine." (1985) 2 *POAC Conference Proceedings* (Danish Hydraulic Institute) 848.

Unknown Waters: A First-Hand Account of the Historic Under-Ice Survey of the Siberian Continental Shelf by USS Queenfish (Tuscaloosa: University of Alabama Press, 2008).

Macnab, Ron, "The Case for Transparency in the Delimitation of the Outer Continental Shelf in Accordance with UNCLOS Article 76." (2004) 35 *Ocean Development and International Law* 1.

"Submarine Elevations and Ridges: Wild Card in the Poker Game of UNCLOS Article 76" (2008) 39 *Ocean Development and International Law* 223.

McRae, Donald M., "Canada and the Delimitation of Maritime Boundaries," in Donald M. McRae and G. Munro (eds.), *Canadian Oceans Policy: National Strategies and the New Law of the Sea* (Vancouver, University of British Columbia Press, 1989).

"Arctic Sovereignty: What Is at Stake?" (2007) 64(1) *Behind the Headlines* 1.

Makkonen, Lasse, *Atmospheric Icing on Sea Structures* (Hanover, NH: US Army Cold Regions Research and Engineering Laboratory, Monograph 84-2, 1984).

Malaurie, Jean, *The Last Kings of Thule: With the Polar Eskimos, as They Face their Destiny* (trans. Adrienne Foulke) (London: Jonathan Cape, 1982).

Mirovitskaya, Natalia S., Margaret Clark, and Ronald G. Purver, "North Pacific Fur Seals: Regime Formation as a Means of Resolving Conflict," in Oran

Young and Gail Osherenko (eds.), *Polar Politics: Creating International Environmental Regimes* (Ithaca, NY: Cornell University Press, 1993).

Mitchell, J. M., Jr., "Visual Range in the Polar Regions with Particular Reference to the Alaskan Arctic." (1956) *Journal of Atmospheric and Terrestrial Physics* 195.

Molenaar, Erik, "Current and Prospective Roles of the Arctic Council System within the Context of the Law of the Sea." (2012) 27 *International Journal of Marine and Coastal Law* 553.

Mulrennan, Monica, and Colin Scott, "Indigenous Rights in Saltwater Environments." (2000) 31 *Development and Change* 681.

Nankivell, Justin DeMowbray, "Arctic Legal Tides: The Politics of International Law in the Northwest Passage," Ph.D. thesis, University of British Columbia, 2010, available at https://circle.ubc.ca/bitstream/handle/2429/26642/ubc_2010_fall_nankivell_justin.pdf?sequence=1.

Neumann, Thilo, "Norway and Russia Agree on Maritime Boundary in the Barents Sea and the Arctic Ocean." (November 9, 2010) 14(34) *ASIL Insight*, available at www.asil.org/files/2010/insights/insights_101109.pdf.

Niimi, Arthur J., "Environmental and Economic Factors Can Increase the Risk of Exotic Species Introductions to the Arctic Region through Increased Ballast Water Discharge." (2004) 33 *Environmental Management* 712.

Nurja, Alfred, "Obama Submits NWFZ Protocols to Senate." (June 2011) *Arms Control Today*, available at www.armscontrol.org/act/2011_06/NWFZ.

Ochoa-Ruiz, Natalia, and Esther Salamanca-Aguado, "Exploring the Limits of International Law Relating to the Use of Force in Self-Defence." (2005) 16 *European Journal of International Law* 499.

O'Connell, Daniel P., *The International Law of the Sea*, vol. 1, ed. Ivan Shearer (Oxford: Clarendon Press, 1982).

O'Driscoll, Cath, "Soot Warming Significant." (2011) 17 *Chemistry and Industry* 10.

Ong, David M., "The 1979 and 1990 Malaysia–Thailand Joint Development Agreements: A Model for International Legal Co-operation in Common Offshore Petroleum Deposits?" (1999) 14 *International Journal of Marine and Coastal Law* 207.

Østreng, Willy, *Delimitation Arrangements in Arctic Seas* (Fridtjof Nansen Institute, Study R007-84, 1985).

Oude Elferink, Alex G., "The 1990 USSR–USA Maritime Boundary Agreement." (1991) 6 *International Journal of Estuarine and Coastal Law* 41.

"Arctic Maritime Delimitations: The Preponderance of Similarities with Other Regions," in Oude Elferink and Donald Rothwell (eds.), *The Law of the Sea and Polar Maritime Delimitation and Jurisdiction* (Dordrecht: Kluwer Law International, 2001).

"Maritime Delimitation between Denmark/Greenland and Norway." (2007) 38 *Ocean Development and International Law* 375.

Oude Elferink, Alex G., and Constance Johnson, "Outer Limits of the Continental Shelf and 'Disputed Areas': State Practice Concerning Article 76(10) of the LOS Convention." (2004) 21 *International Journal of Marine and Coastal Law* 466.

Pearson, Lester B., "Canada Looks Down North." (1946) 24 *Foreign Affairs* 638.

Pedersen, Torbjørn, "The Svalbard Continental Shelf Controversy: Legal Disputes and Political Rivalries." (2006) 37 *Ocean Development and International Law* 339.

Peterson, Alexander M., "Sino-Japanese Cooperation in the East China Sea: A Lasting Arrangement?" (2009) 42 *Cornell International Law Journal* 441.

Petrow, Richard, *Across the Top of Russia: The Cruise of the USCGC Northwind into the Polar Seas North of Siberia* (London: Hodder and Stoughton, 1968).

Pew Environmental Group, "Oil Spill Prevention and Response in the US Arctic Ocean: Unexamined Risks, Unacceptable Consequences." (November 2010), available at www.pewtrusts.org/uploadedFiles/wwwpewtrustsorg/Reports/ Protecting_ocean_life/PEW-1010_ARTIC_Report.pdf.

"More than 2,000 Scientists Worldwide Urge Protection of Central Arctic Ocean Fisheries." (April 2012), available at www.oceansnorth.org/arctic-fisheries-letter.

Pharand, Donat, *Canada's Arctic Waters in International Law* (Cambridge University Press, 1988).

"Delimitation Problems of Canada (Second Part)," in Donat Pharand and Umberto Leanza (eds.), *The Continental Shelf and the Exclusive Economic Zone: Delimitation and Legal Regime* (Dordrecht: Martinus Nijhoff, 1993), 171.

"The Arctic Waters and the Northwest Passage: A Final Revisit." (2007) 38 *Ocean Development and International Law* 3.

Pharand, Donat, and Leonard Legault, *The Northwest Passage: Arctic Straits* (Dordrecht: Martinus Nijhoff, 1984).

Plaut, Shayna, "'Cooperation Is the Story' – Best Practices of Transnational Indigenous Activism in the North." (2012) 16 *International Journal of Human Rights* 193.

Quinn, P. K., et al., *The Impact of Black Carbon on the Arctic Climate* (Oslo: Arctic Monitoring and Assessment Programme, 2011).

Ramseur, Jonathan L., "Liability and Compensation Issues Raised by the 2010 Gulf Oil Spill." Congressional Research Service, March 11, 2011, available at http://assets.opencrs.com/rpts/R41679_20110311.pdf.

Reid, Robert S., "The Canadian Claim to Sovereignty over the Waters of the Arctic." (1974) 12 *Canadian Yearbook of International Law* 111.

Riddell-Dixon, Elizabeth, "Canada and Arctic Politics: The Continental Shelf Extension." (2008) 39 *Ocean Development and International Law* 343.

Roche, Douglas, and Ernie Regehr, "Canada, NATO and Nuclear Weapons." Project Ploughshares Working Paper 01-3 (2001), available at www. ploughshares.ca/content/canada-nato-and-nuclear-weapons.

Roth, R. R., "Sovereignty and Jurisdiction over Arctic Waters." (1990) 28 *Alberta Law Review* 845.

Rothwell, Donald R., *Maritime Boundaries and Resource Development: Options for the Beaufort Sea* (Calgary: Canadian Institute of Resources Law, 1988).

The Polar Regions and the Development of International Law (Cambridge University Press, 1996).

Russell, Dawn, "International Ocean Boundary Issues and Management Arrangements," in David VanderZwaag (ed.), *Canadian Ocean Law and Policy* (Toronto: Butterworths, 1992).

Ruys, Tom, *"Armed Attack" and Article 51 of the UN Charter: Evolutions in Customary Law and Practice* (Cambridge University Press, 2010).

Sahlins, Peter, *Boundaries: The Making of France and Spain in the Pyrenees* (Berkeley: University of California Press, 1989).

Samuels, Joel H., "Condominium Arrangements in International Practice: Reviving an Abandoned Concept of Boundary Dispute Resolution." (2007–2008) 29 *Michigan Journal of International Law* 727.

Schofield, Clive, "Australia's Final Frontiers? Developments in the Delimitation of Australia's International Maritime Boundaries." (2008) 158 *Maritime Studies* 2.

"The Trouble with Islands: The Definition and Role of Islands and Rocks in Maritime Boundary Delimitation," in S. Y. Hong and Jon Van Dyke (eds.), *Maritime Boundary Disputes, Settlement Processes, and the Law of the Sea* (The Hague: Martinus Nijhoff, 2009).

Scott, Colin, and Monica Mulrennan, "Reconfiguring Mare Nullius: Torres Strait Islanders, Indigenous Sea Rights and the Divergence of Domestic and International Norms," in Mario Blaser, *et al.* (eds.), *Indigenous Peoples and Autonomy: Insights for a Global Age* (Vancouver: UBC Press, 2010).

Scovazzi, Tullio, "New Developments Concerning Soviet Straight Baselines." (1988) 3 *International Journal of Estuarine and Coastal Law* 37.

The Evolution of the International Law of the Sea: New Issues, New Challenges (The Hague: Martinus Nijhoff, 2001).

Scrivener, David, "Arctic Environmental Cooperation in Transition." (1999) 35(192) *Polar Record* 51.

Shah, Niaz A., "Self-Defence, Anticipatory Self-Defence and Pre-emption: International Law's Response to Terrorism." (2007) 12 *Journal of Conflict and Security Law* 95.

Shaw, Glen E., "The Arctic Haze Phenomenon." (August 16, 1995) 76 *Bulletin of the American Meteorological Society* 2403.

Shi, Lei, "Successful Use of the Tacit Acceptance Procedure to Effectuate Progress in International Maritime Law." (1998–1999) 11 *University of San Francisco Maritime Law Journal* 299.

Shusterich, K. M., "International Jurisdictional Issues in the Arctic Ocean," in W. E. Westermeyer and K. M. Shusterich (eds.), *United States Arctic Interests: The 1980s and 1990s* (New York: Springer-Verlag, 1984).

Sillanpää, Lennard, *Impact of International Law on Indigenous Rights in Northern Europe* (Ottawa: Indian and Northern Affairs Canada, 1992).

Simon, Mary, "Inuit and the Canadian Arctic: Sovereignty Begins at Home." (2009) 43 *Journal of Canadian Studies* 250.

Skogan, John Kristen, "The Evolution of the Four Soviet Fleets 1968–1987," in John Kristen Skogan and Arne Olav Brundtland, *Soviet Seapower in Northern Waters: Facts, Motivation, Impact and Responses* (London: Pinter, 1990).

Smith, Robert W., "United States–Russia Maritime Boundary," in Gerald Henry Blake (ed.), *Maritime Boundaries* (London: Routledge, 1994).

Sohn, Louis B., "Baseline Considerations," in Jonathan I. Charney and Lewis M. Alexander (eds.), *International Maritime Boundaries*, vol. 1 (Dordrecht: Martinus Nijhoff, 1993).

Sorensen, Christina, "Drug Trafficking on the High Seas: A Move Toward Universal Jurisdiction under International Law." (1990) 4 *Emory International Law Review* 207.

Speca, Anthony, "Nunavut, Greenland and the Politics of Resource Revenues." (May 2012) *Policy Options* 62, available at www.irpp.org/po/archive/may12/speca.pdf.

"In the Belly of the Whaling Commission." *Northern Public Affairs*, June 18, 2012, available at www.northernpublicaffairs.ca/index/in-the-belly-of-the-whaling-commission/.

Springer, A. L., "Do Fences Make Good Neighbours? The Gulf of Maine Revisited." (1994) 6 *International Environmental Affairs* 223.

Stabrun, Kristoffer, "The Grey Zone Agreement of 1978: Fishery Concerns, Security Challenges and Territorial Interests." Fridtjof Nansen Institute Report 13/2009, available at www.fni.no/doc&pdf/FNI-R1309.pdf.

Stevenson, Christopher, "Hans Off! The Struggle for Hans Island and the Potential Ramifications for International Border Dispute Resolution." (2007) 30 *Boston College International and Comparative Law Review* 263.

Stirling, Ian, *Polar Bears: The Natural History of a Threatened Species* (Markham, Ont.: Fitzhenry and Whiteside, 2011).

Stirling, Ian, and Andrew E. Derocher, "Effects of Climate Warming on Polar Bears: A Review of the Evidence." (2012) 18(9) *Global Change Biology* 2694.

Stirling, Ian, and Claire Parkinson, "Possible Effects of Climate Warming on Selected Populations of Polar Bears (*Ursus maritimus*) in the Canadian Arctic." (2006) 59 *Arctic* 261.

Stokke, Olav Schram, "Sub-regional Cooperation and Protection of the Arctic Marine Environment: The Barents Sea," in Davor Vidas (ed.), *Protecting the Polar Marine Environment: Law and Policy for Pollution Prevention* (Cambridge University Press, 2000), chap. 6.

Tester, Frank, and Peter Kulchyski, *Tammarniit (Mistakes): Inuit Relocation in the Eastern Arctic, 1939–63* (Vancouver: University of British Columbia Press, 1994).

Thorleifsson, Thorleif Tobuas, "Norway 'must really drop their absurd claims such as that to the Otto Sverdrup Islands.' Bi-Polar International Diplomacy: The Sverdrup Islands Question, 1902–1930," MA thesis, Simon Fraser University, 2006, available at http://ir.lib.sfu.ca/retrieve/3720/etd2367.pdf.

Tingle, Christopher, "Submarine Accidents: A 60-Year Statistical Assessment." (2009) *Professional Safety: Journal of the American Society of Safety Engineers* 31.

Trudeau, Pierre, "Remarks to the Press Following the Introduction of Legislation on Arctic Pollution, Territorial Sea and Fishing Zones in the Canadian House of Commons on April 8, 1970." (1970) 9 ILM 600.

Ulfstein, Geir, "Spitsbergen/Svalbard," in Rudiger Wolfrum (ed.), *Max Planck Encyclopedia of Public International Law* (Oxford University Press, 2012).

Ünlü, Nihan, *The Legal Regime of the Turkish Straits* (The Hague: Martinus Nijhoff, 2002).

Van Dyke, Jon M., "The Disappearing Right to Navigational Freedom in the Exclusive Economic Zone." (2005) 29 *Marine Policy* 107.

"Canada's Authority to Prohibit LNG Vessels from Passing through Head Harbor Passage to US Ports." (2008–2009) 14 *Ocean and Coastal Law Journal* 45.

Verhoef, Jacob, and Dick MacDougall, "Delineating Canada's Continental Shelf According to the United Nations Convention on the Law of the Sea." (2008) 3 *Journal of Ocean Technology* 1.

Vidas, Davor (ed.), *Protecting the Polar Marine Environment: Law and Policy for Pollution Prevention* (Cambridge University Press, 2000).

Wadhams, Peter, "Arctic Ice Cover, Ice Thickness and Tipping Points." (2012) 41 *AMBIO: A Journal of the Human Environment* 1.

Wegge, Njord, "The EU and the Arctic: European Foreign Policy in the Making." (2012) 3 *Arctic Review on Law and Politics* 6.

"Politics between Science, Law and Sentiments: Explaining the European Union's Ban on Trade in Seal Products." (2012) 6 *Environmental Politics* 1.

Weil, Prosper, *The Law of Maritime Delimitation – Reflections* (Cambridge: Grotius Publications, 1989).

Wells, Robert D., "The Icy Nyet." (1968) 94 (782) *US Naval Institute Proceedings* 73.

Wendt, Alexander, *Social Theory of International Politics* (Cambridge University Press, 1999).

Wezeman, Siemon T., "Military Capabilities in the Arctic." SIPRI Background Paper, Stockholm, March 2012, available at http://books.sipri.org/product_info?c_product_id=442.

Wilkening, Ken, "Science and International Environmental Nonregimes: The Case of Arctic Haze." (2011) 28 *Review of Policy Research* 131, available at www.highbeam.com/doc/1G1-253536411.html.

Wilson, Gary N., "Inuit Diplomacy in the Circumpolar North." (2007) 13 *Canadian Foreign Policy Journal* 65.

Woehrling, José, "Les Revendications du Canada sur les eaux de l'archipel de l'Arctique et l'utilisation immémoriale des glaces par les Inuit." (1987) 30 *German Yearbook of International Law* 120.

World Wildlife Fund, "Drilling for Oil in the Arctic: Too Soon, Too Risky." December 2010, available at www.worldwildlife.org/what/wherewework/arctic/WWFBinaryitem18711.pdf.

Young, Nigel, "Peace Movements in History: Perspectives from Social Movements," in S. Mendlovitz and R. B. Walker (eds.), *Towards a Just World Peace* (London: Butterworths, 1987).

Young, Oran, "Governing the Arctic: From Cold War Theatre to Mosaic of Cooperation." (2005) 11 *Global Governance* 9.

Young, Oran, and Gail Osherenko, *Polar Politics: Creating International Environmental Regimes* (Ithaca, NY: Cornell University Press, 1993).

Index

United Nations Sanctions and the Rule of Law
Jeremy Farrall

National Law in WTO Law: Effectiveness and Good Governance in the World Trading System
Sharif Bhuiyan

The Threat of Force in International Law
Nikolas Stürchler

Indigenous Rights and United Nations Standards
Alexandra Xanthaki

International Refugee Law and Socio-Economic Rights
Michelle Foster

The Protection of Cultural Property in Armed Conflict
Roger O'Keefe

Interpretation and Revision of International Boundary Decisions
Kaiyan Homi Kaikobad

Multinationals and Corporate Social Responsibility: Limitations and Opportunities in International Law
Jennifer A. Zerk

Judiciaries within Europe: A Comparative Review
John Bell

Law in Times of Crisis: Emergency Powers in Theory and Practice
Oren Gross and Fionnuala Ní Aoláin

Vessel-Source Marine Pollution: The Law and Politics of International Regulation
Alan Tan

Enforcing Obligations Erga Omnes in International Law
Christian J. Tams

Non-Governmental Organisations in International Law
Anna-Karin Lindblom

Democracy, Minorities and International Law
Steven Wheatley

Prosecuting International Crimes: Selectivity and the International Law Regime
Robert Cryer

Compensation for Personal Injury in English, German and Italian Law: A Comparative Outline
Basil Markesinis, Michael Coester, Guido Alpa, Augustus Ullstein

Dispute Settlement in the UN Convention on the Law of the Sea
Natalie Klein

The International Protection of Internally Displaced Persons
Catherine Phuong

Imperialism, Sovereignty and the Making of International Law
Antony Anghie

Necessity, Proportionality and the Use of Force by States
Judith Gardam

International Legal Argument in the Permanent Court of International Justice: The Rise of the International Judiciary
Ole Spiermann

Great Powers and Outlaw States: Unequal Sovereigns in the International Legal Order
Gerry Simpson

Local Remedies in International Law
C. F. Amerasinghe

Reading Humanitarian Intervention: Human Rights and the Use of Force in International Law
Anne Orford

Conflict of Norms in Public International Law: How WTO Law Relates to Other Rules of International Law
Joost Pauwelyn

CPSIA information can be obtained at www.ICGtesting.com
Printed in the USA
LVOW12s2305050814

397739LV00016B/280/P